PoseMuse
PO Box 2105
Edwards, CO 81632 USA
PoseMuse.com
posemuse@gmail.com

Ordering Information:
Available on Amazon.com in paperback and Kindle formats, and Gumroad in pdf format via PoseMuse.com. Special discounts are available on quantity purchases by businesses, corporations, associations, and others. For details, contact PoseMuse above.

Publisher's Cataloging-in-Publication Data:
Martin, Justin R.
Poses for Artists Volume 5 - Hands, Skulls, Pin-ups & Various Poses: An essential reference for figure drawing and the human form. Inspiring Art and Artists Series / Justin R. Martin.
1. Nonfiction - Art - Techniques - Drawing
2. Nonfiction - Art - Reference
3. Nonfiction - Art - Illustration

First Edition, First Printing 2019
ISBN 9781076190581
Imprint: Independently published
14 13 12 11 10 9 8 7 6 5 4 3 2 1
Printed in the United States of America

Introduction

The poses included in the Poses for Artists Book Series, were mostly first available online to encourage all artists to create. The purpose of sharing the poses is to help artists get over the long, and sometimes painful, 'artists-block' that occurs at the very beginning of a new drawing. Staring at that blank page can be DAUNTING. These poses are here to jump-start the whole process.

If you draw, you know the fear of wasting energy staring at a blank page. Use these poses to side-step the problem, and get drawing.

These books are not step-by-step drawing tutorials. There are PLENTY of those out there. These books are raw creative inspiration to get you moving forward.

Thank you for supporting our project by purchasing this book. We keep creating new poses because we all know the need to create. Keep drawing, and share your work, so others can be inspired by you!

Table of Contents

Crouching Poses

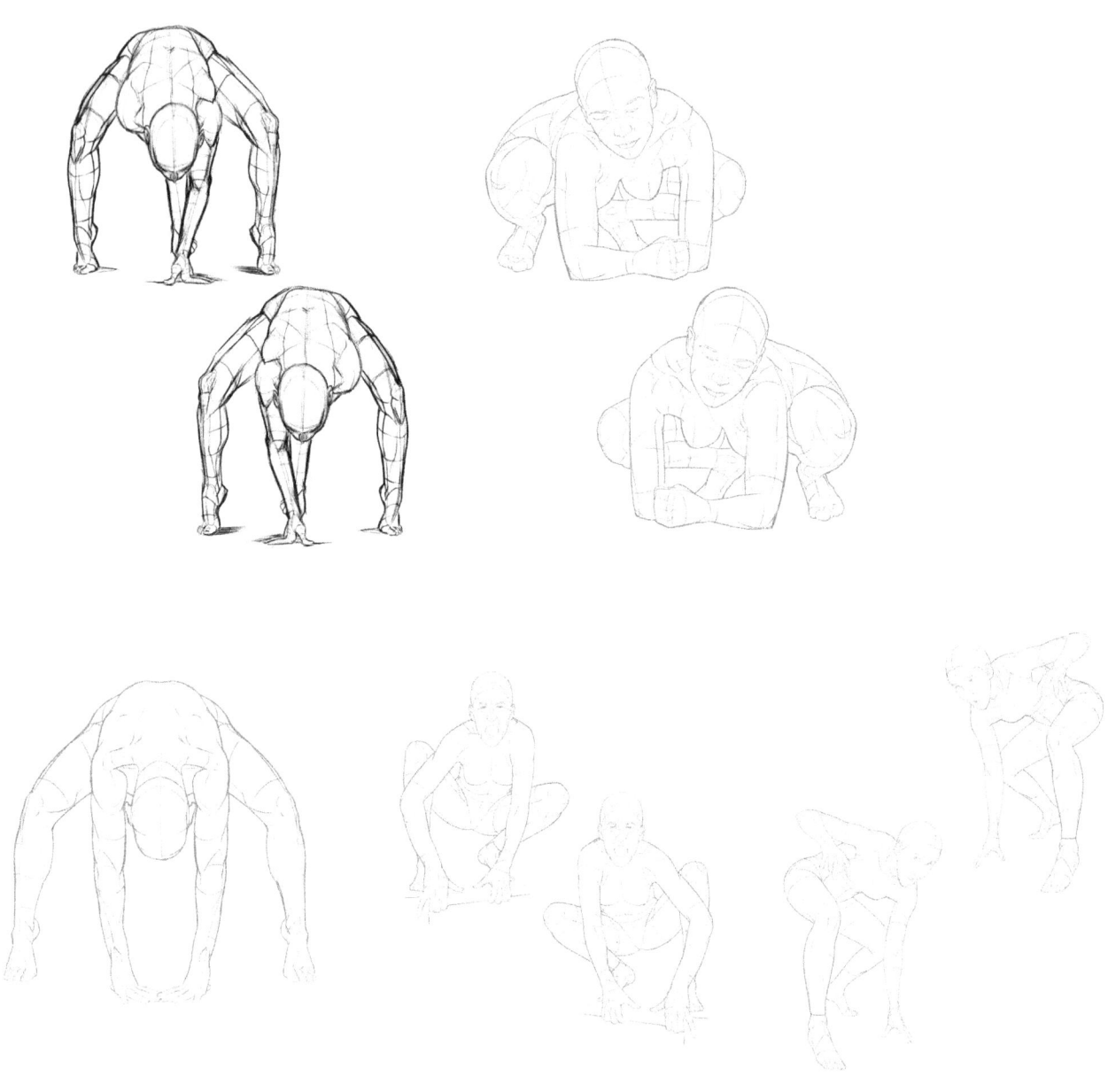

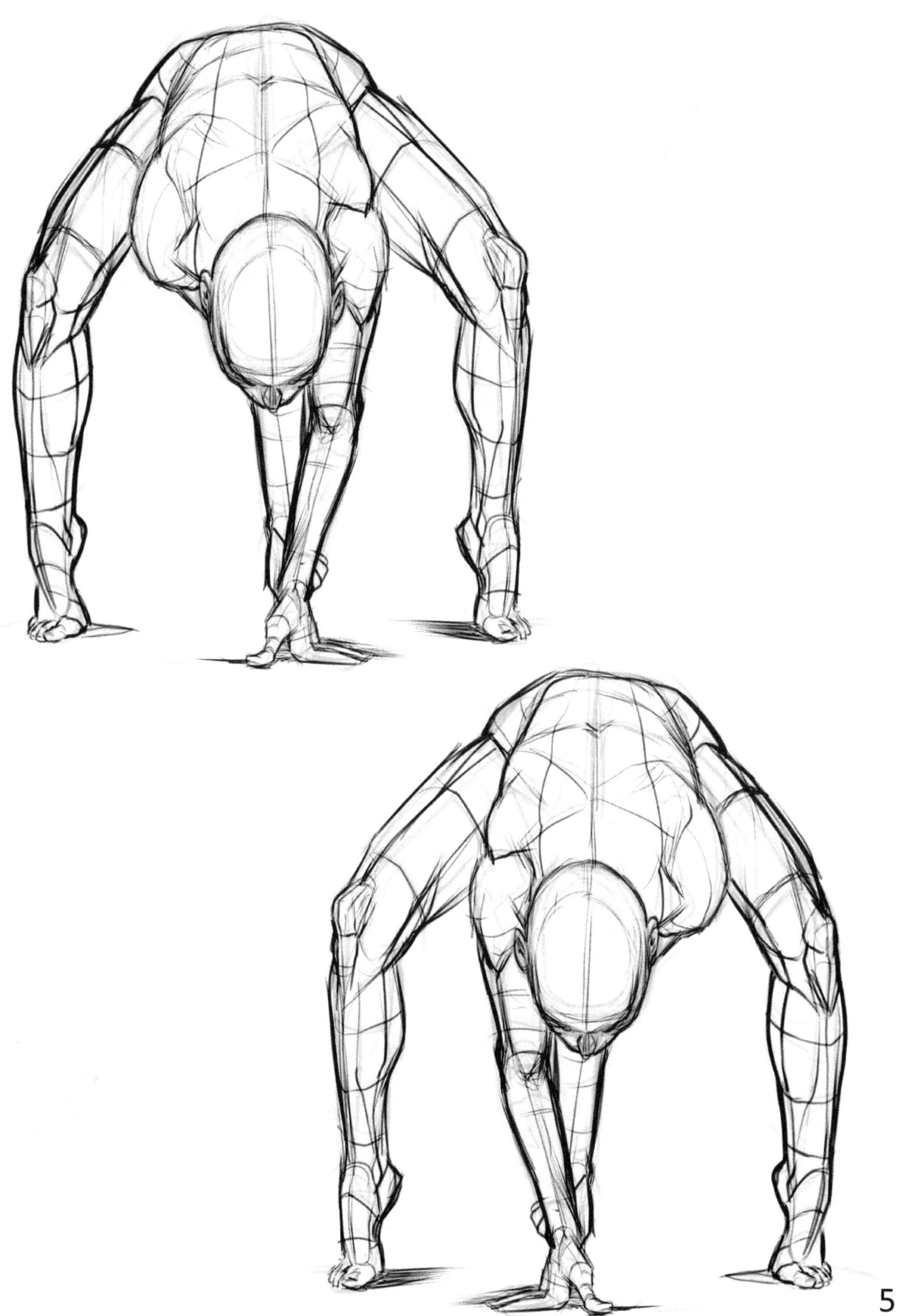

5

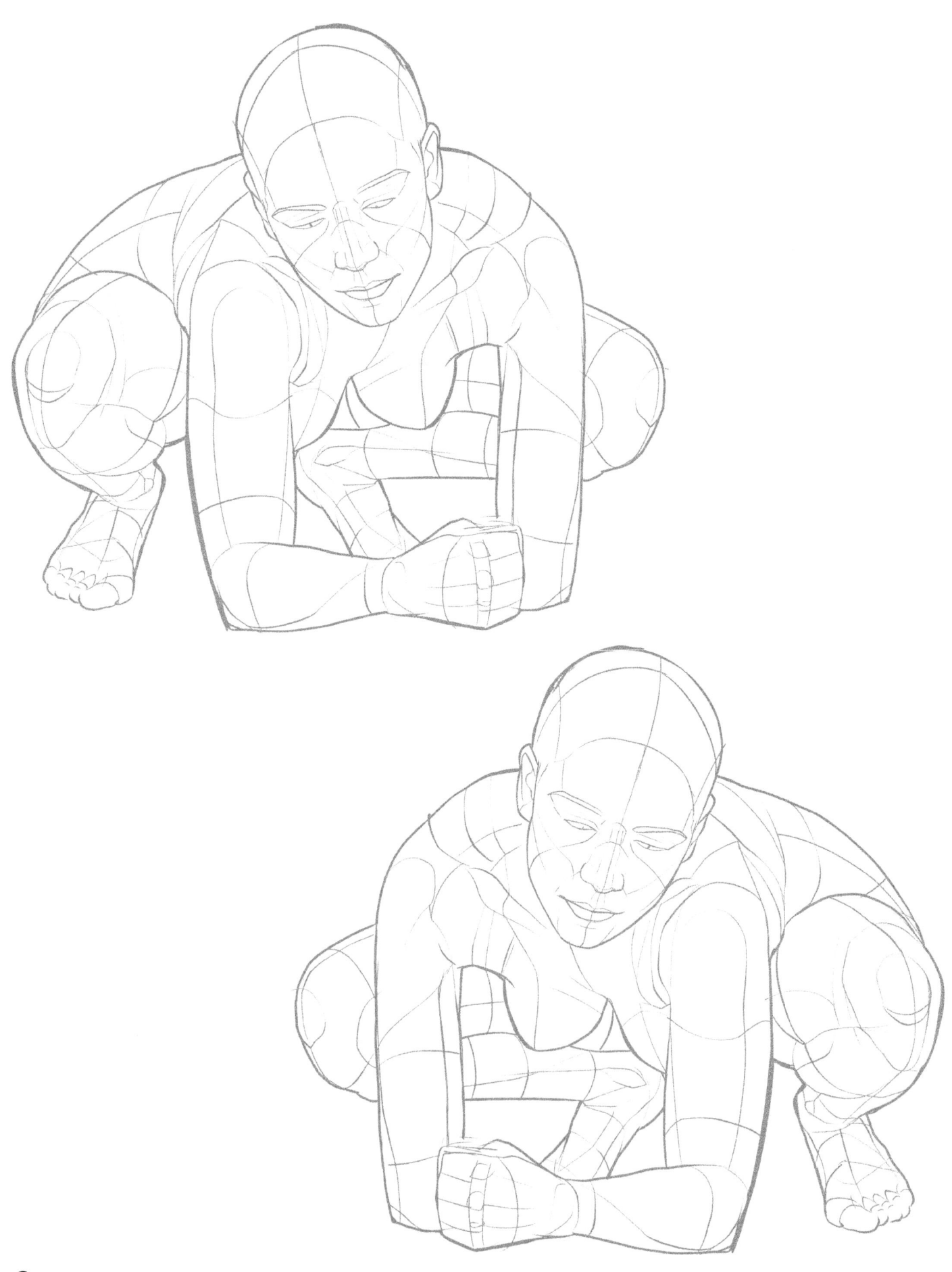

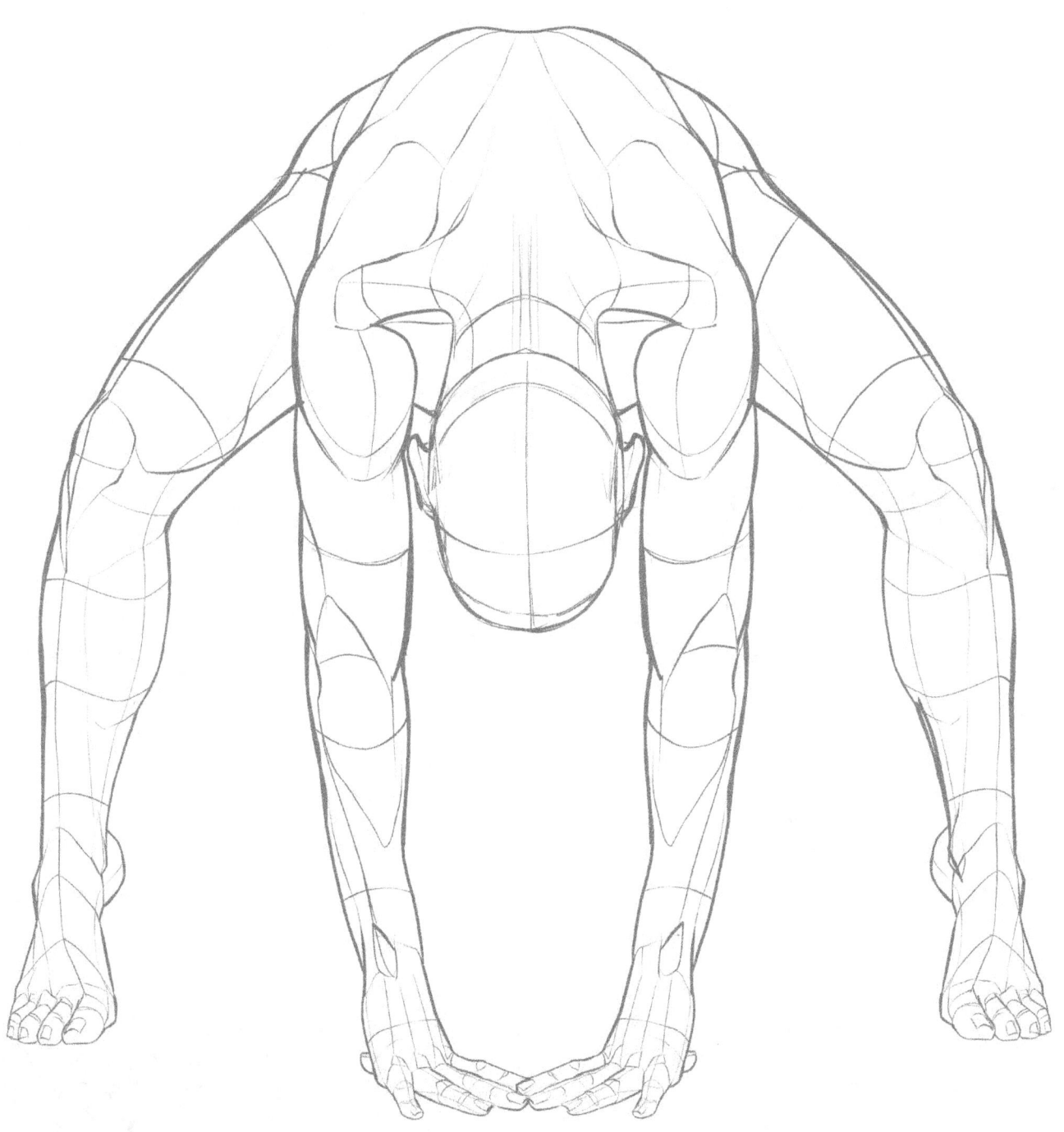

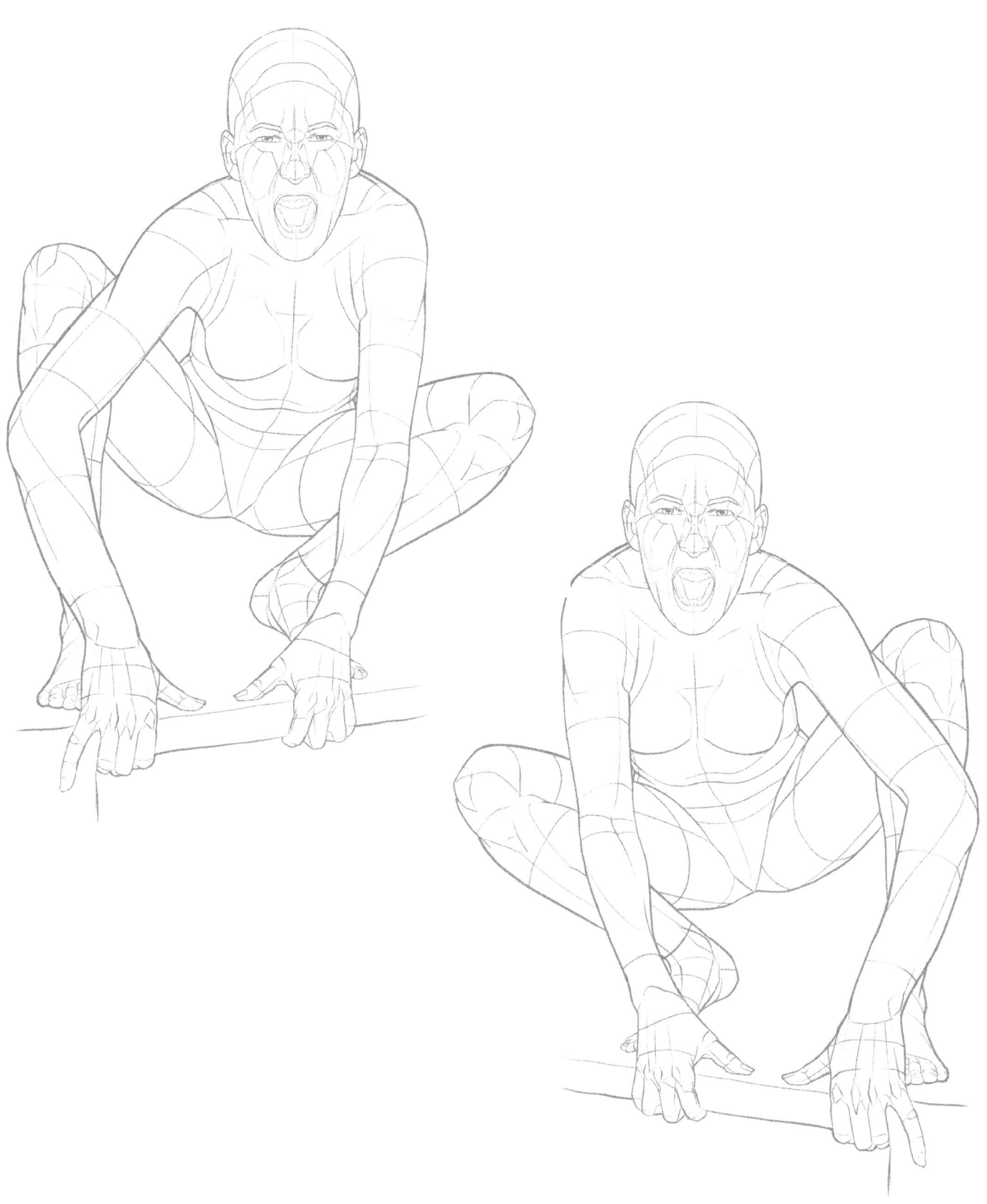

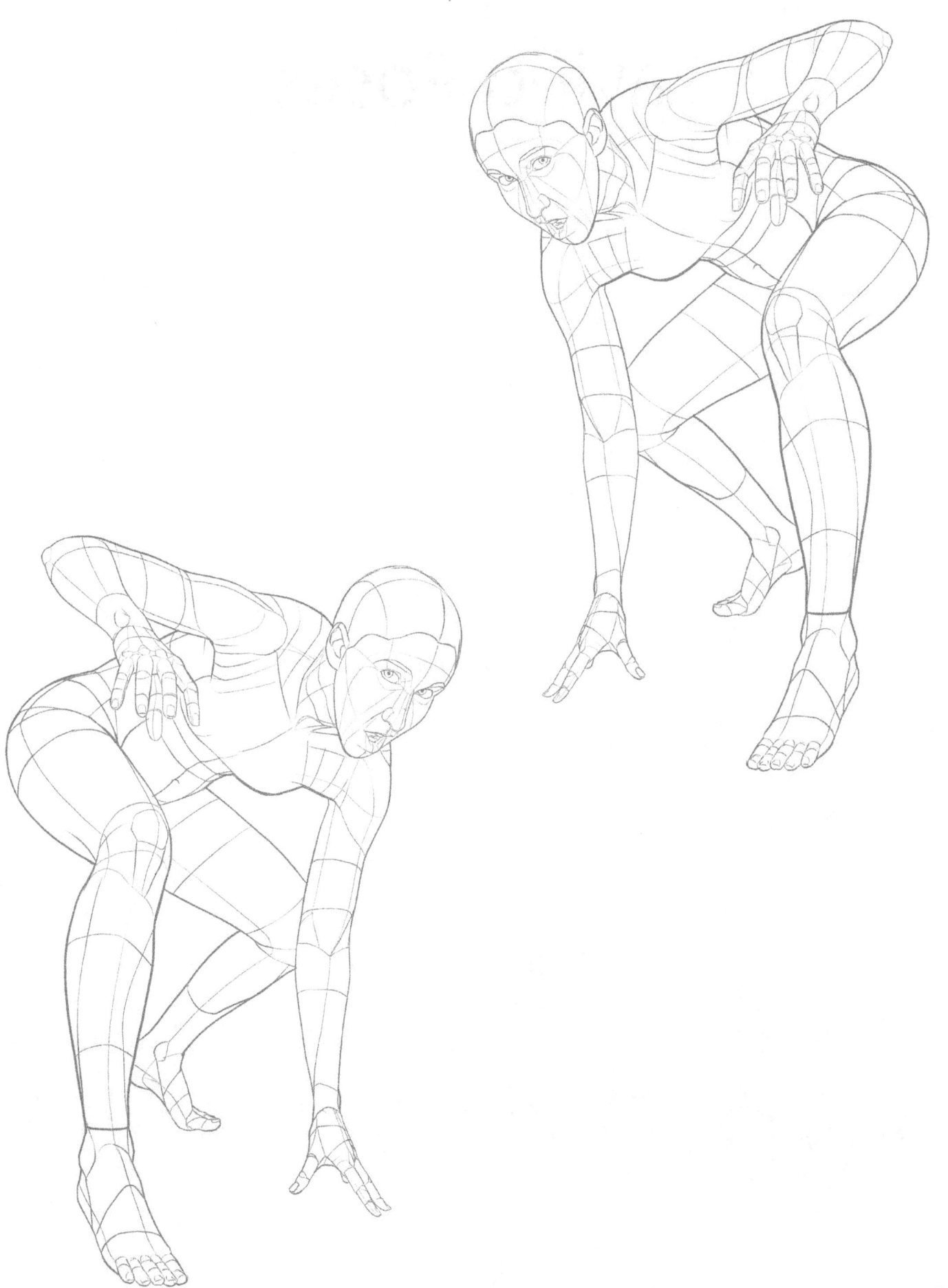

9

Laying Poses

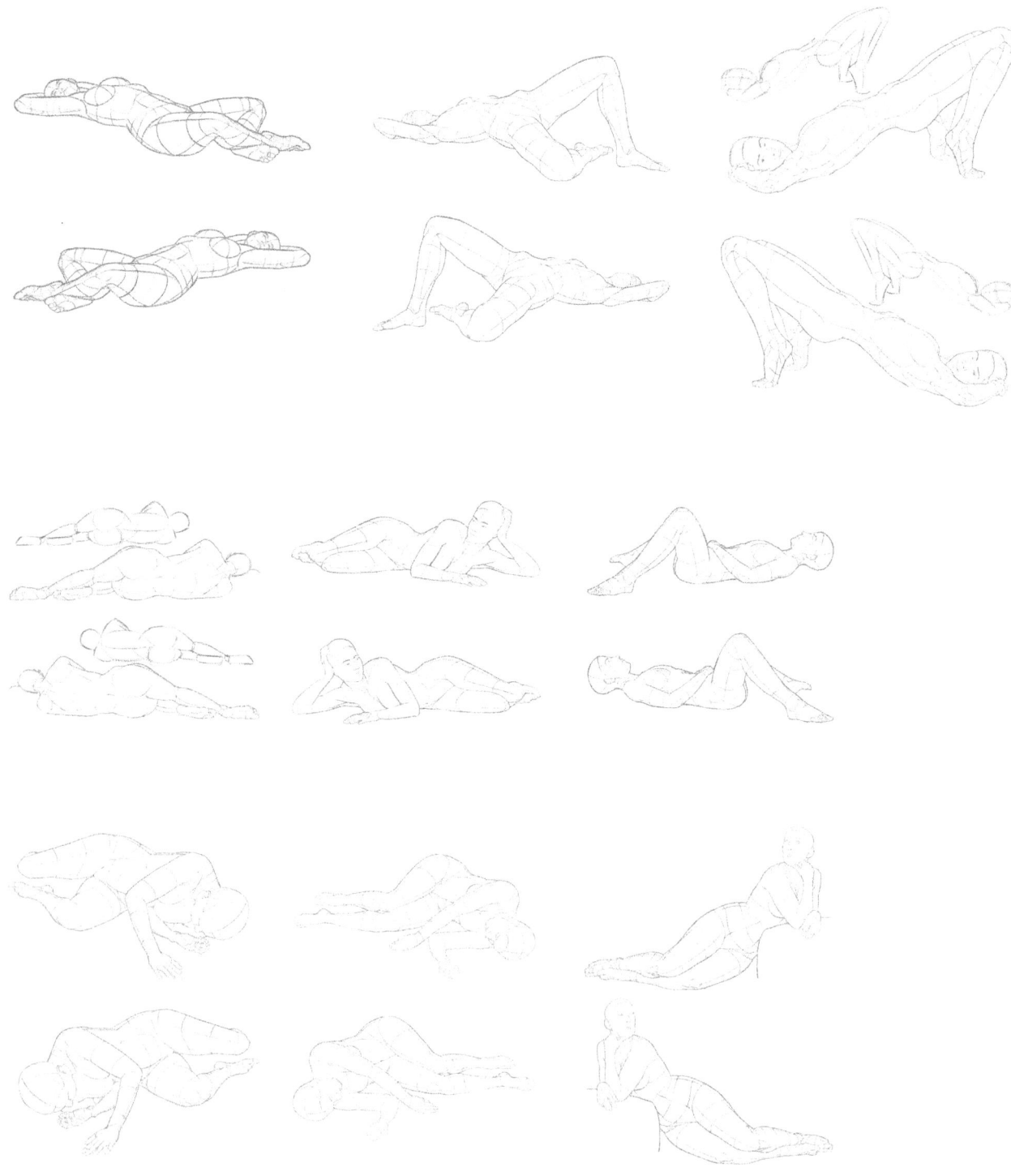

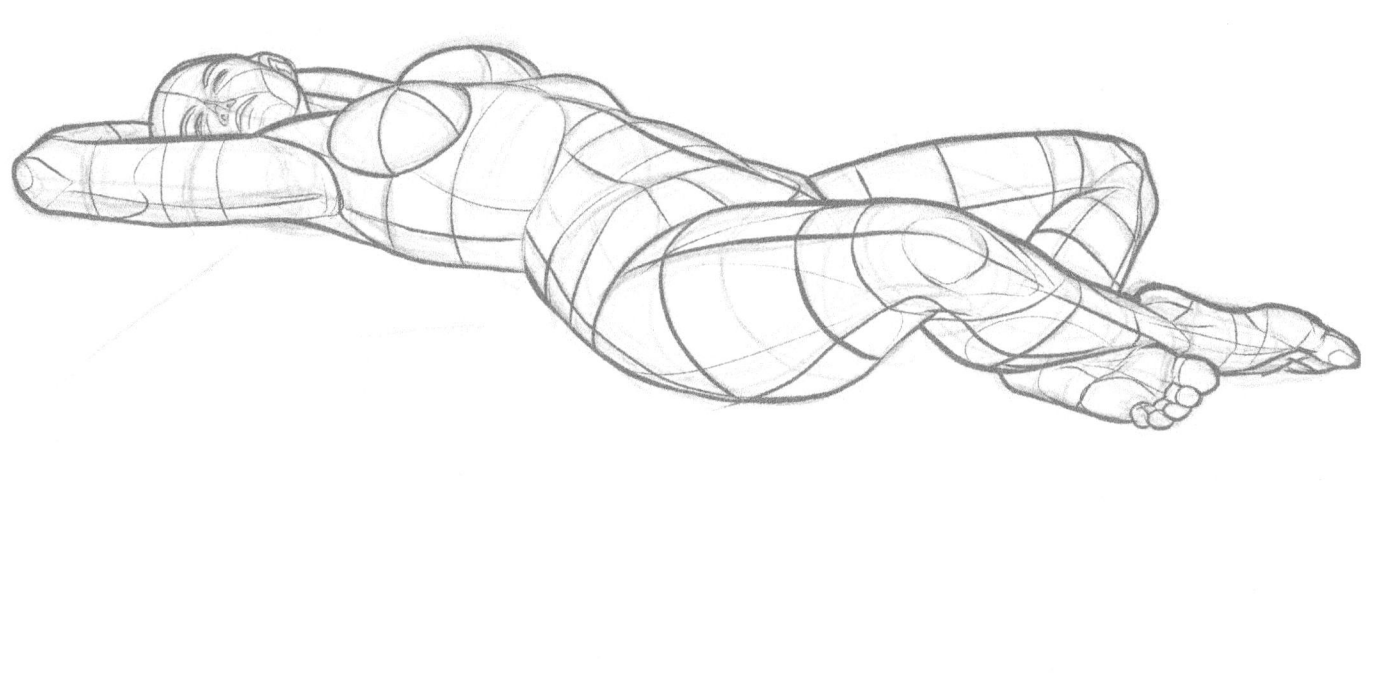

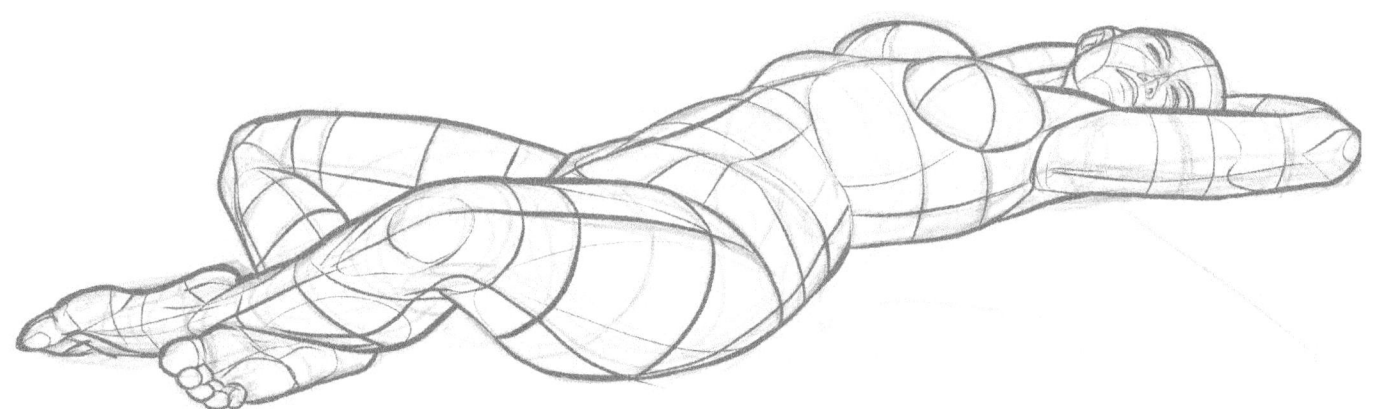

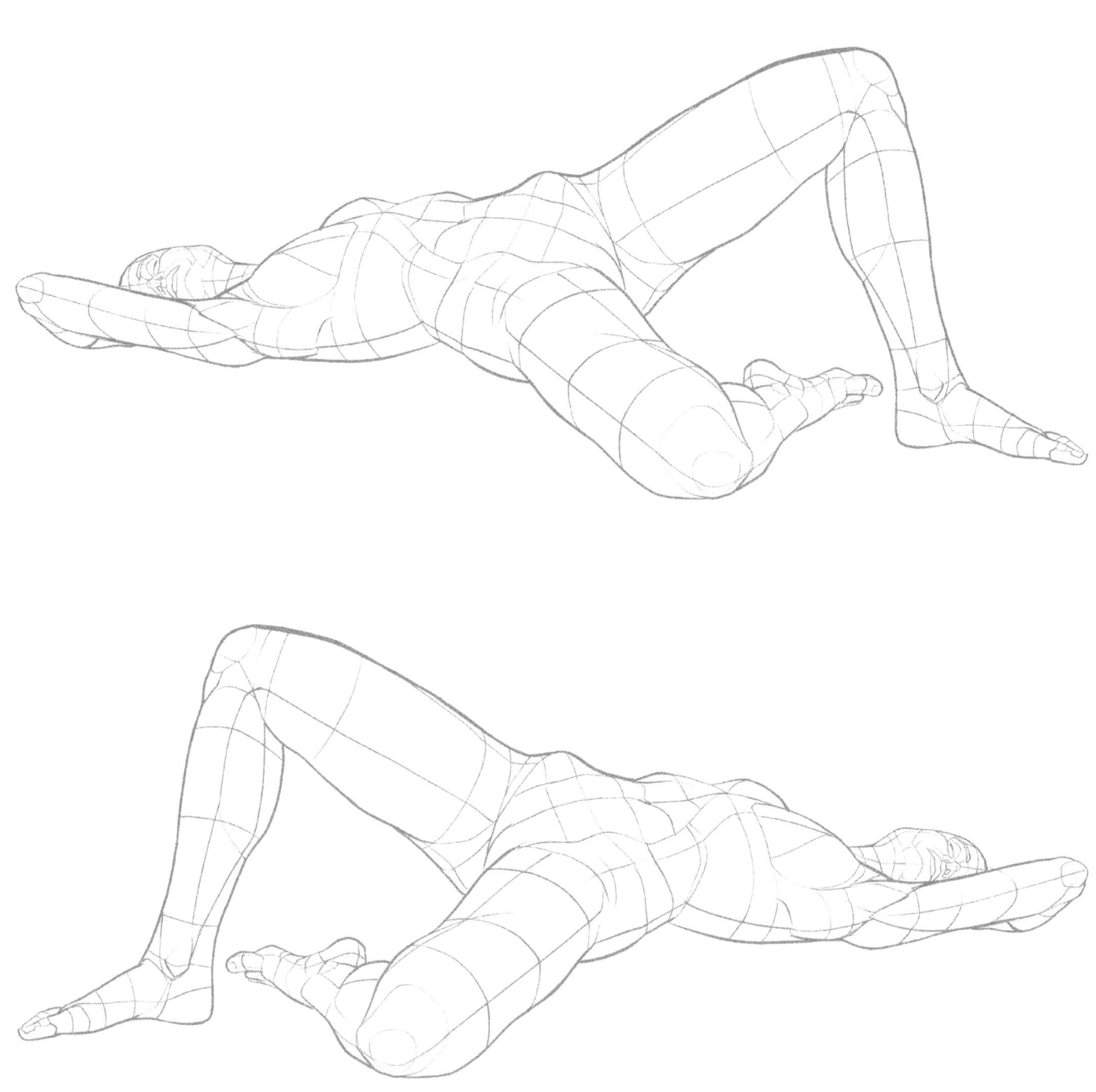

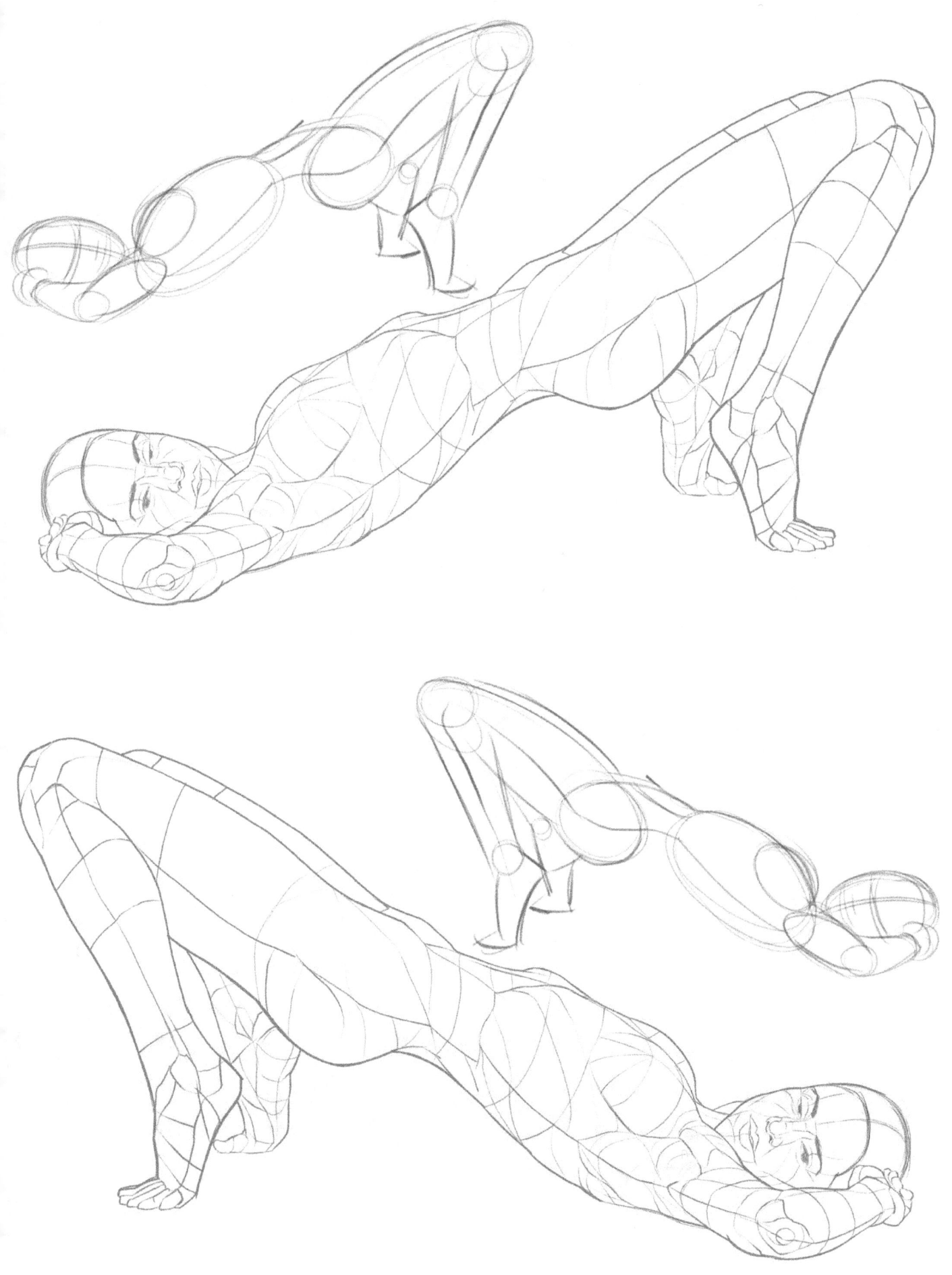

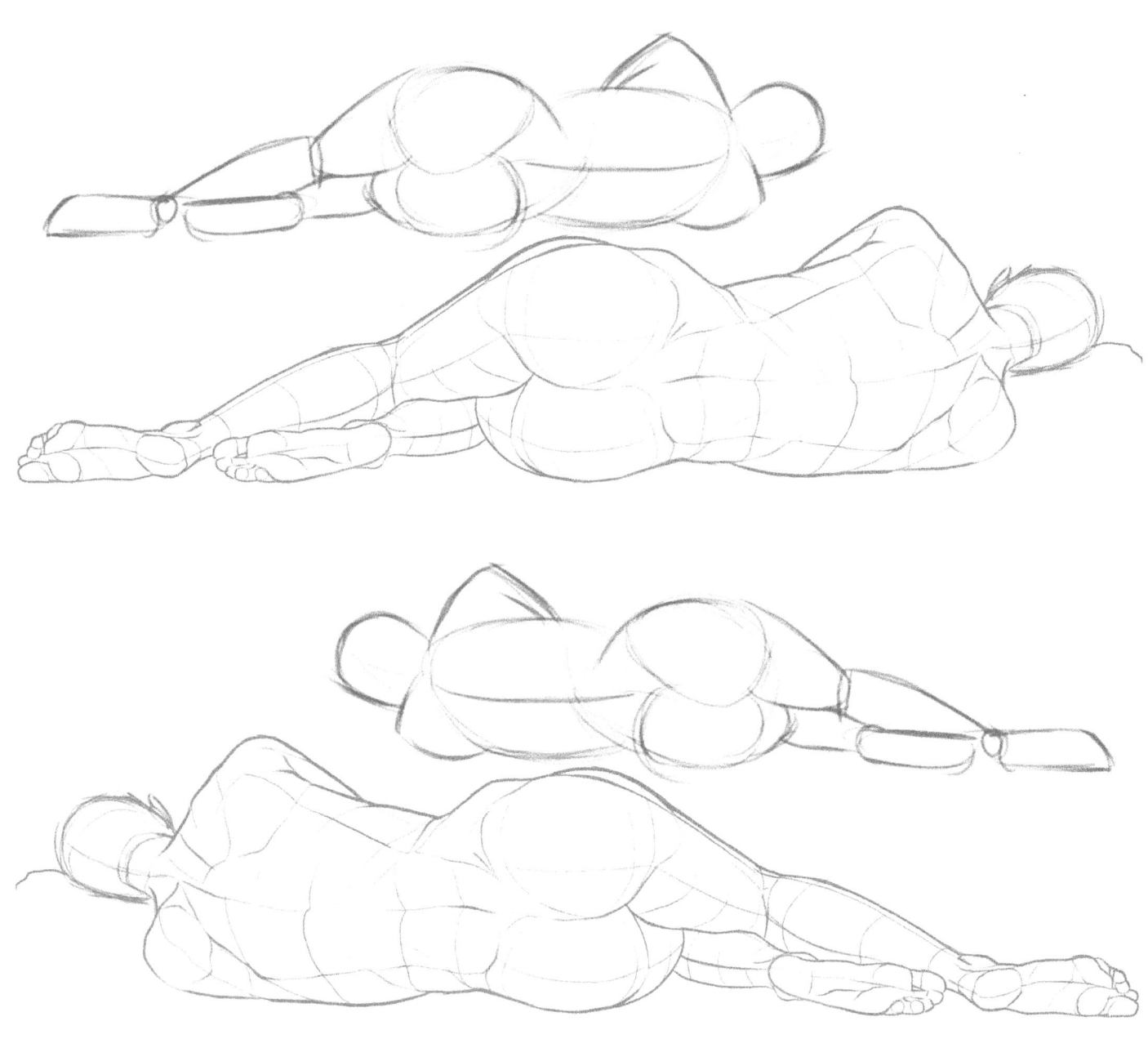

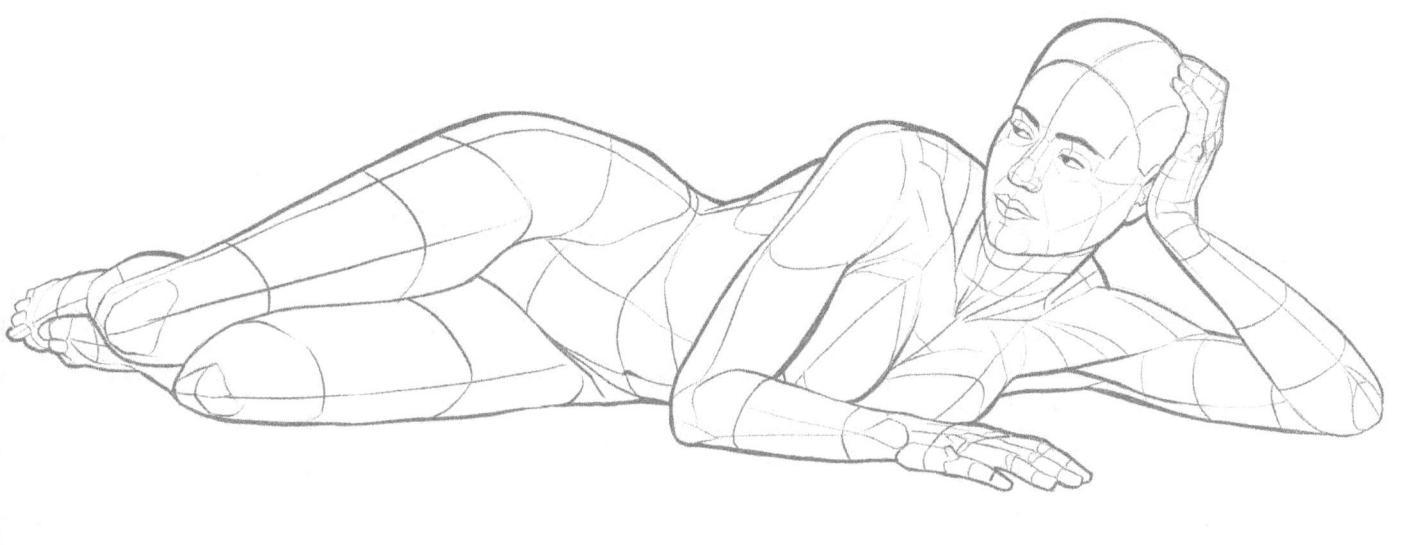

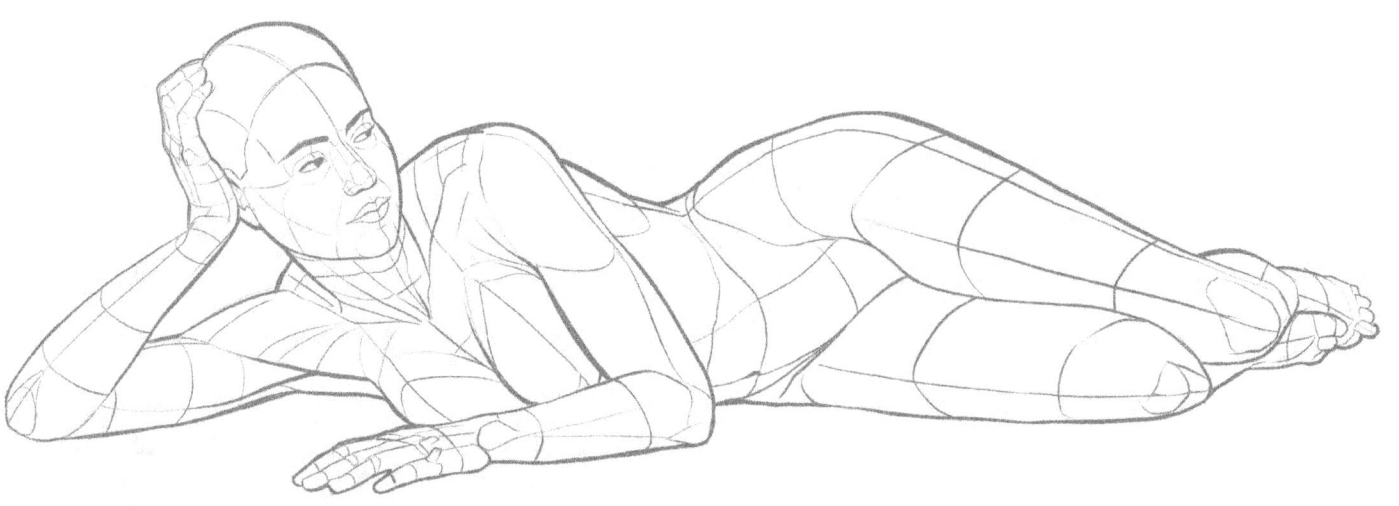

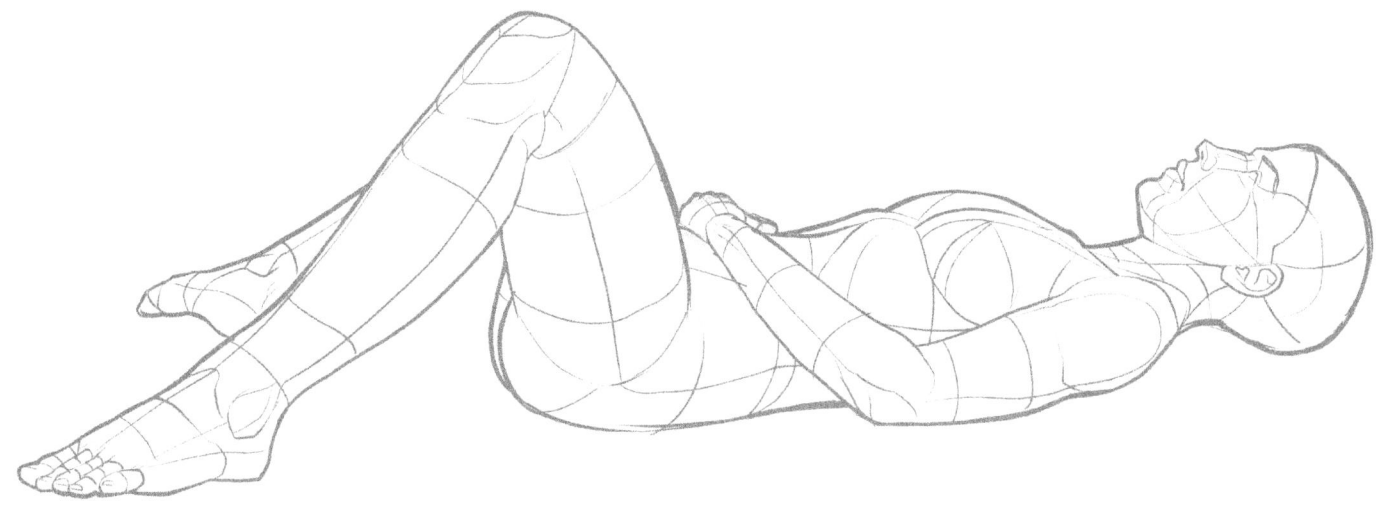

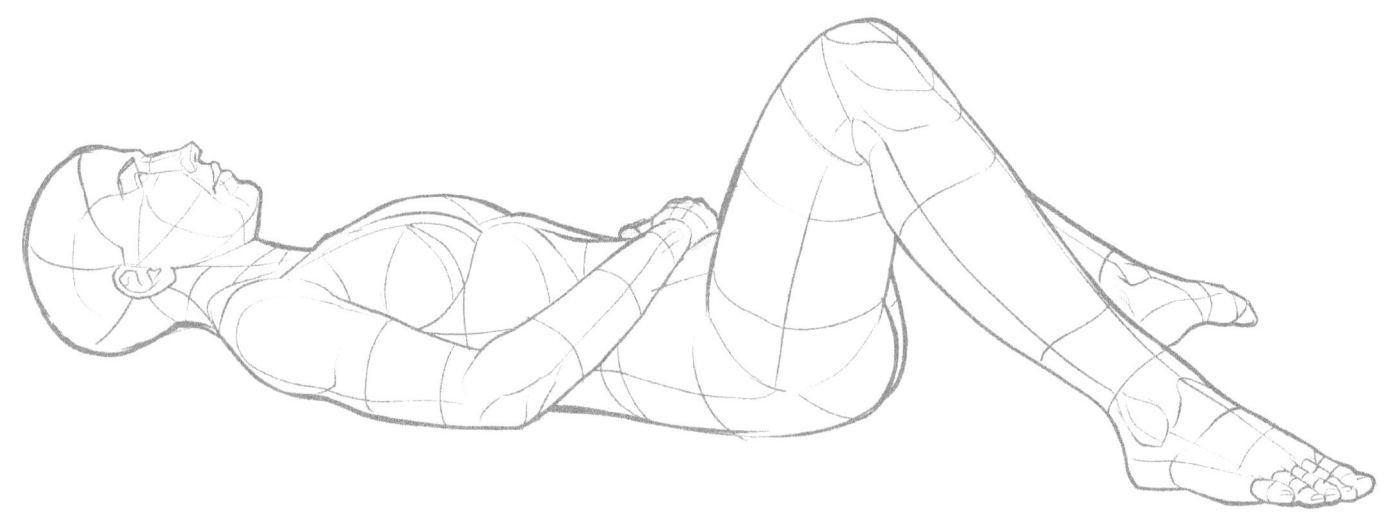

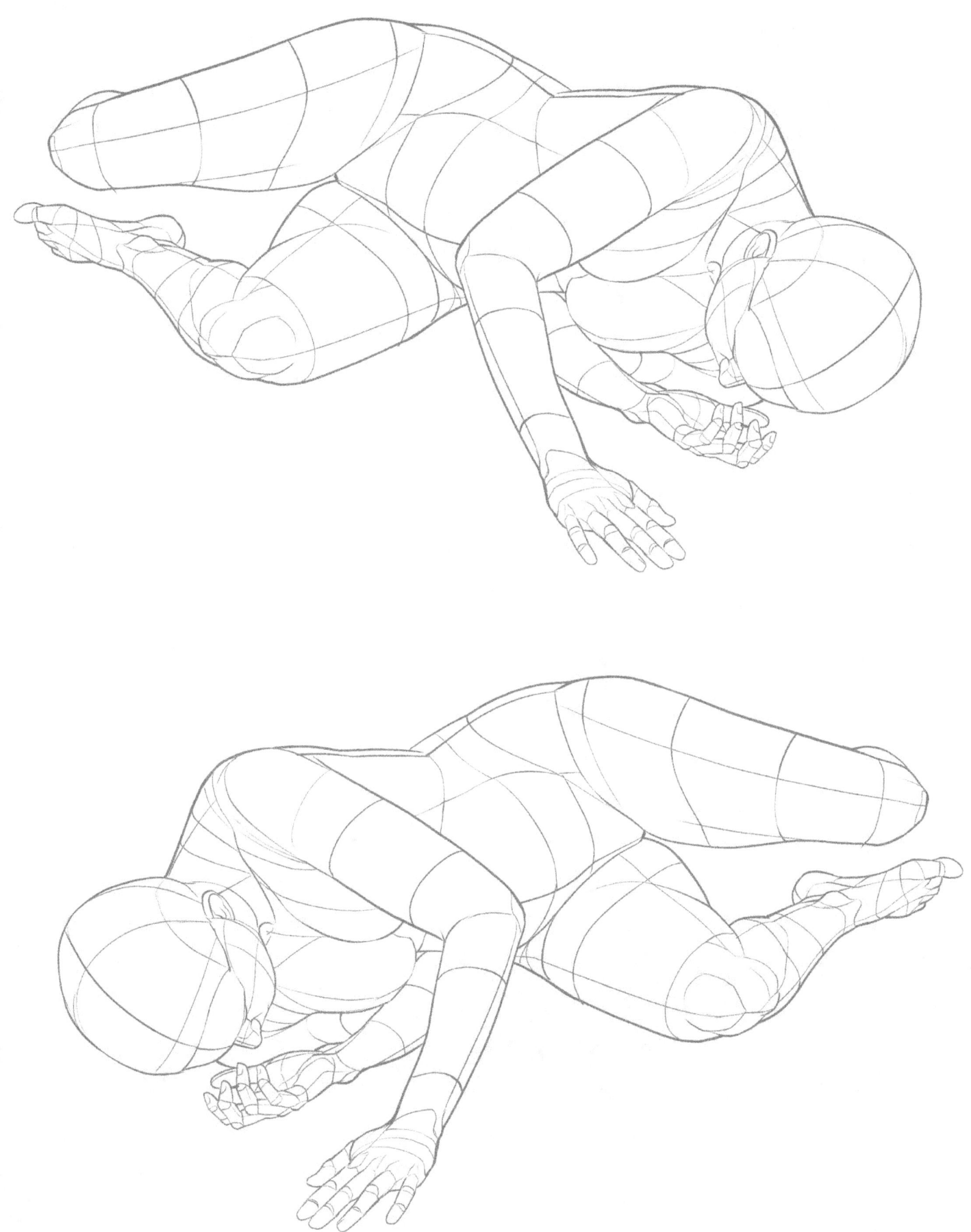

17

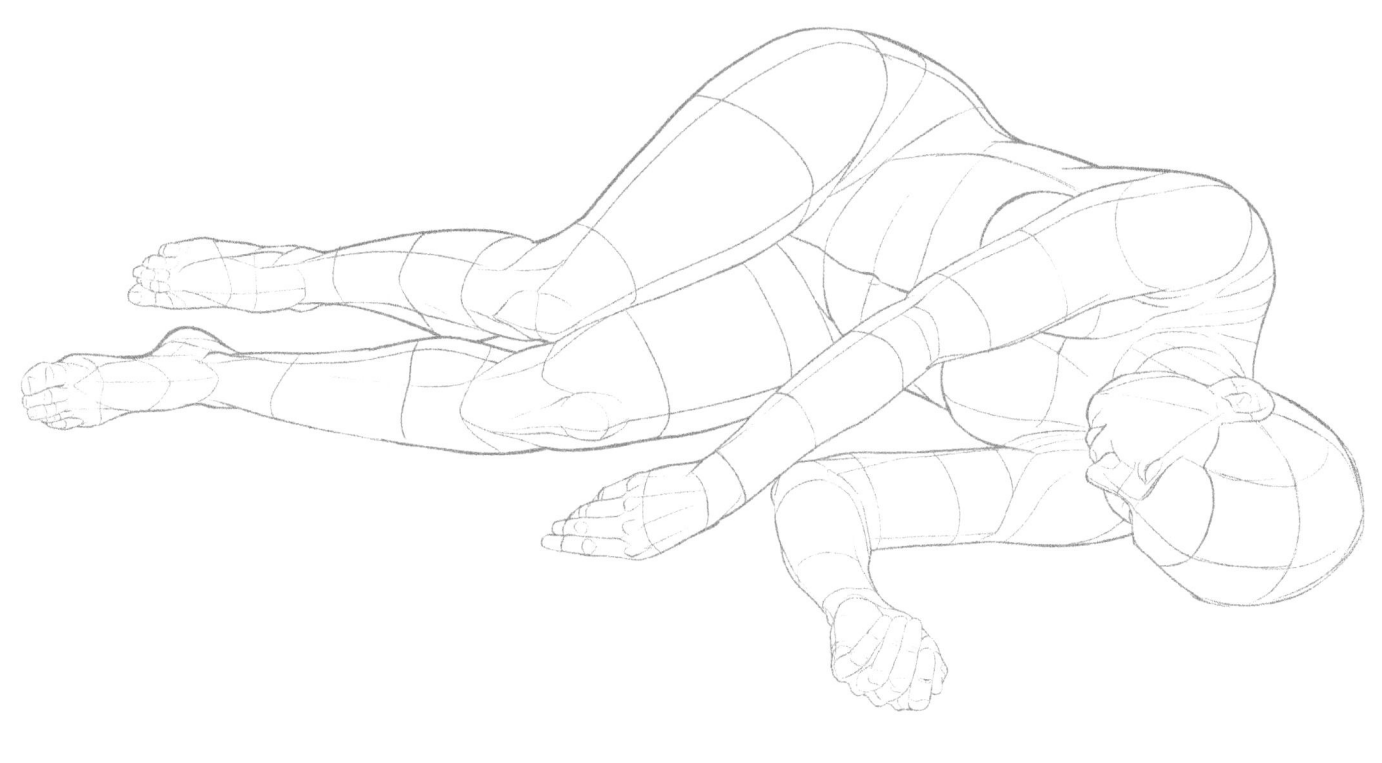

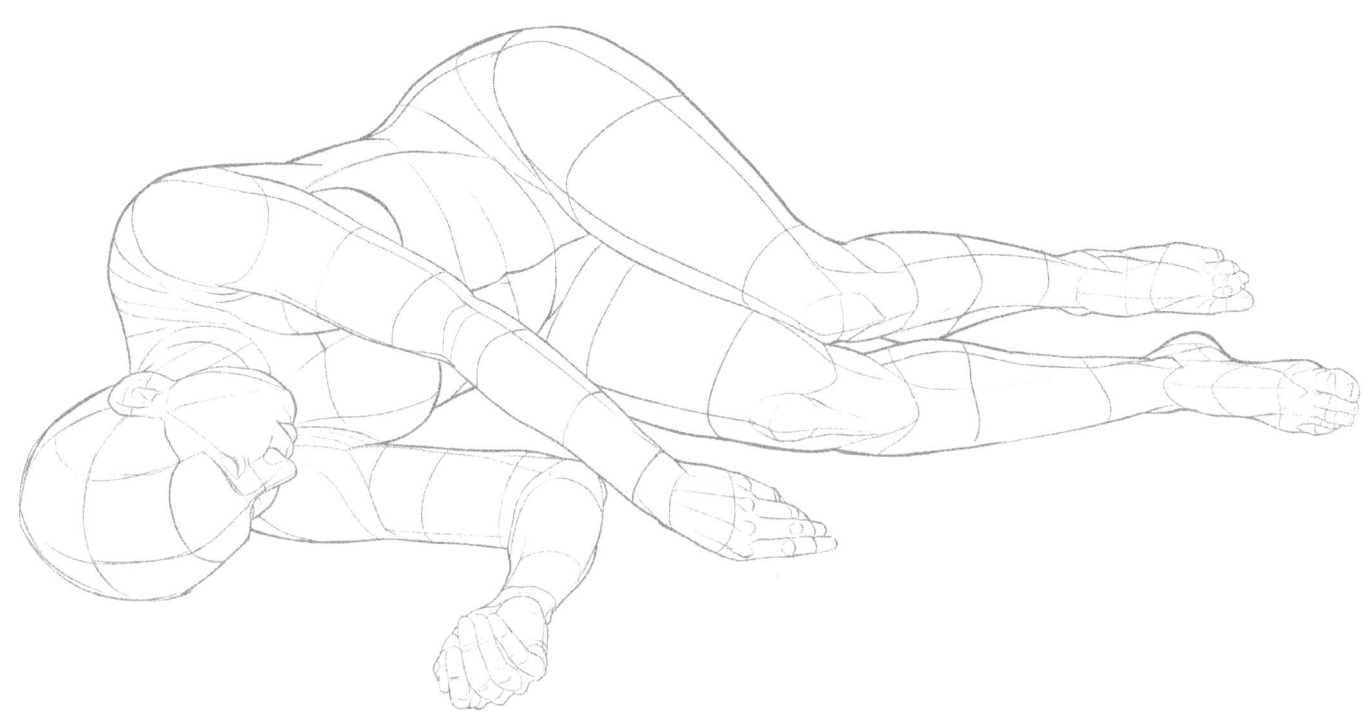

18

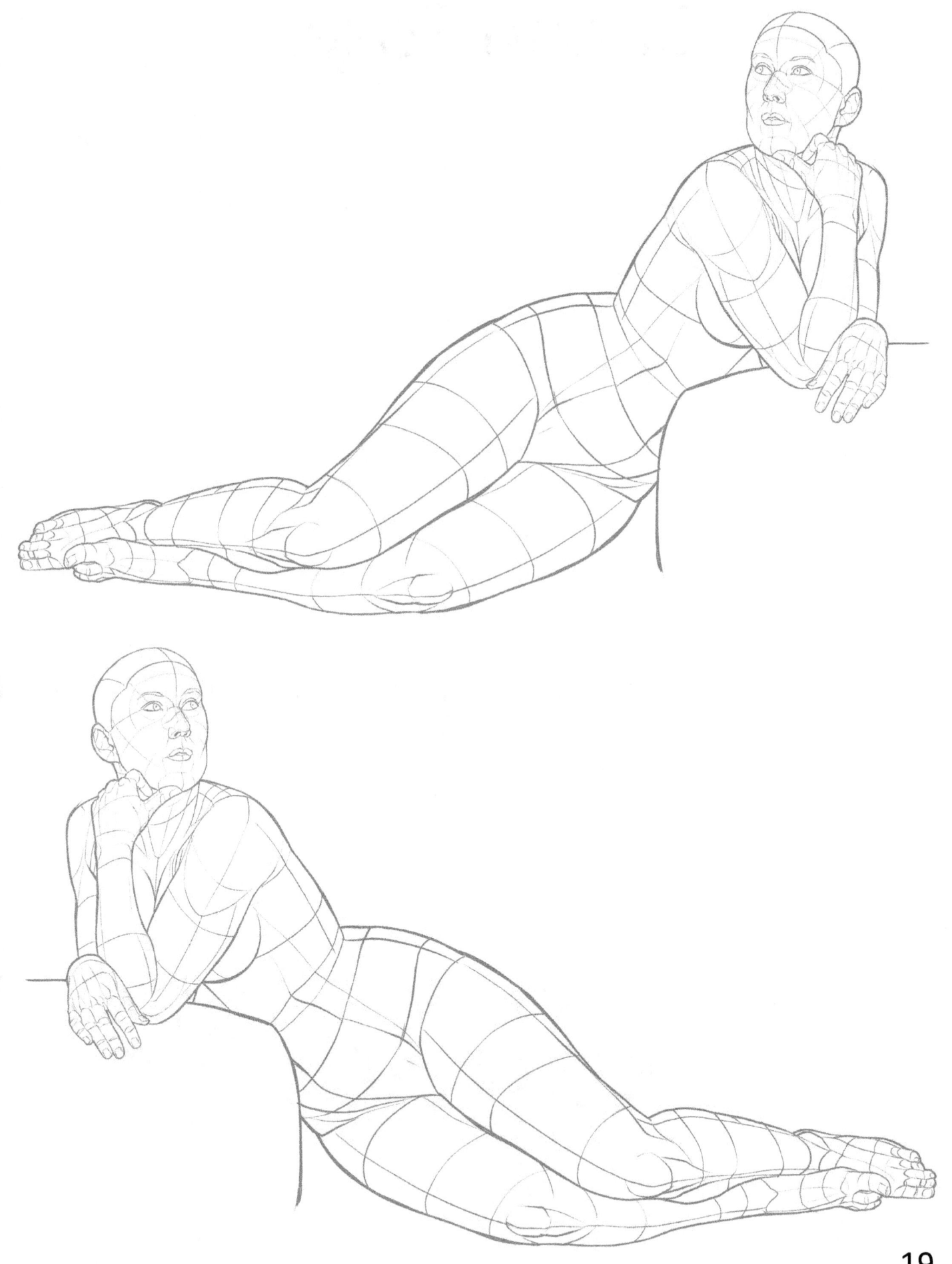

19

Sitting Poses

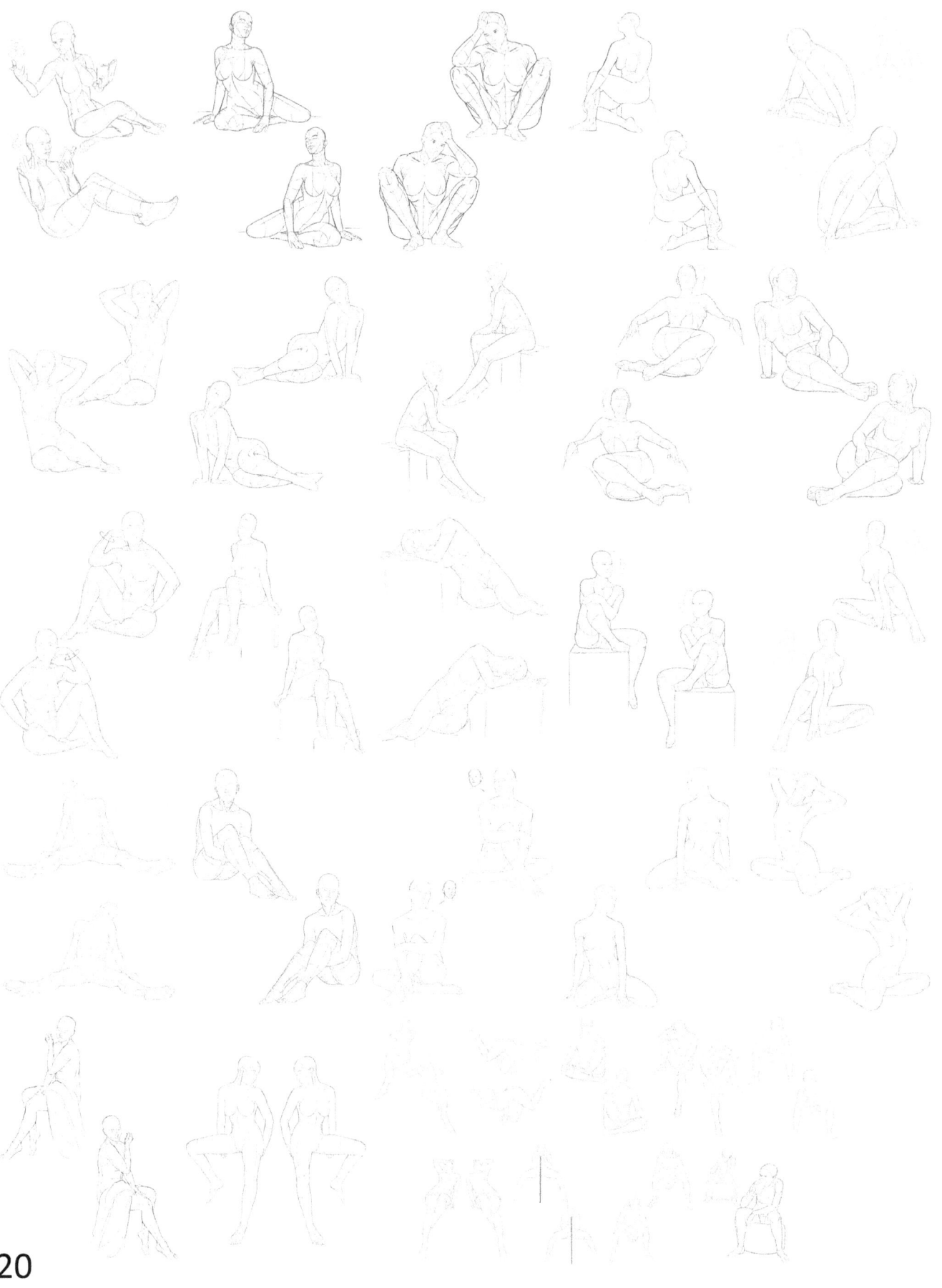

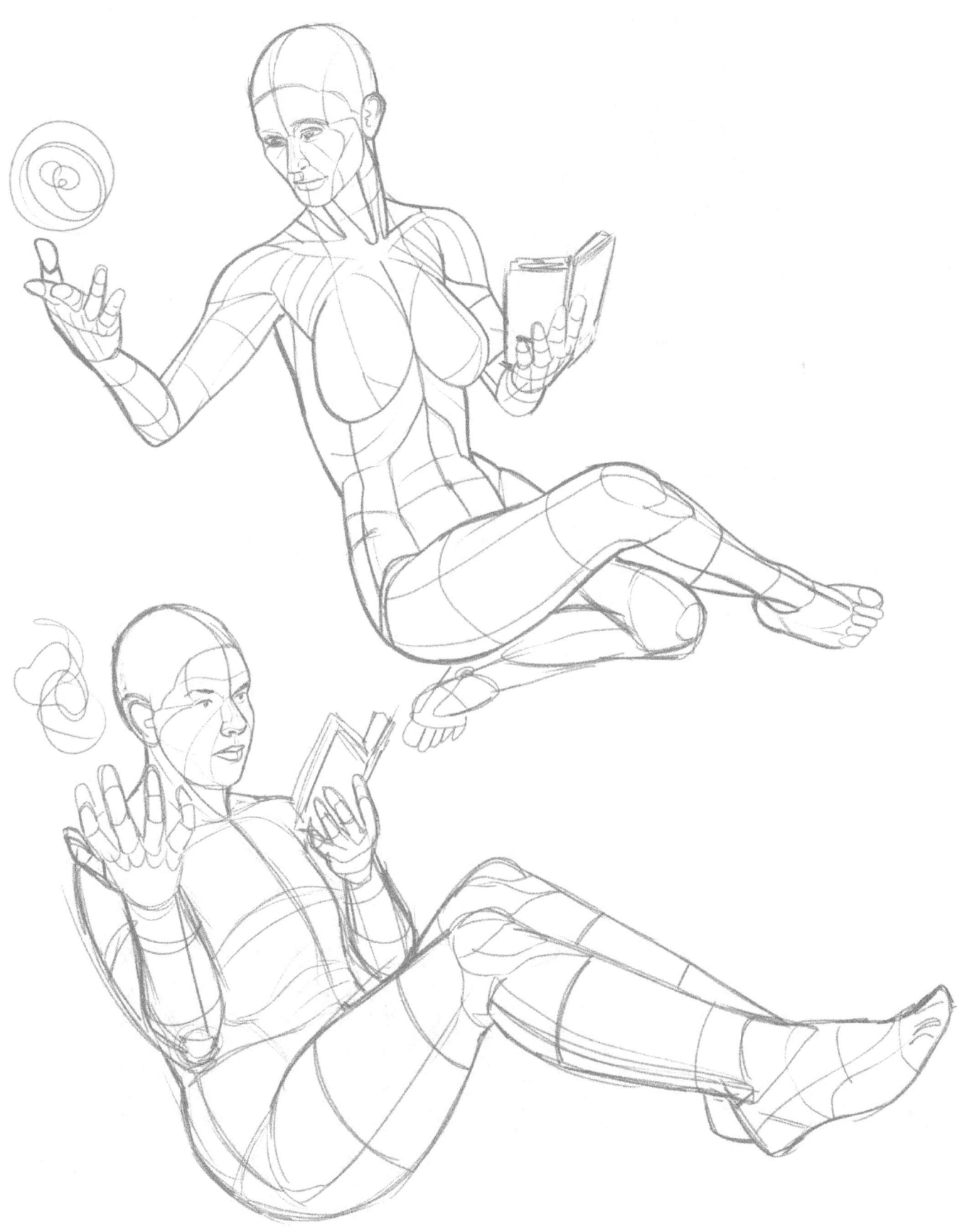

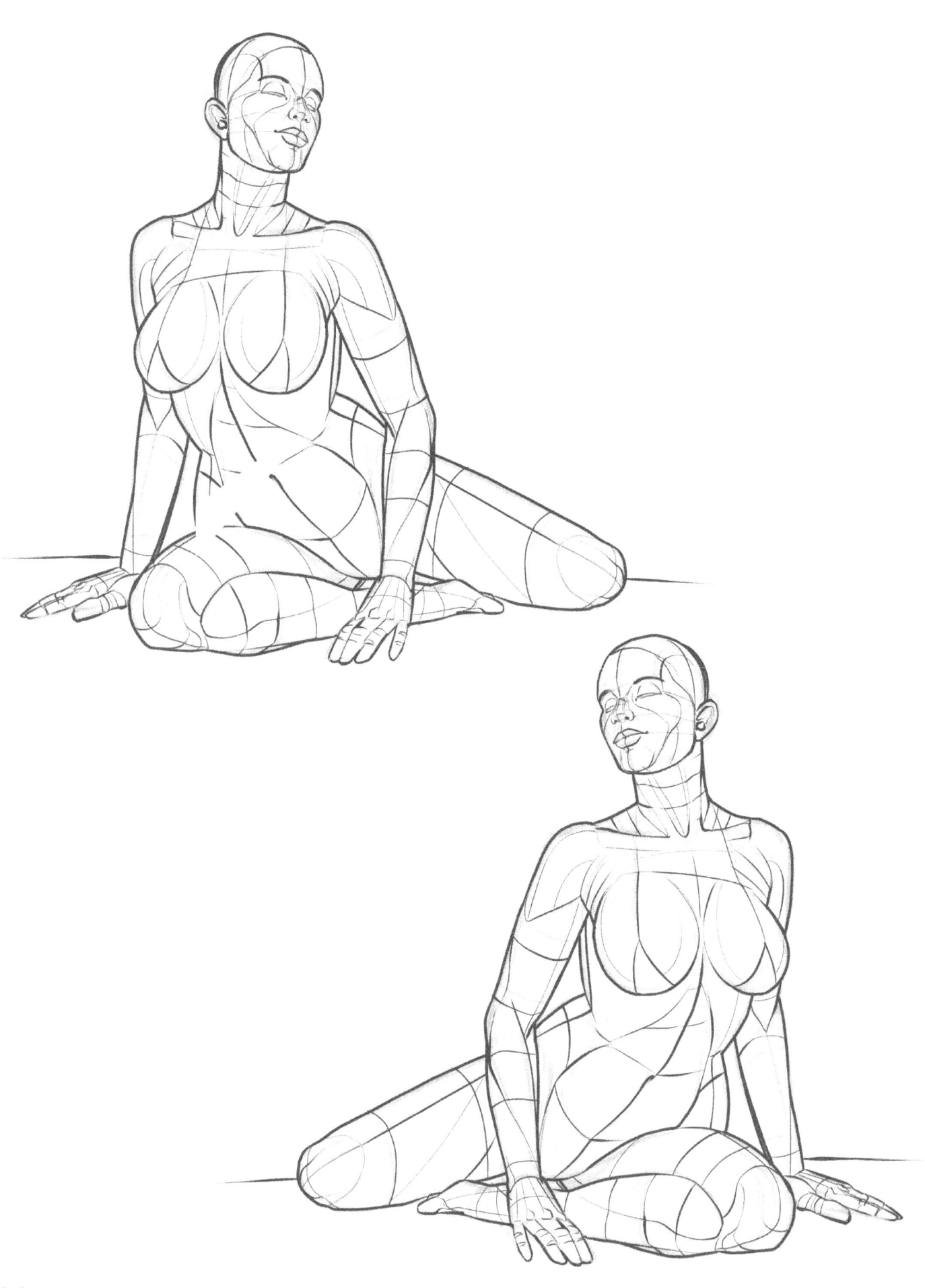

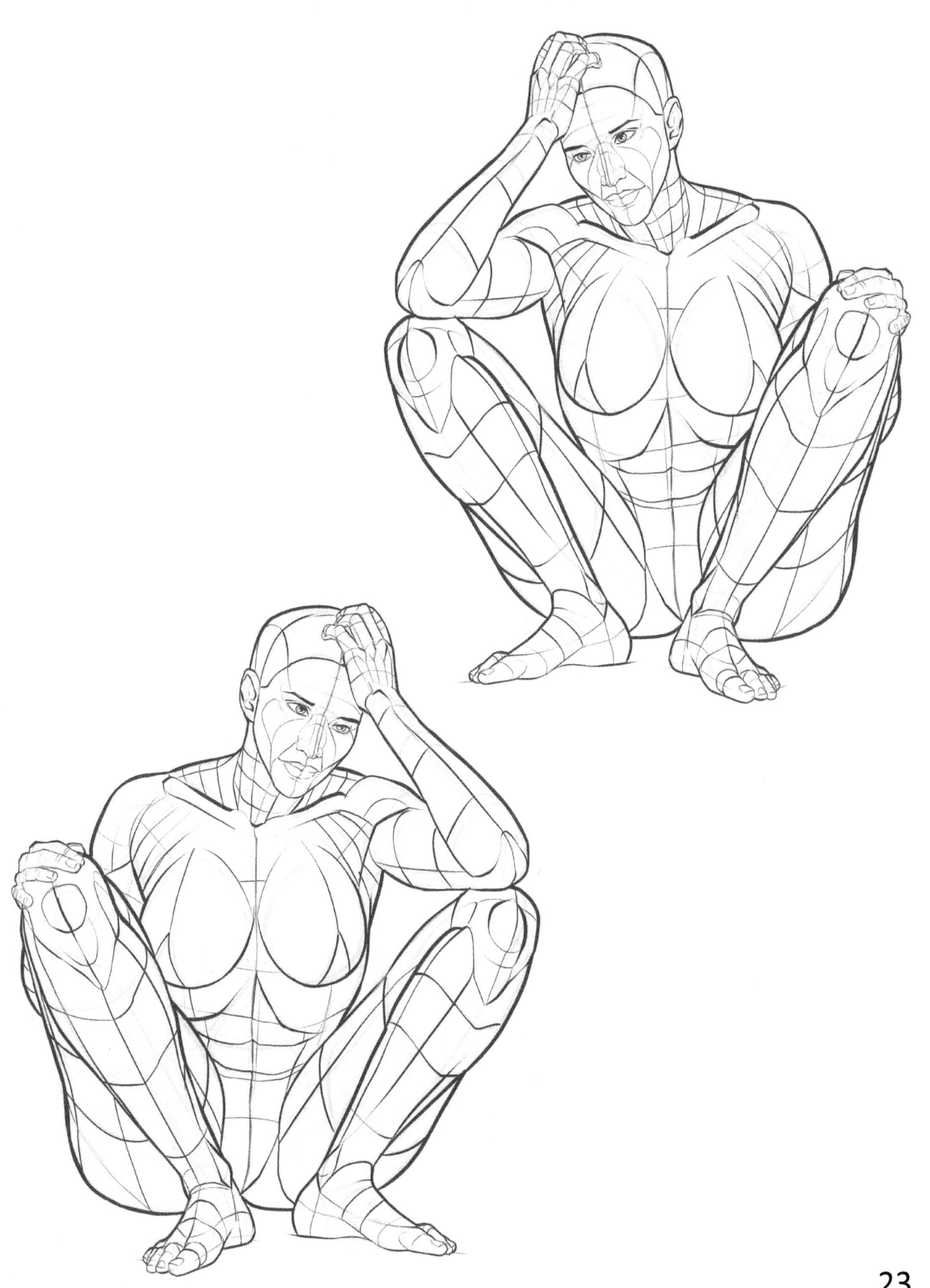

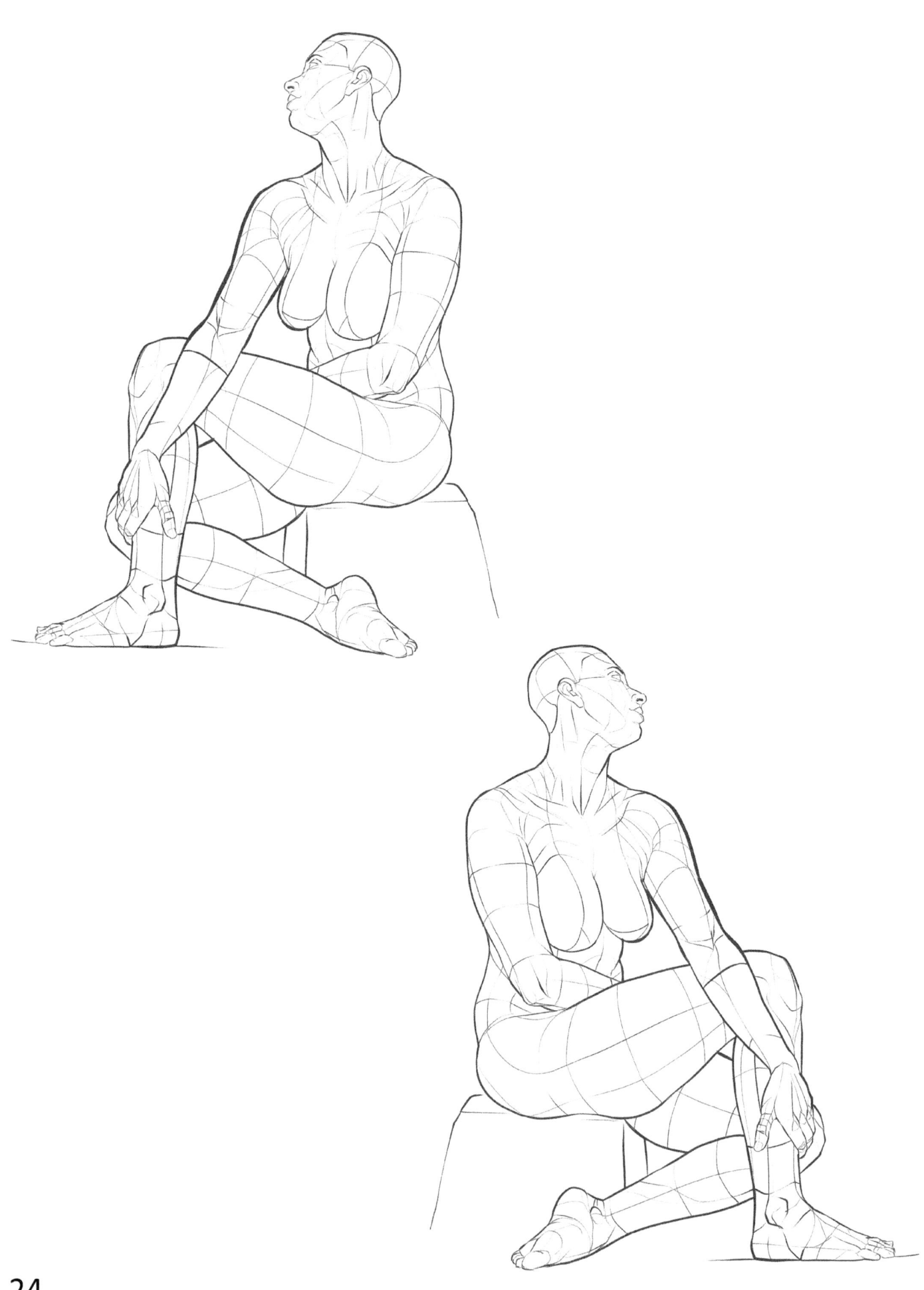

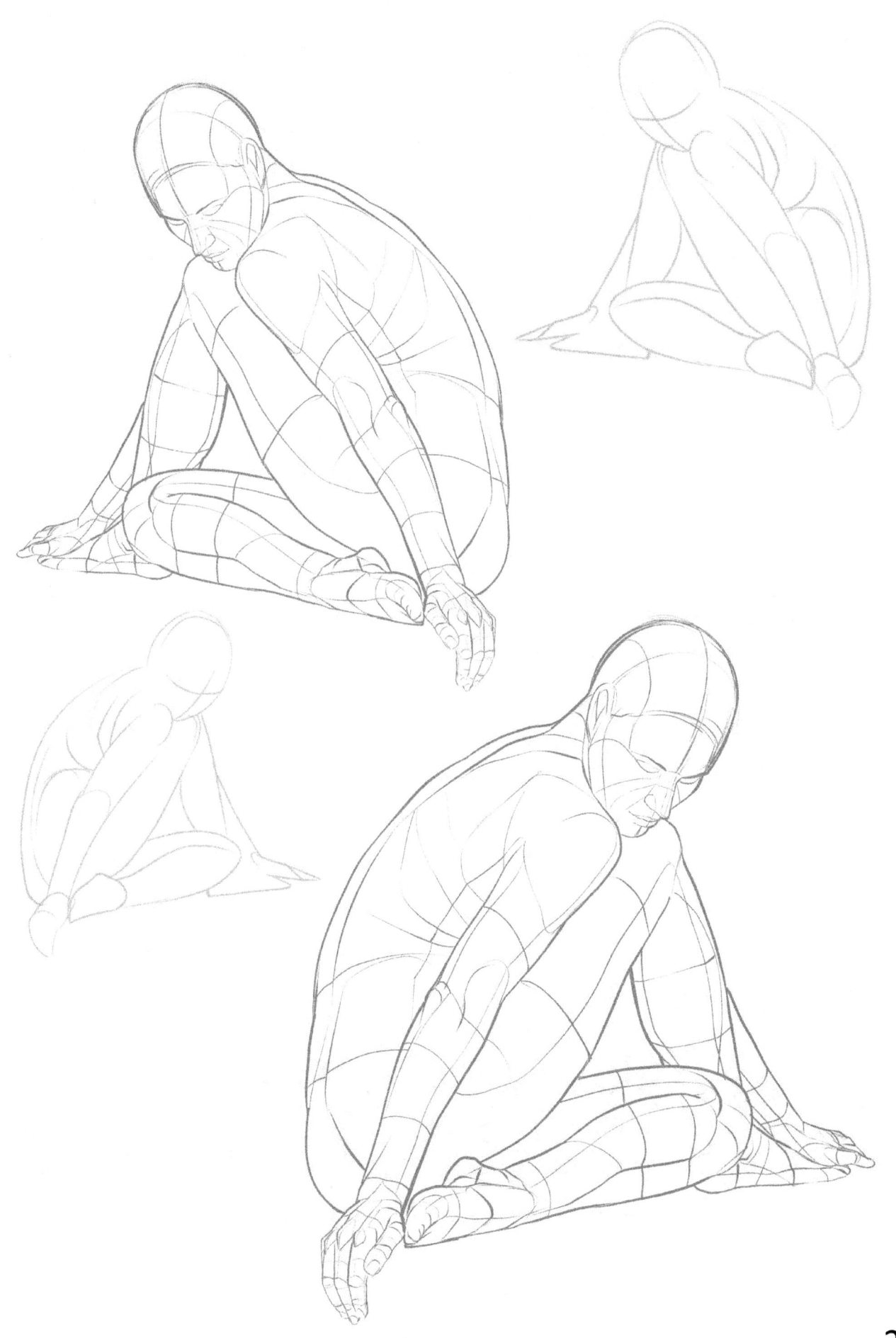

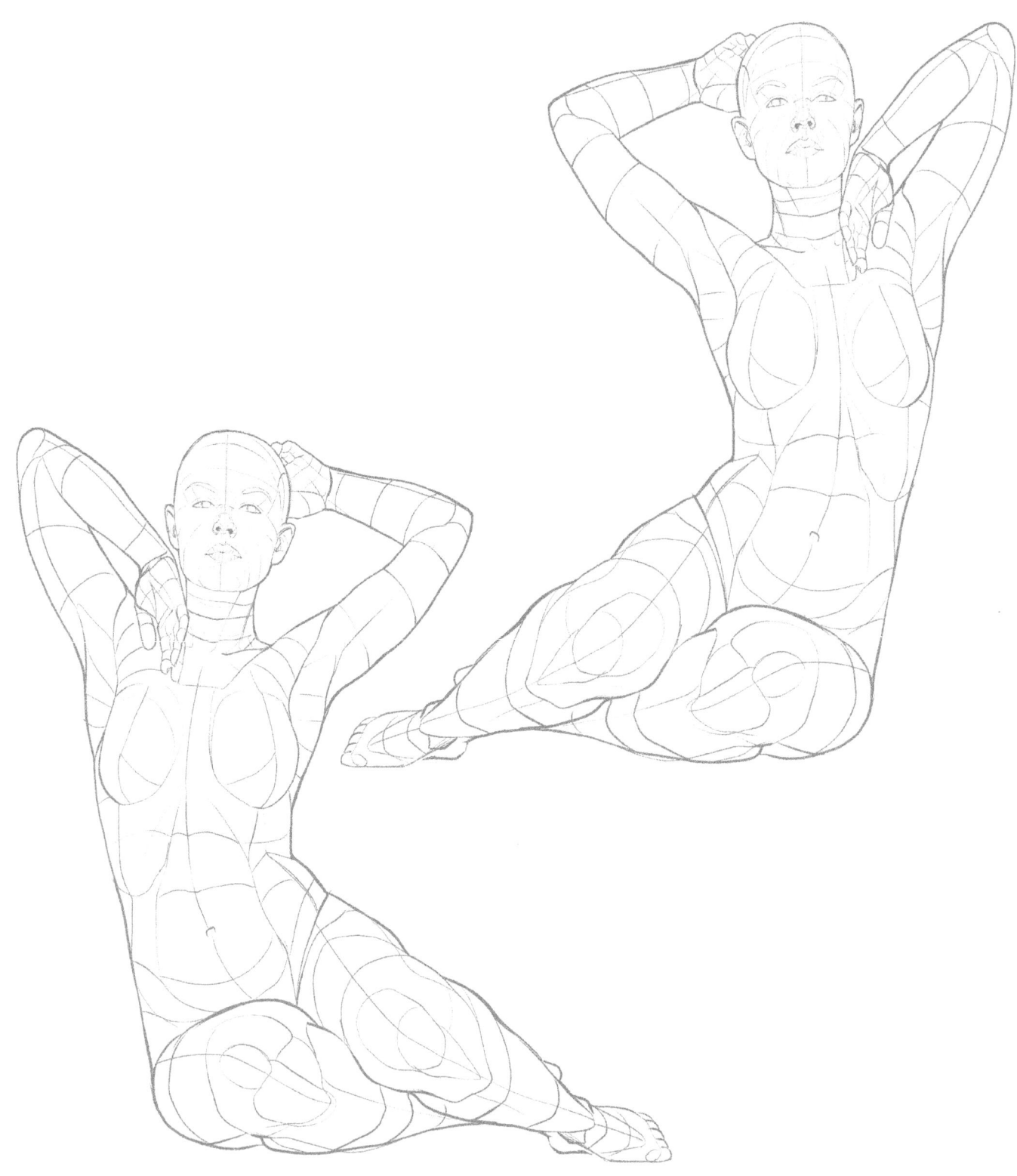

26

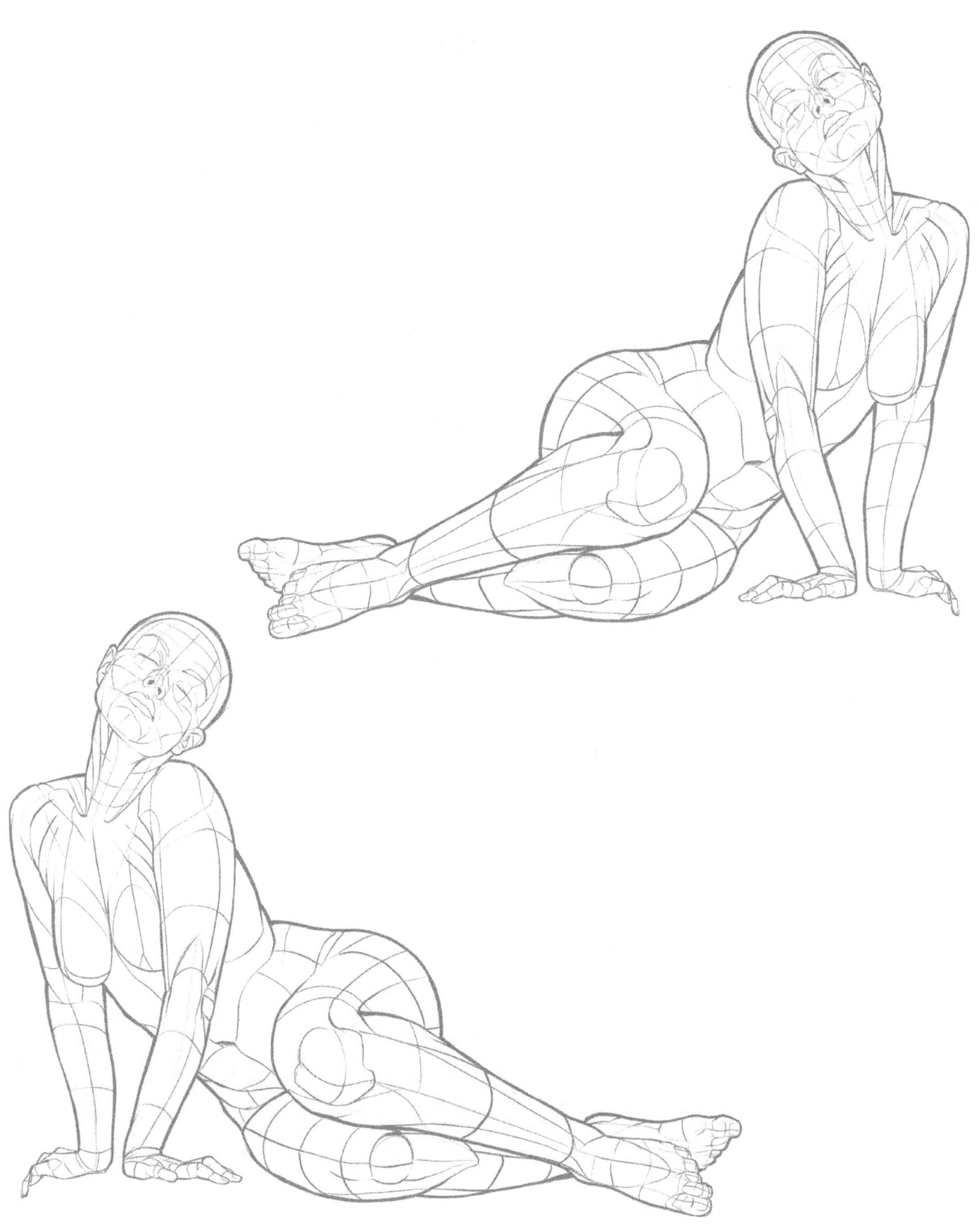

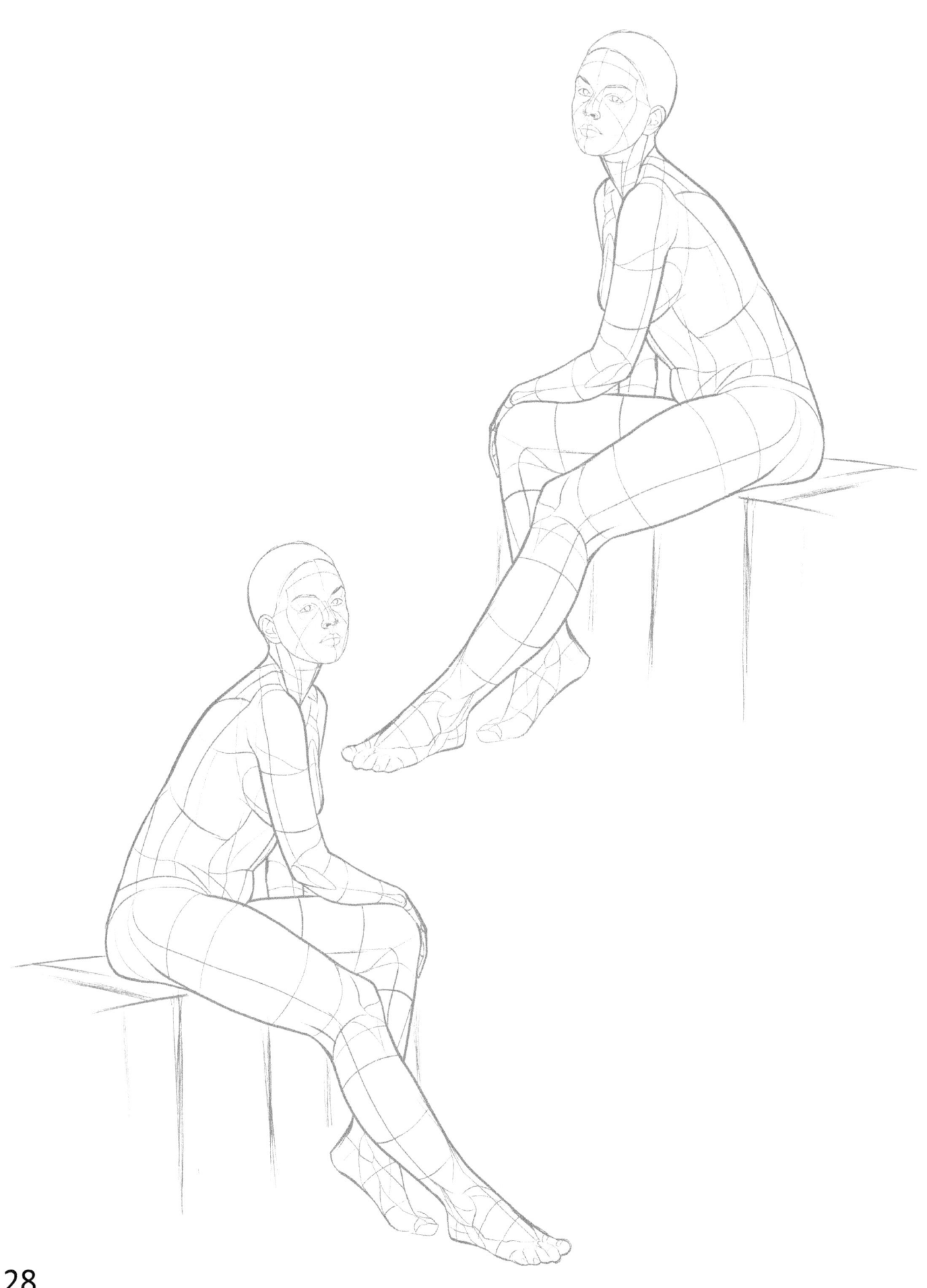

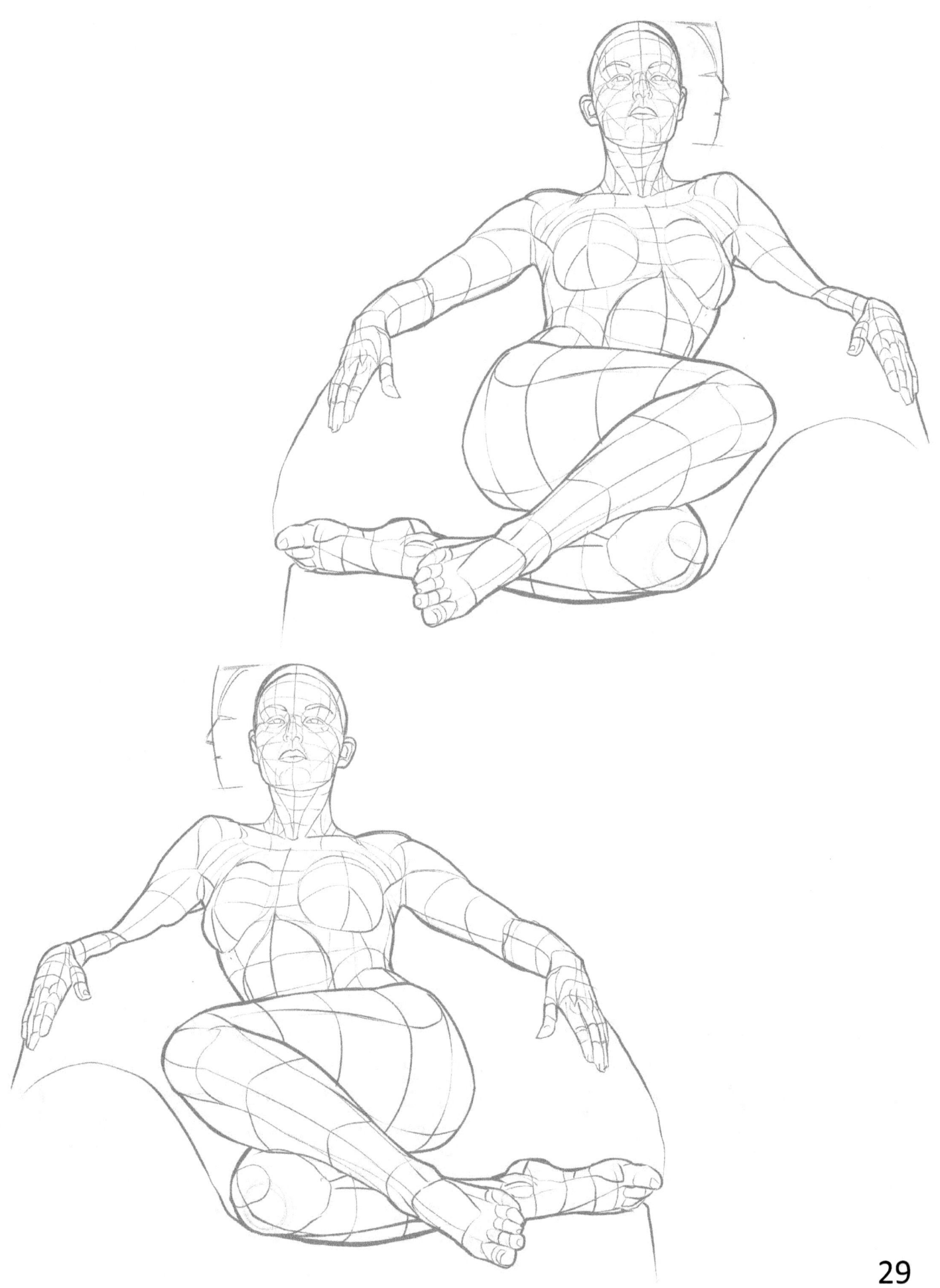

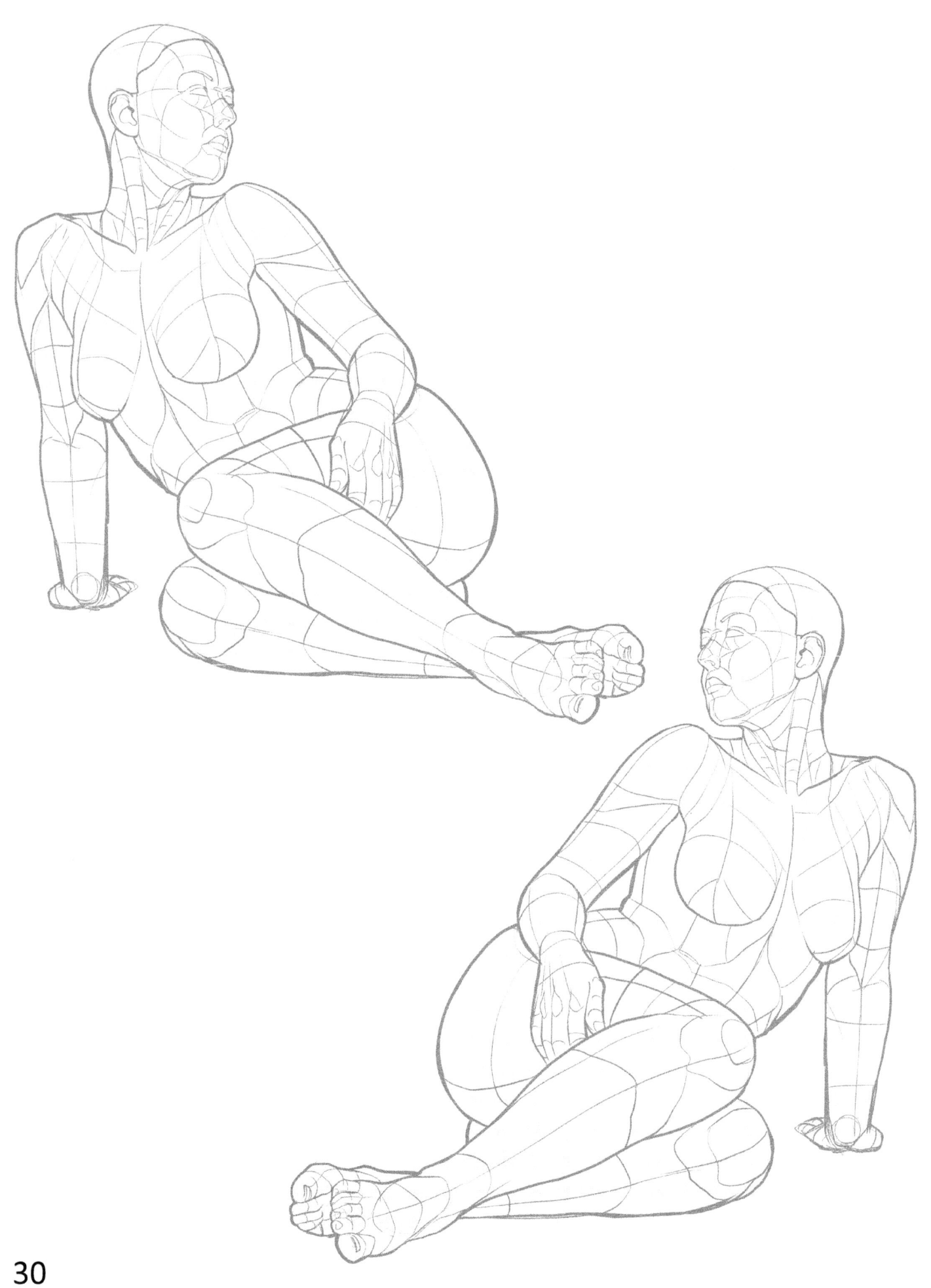

30

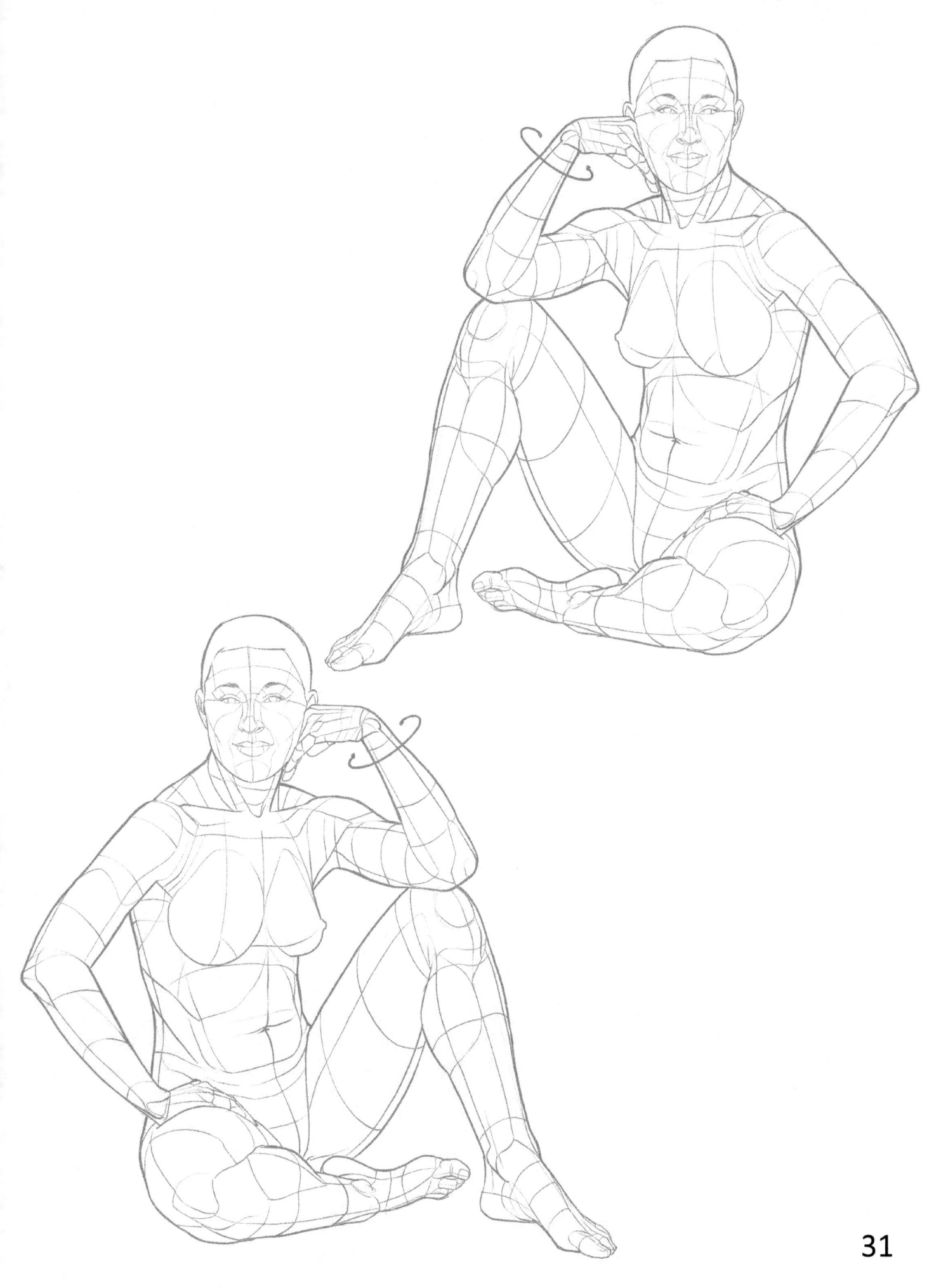

31

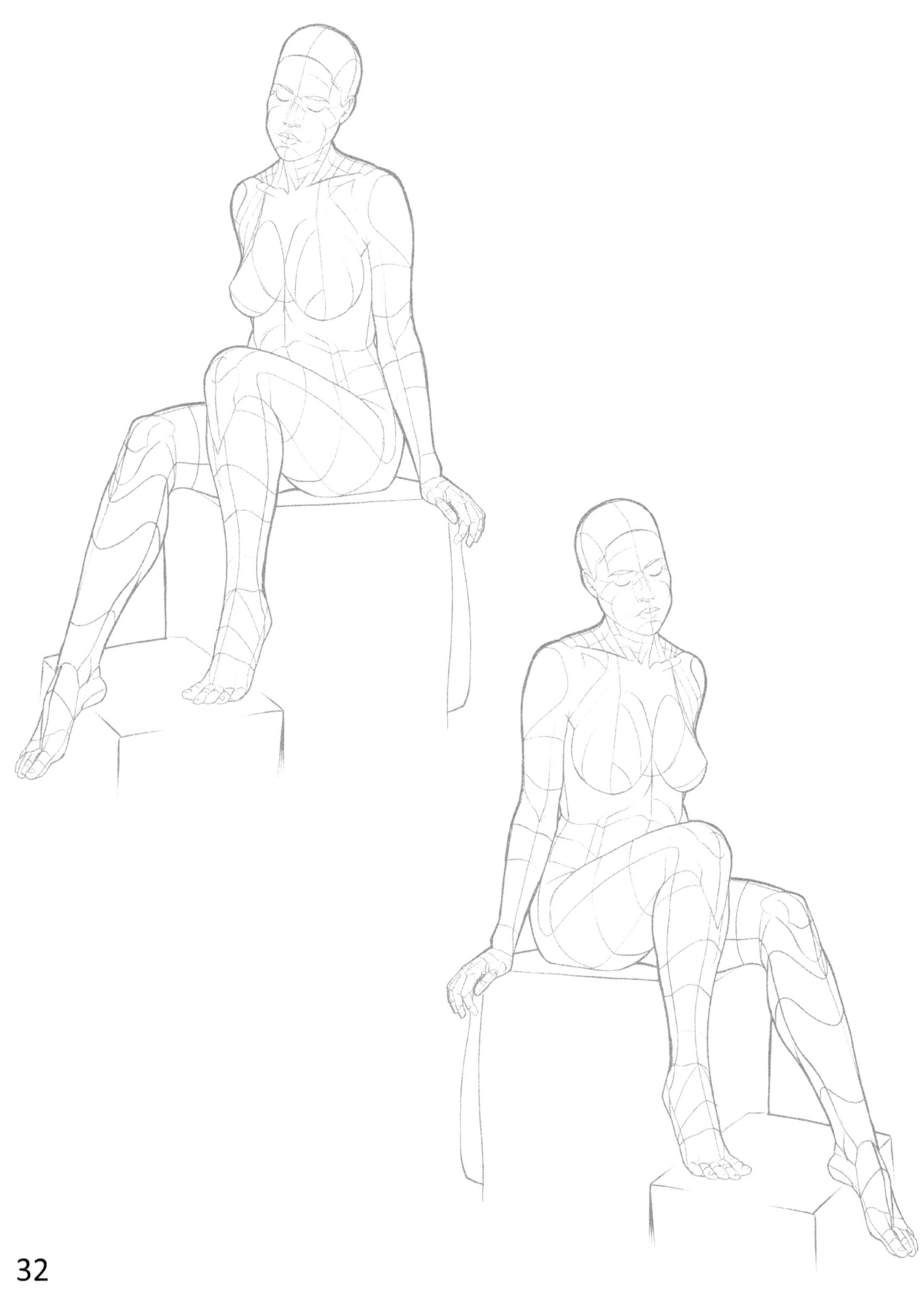

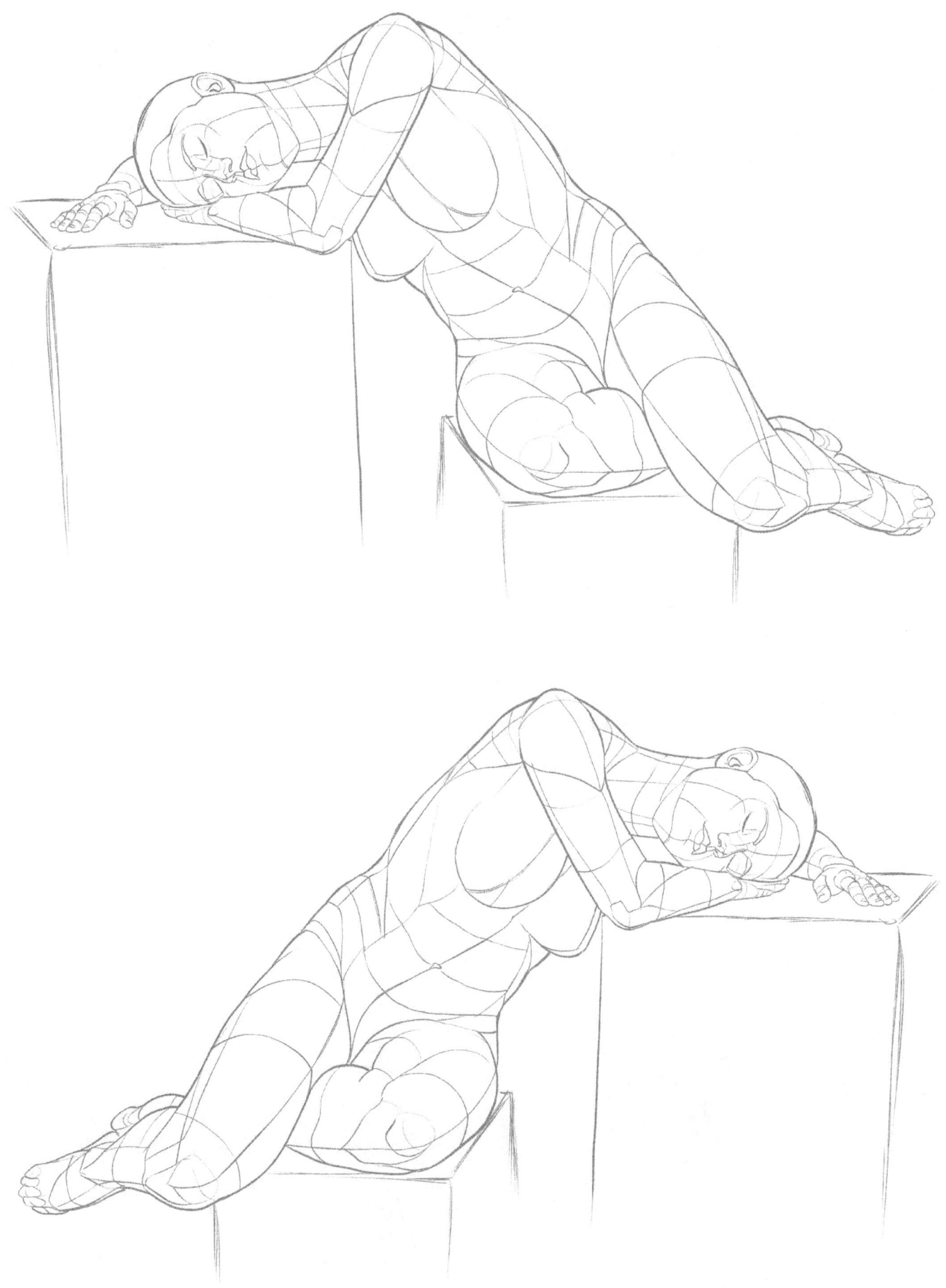

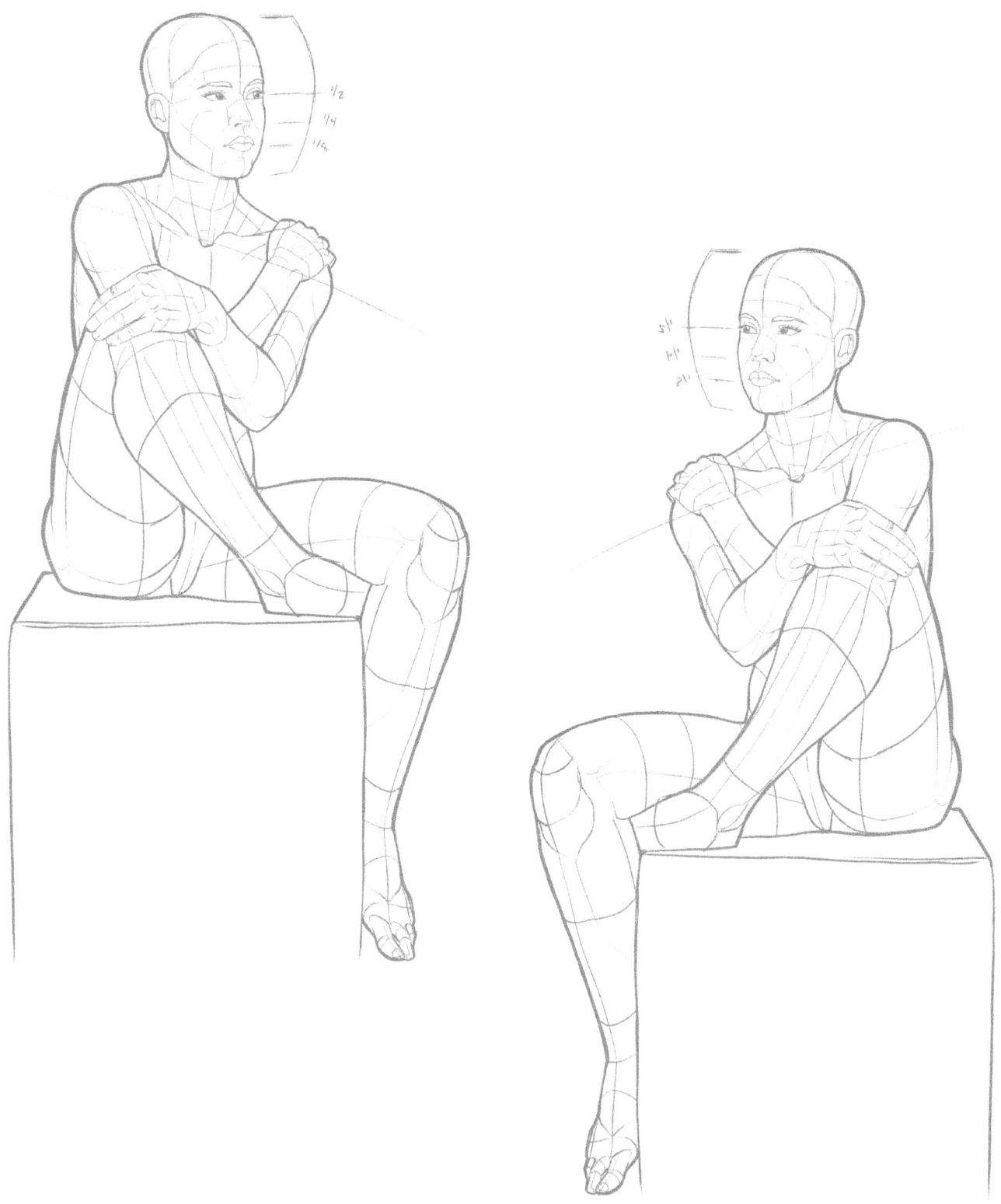

1/2
1/4
1/4

1/2
1/4
1/4

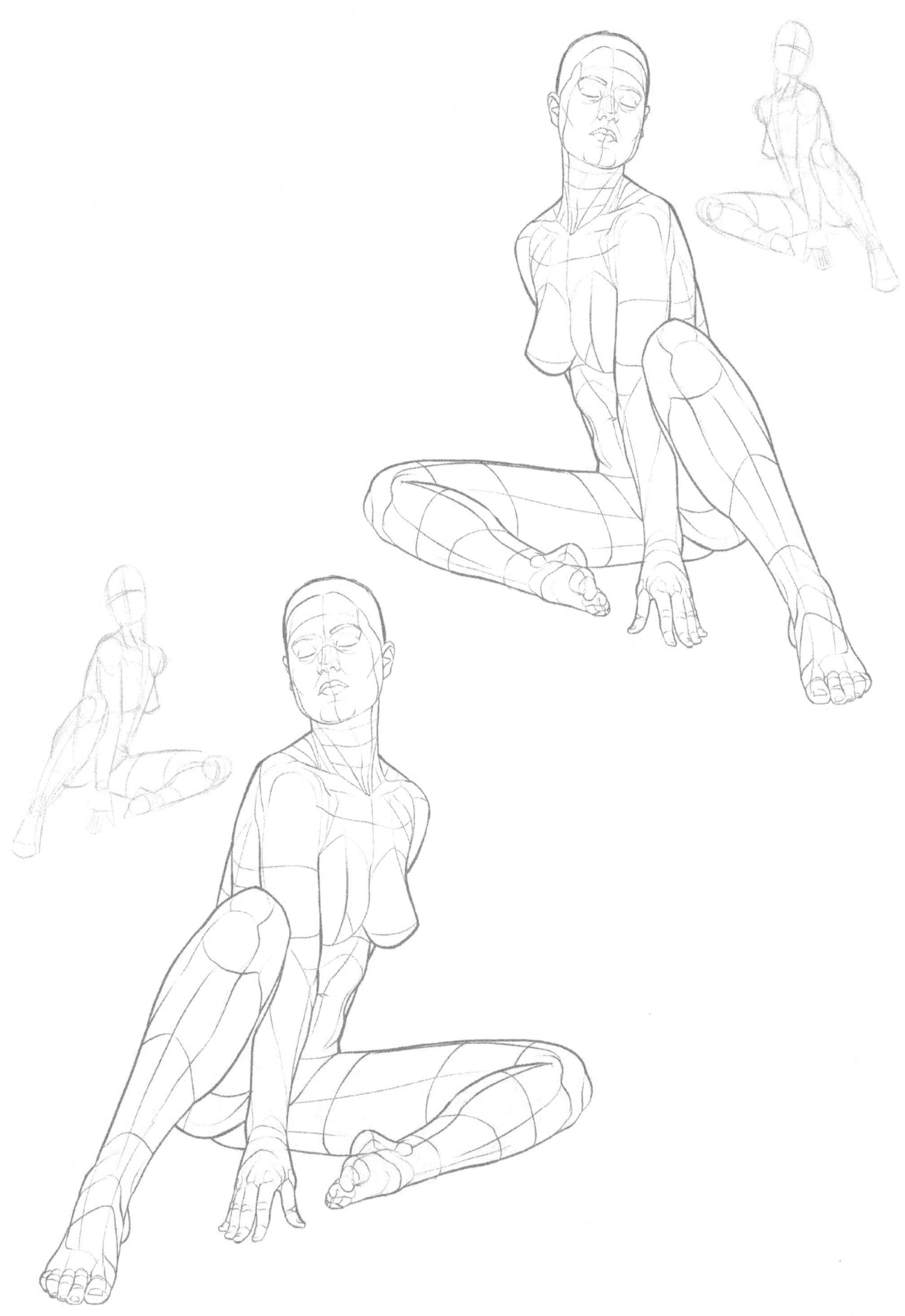

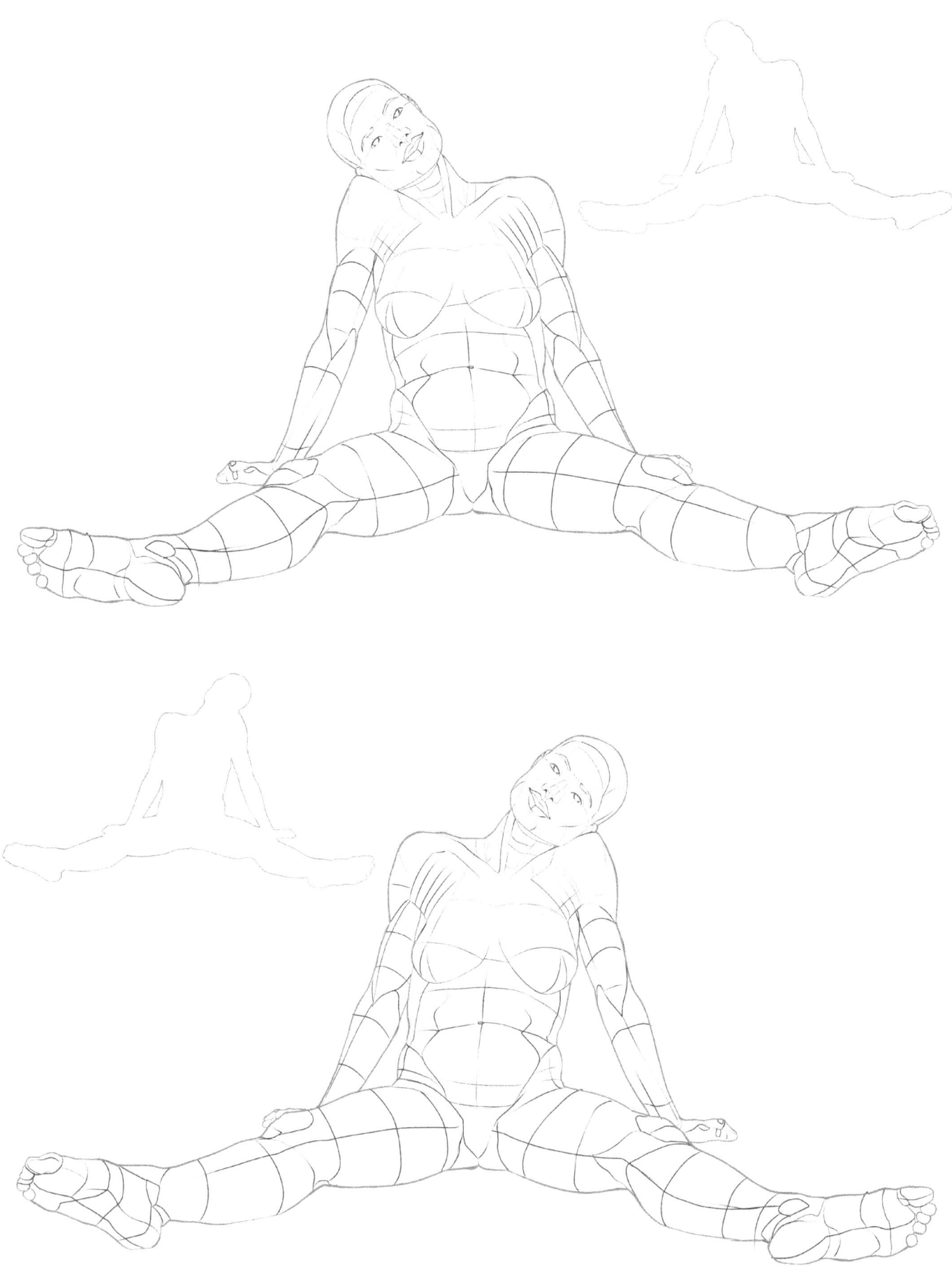

36

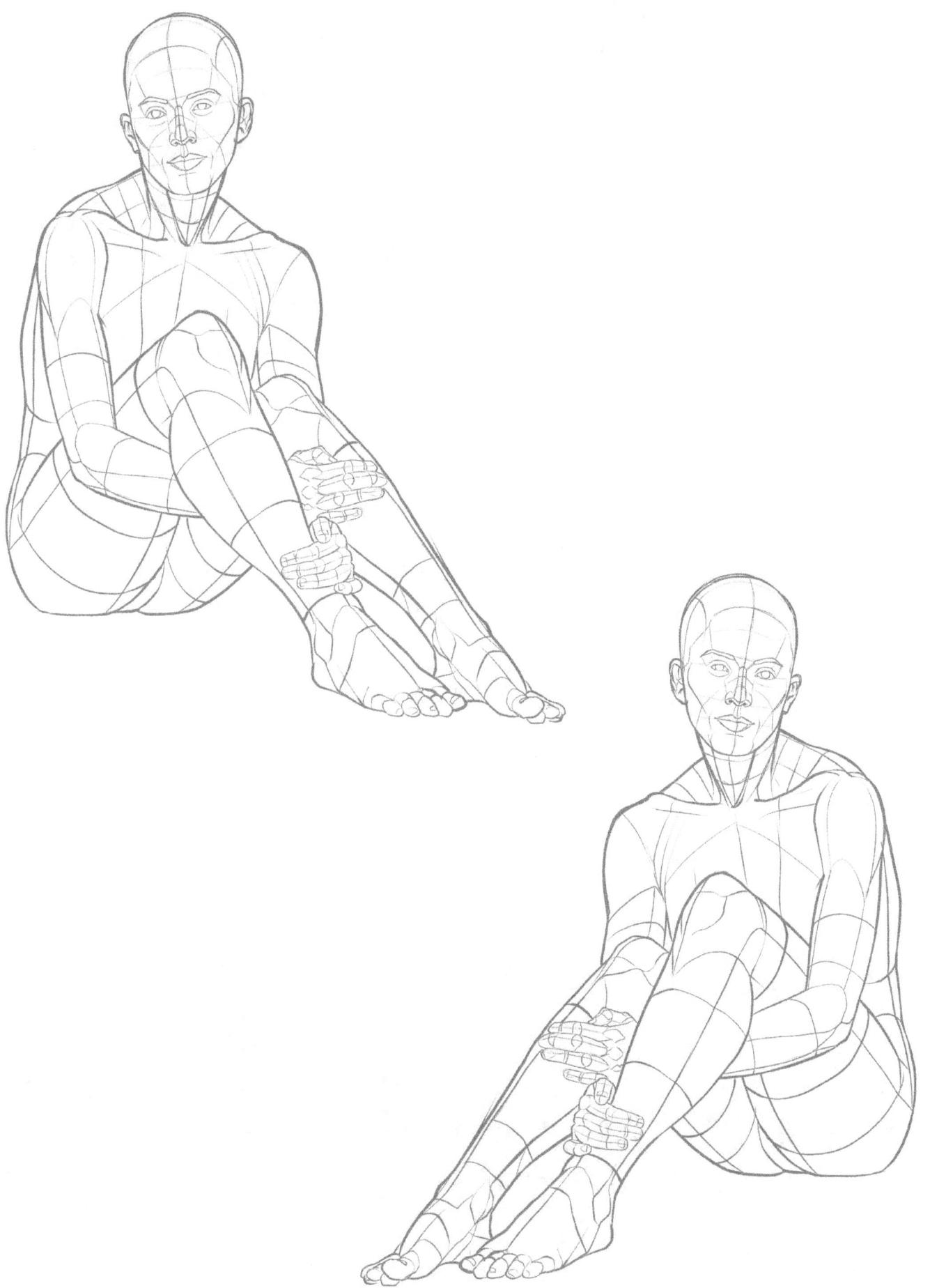

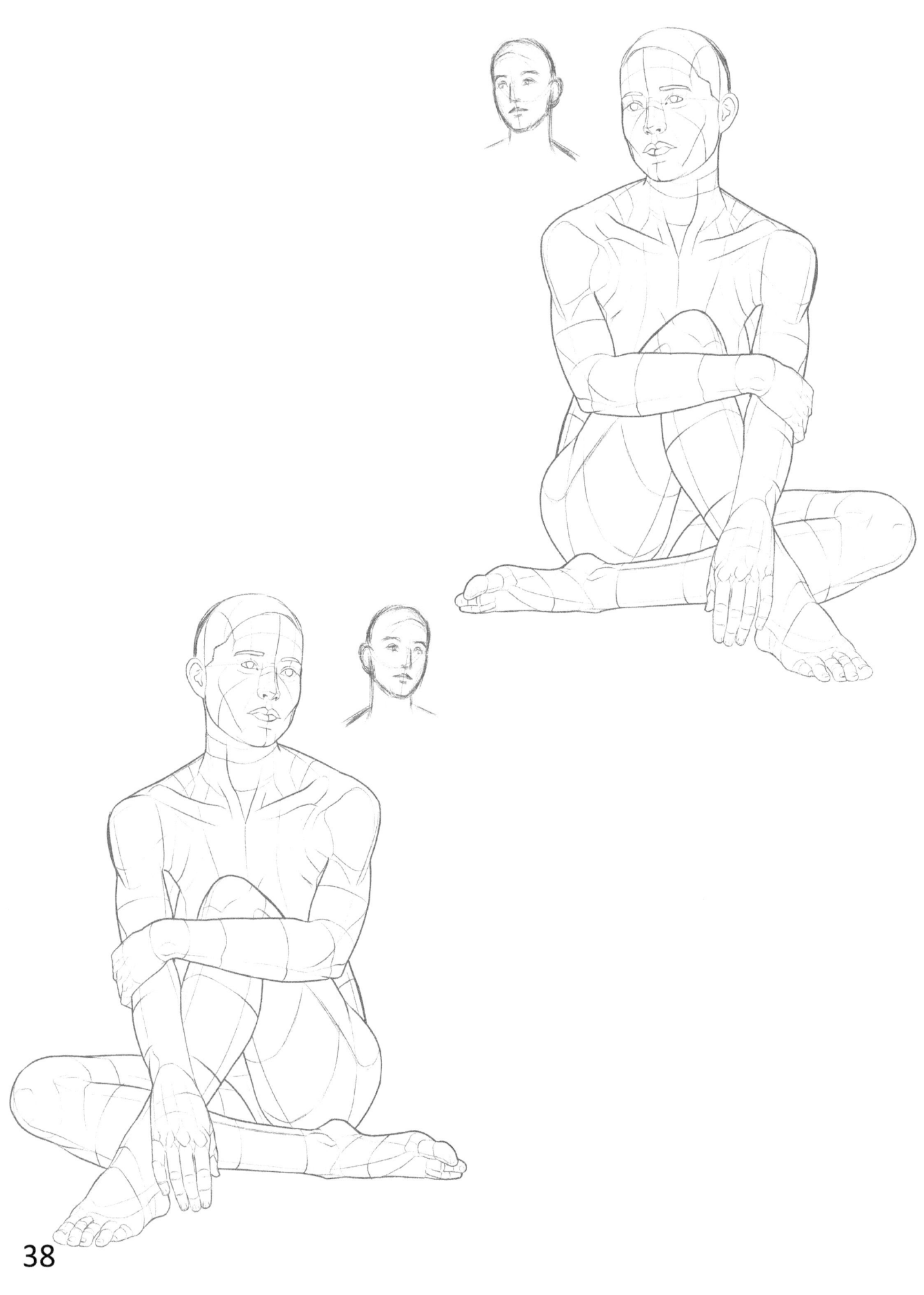

38

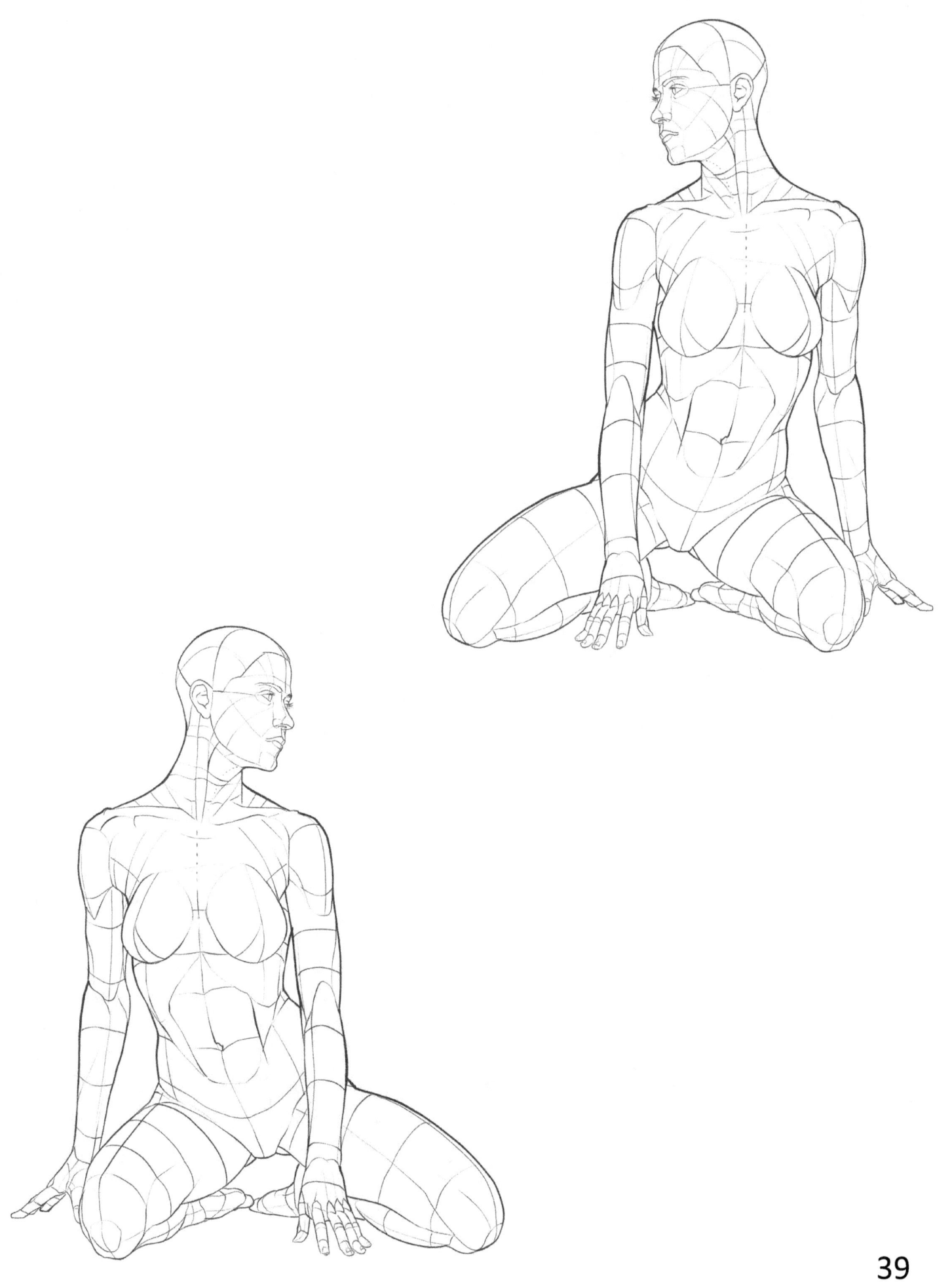

39

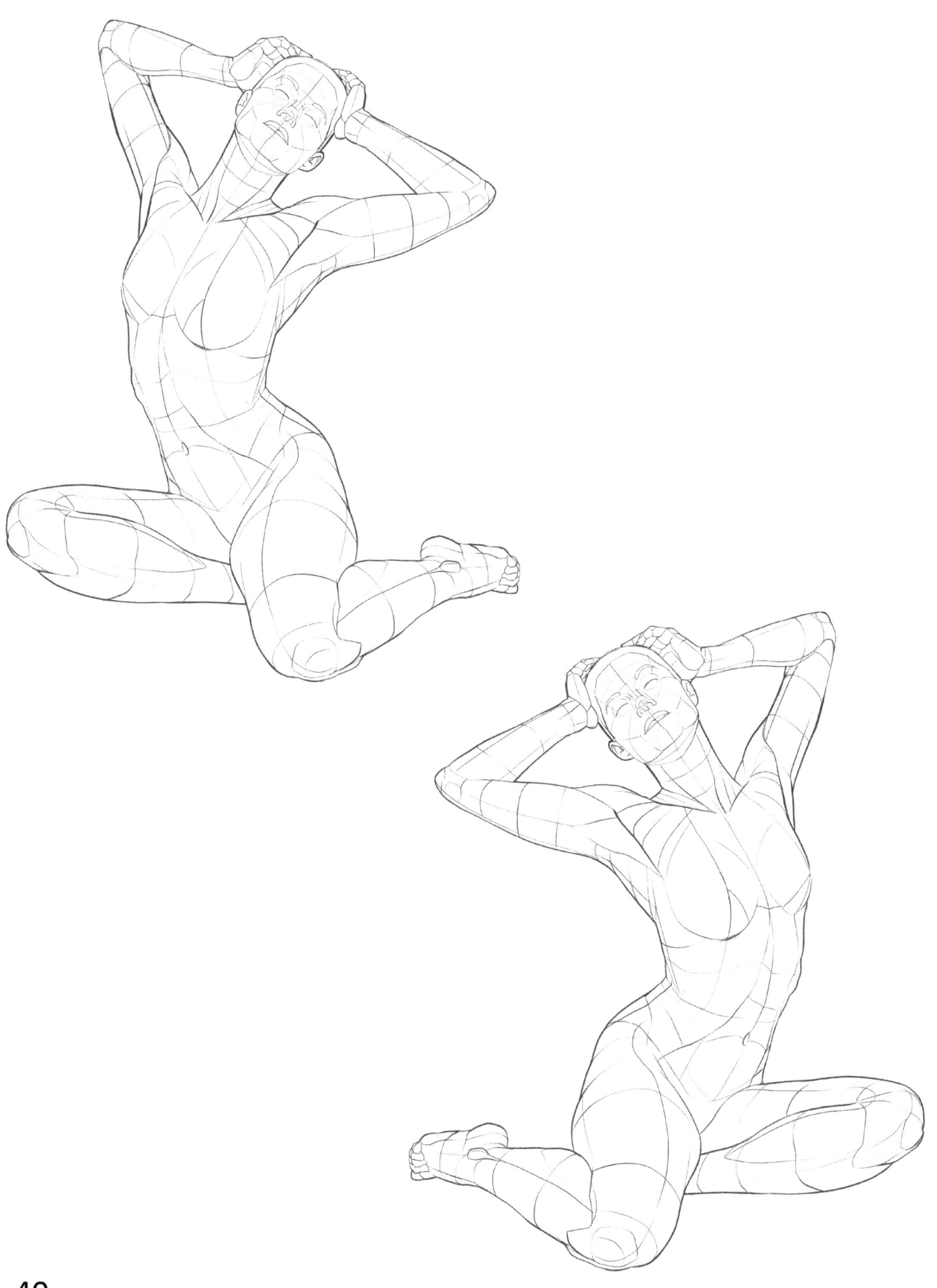

40

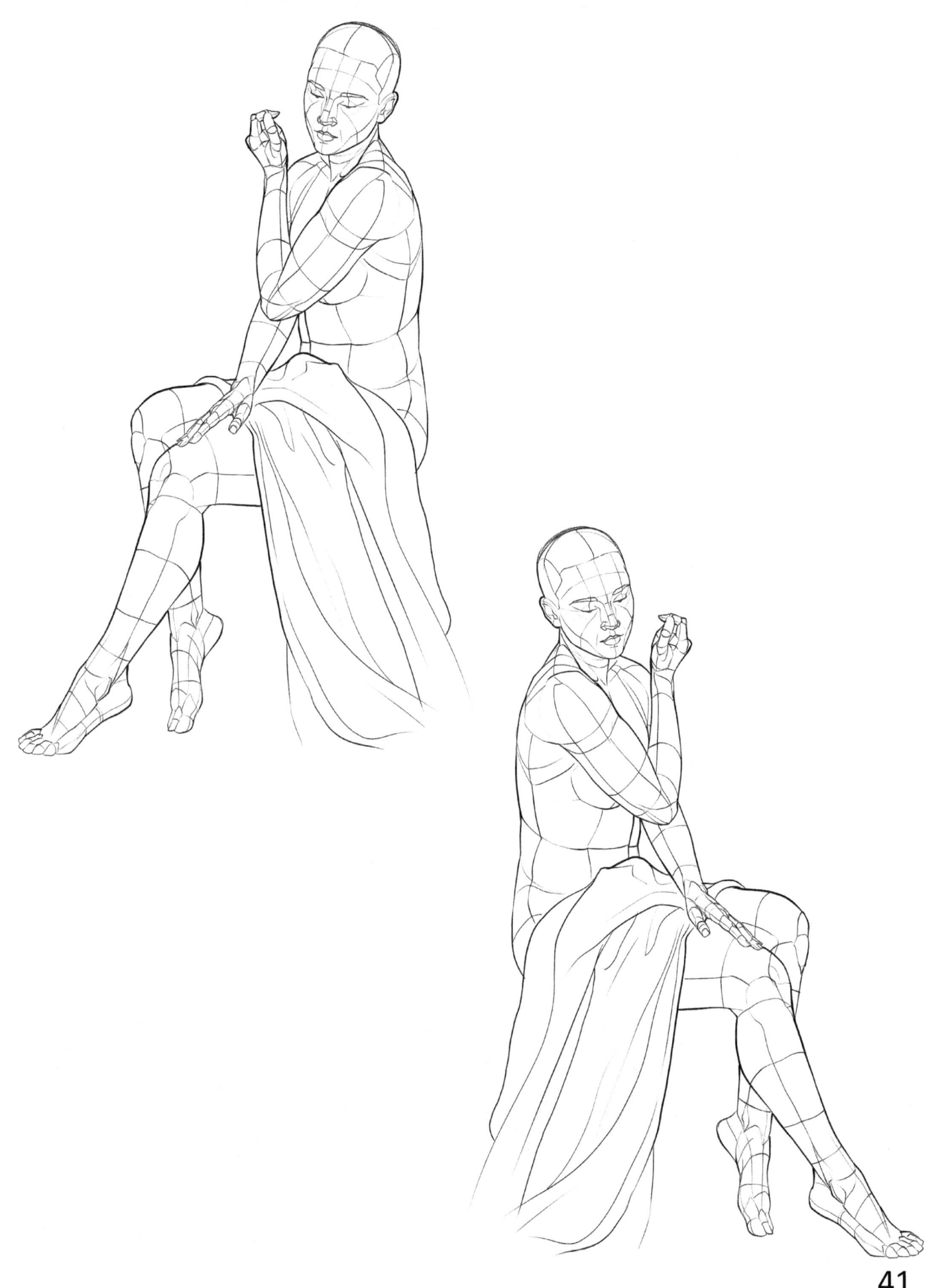

41

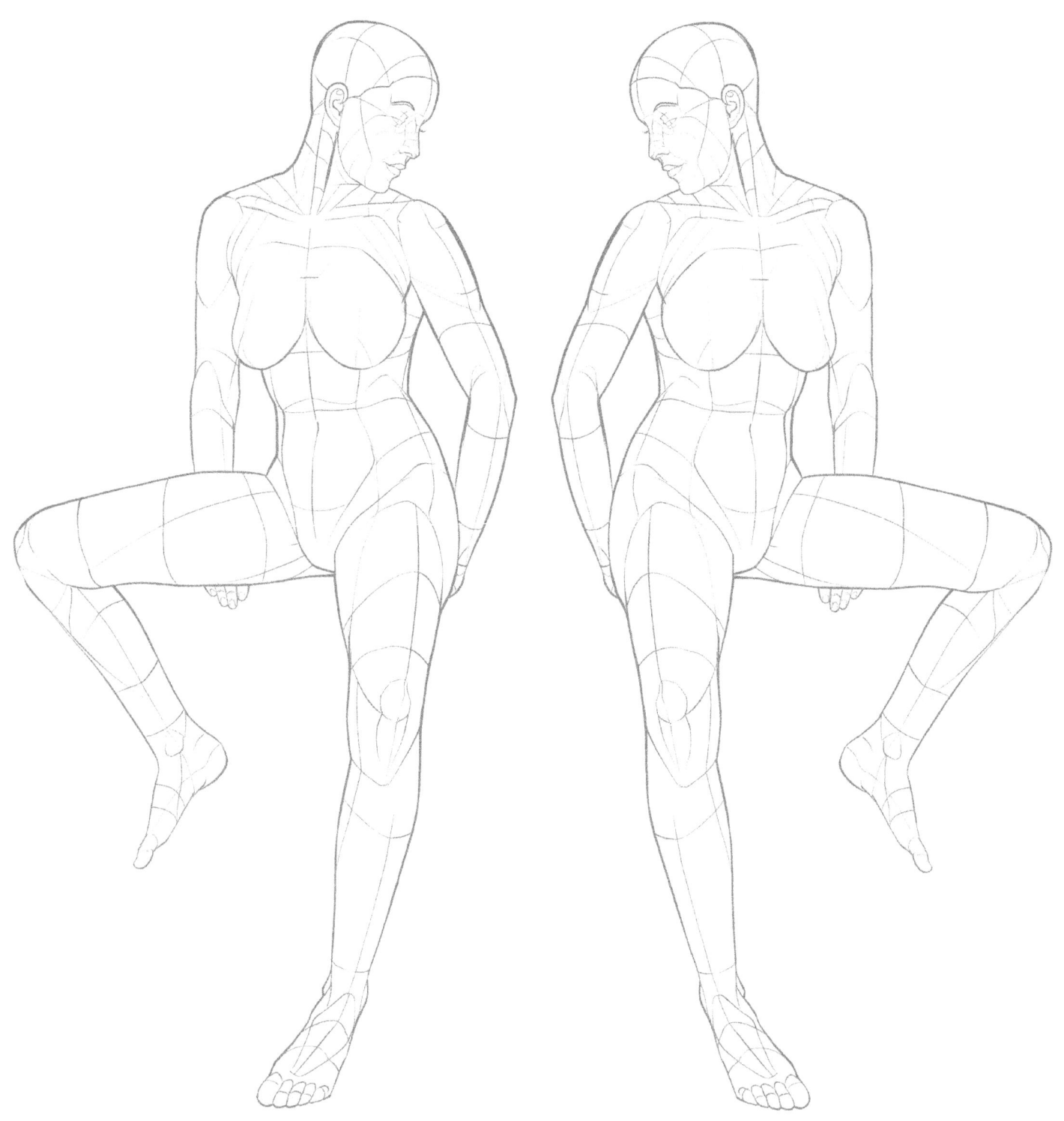

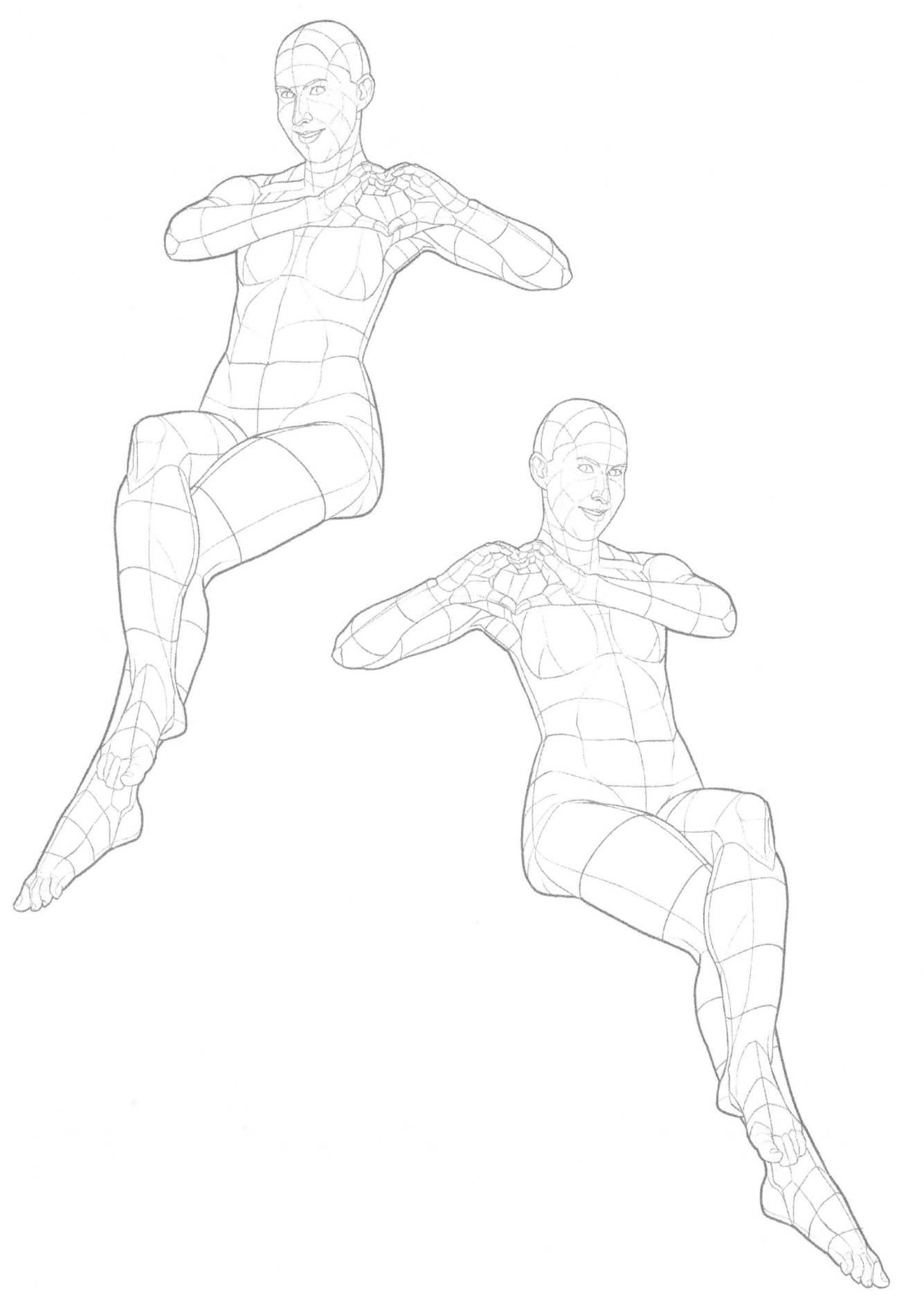

43

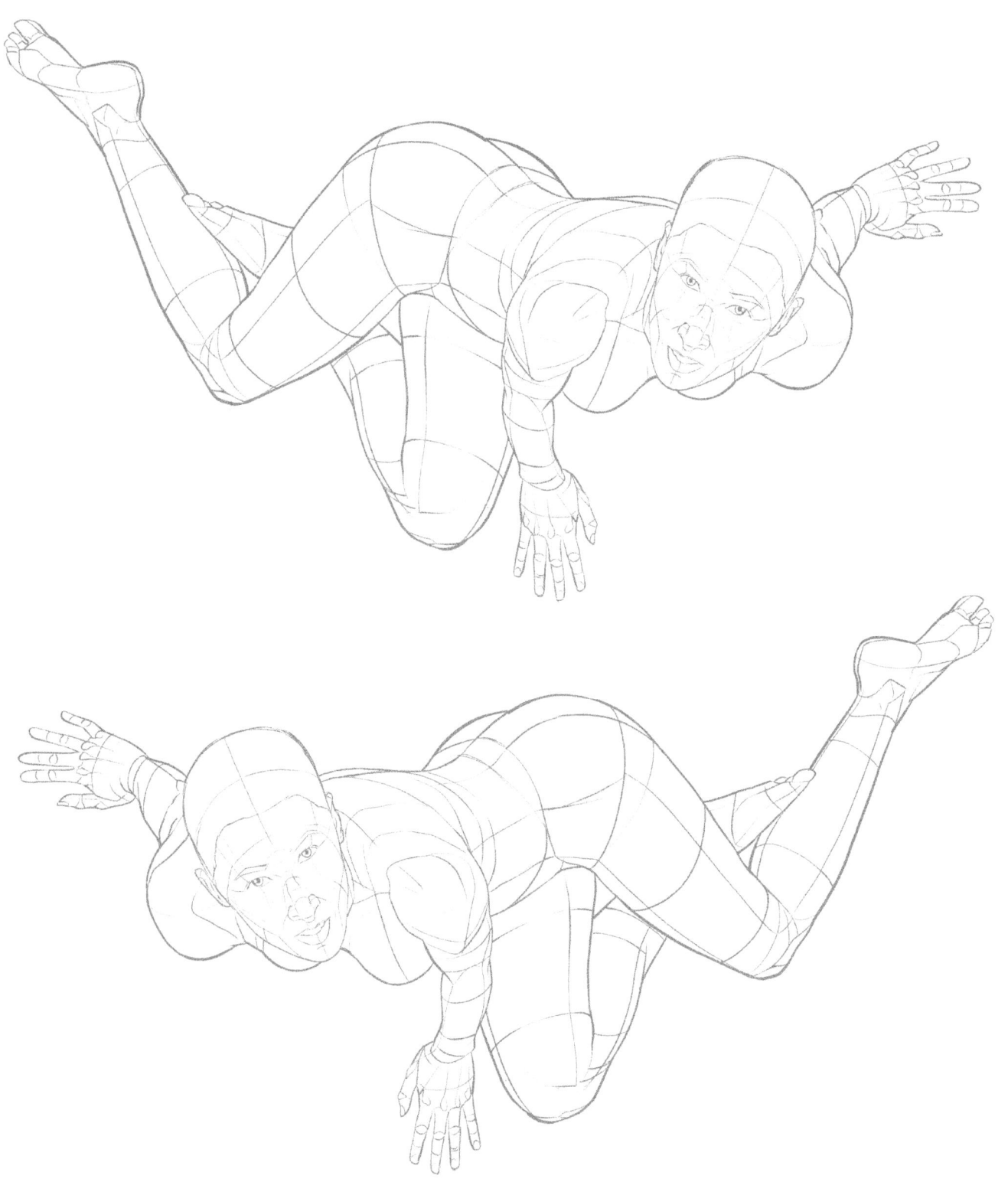

44

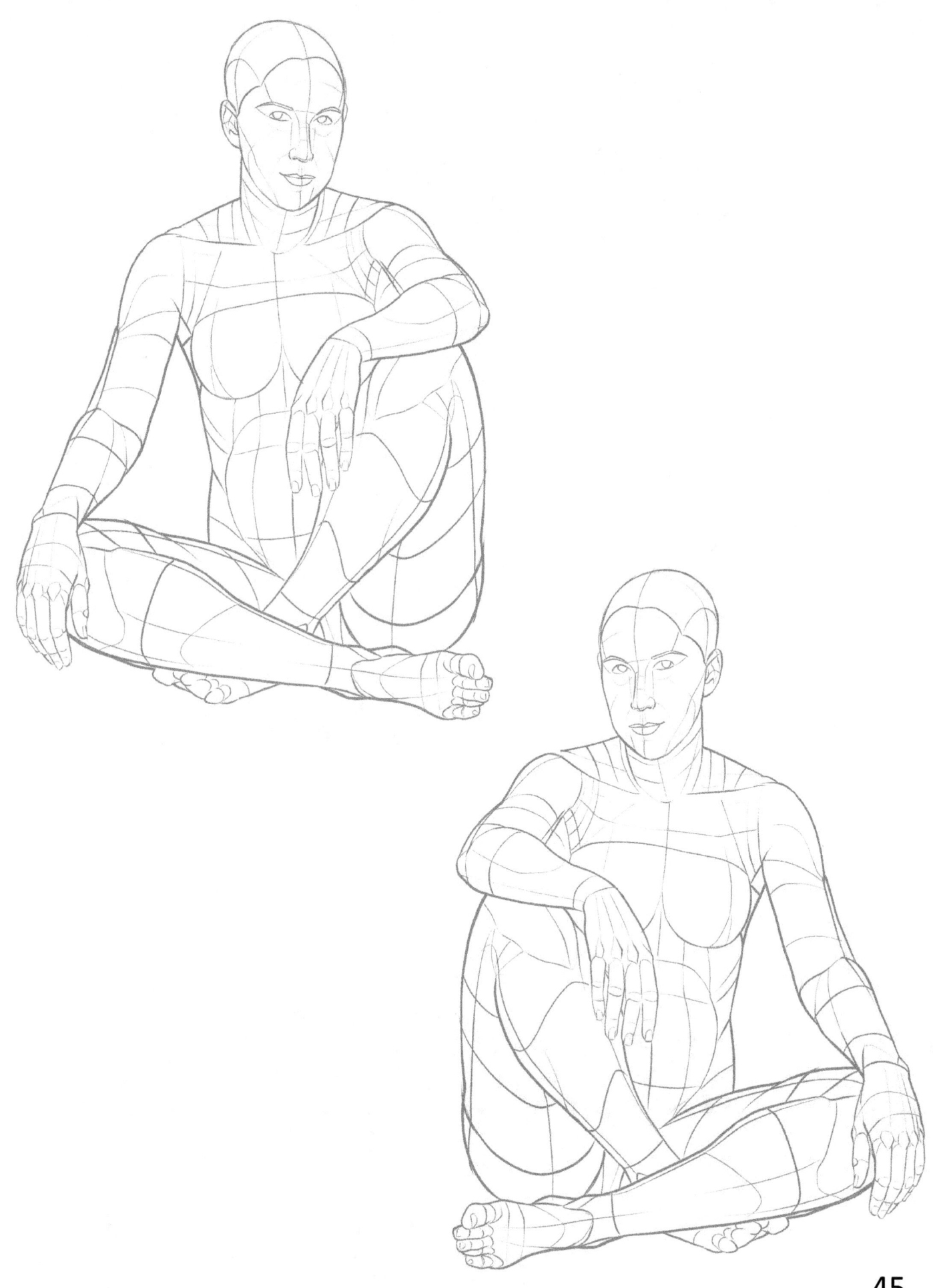

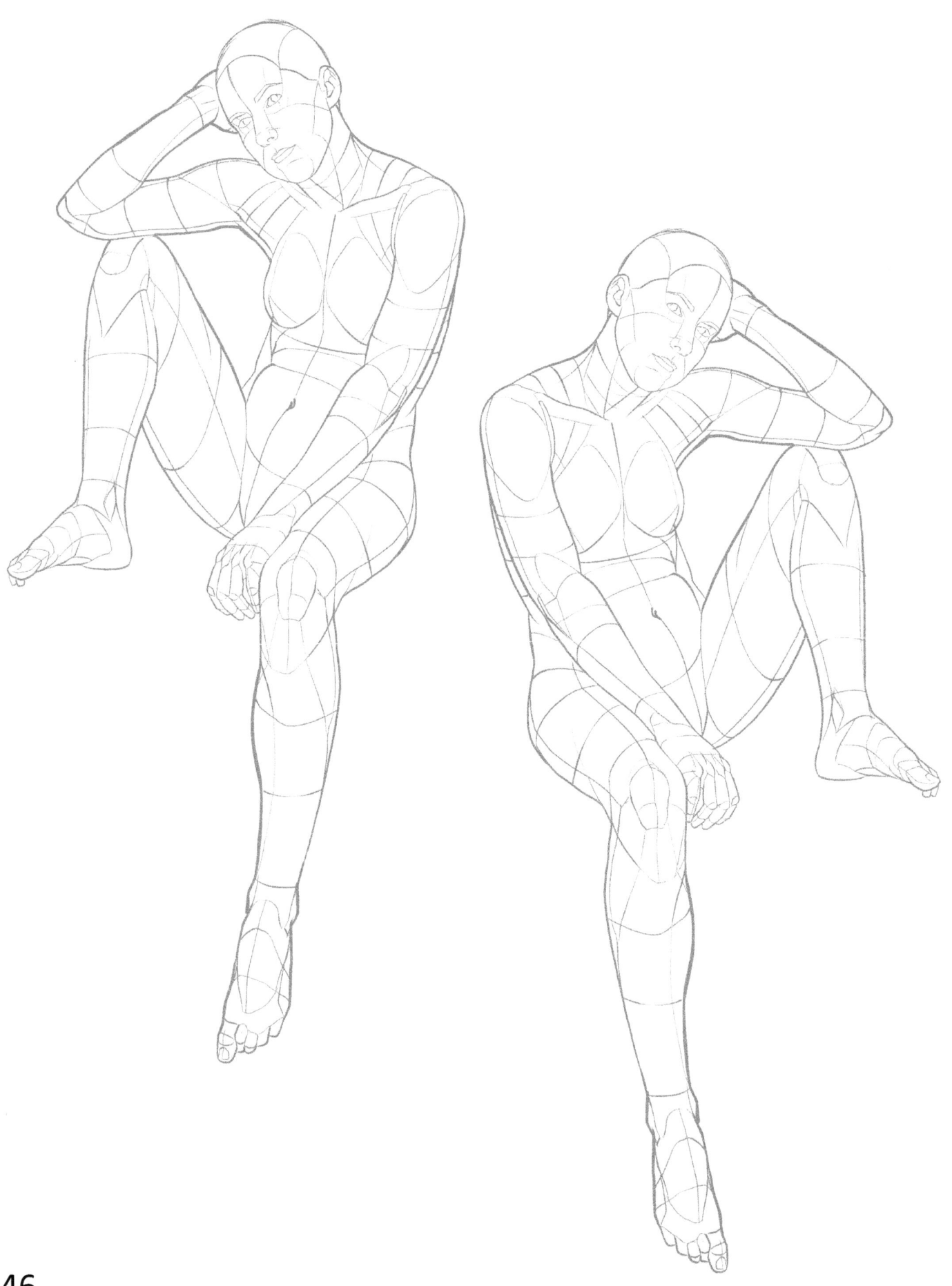

46

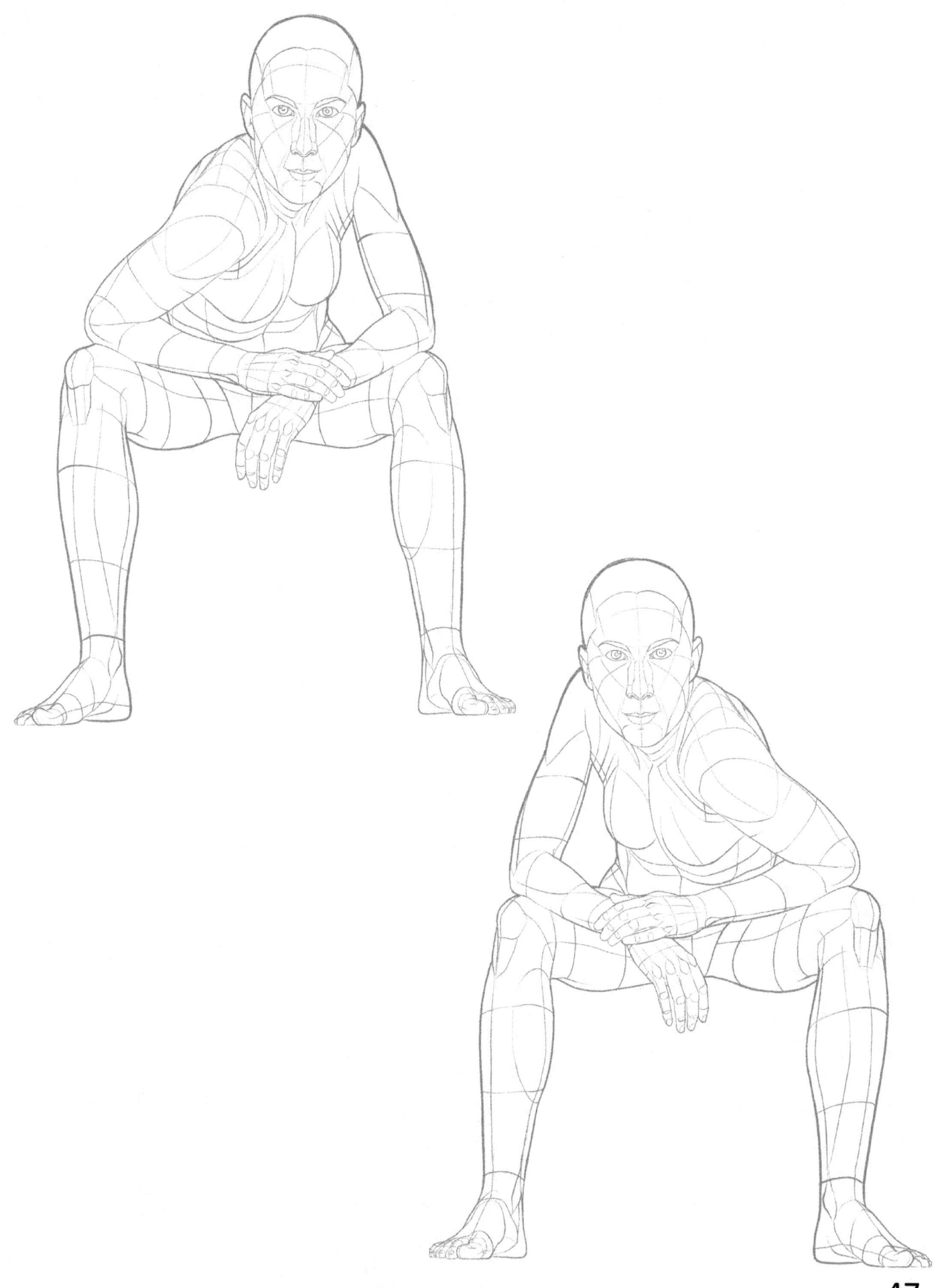

47

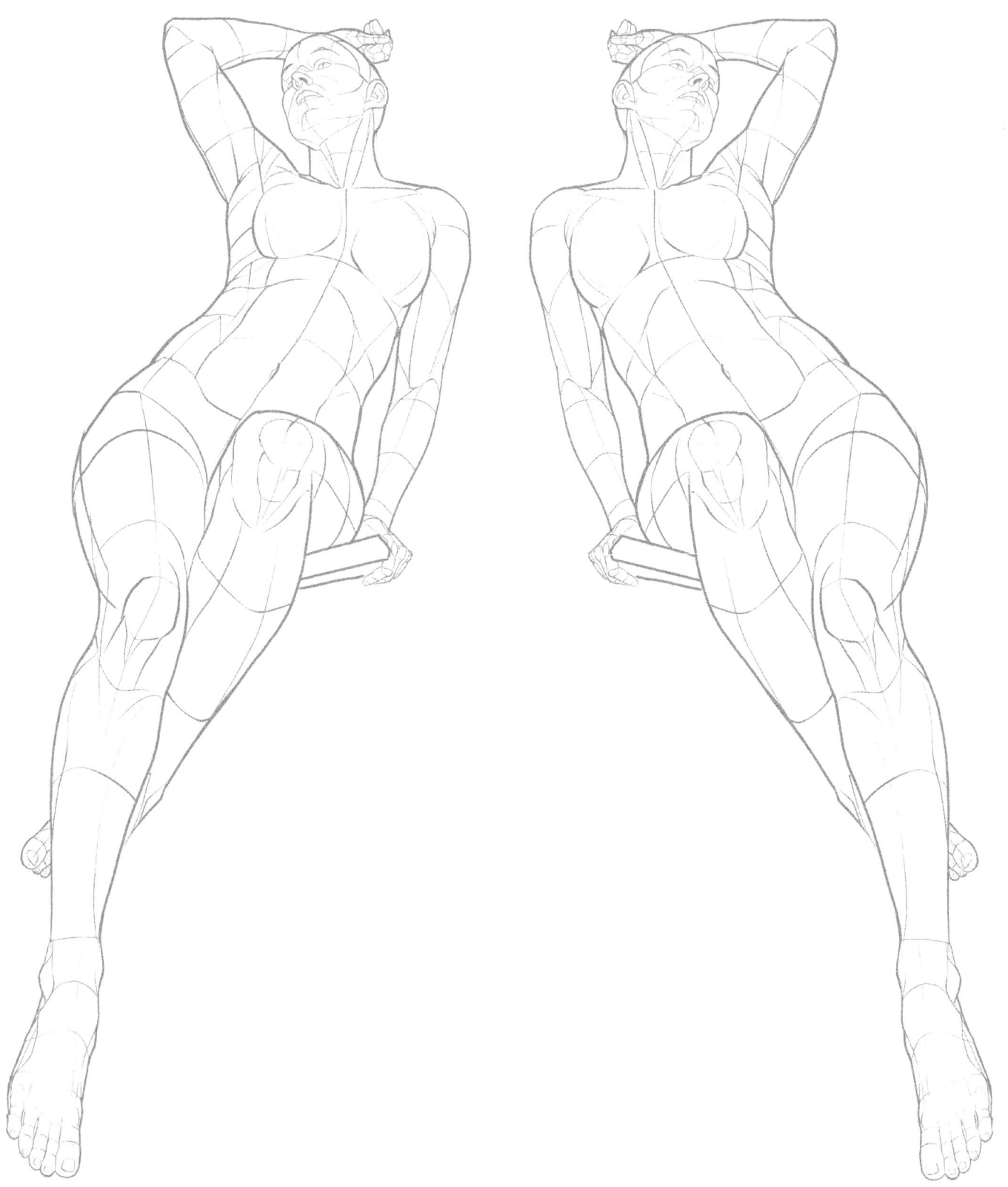

48

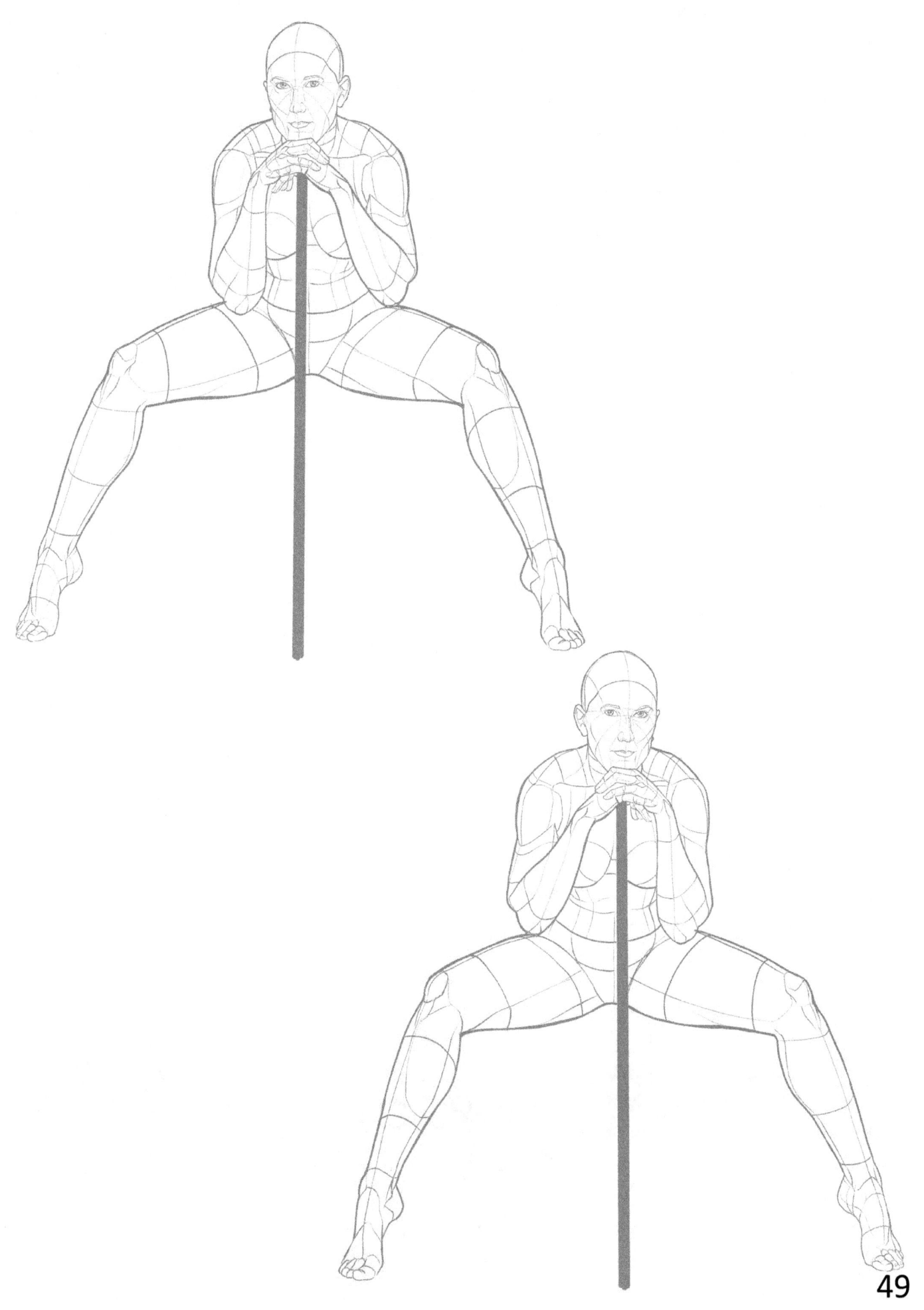

49

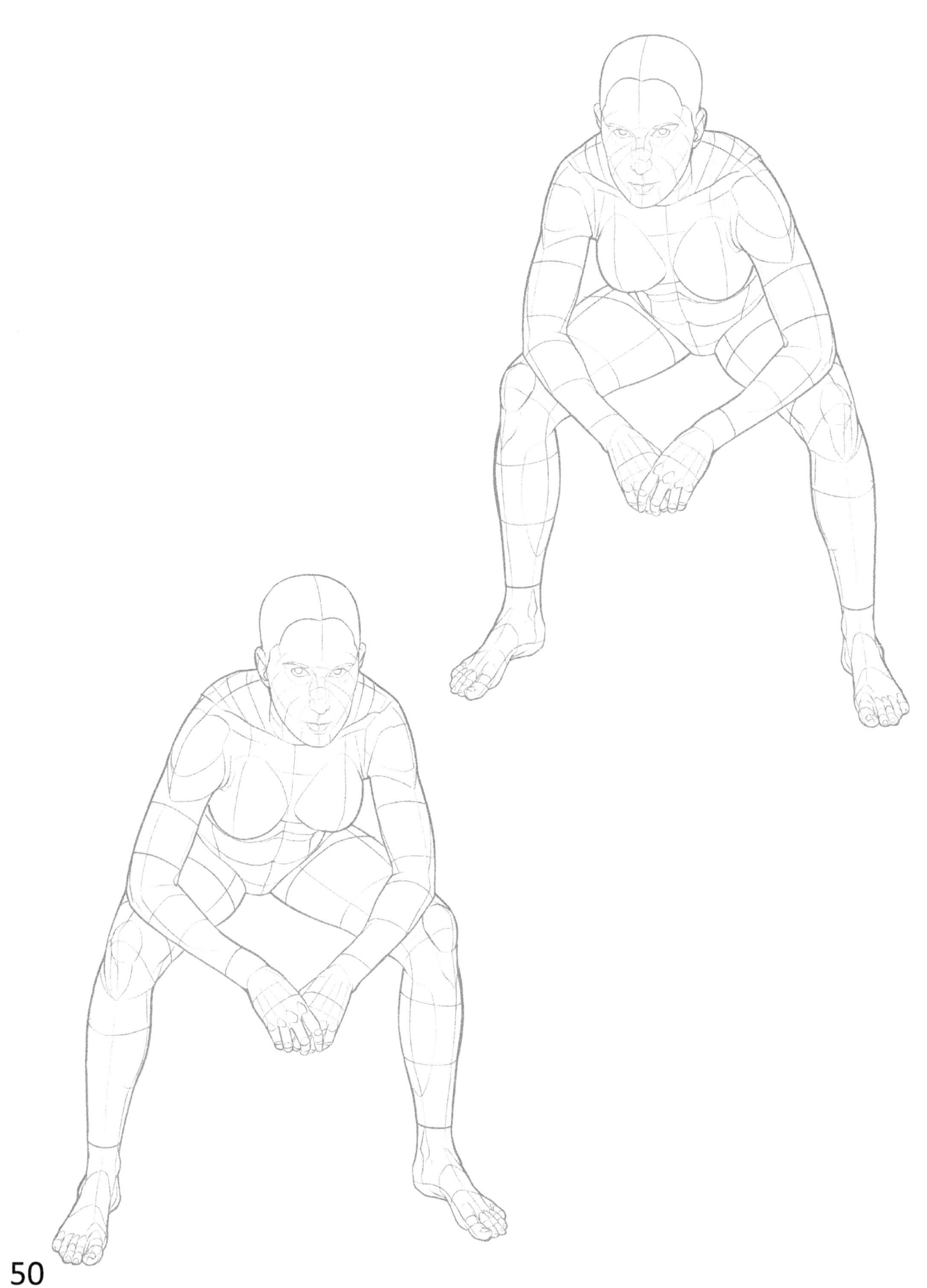

50

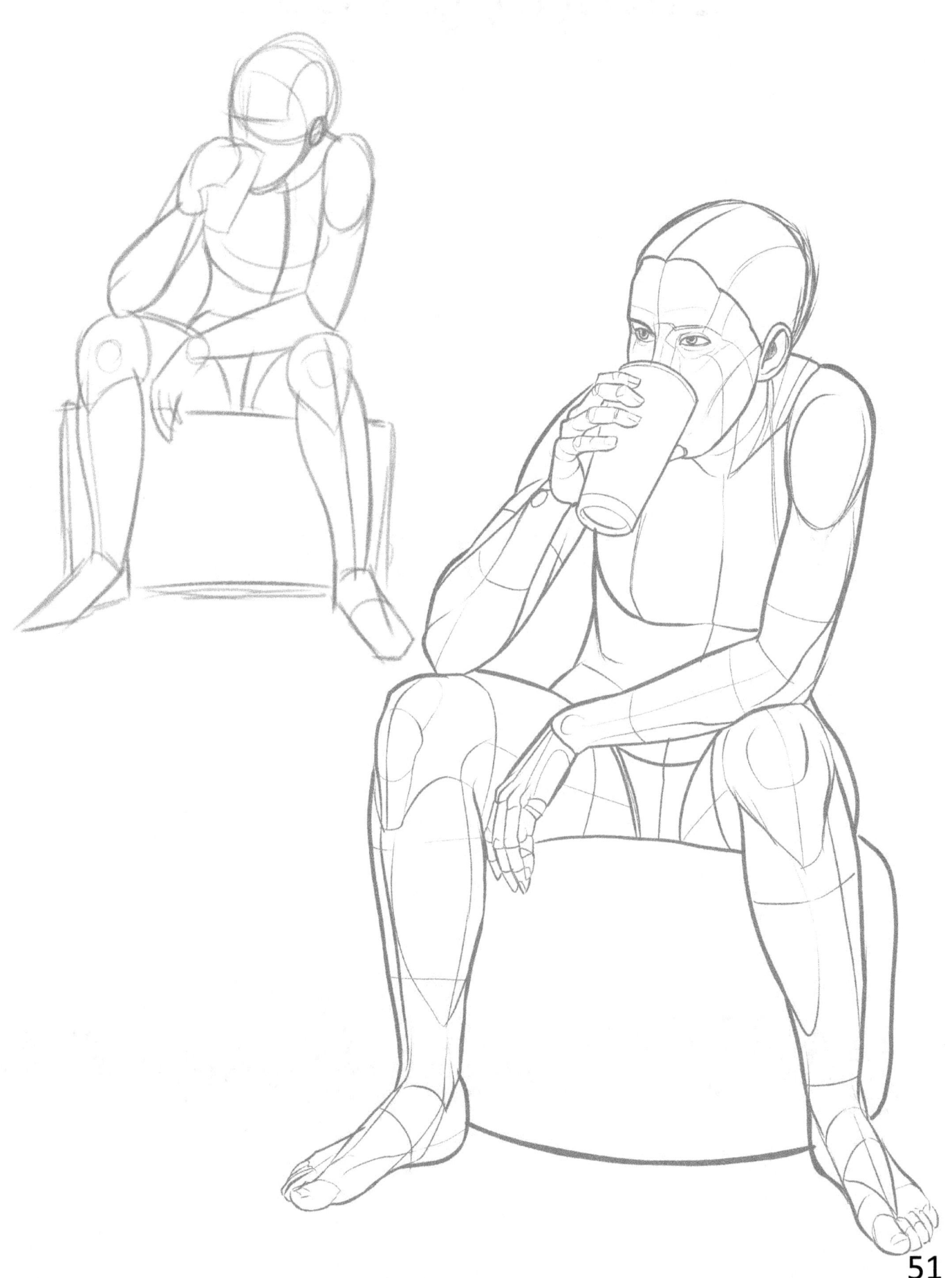

51

Standing Poses

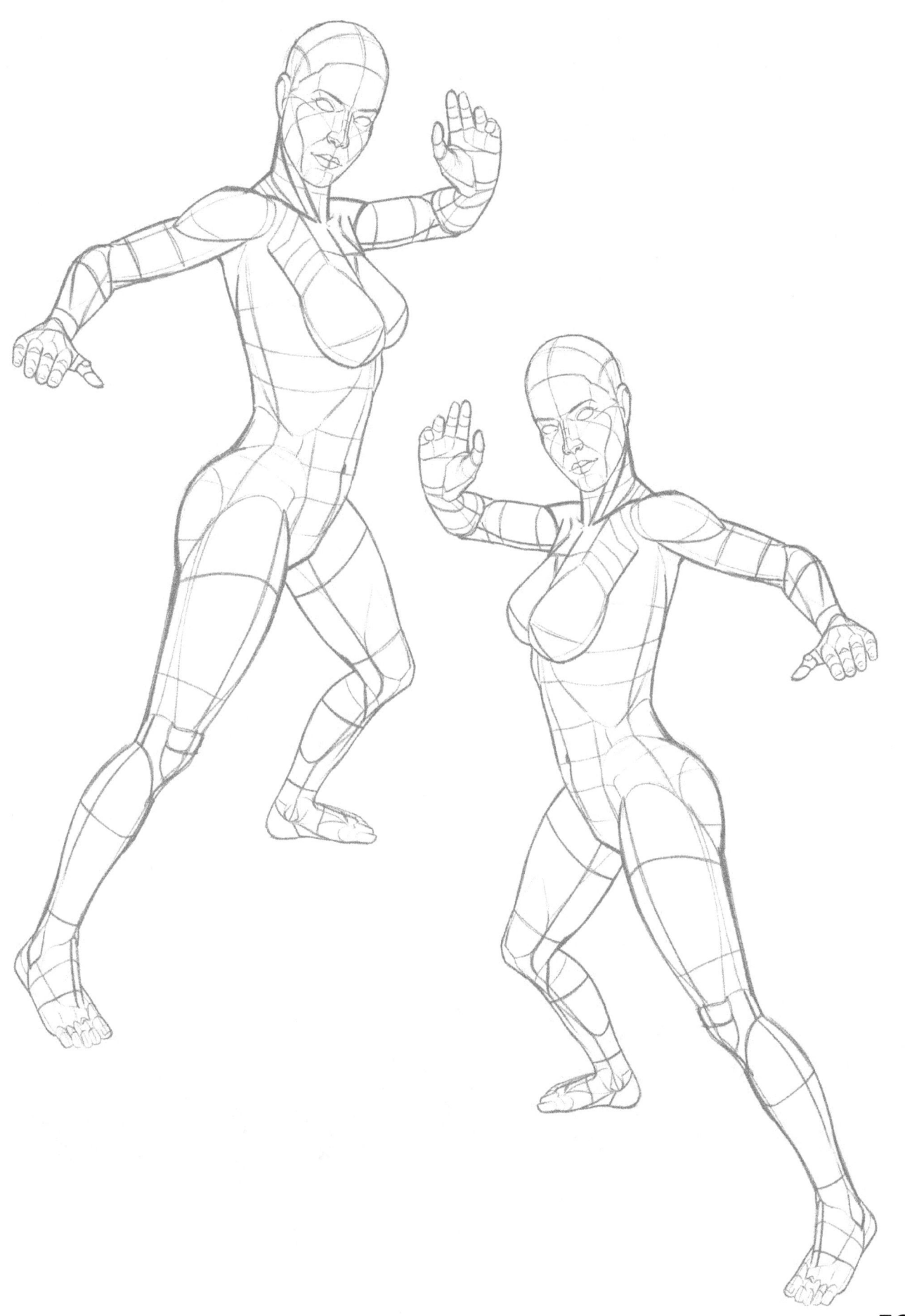

53

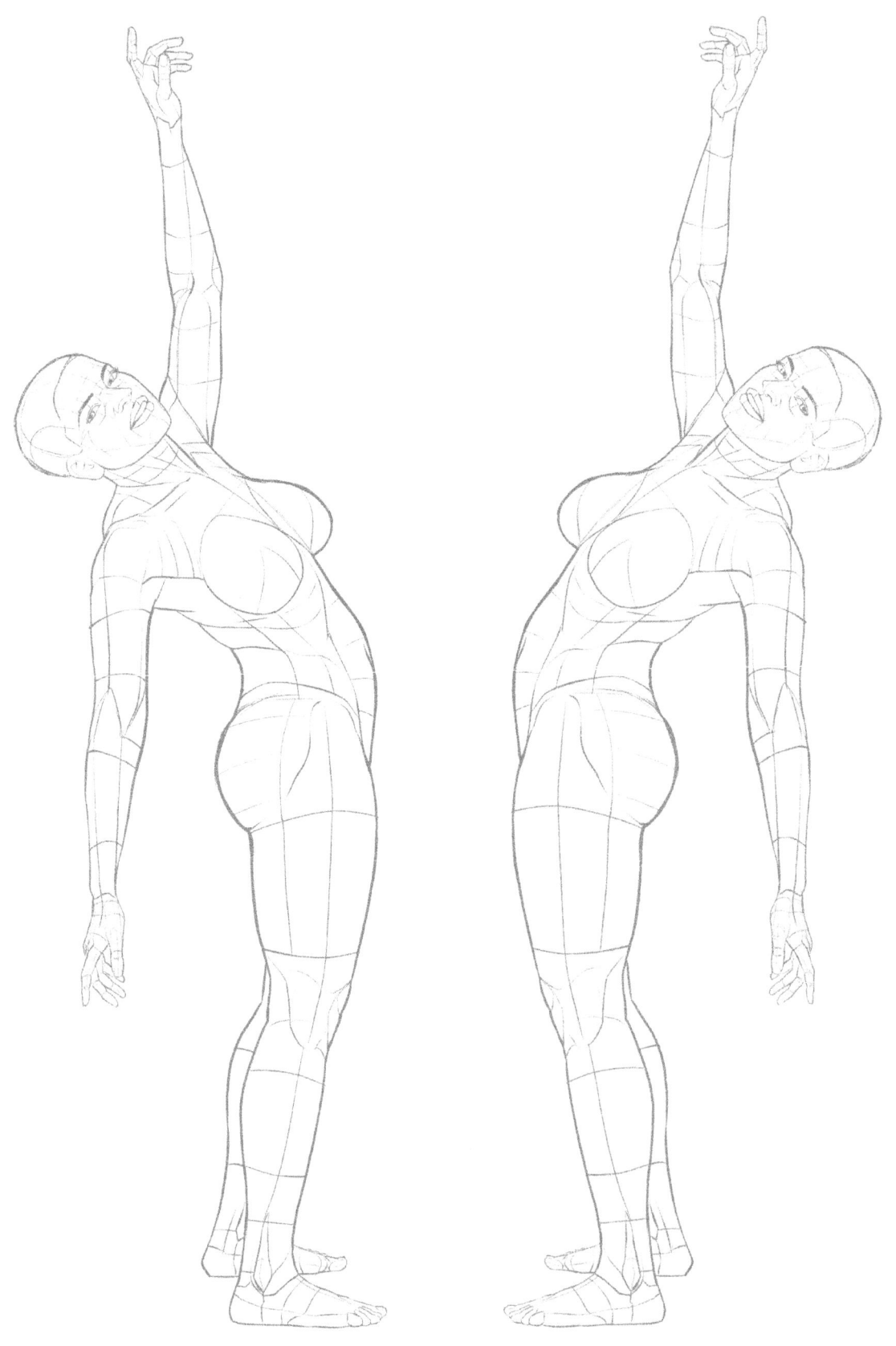

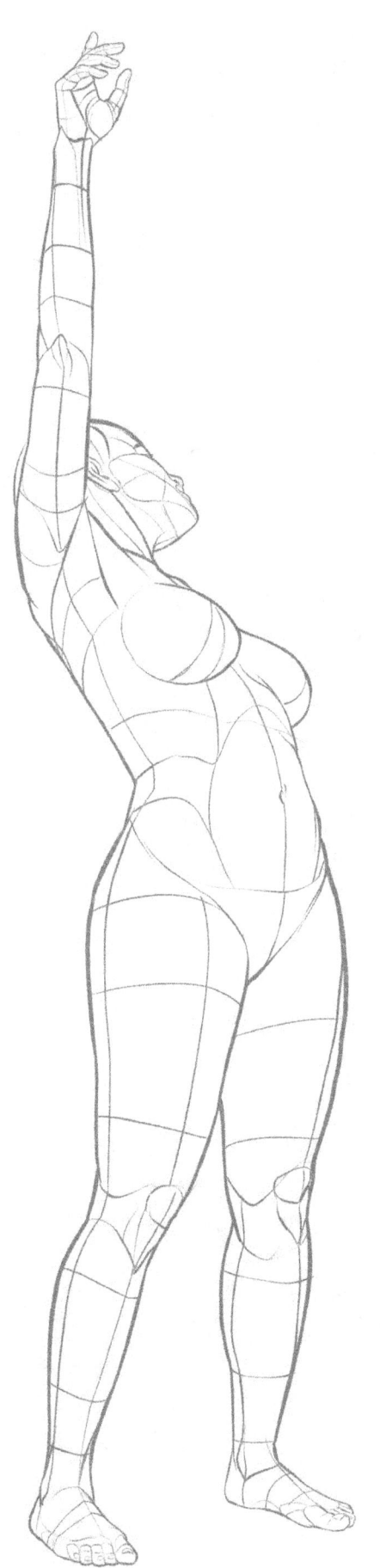
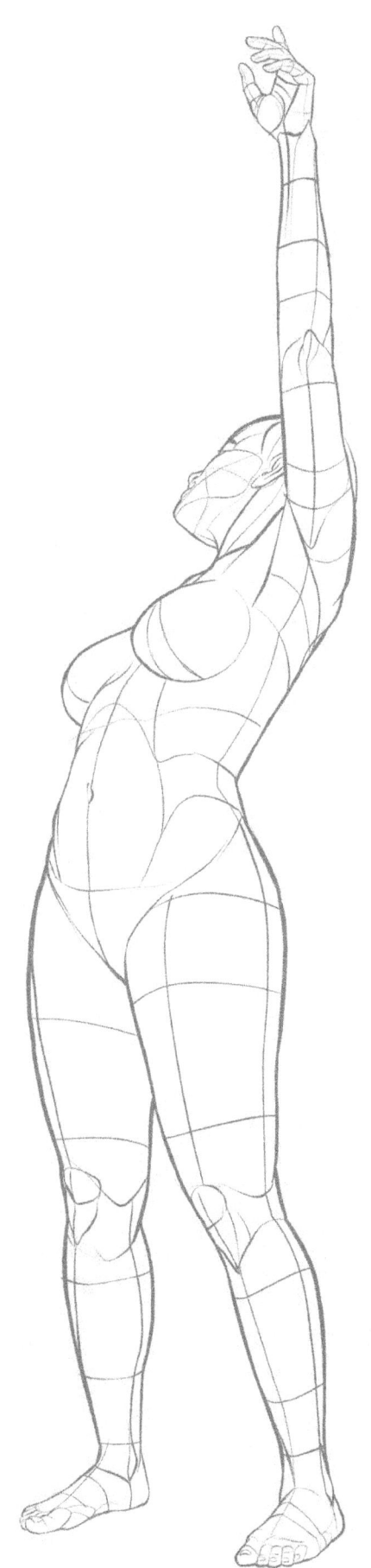

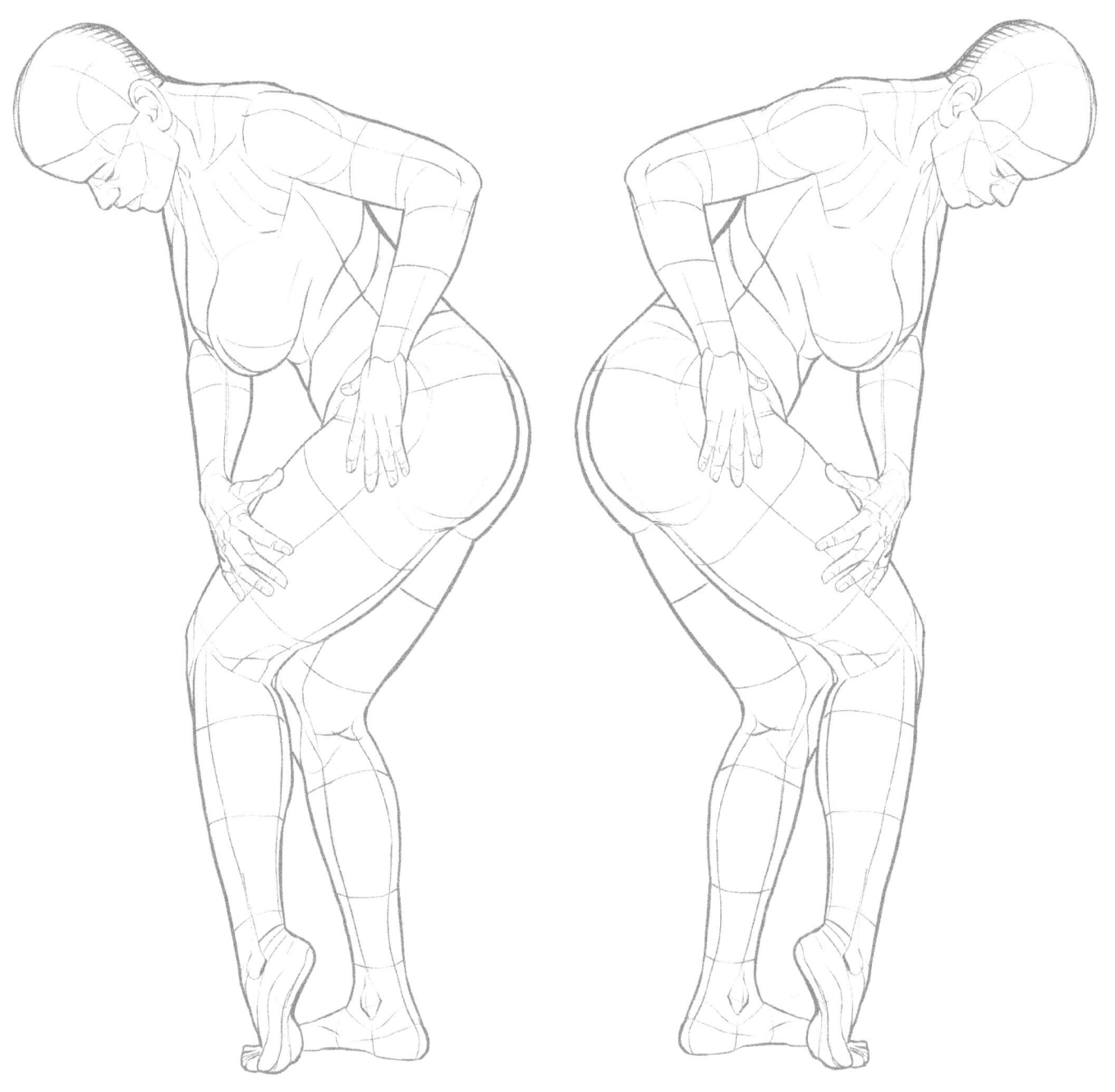

56

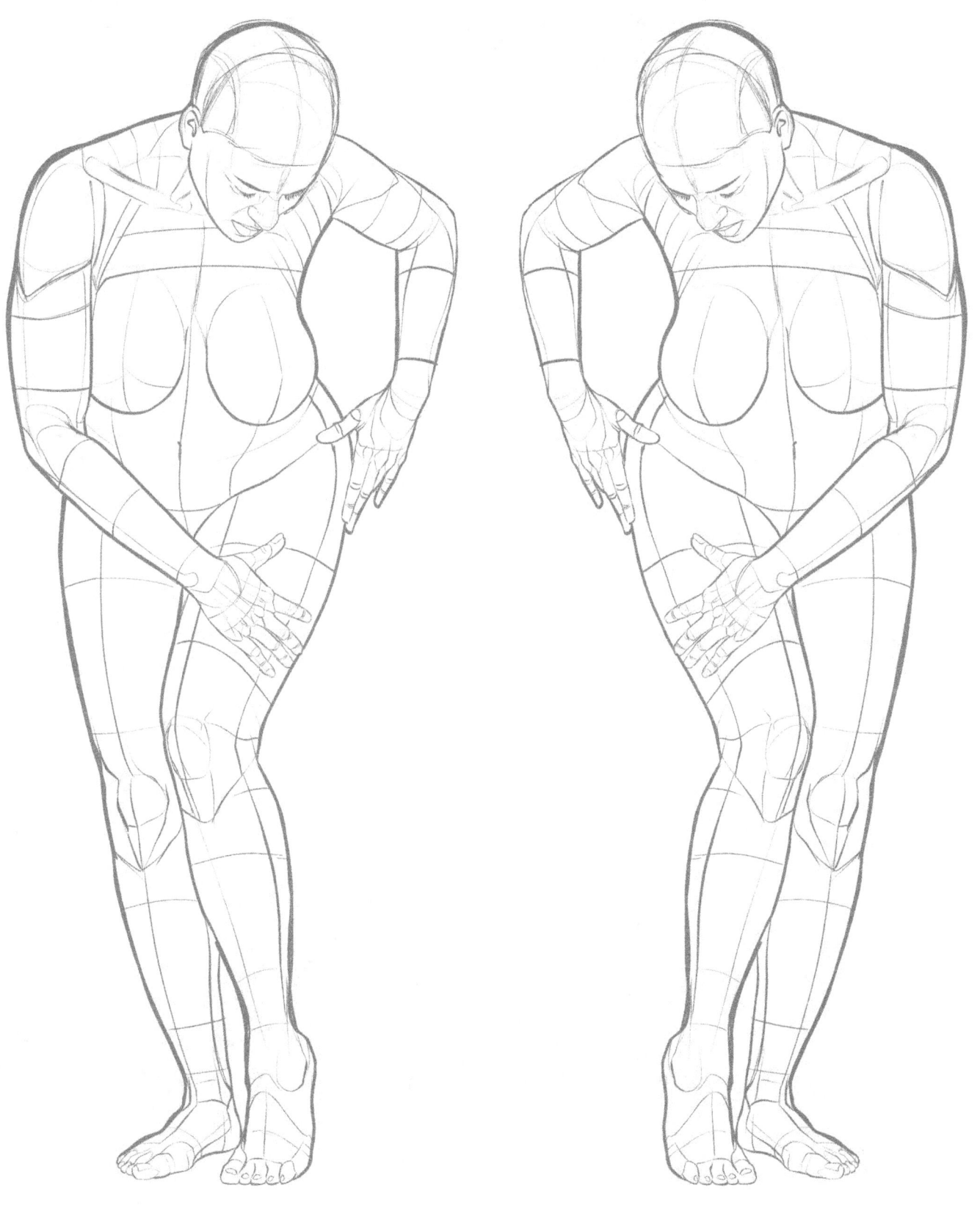

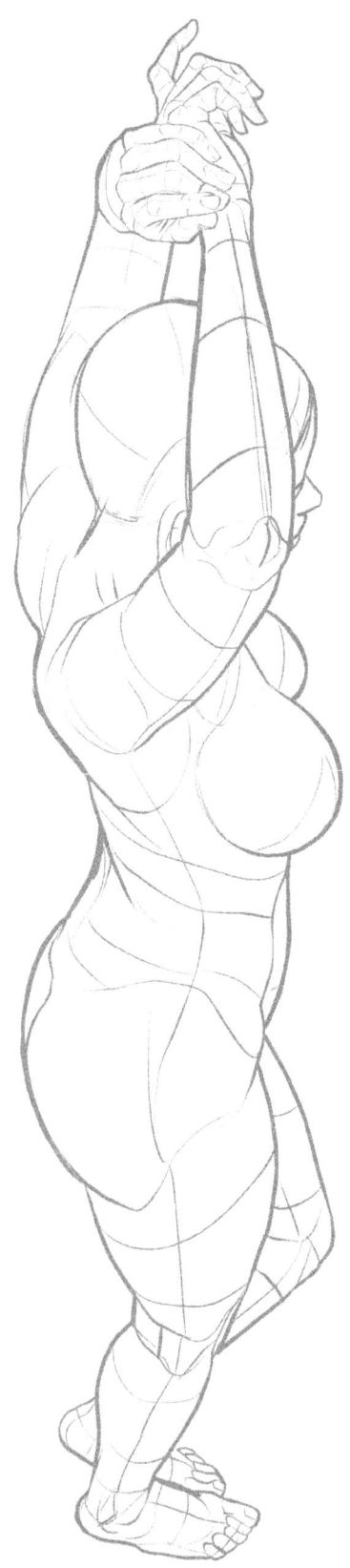
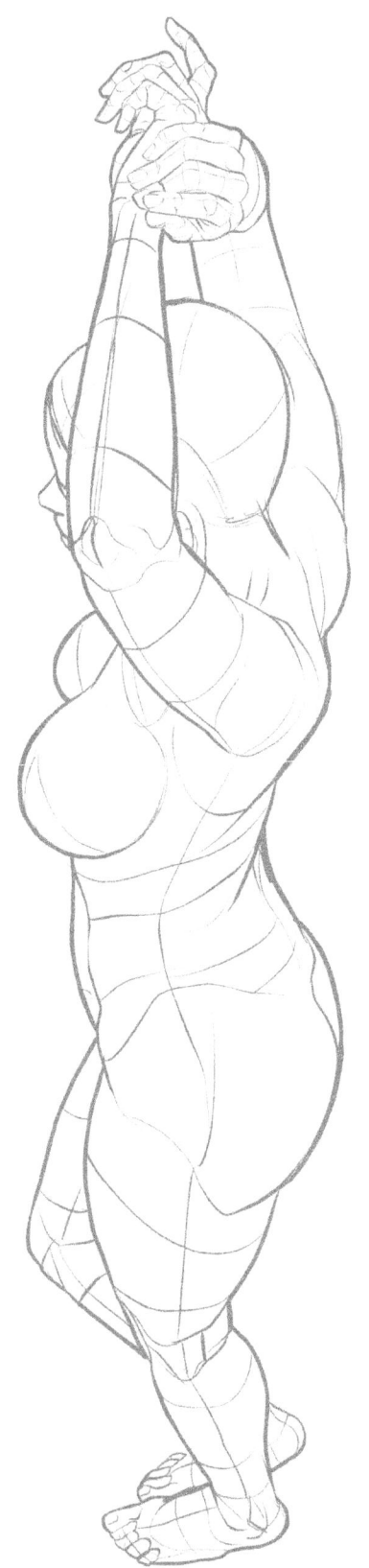

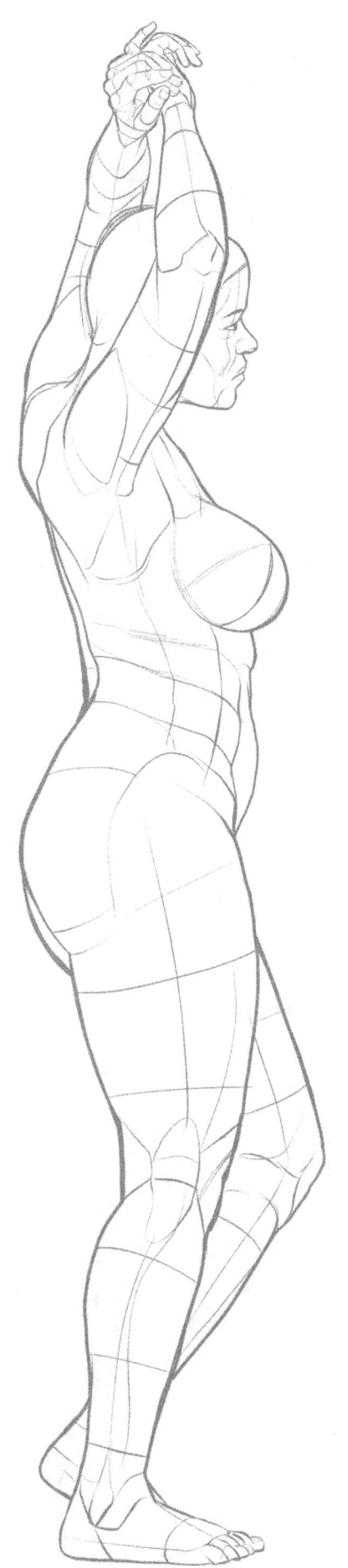
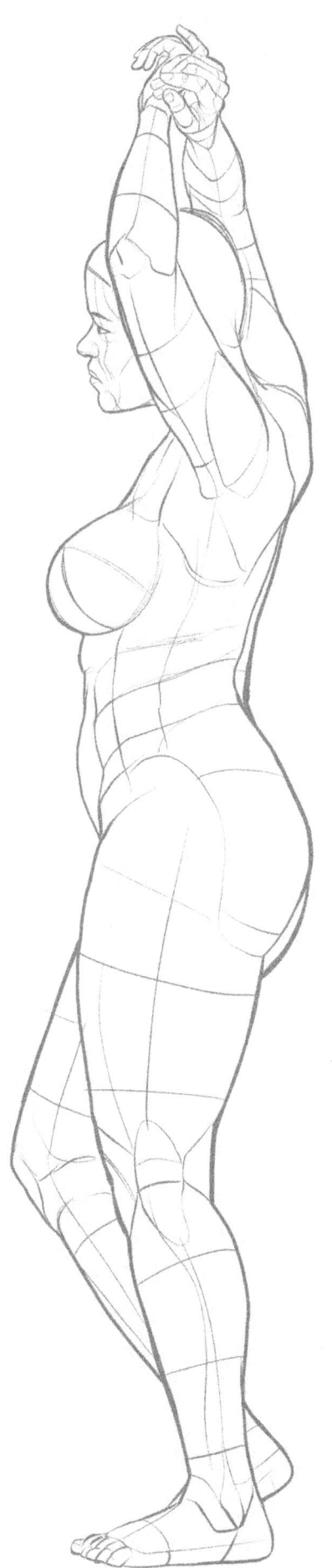

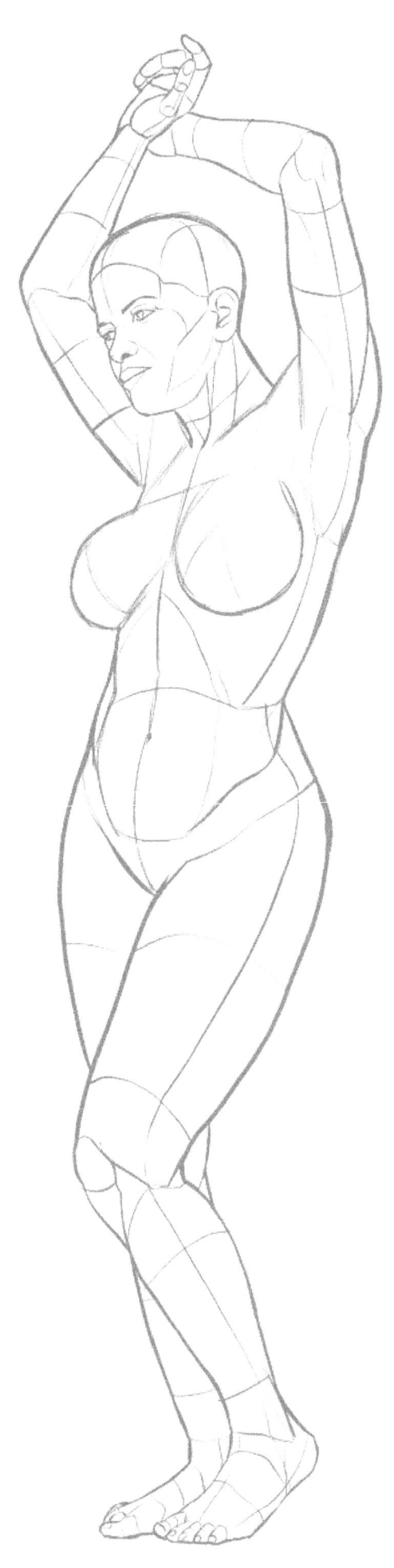
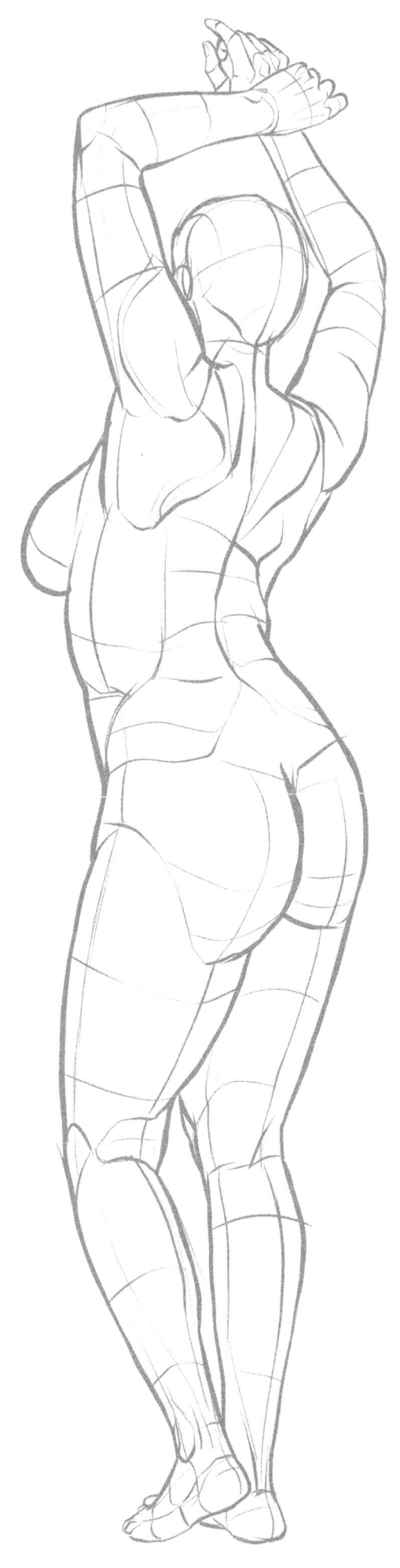

60

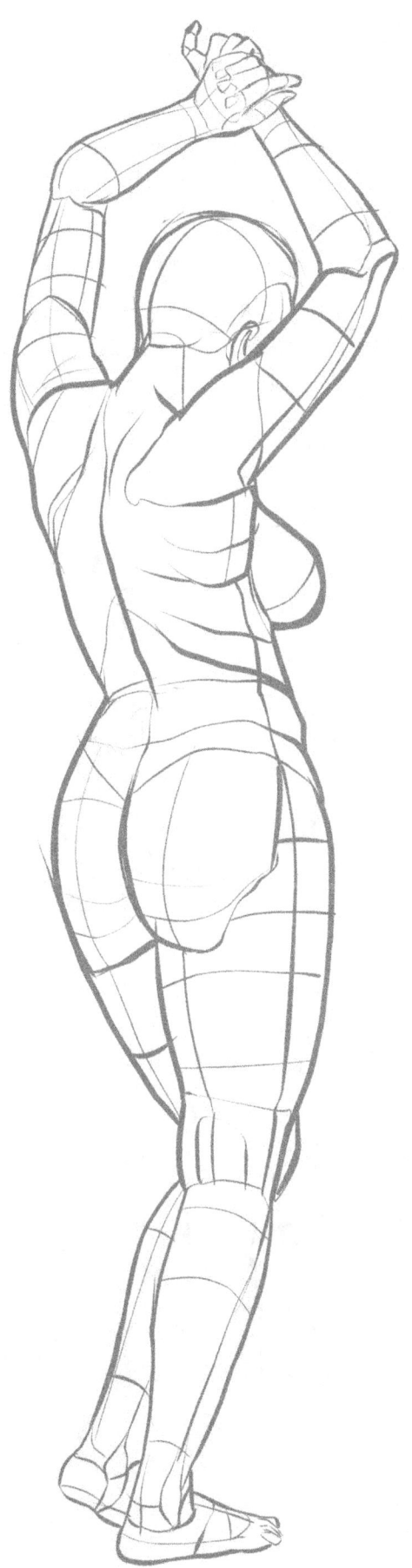
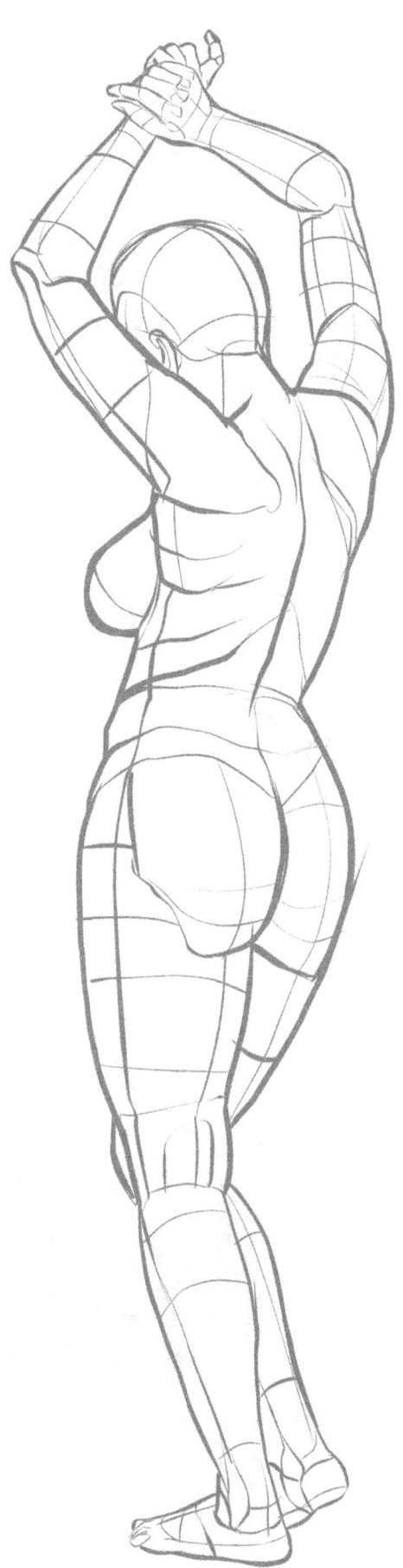

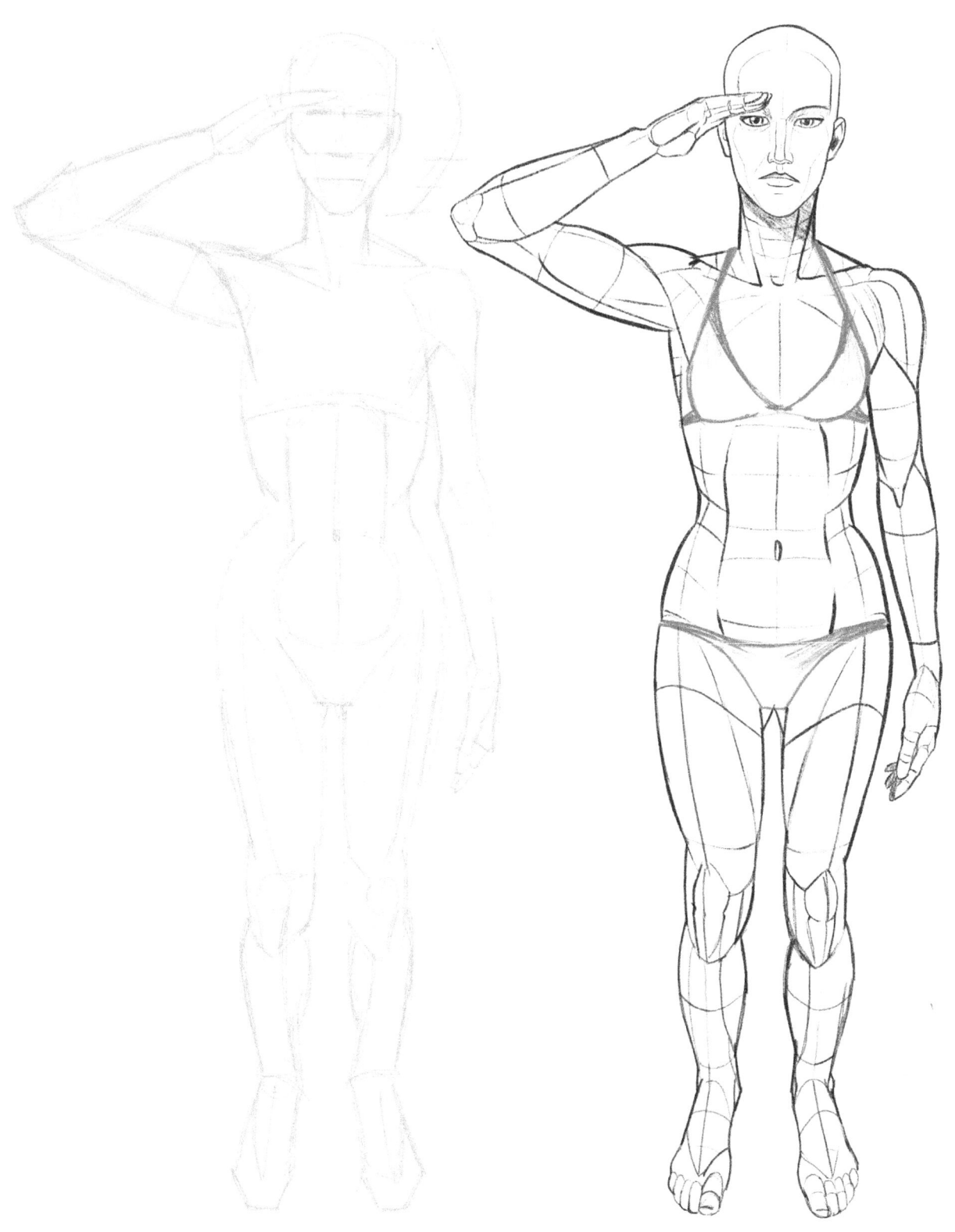

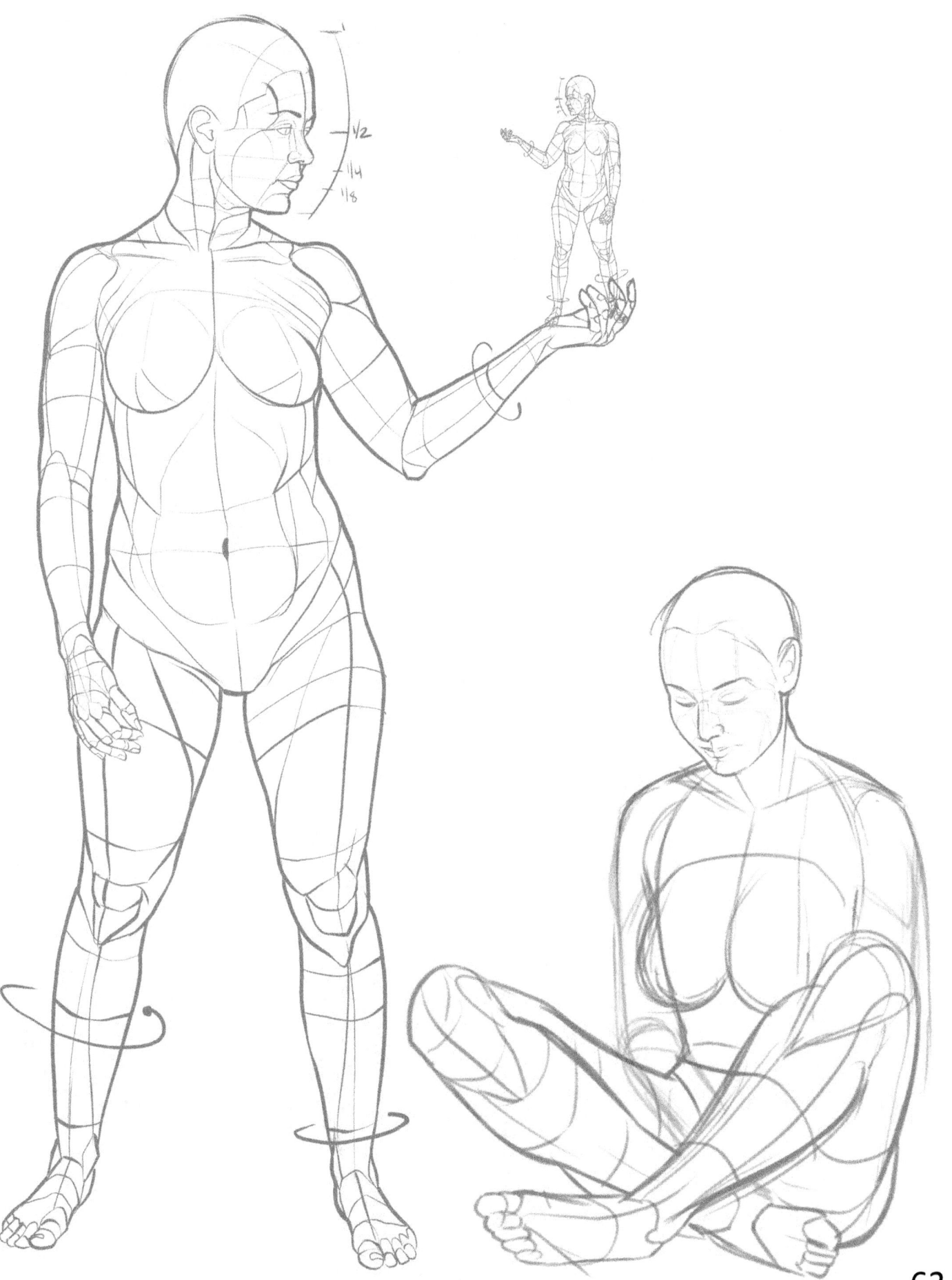

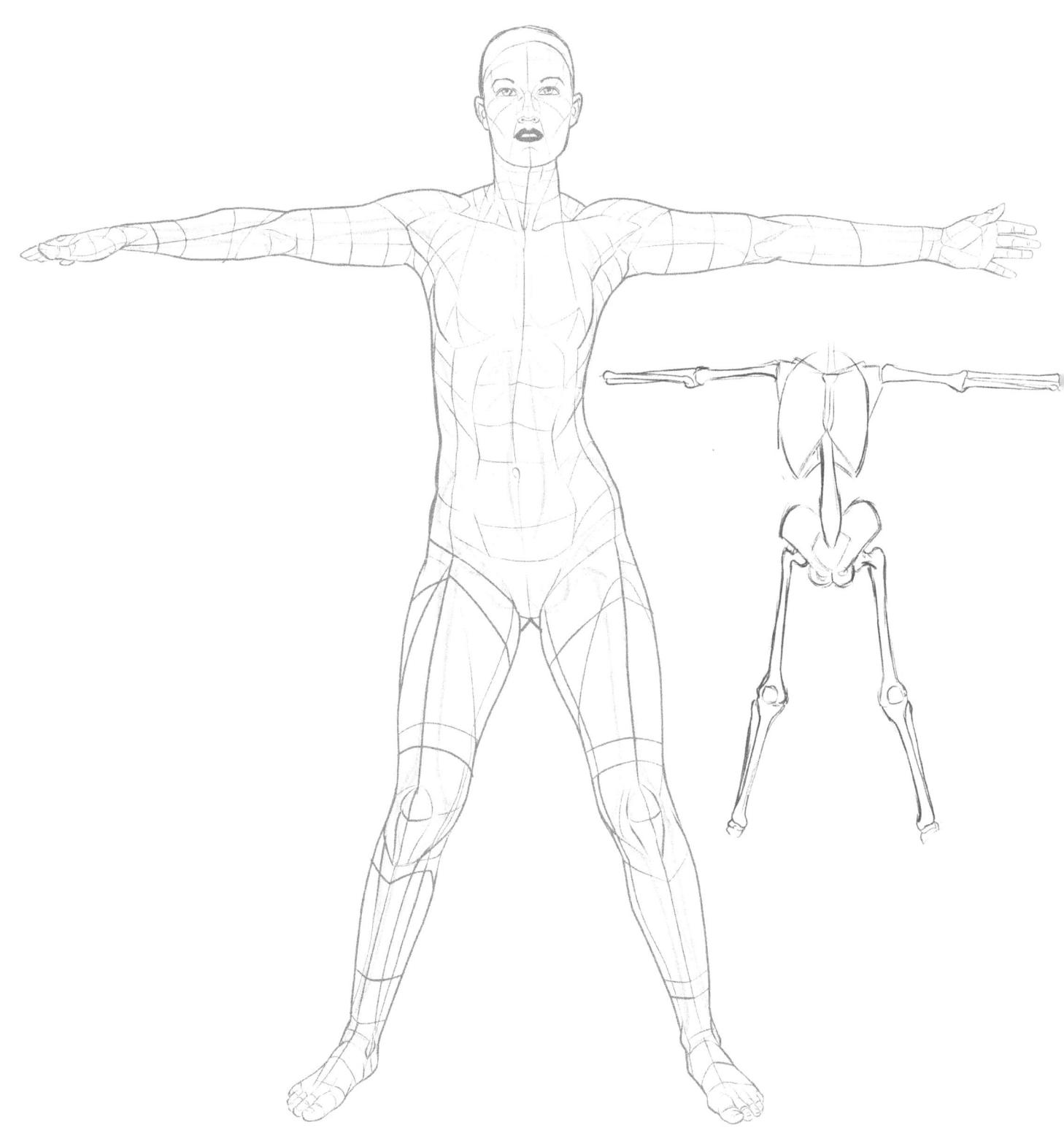

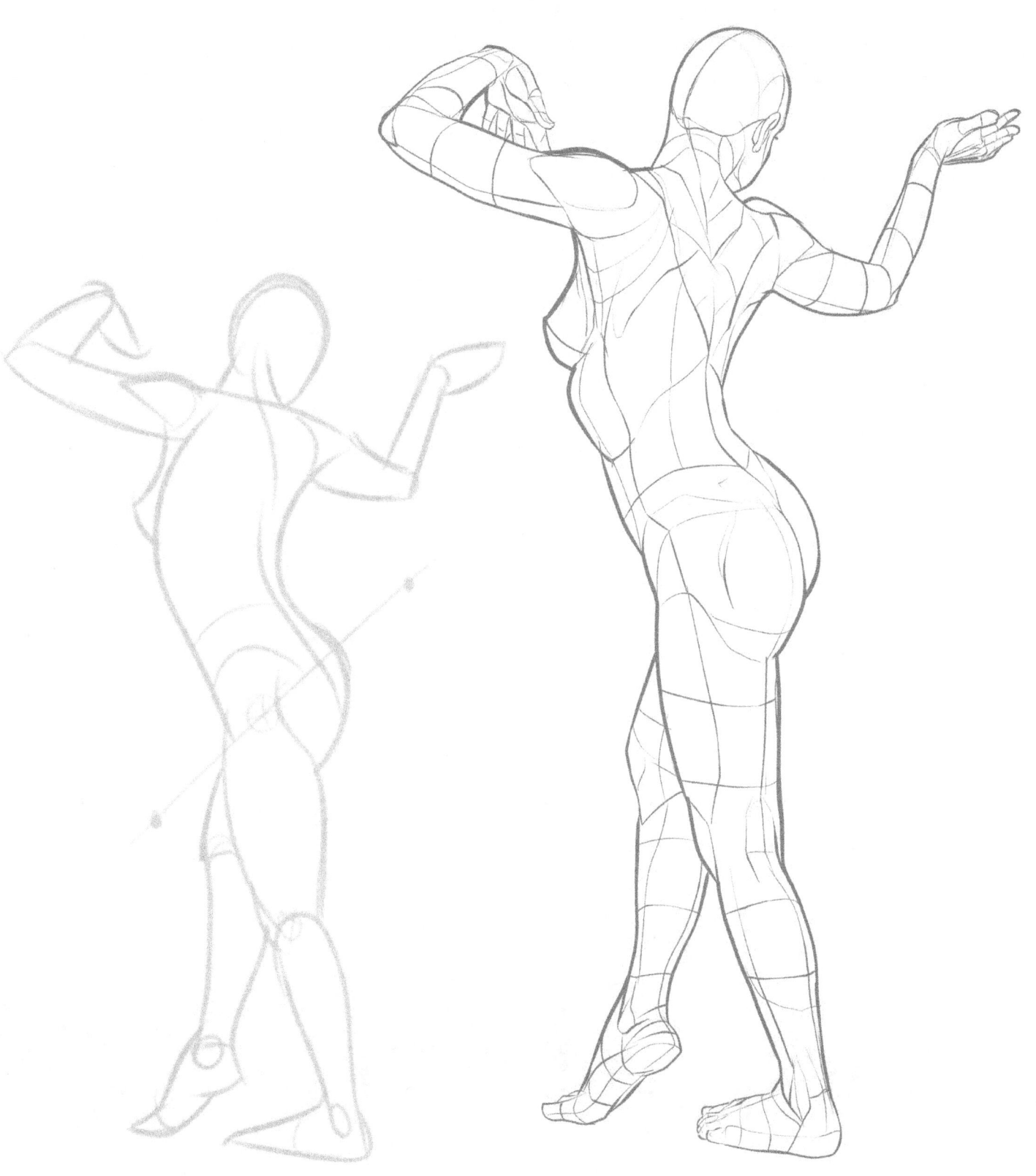

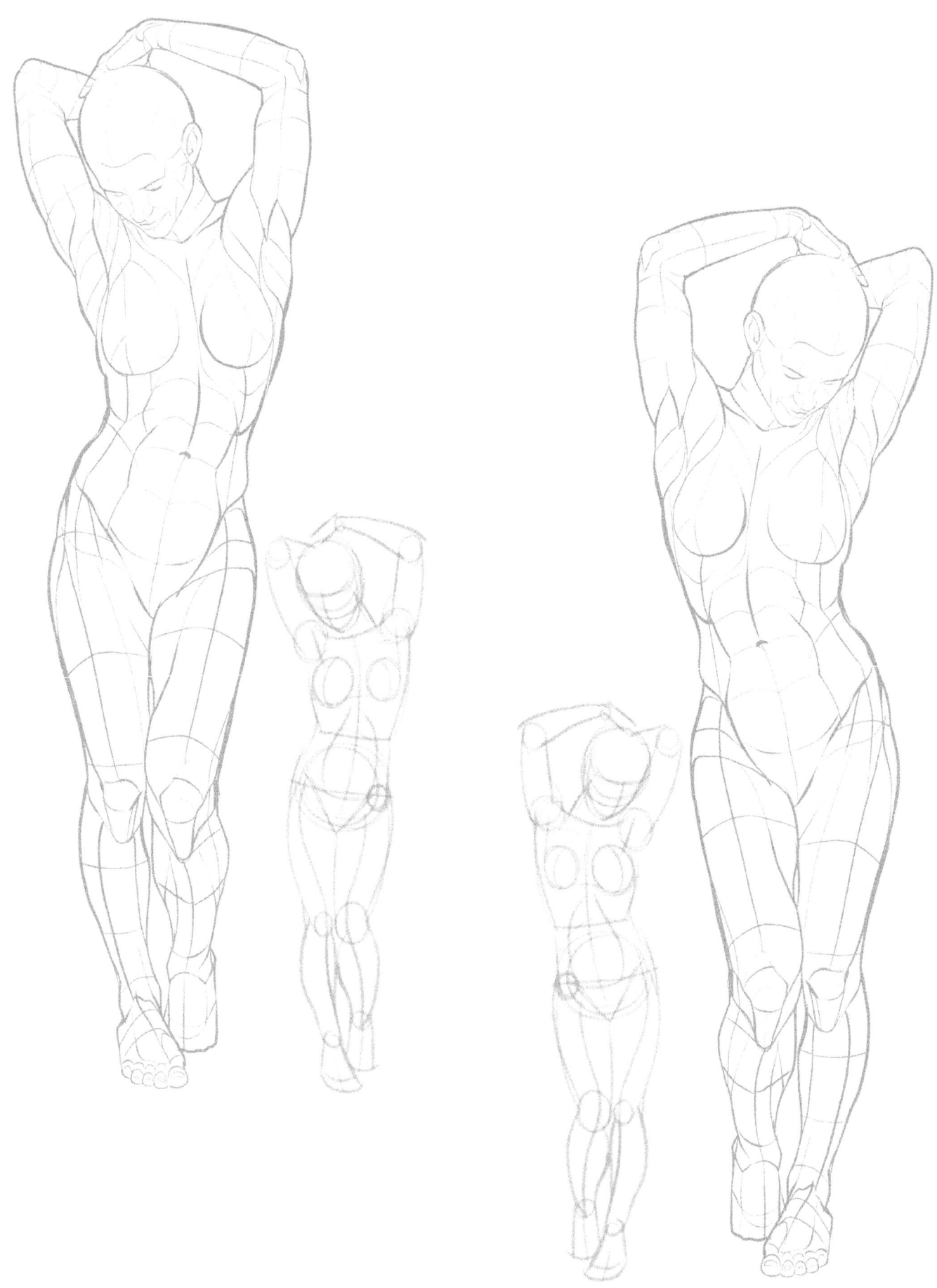

66

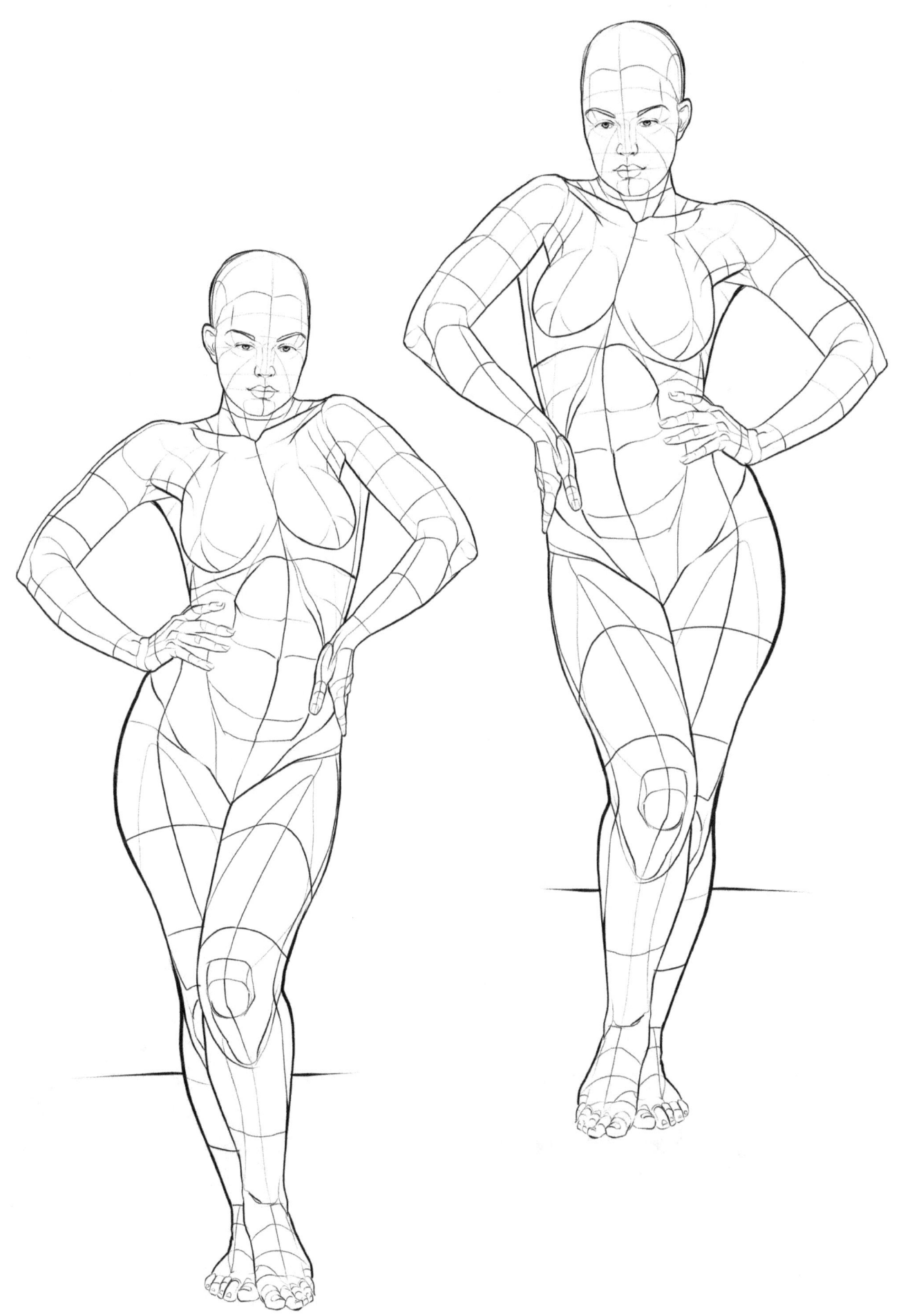

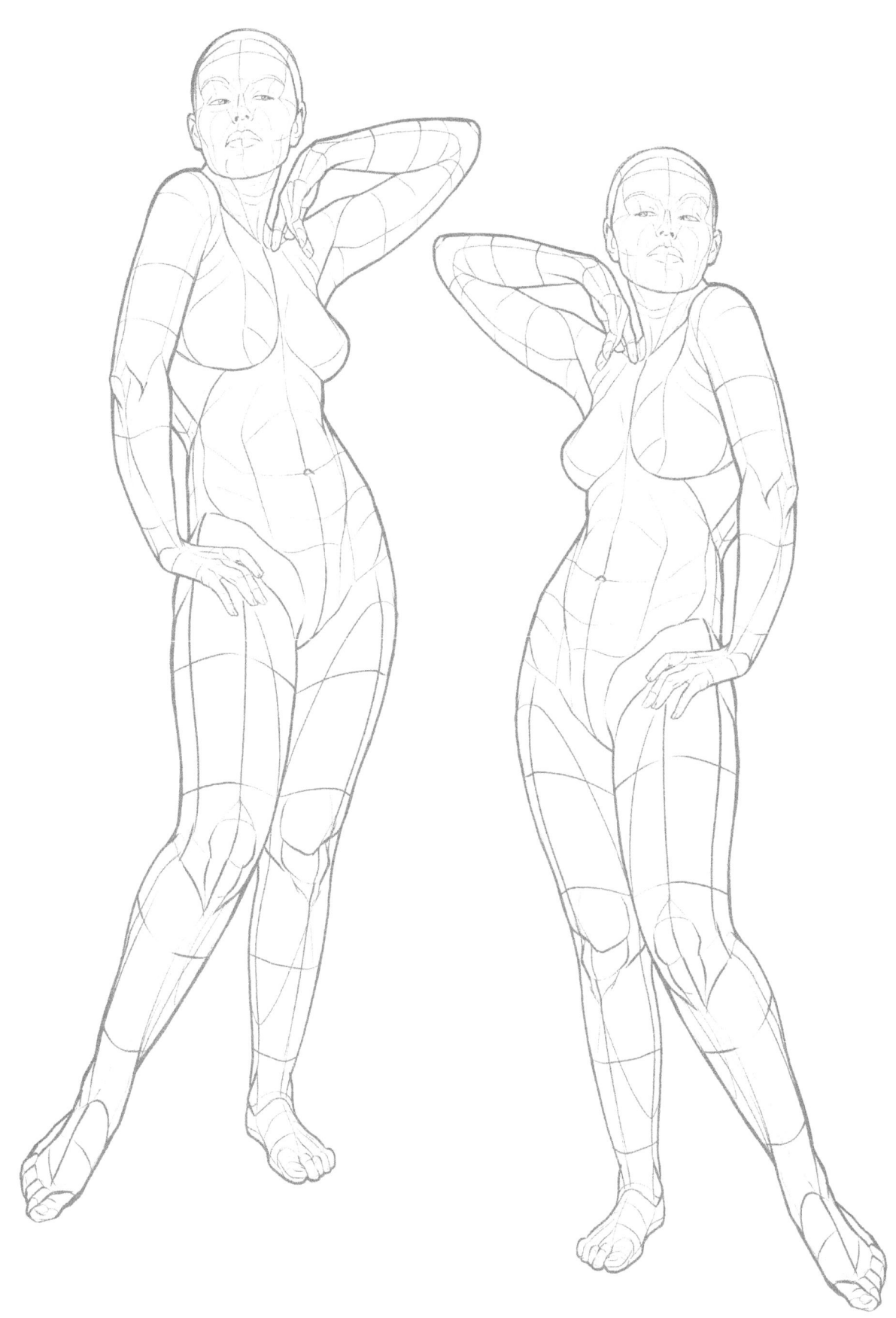

68

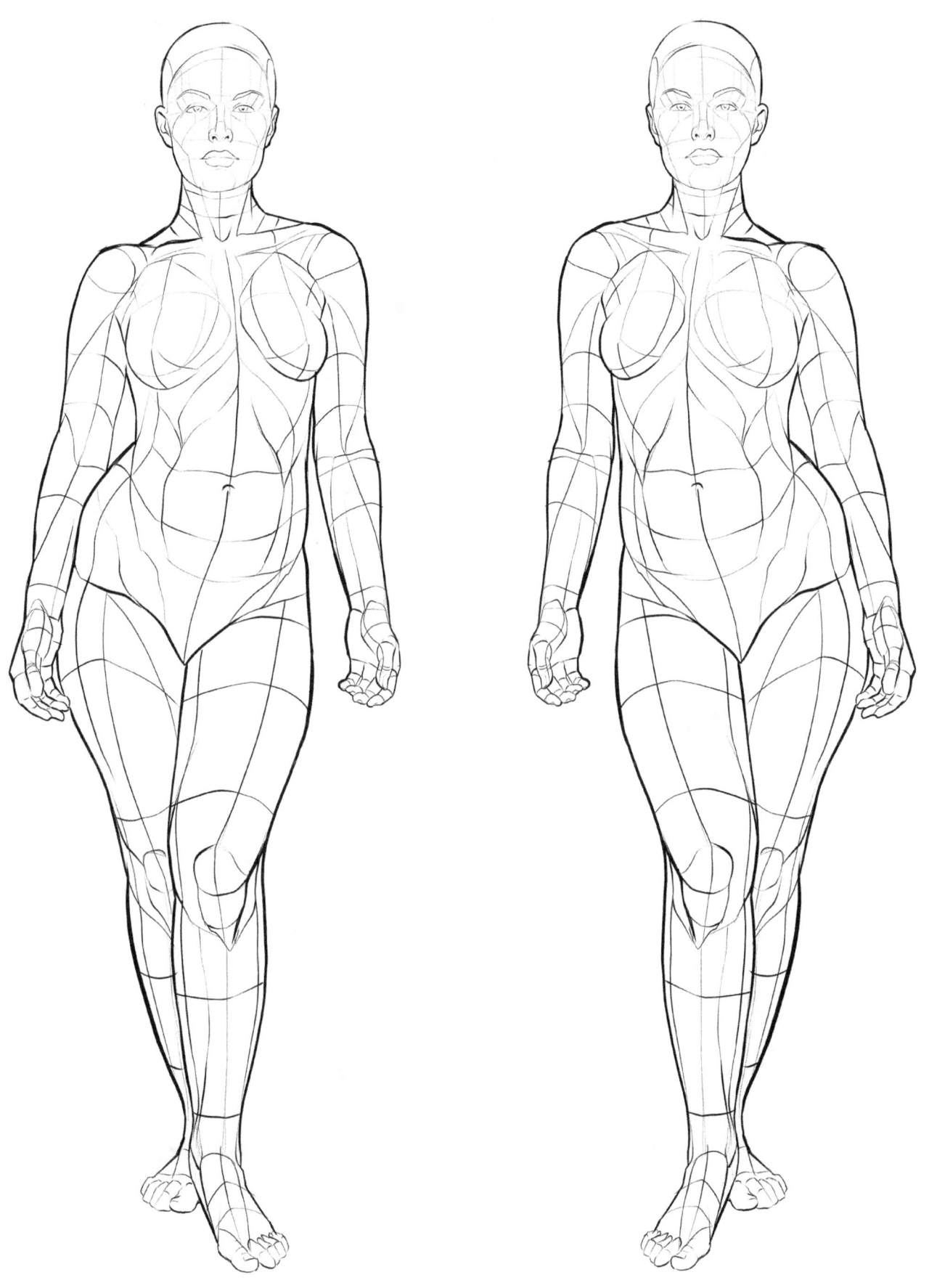

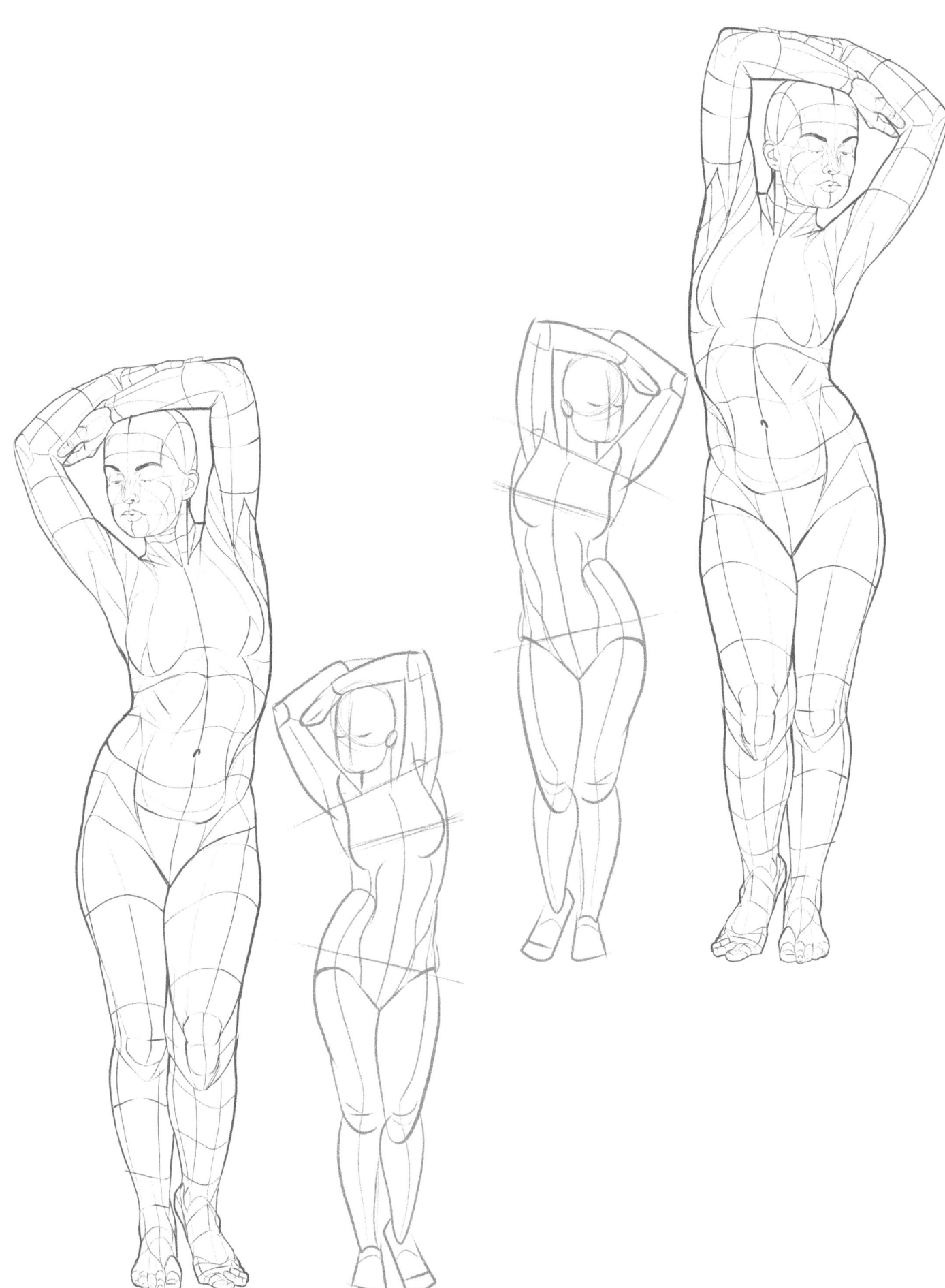

70

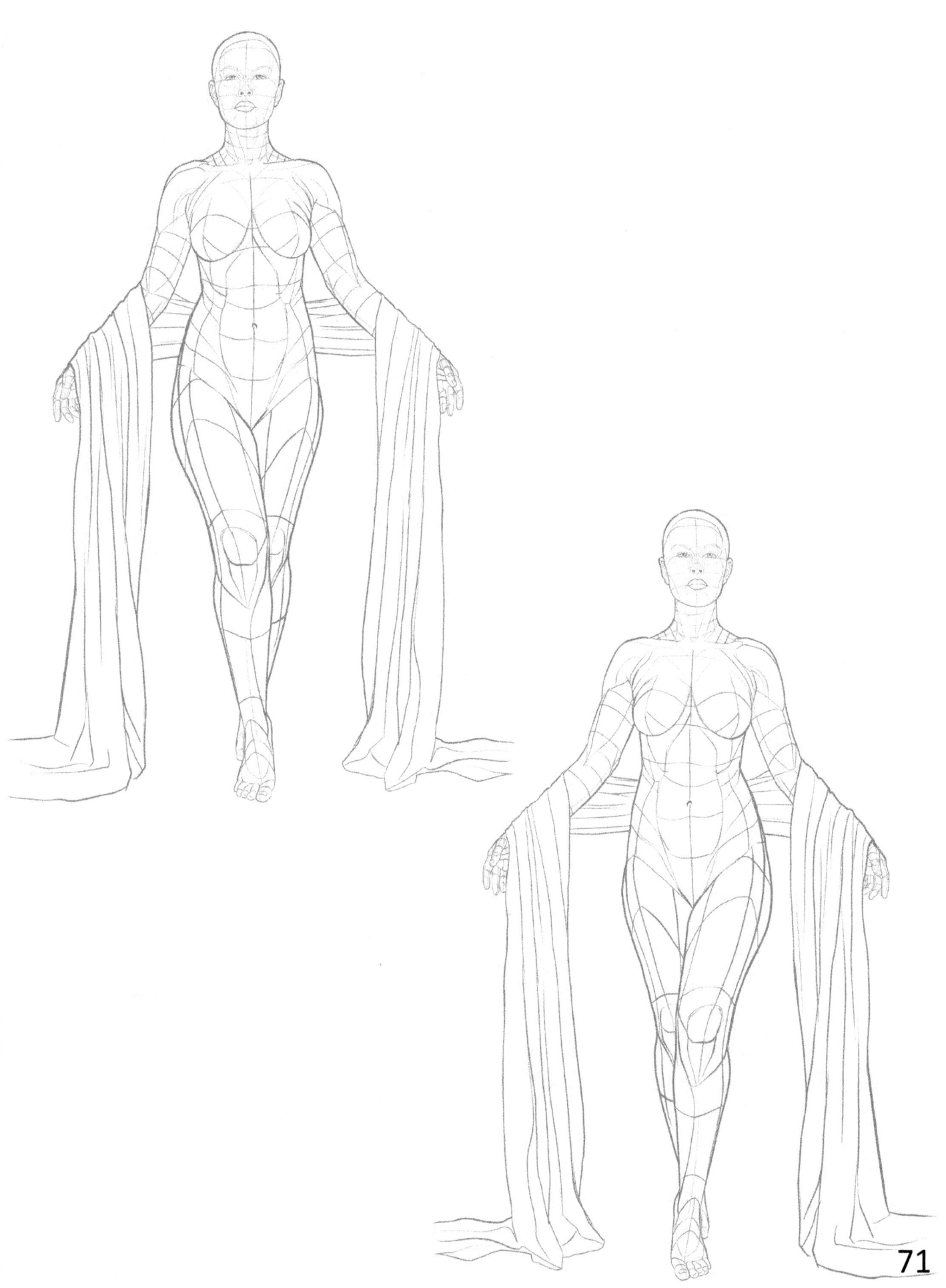

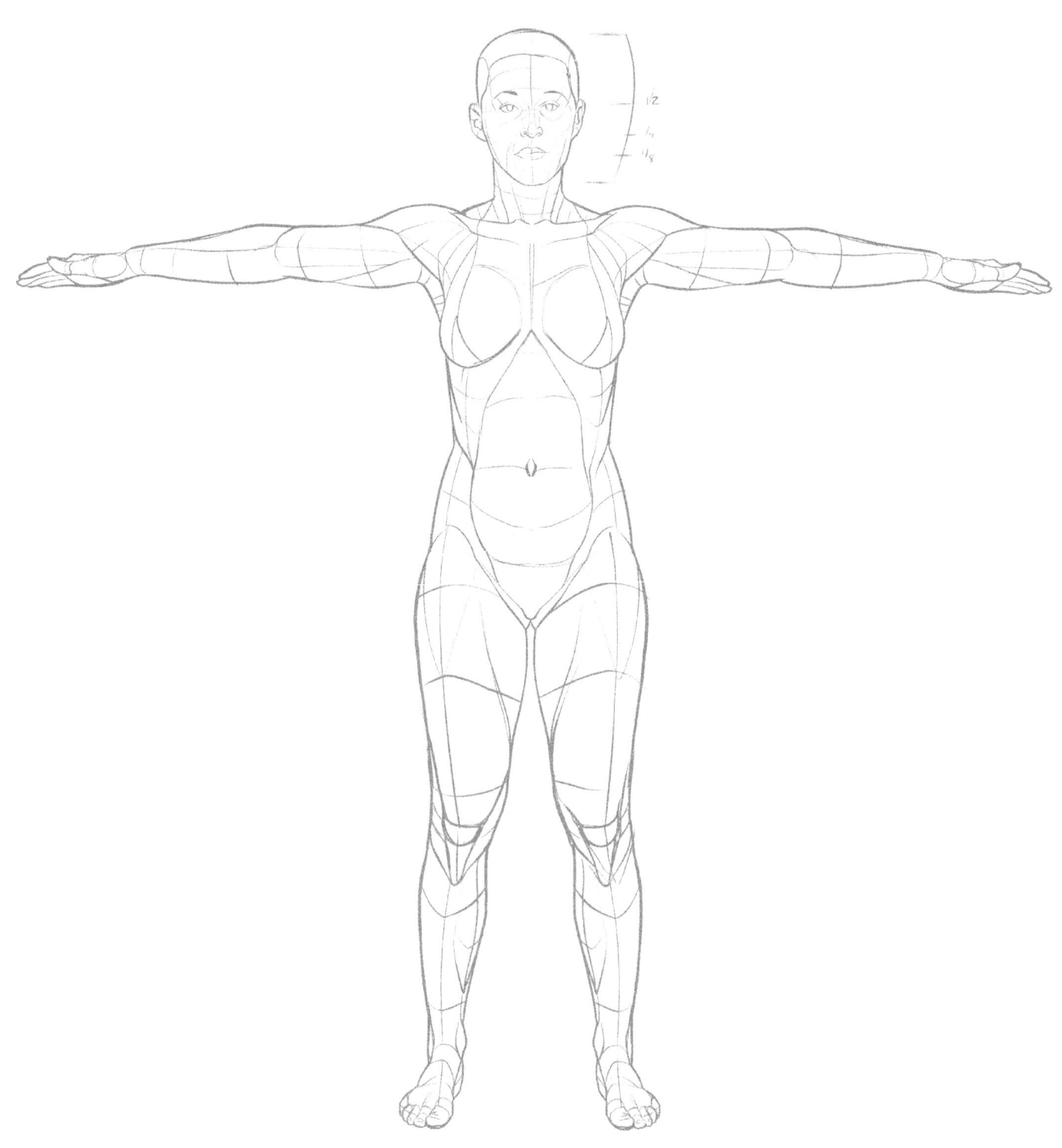

½
¼
⅛

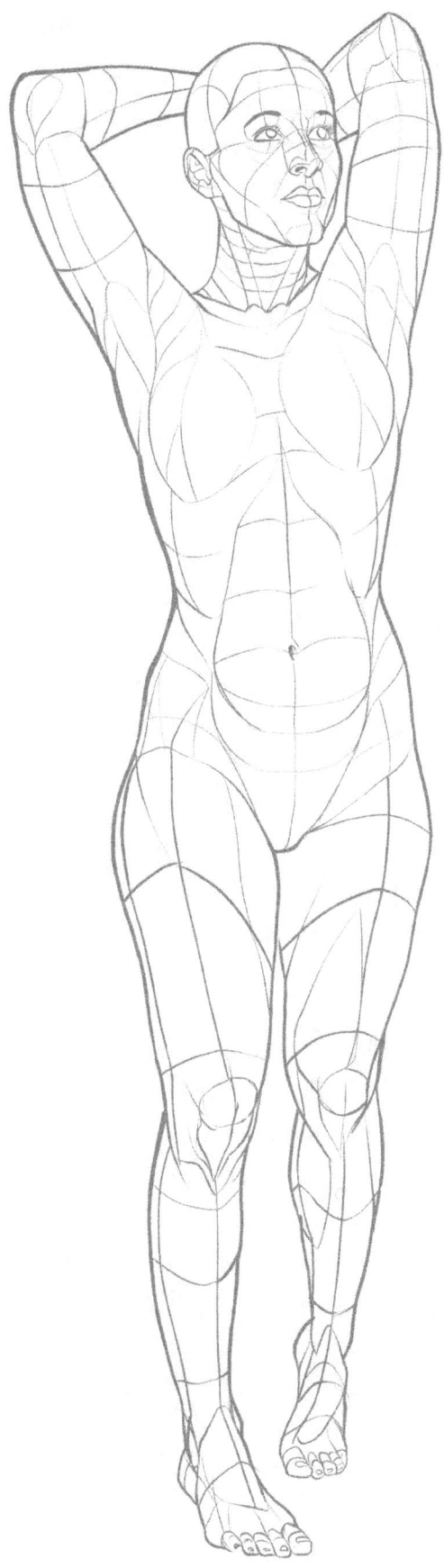 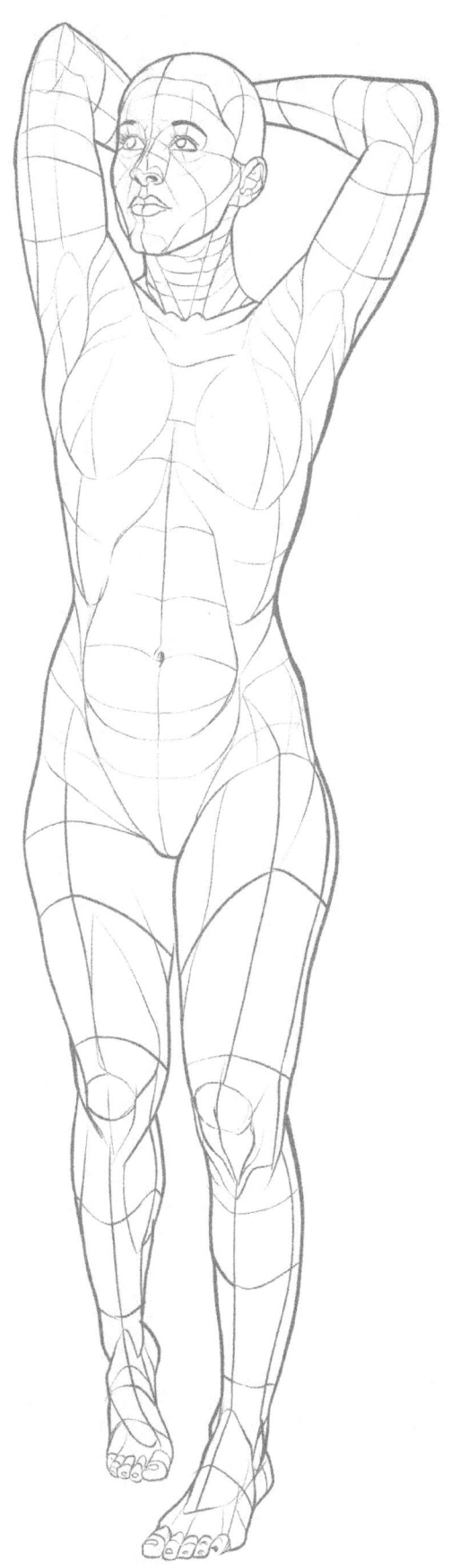

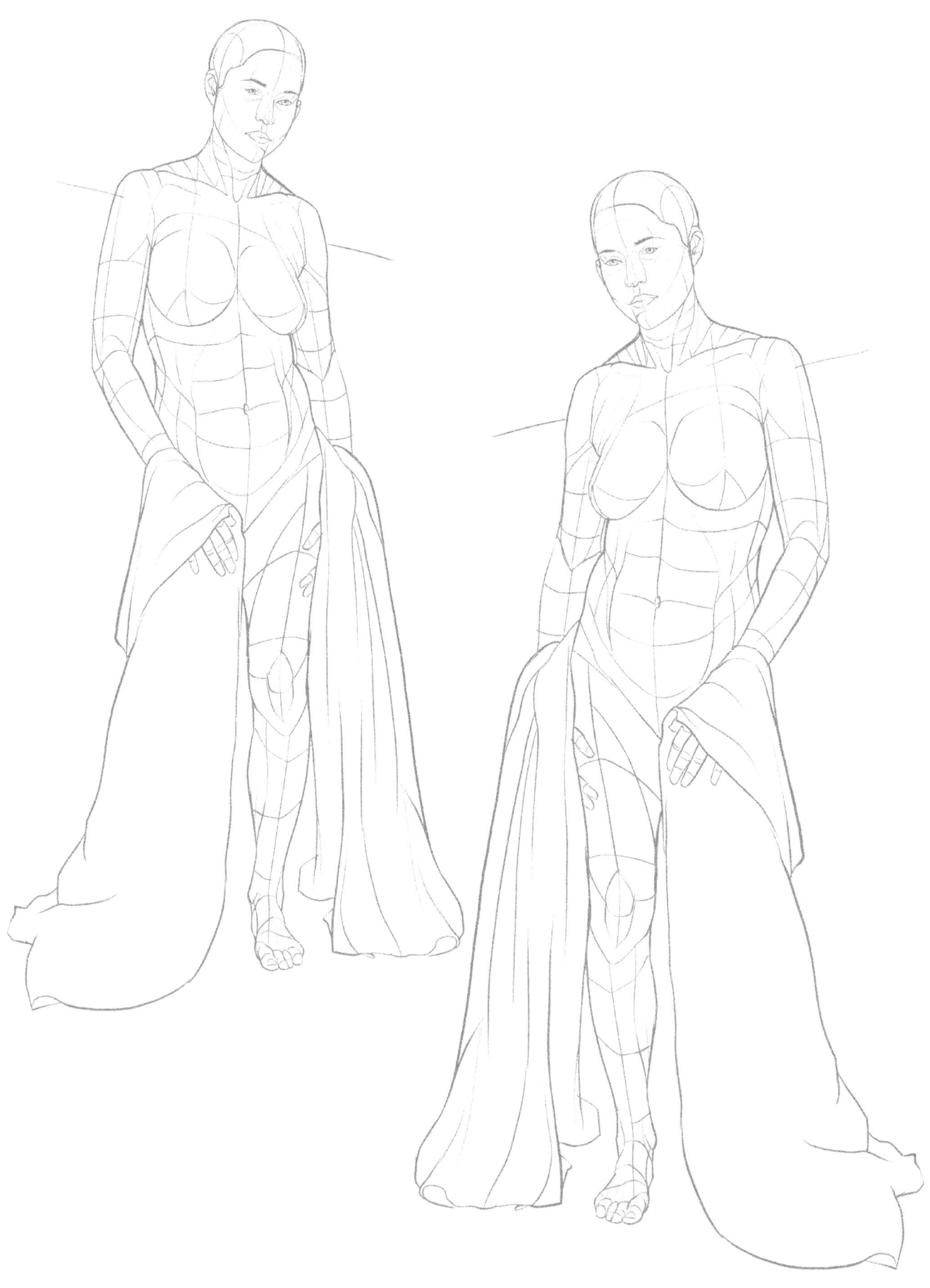

74

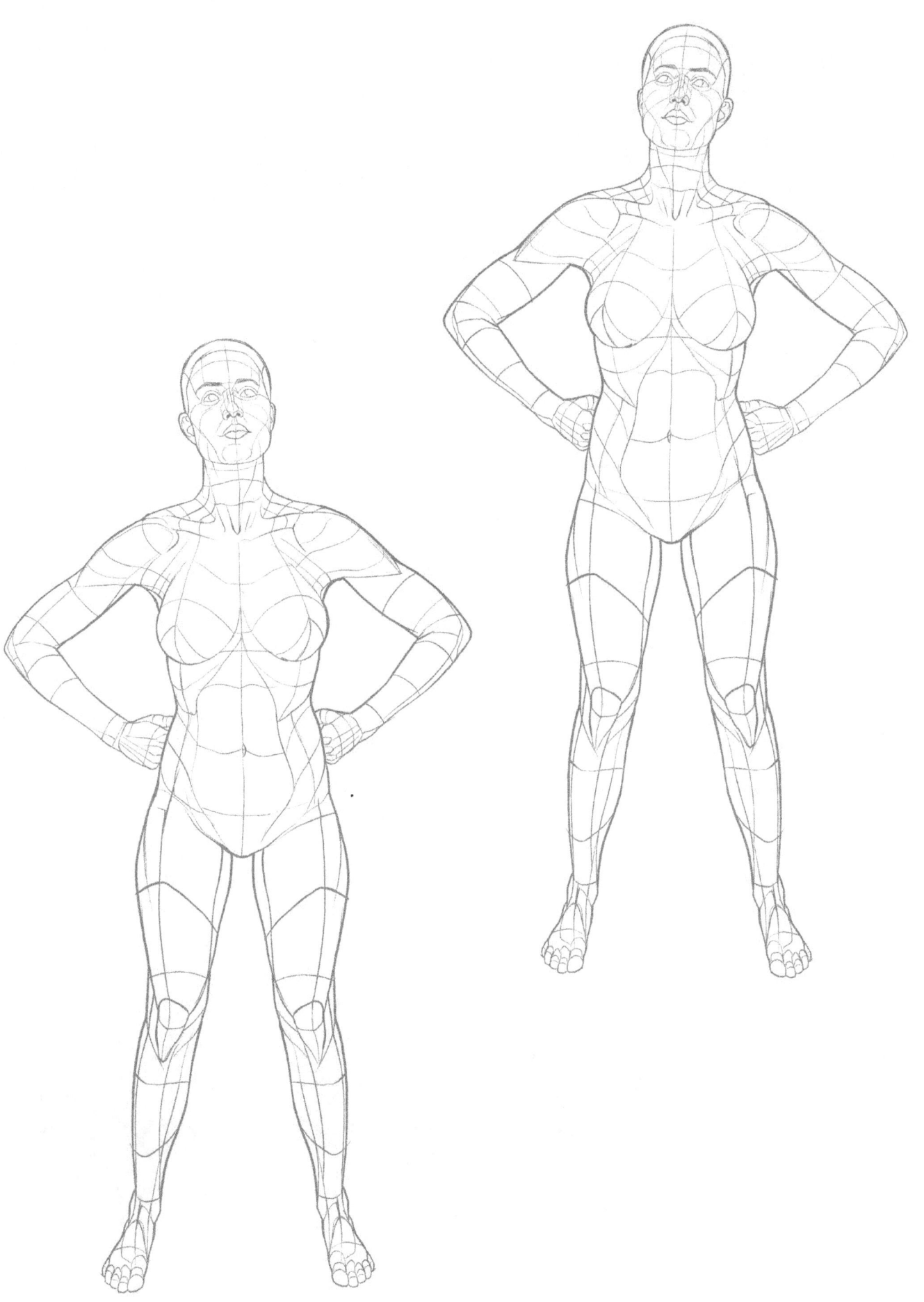

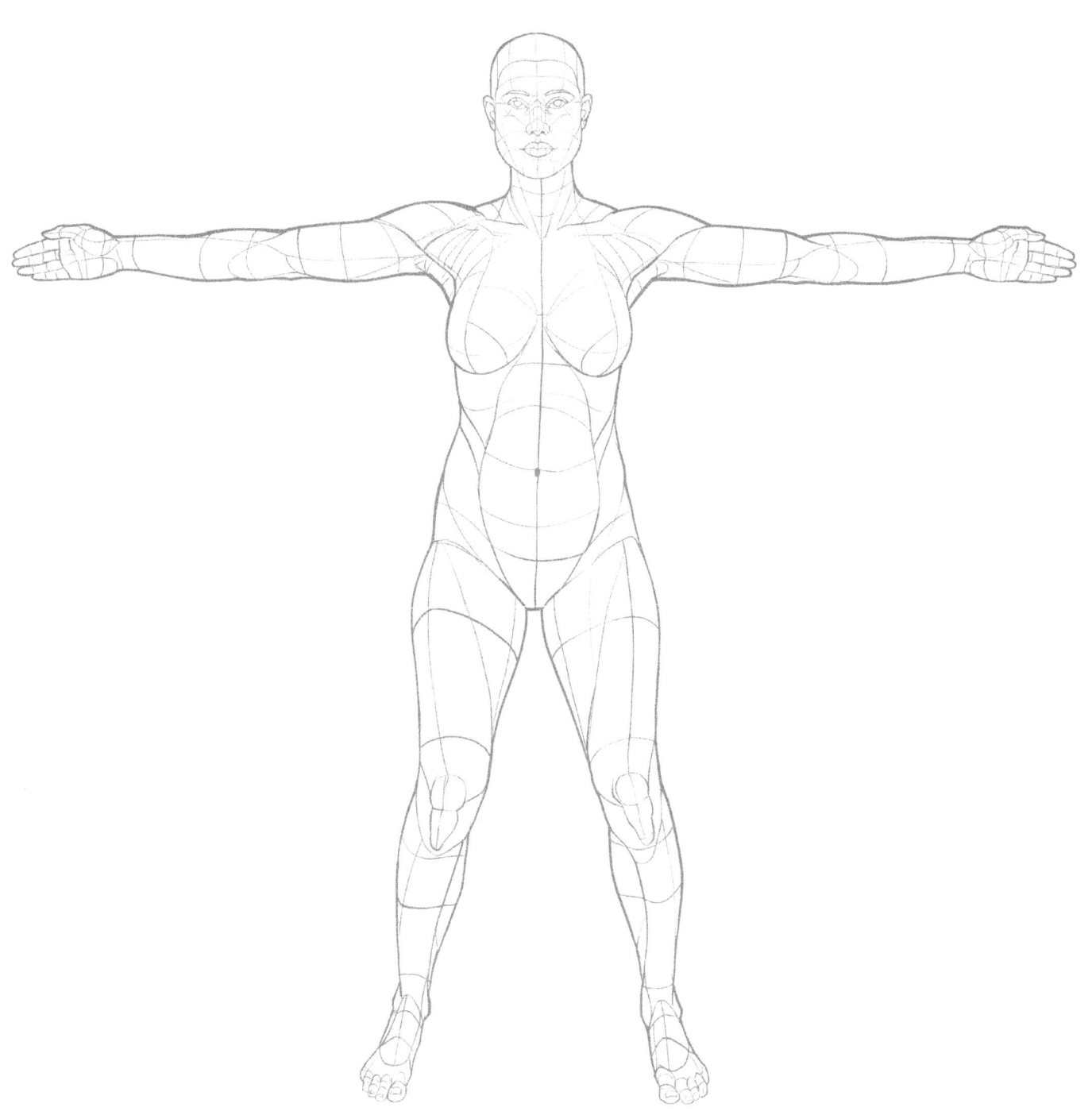

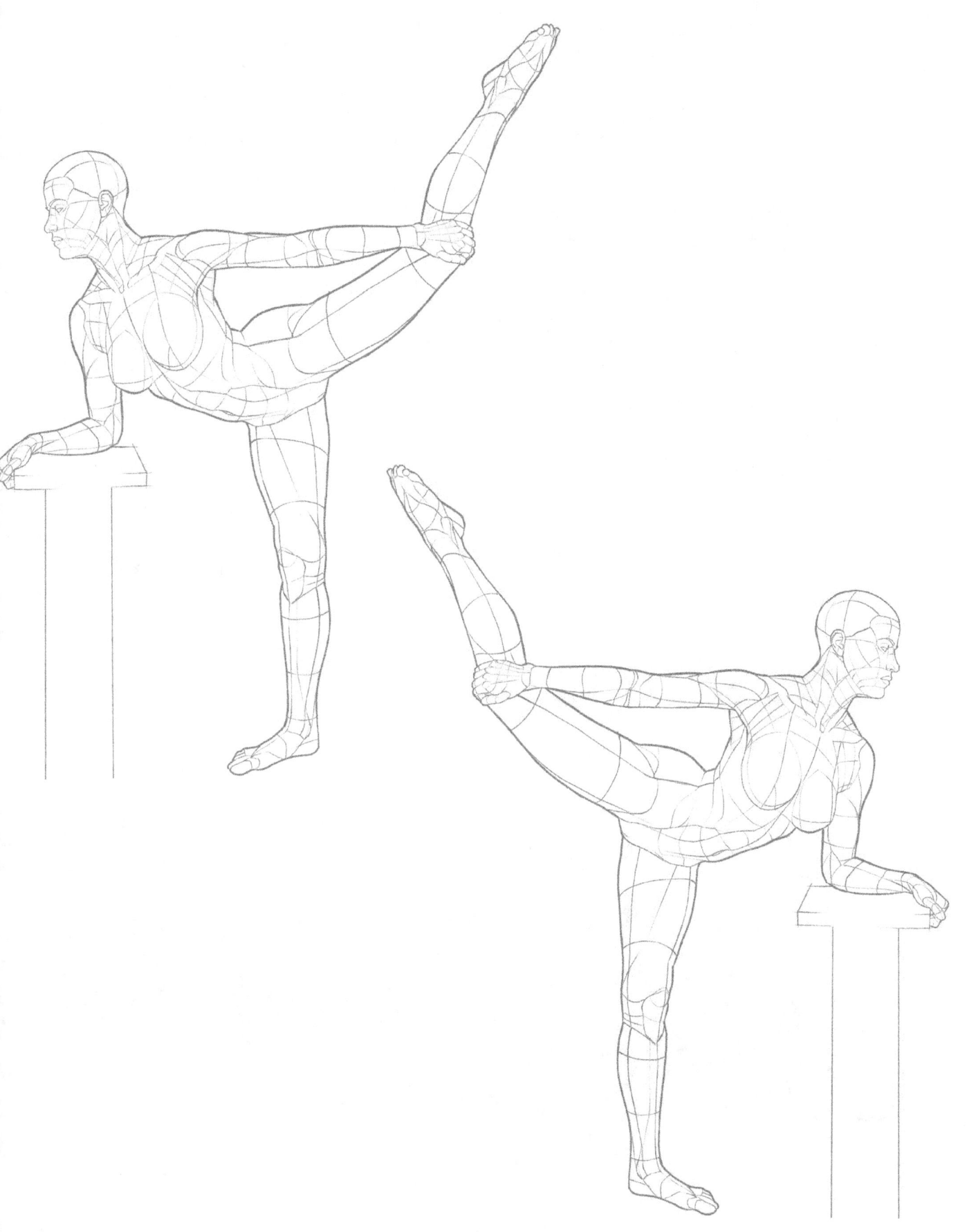

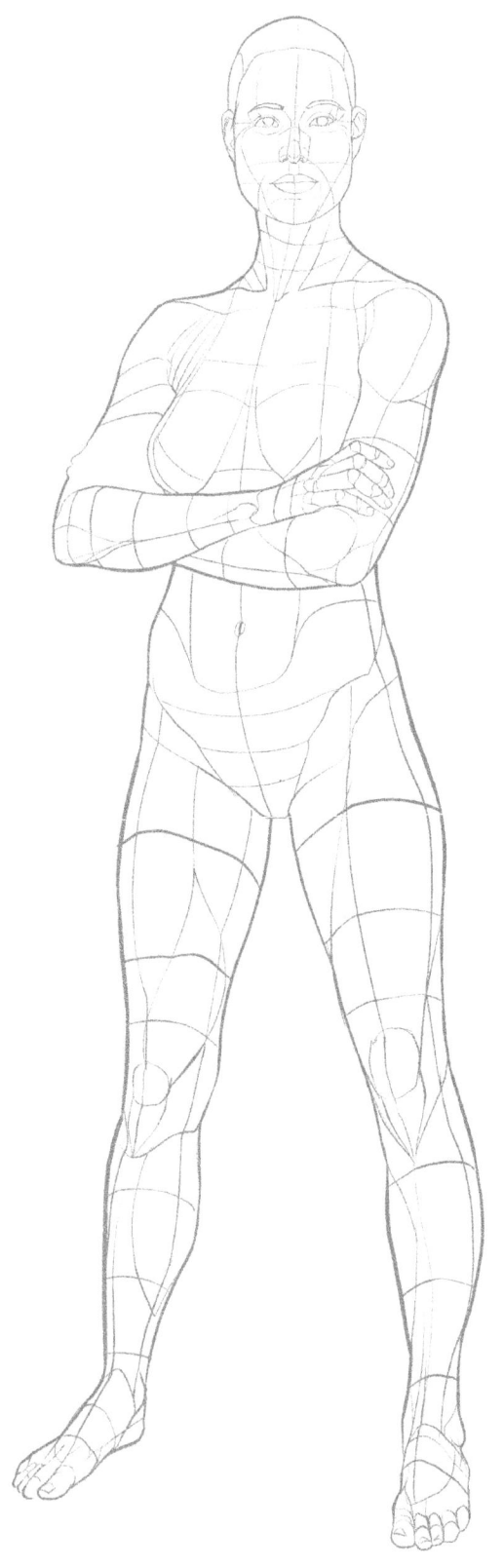
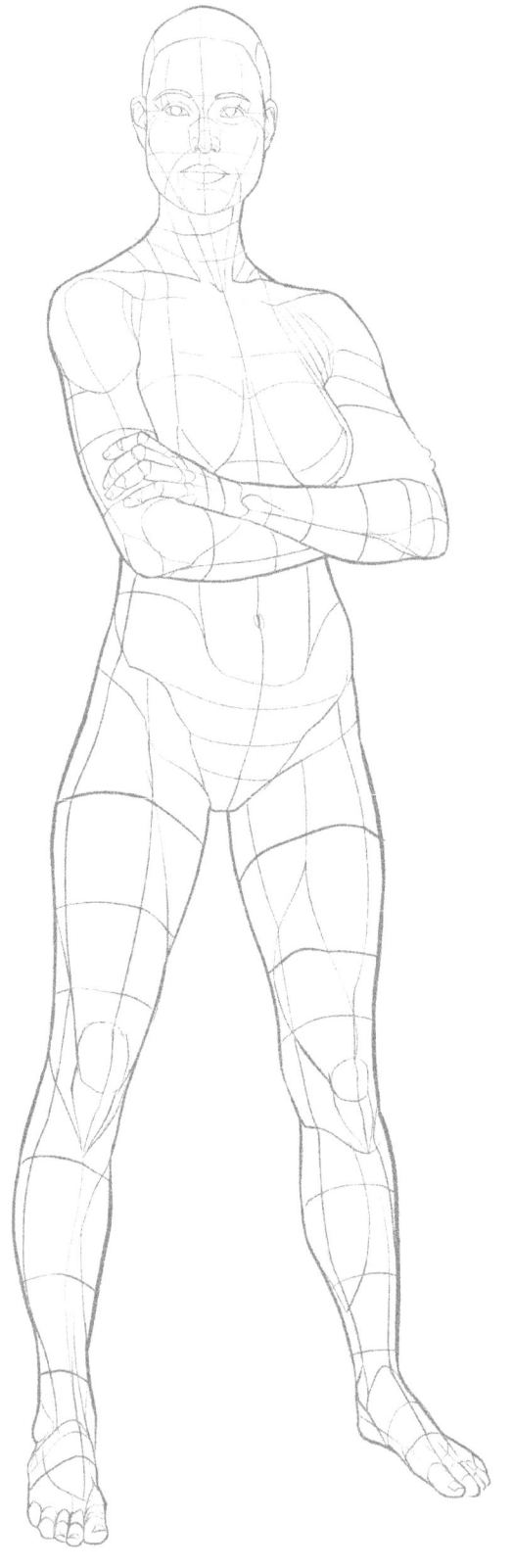

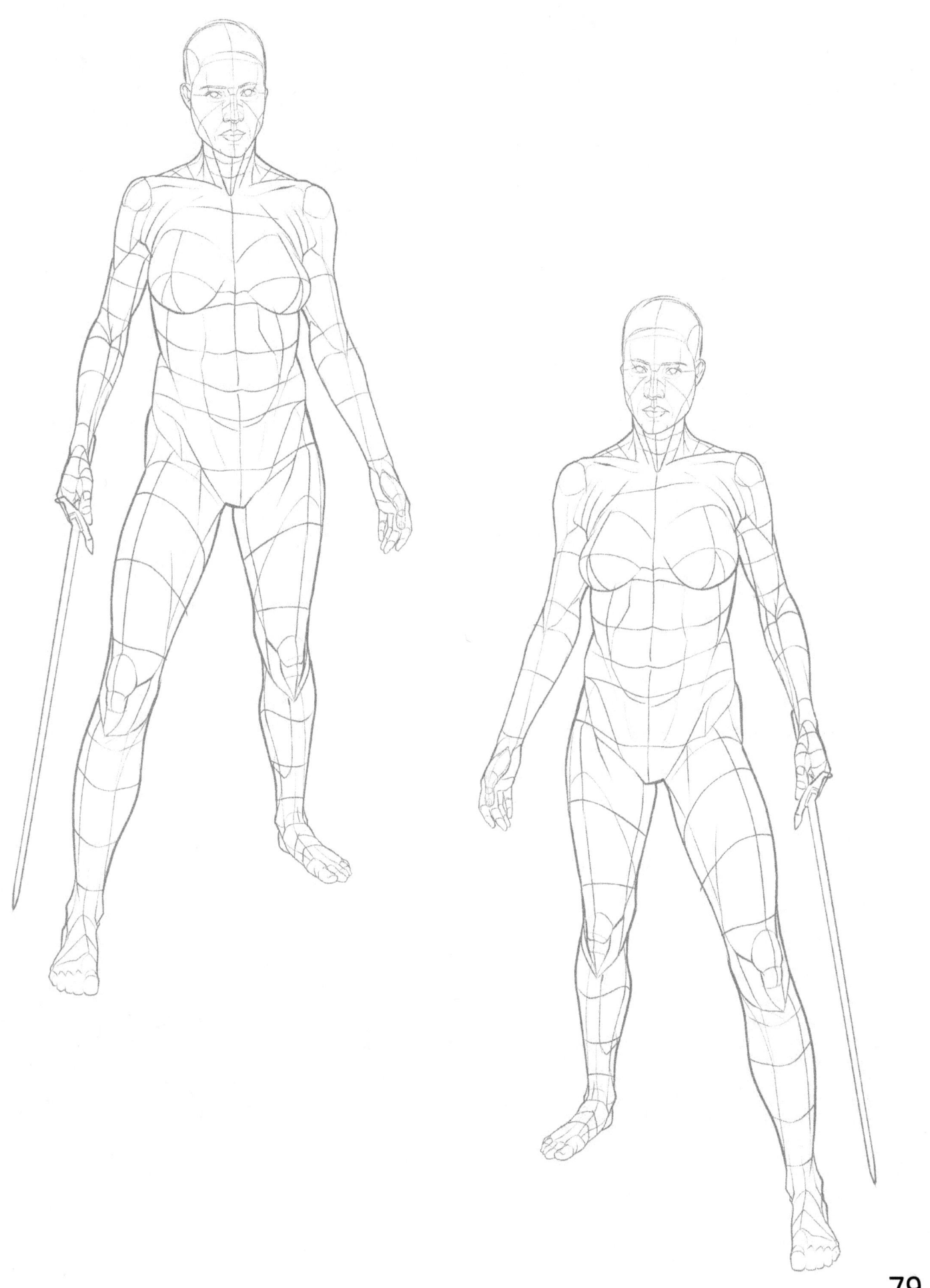

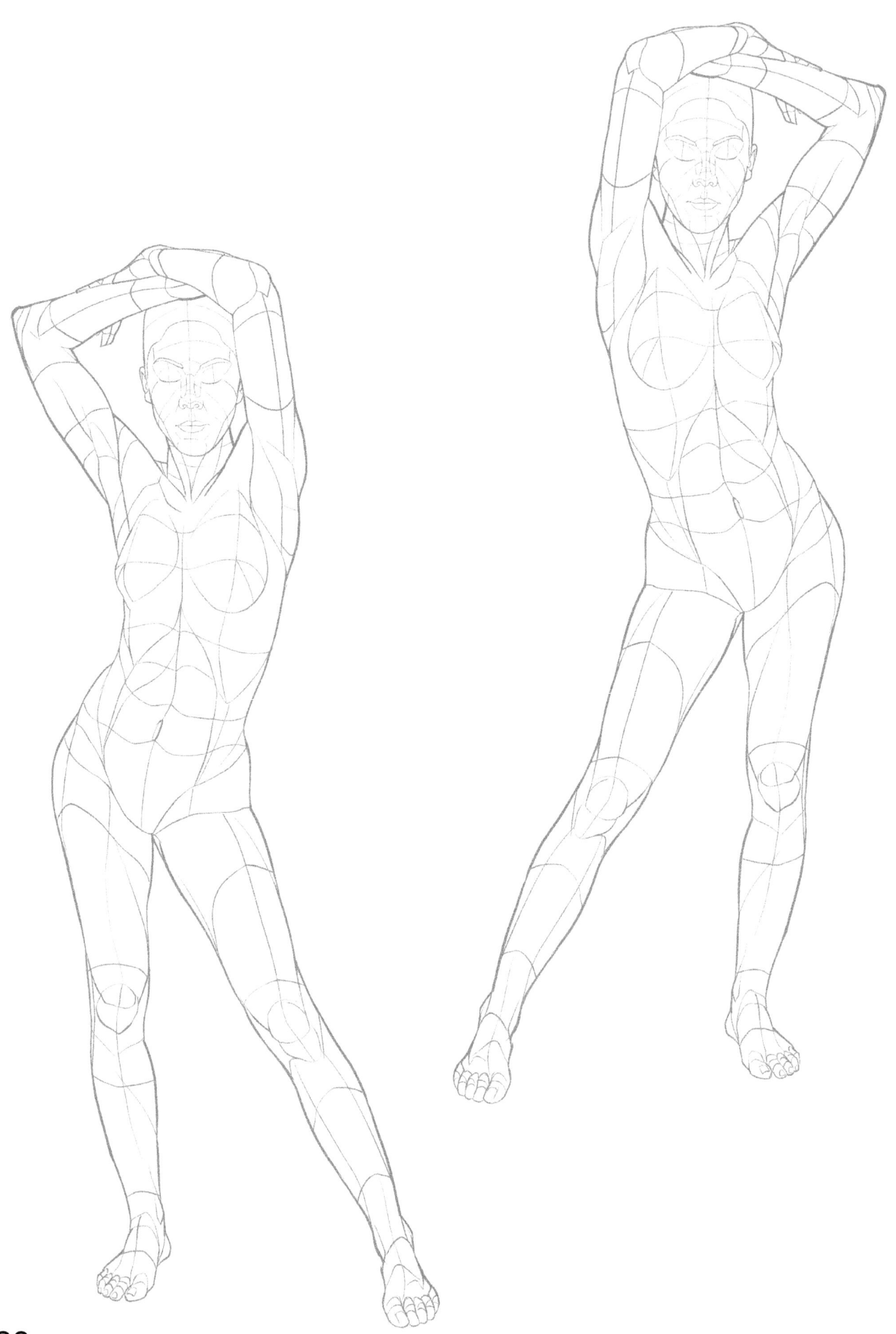

80

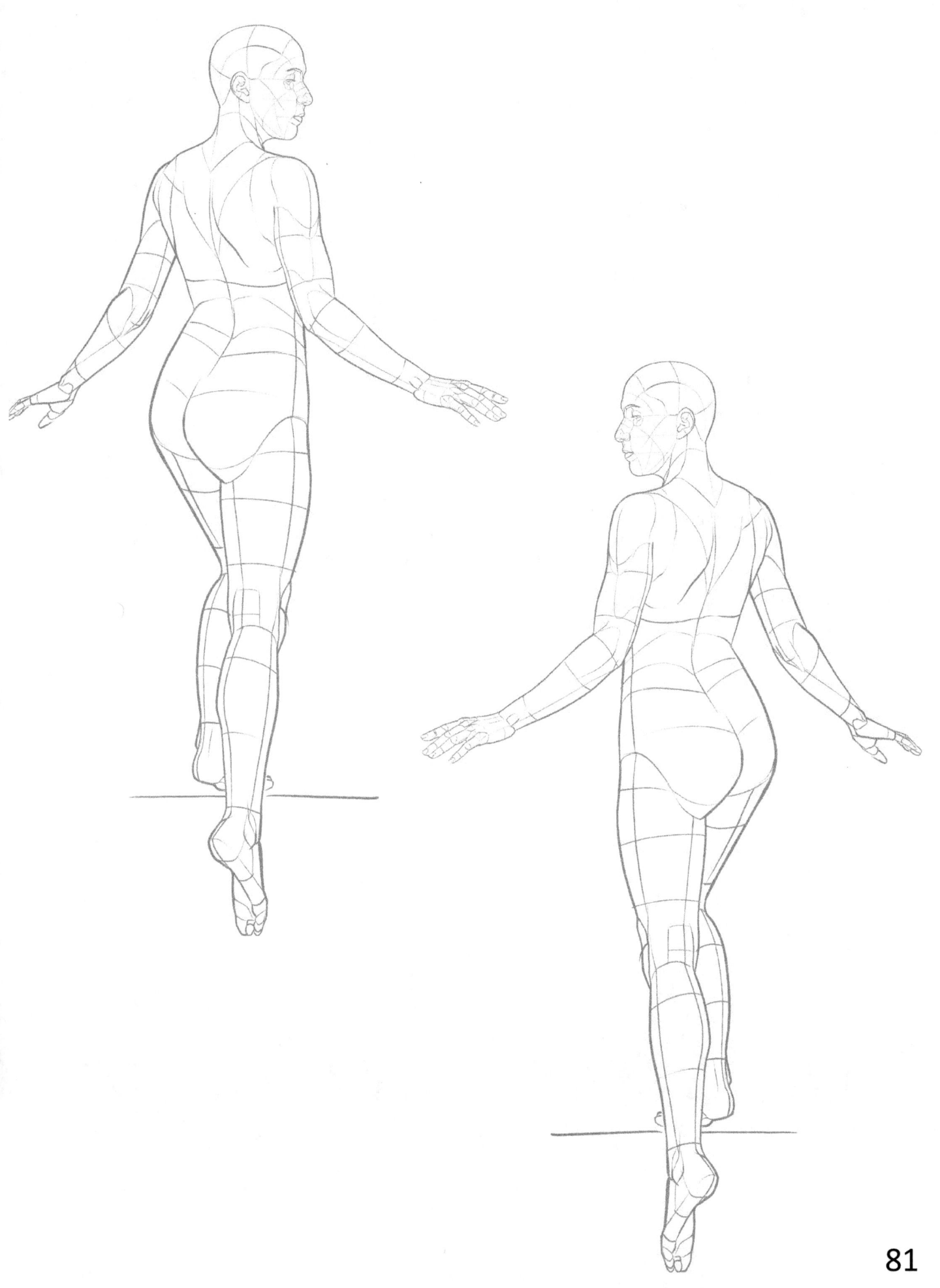

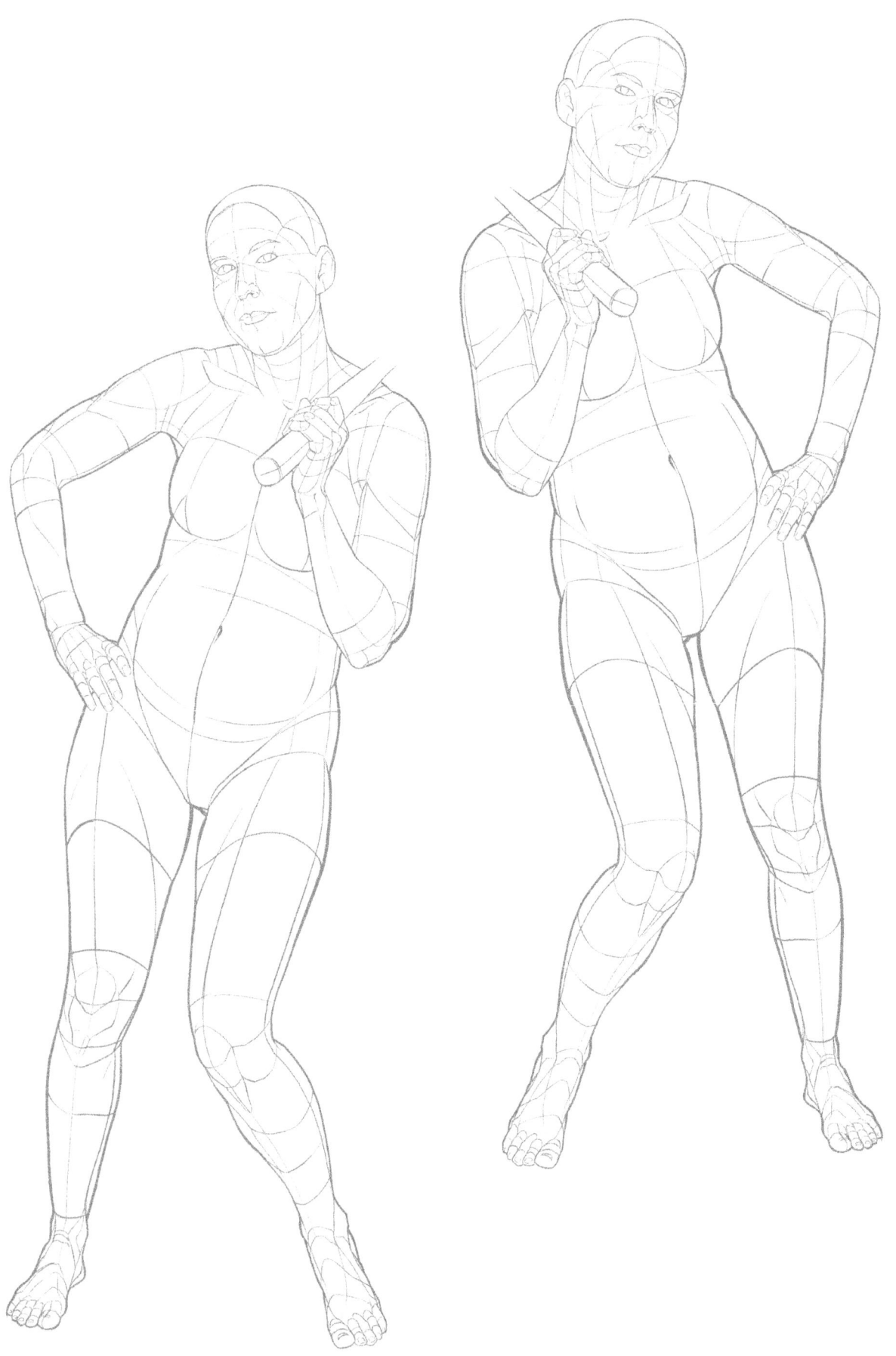

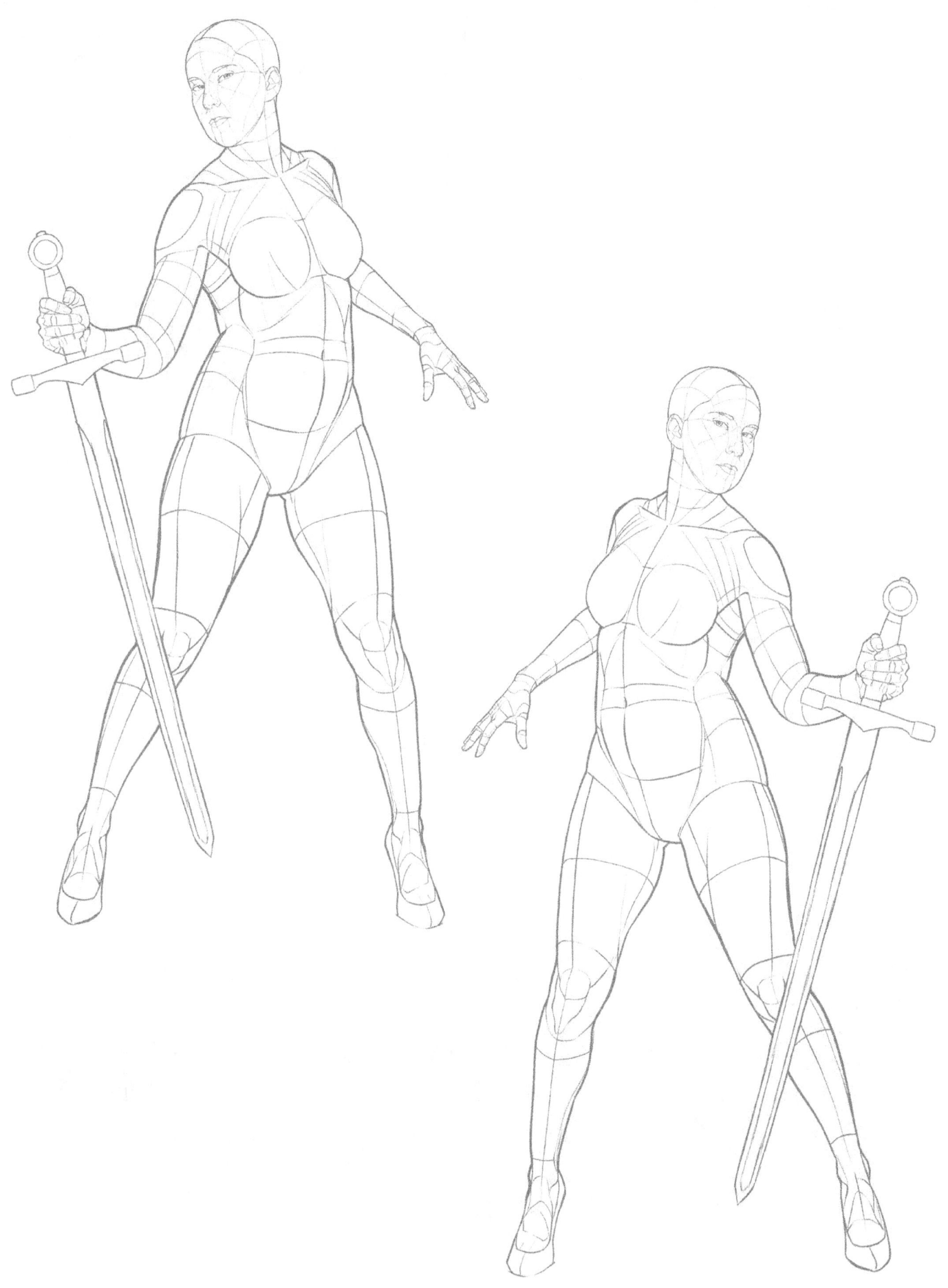

83

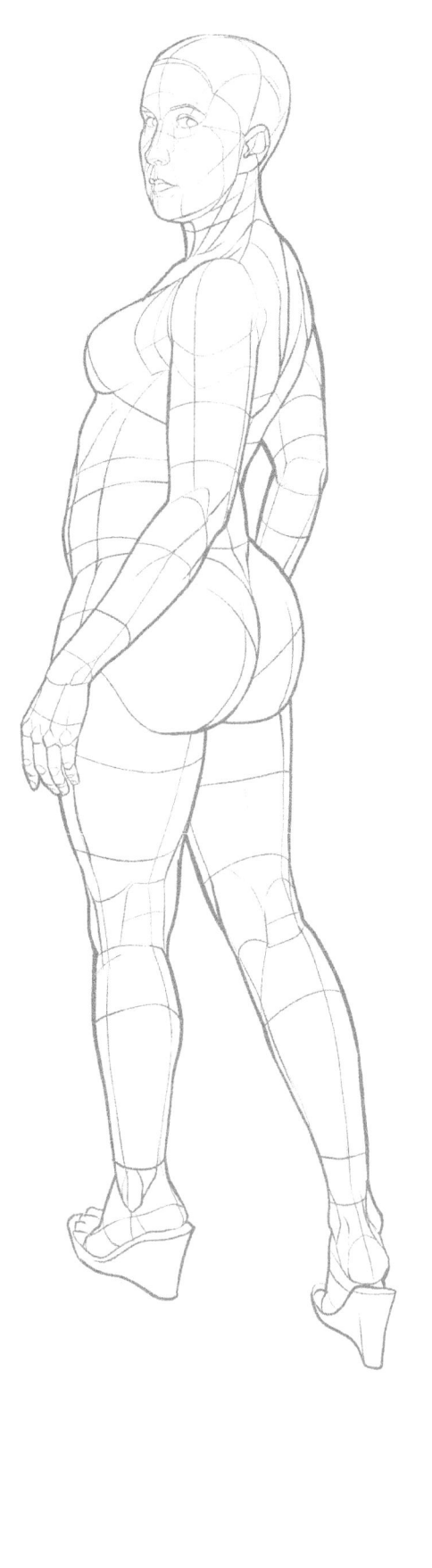
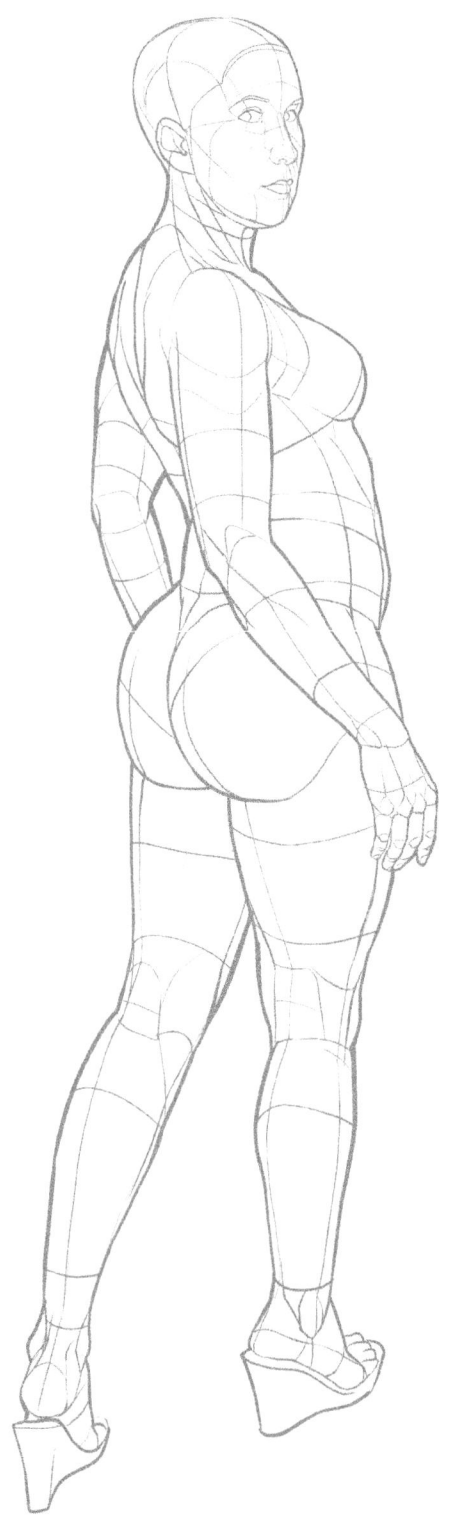

84

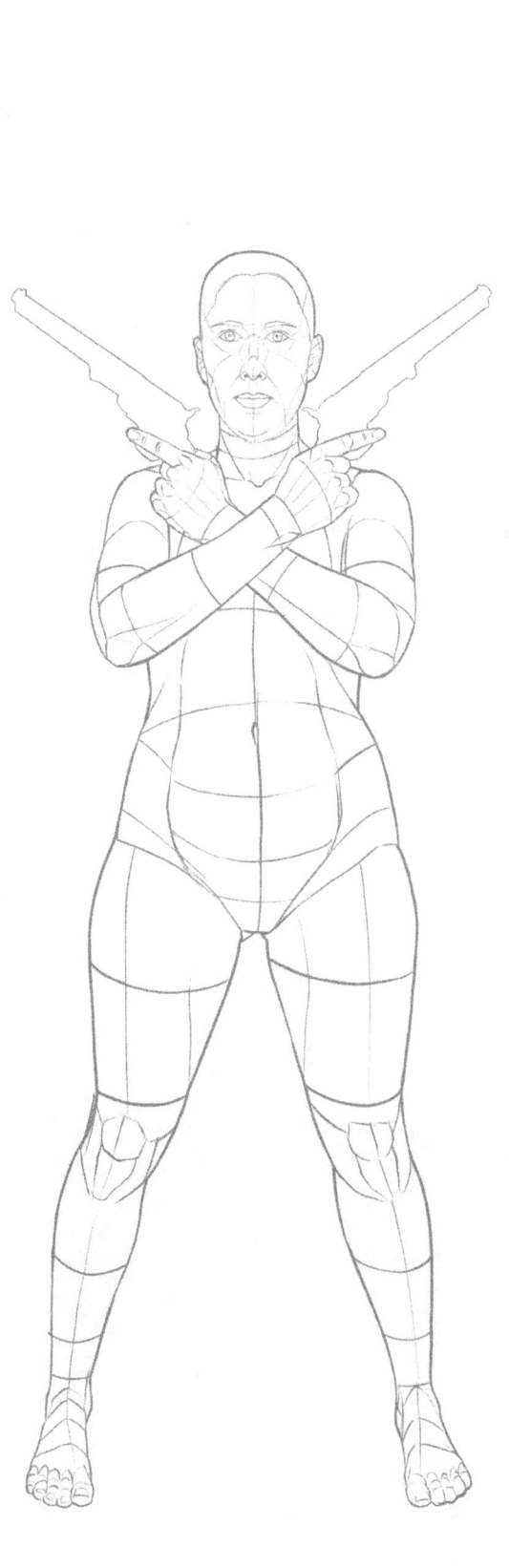
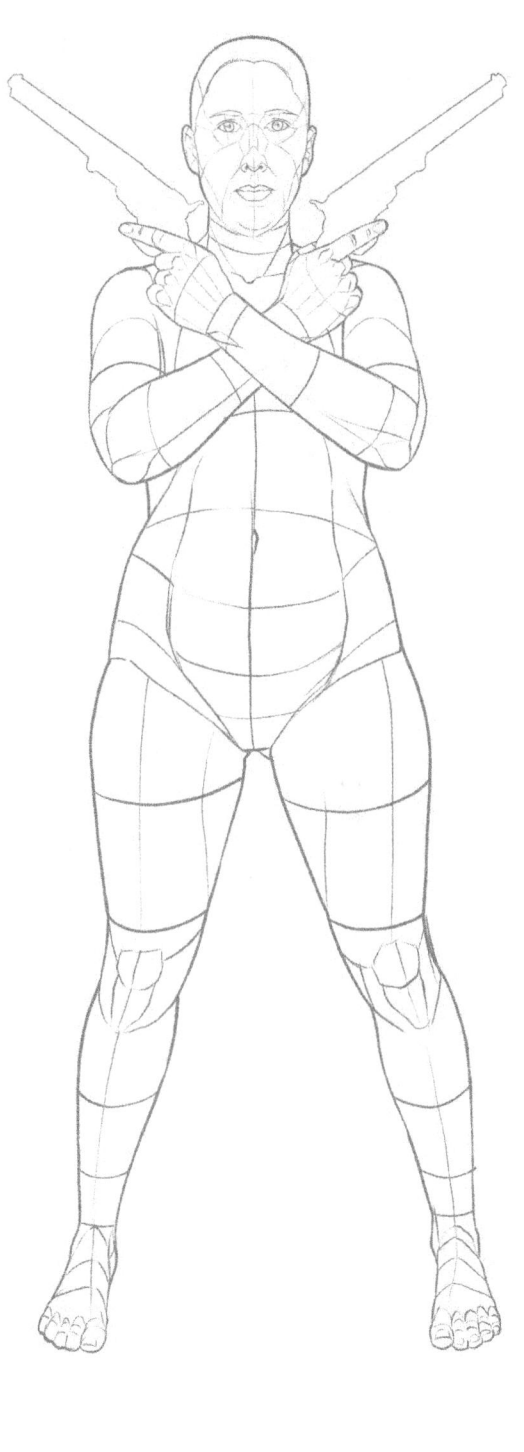

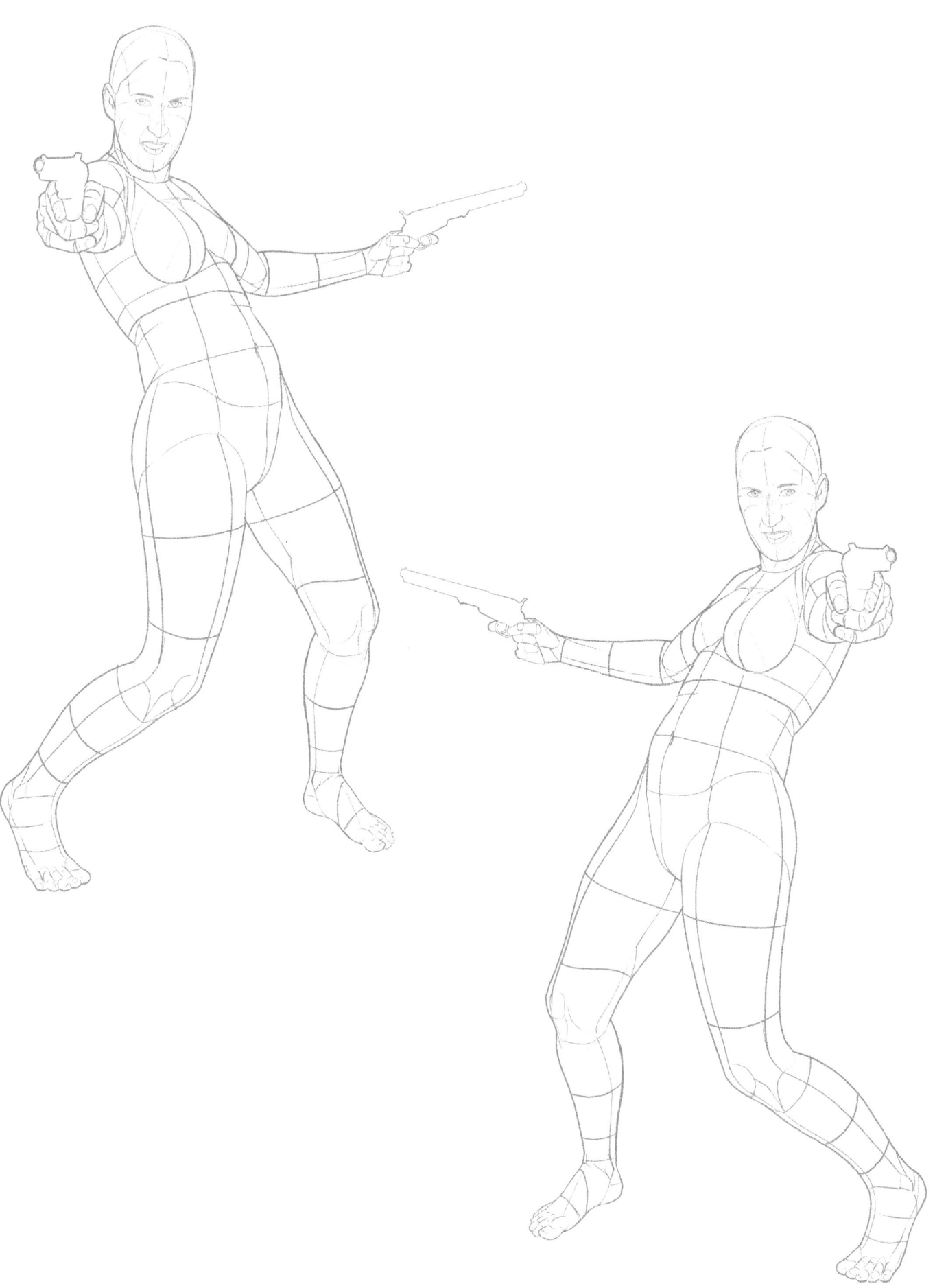

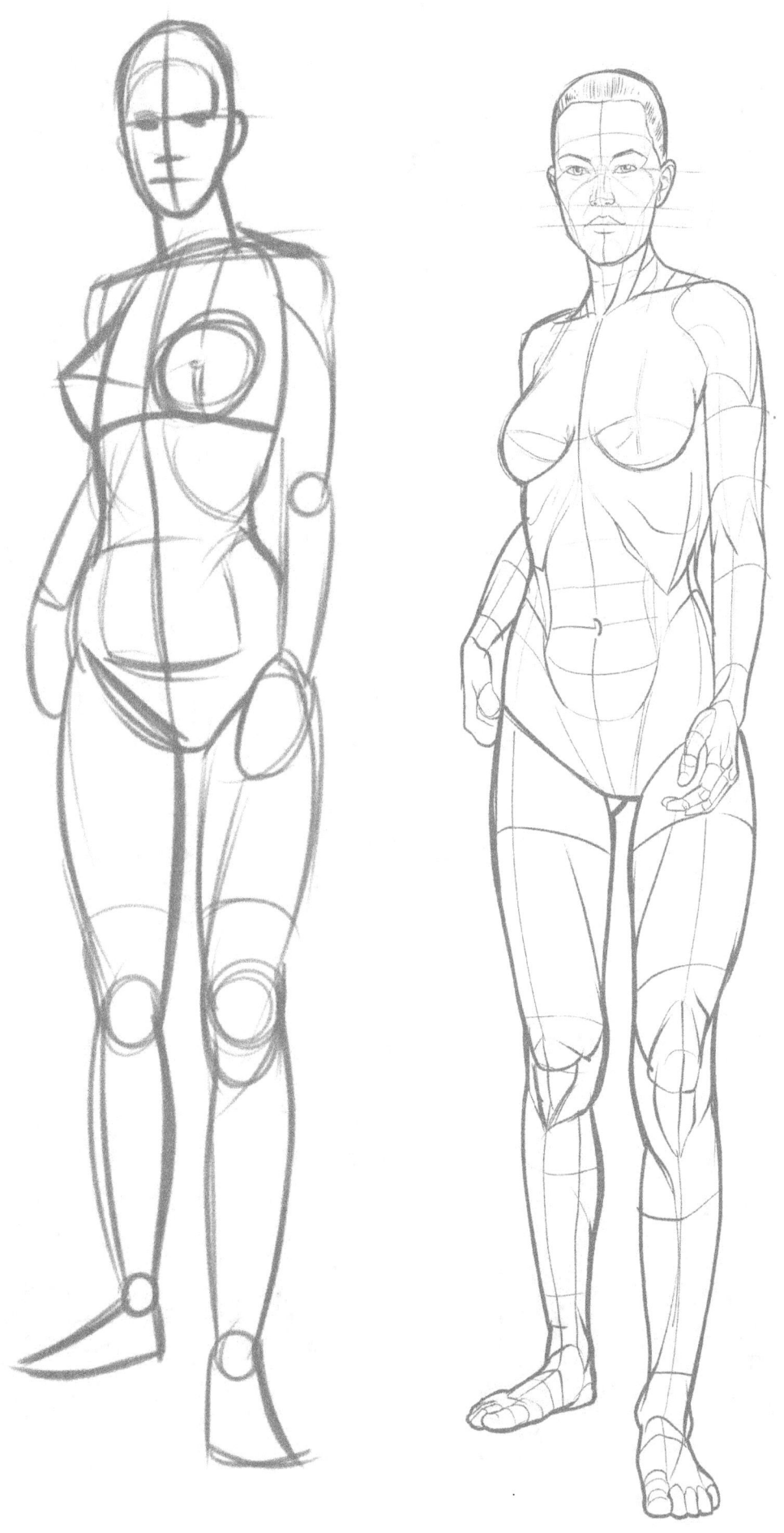

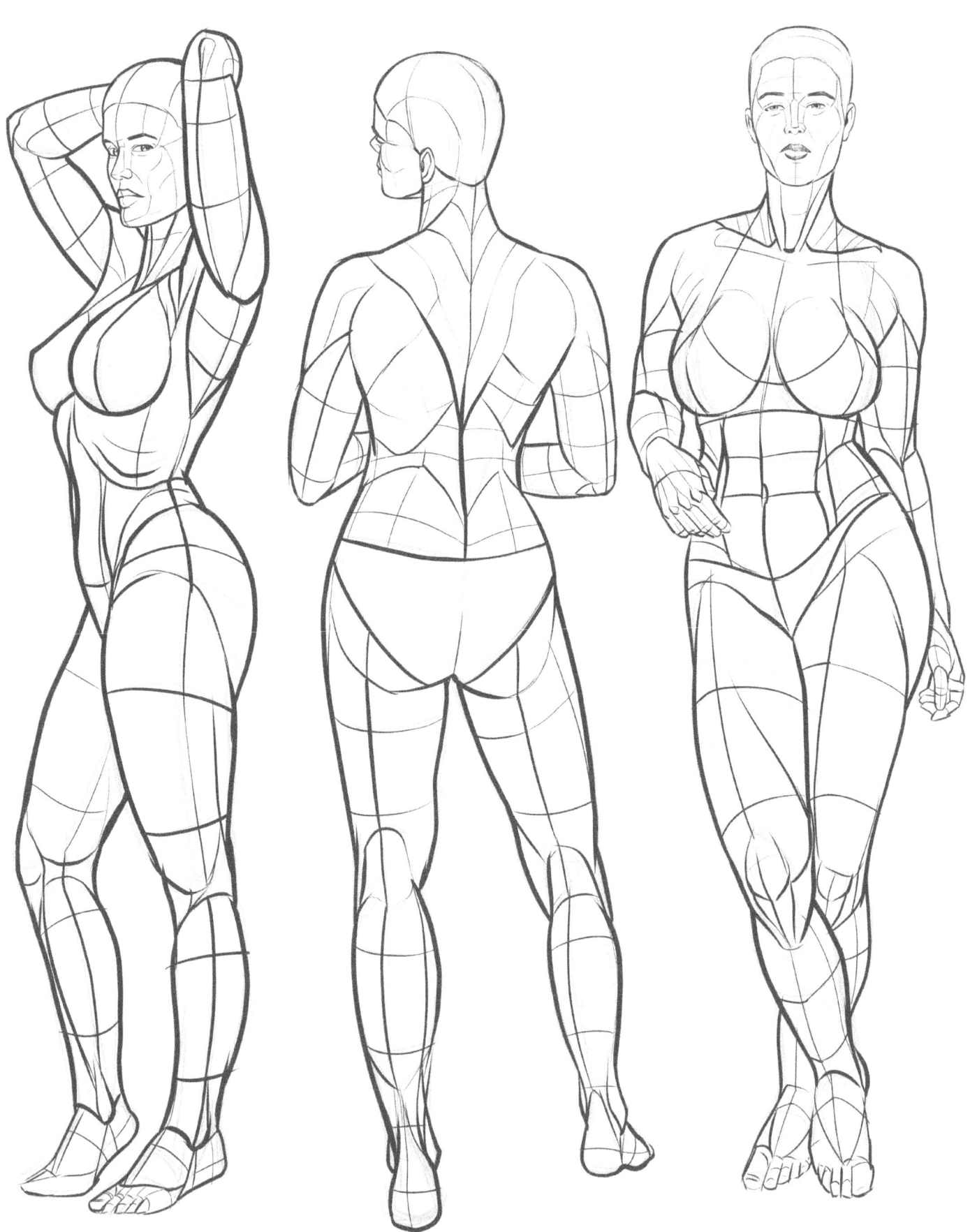

88

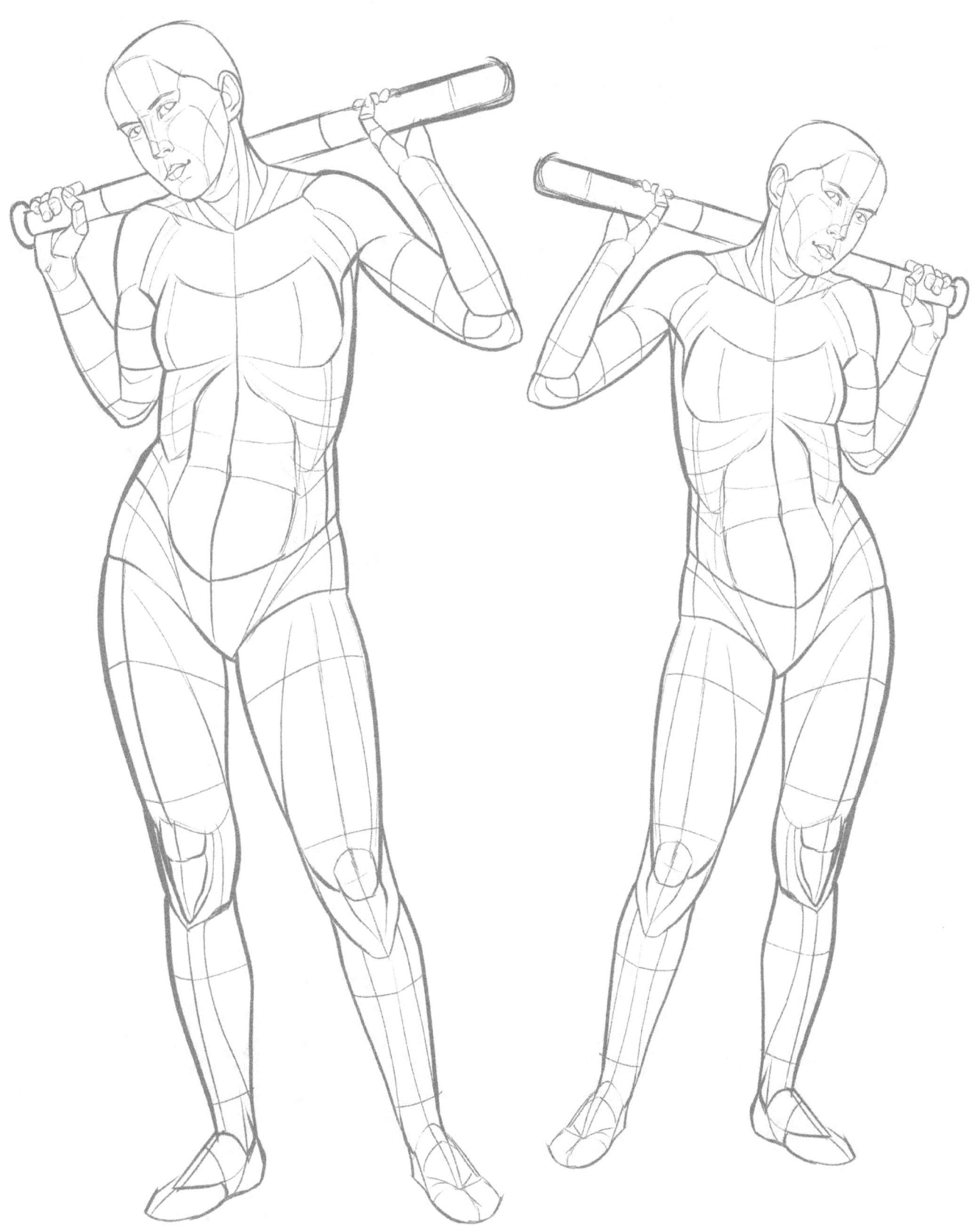

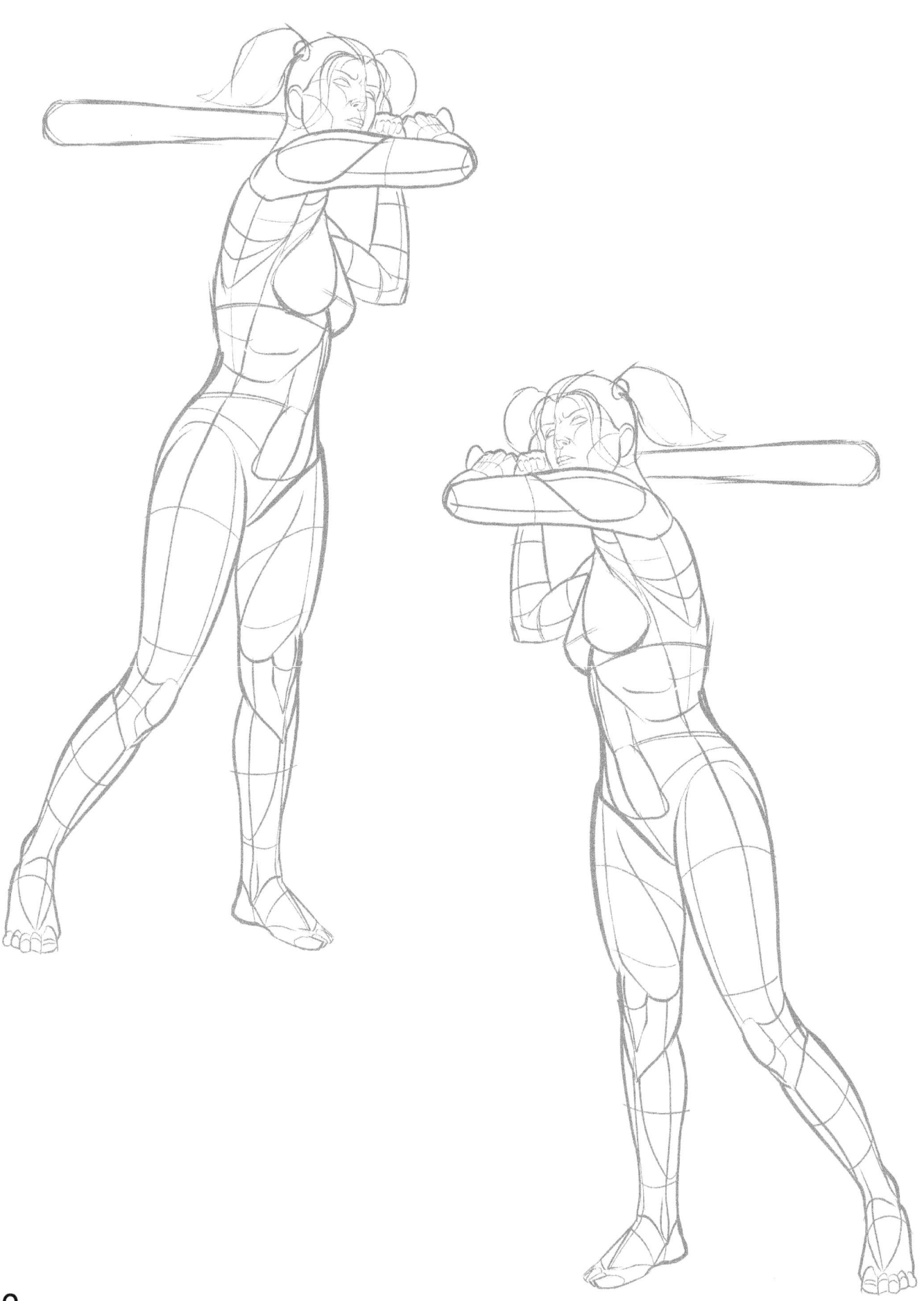

90

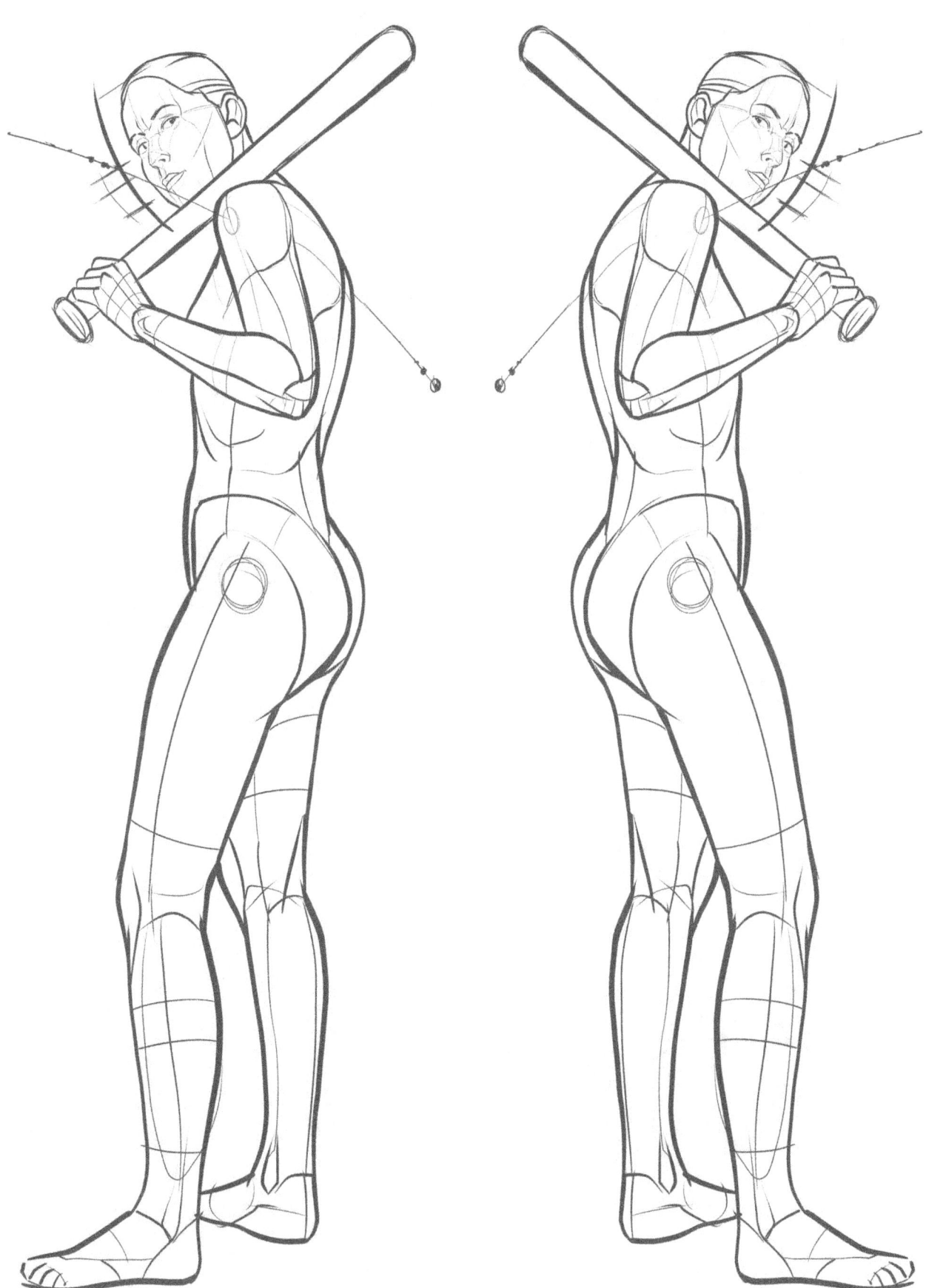

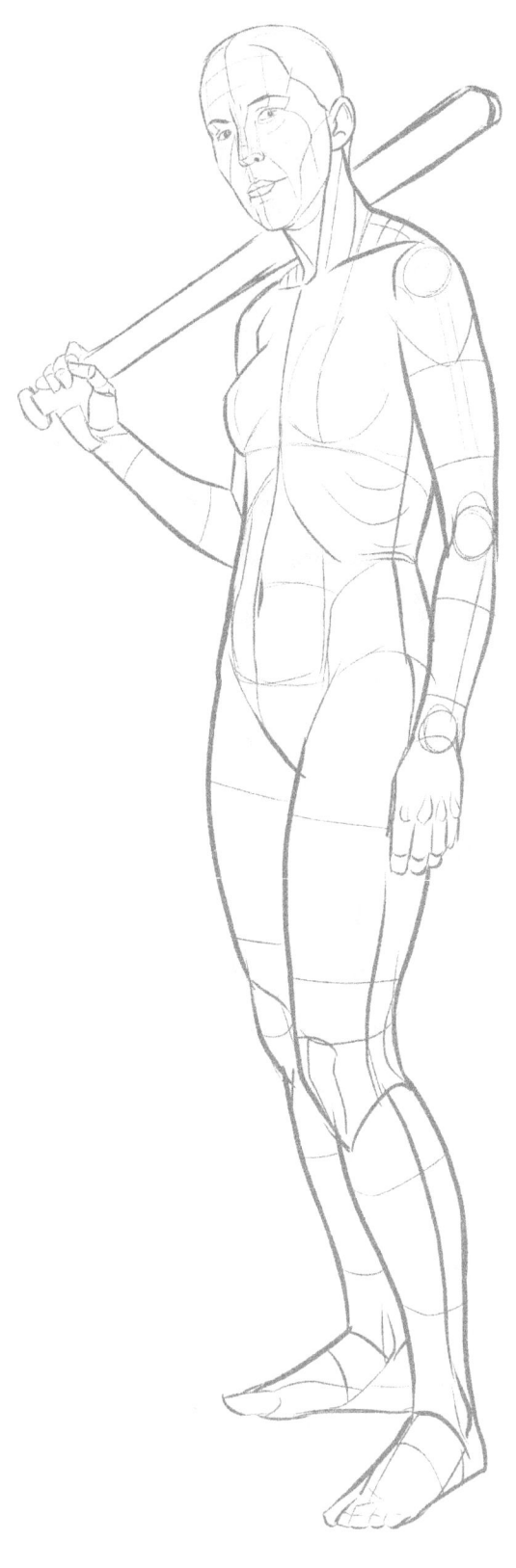
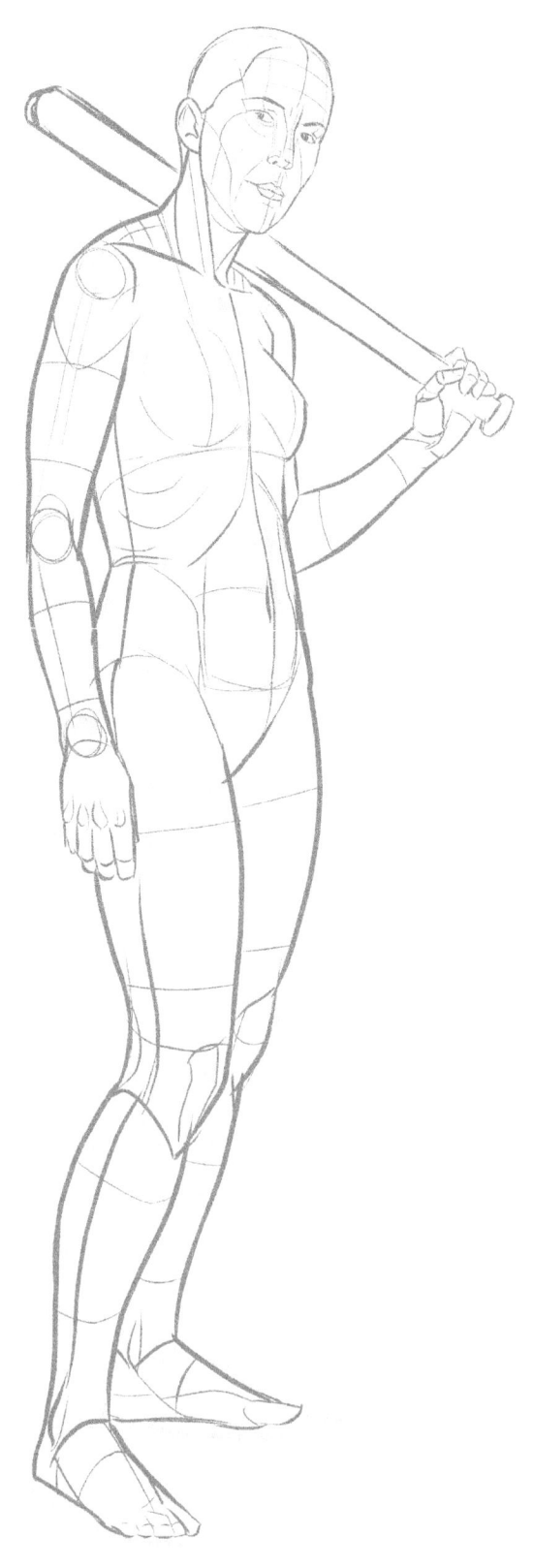

92

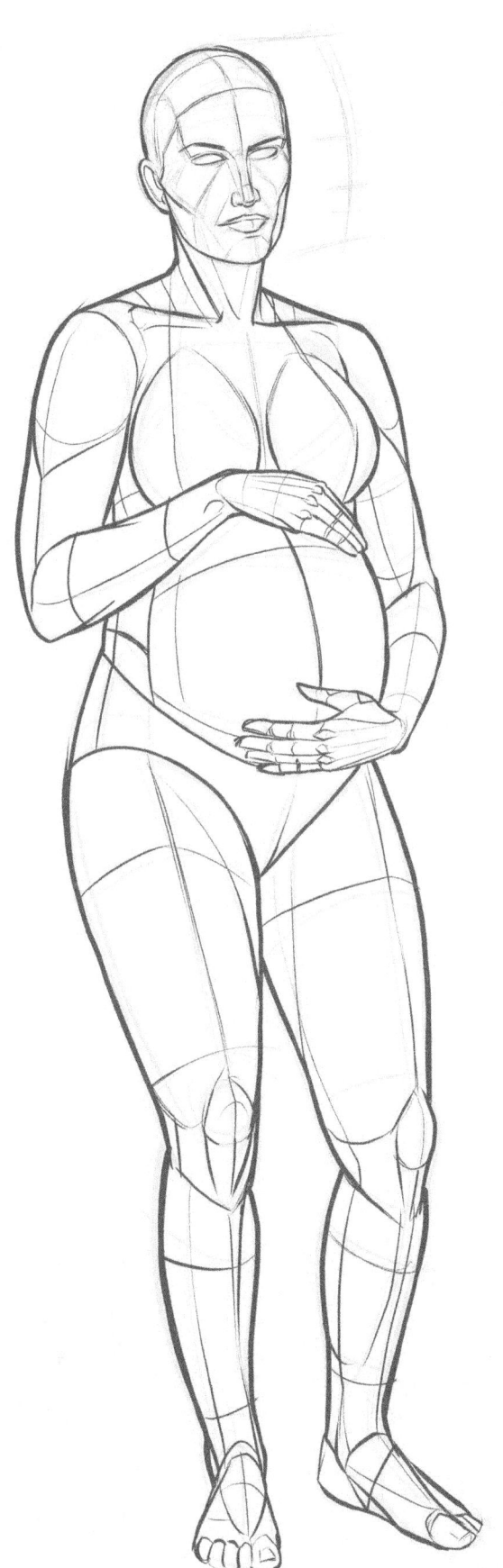
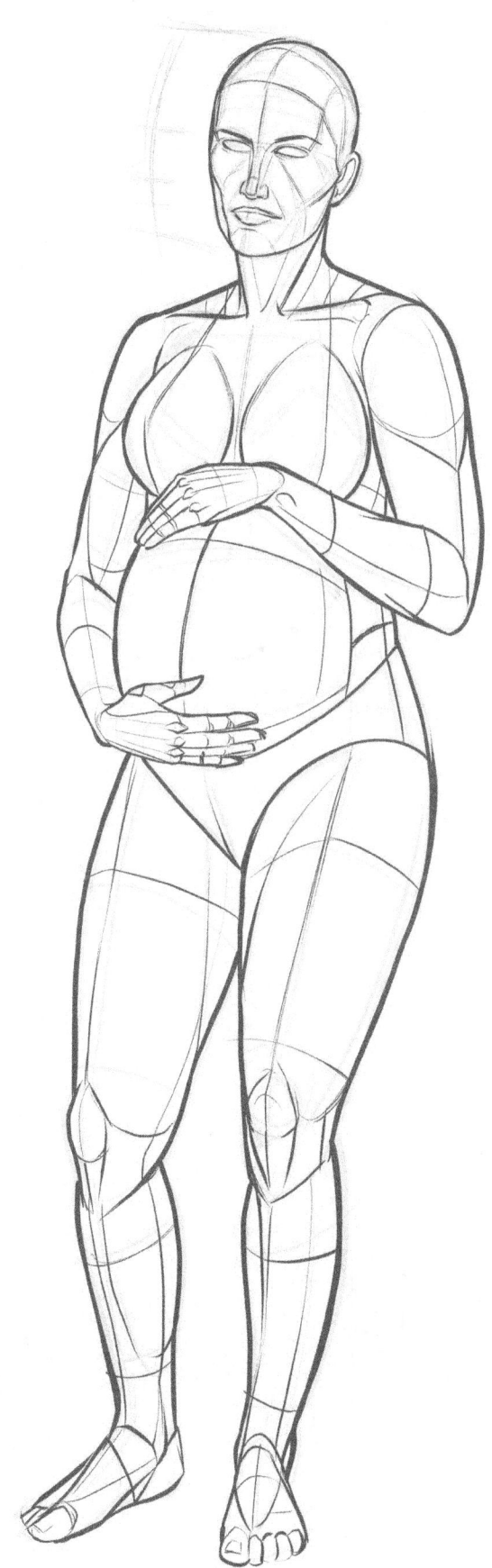

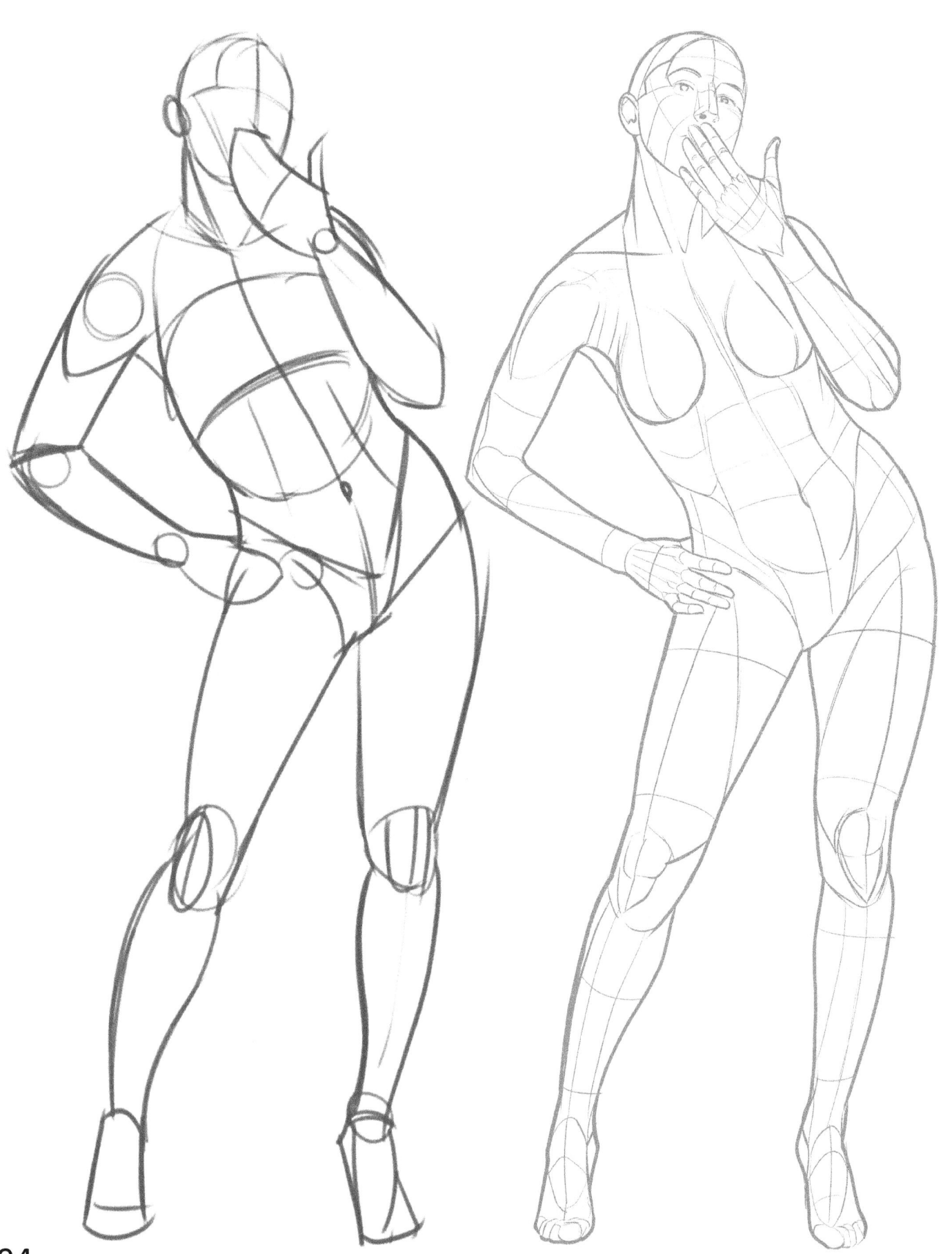

94

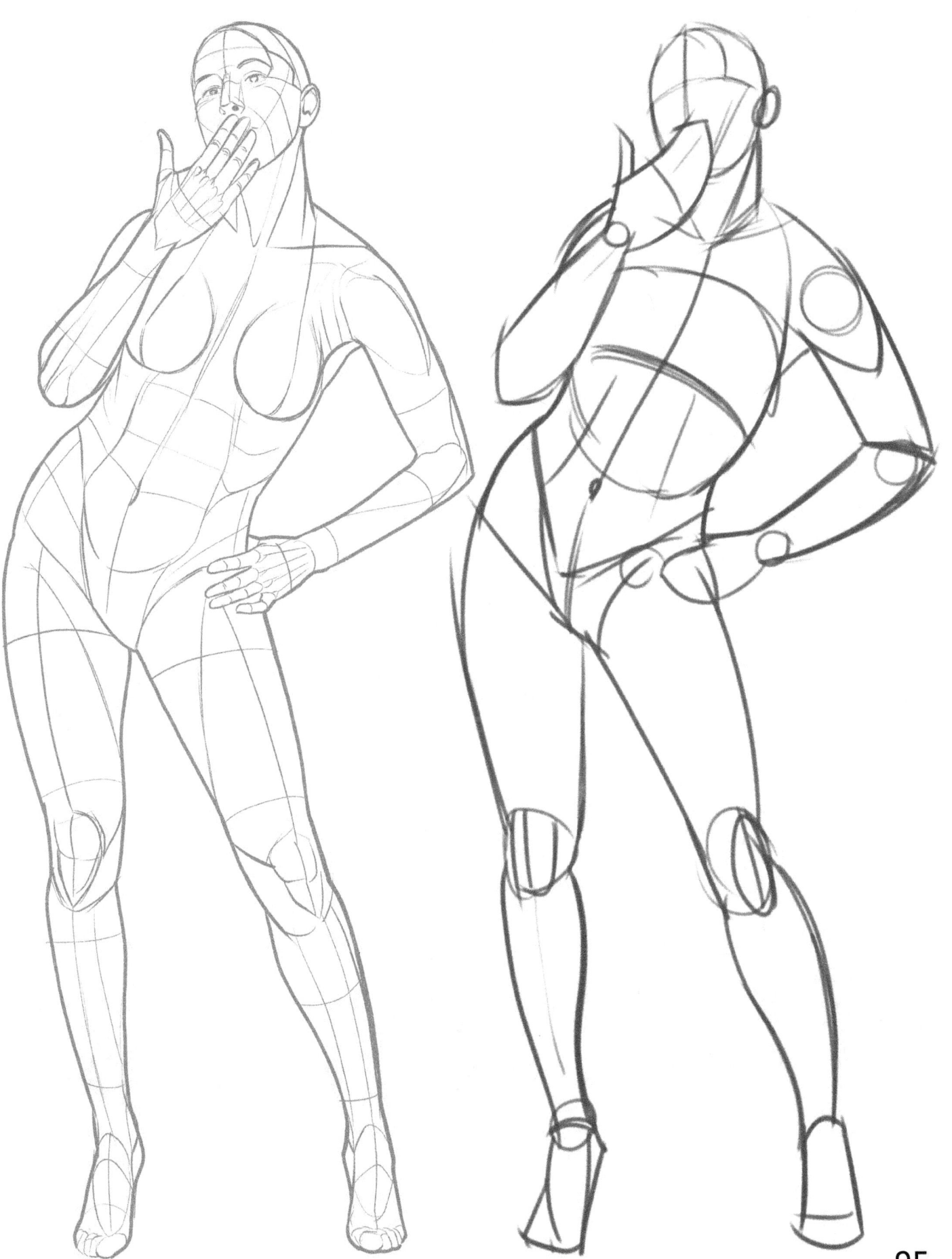

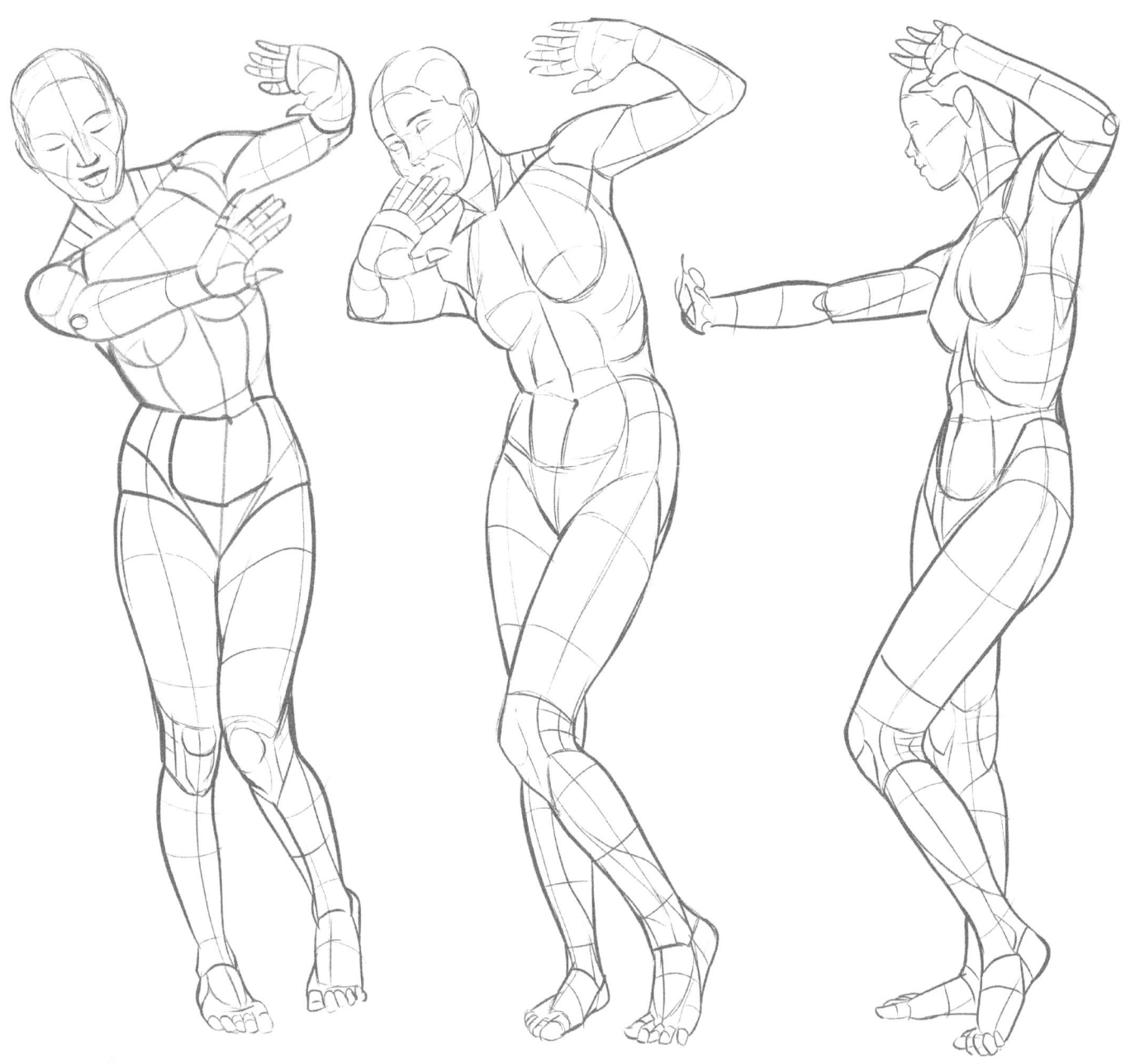

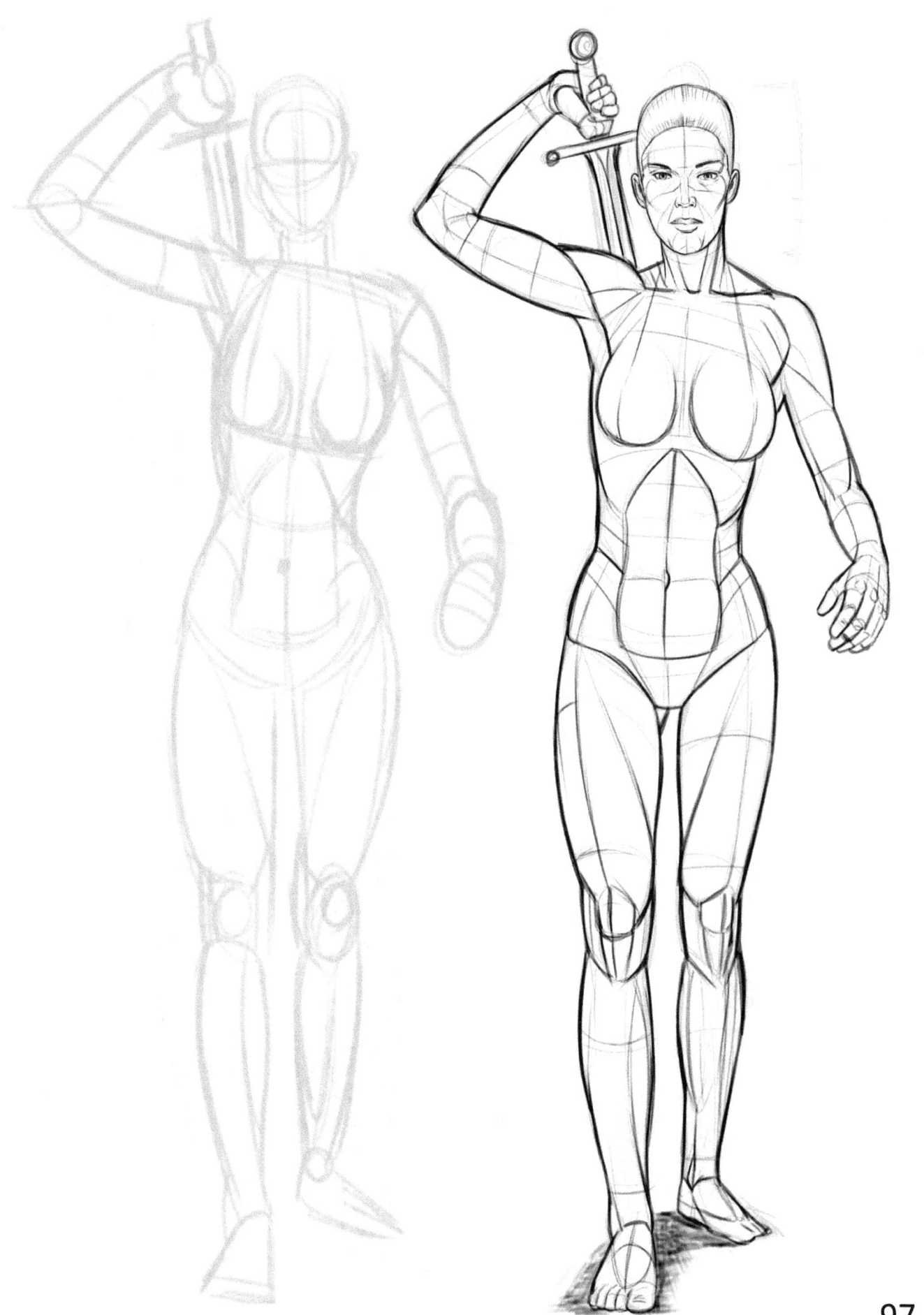

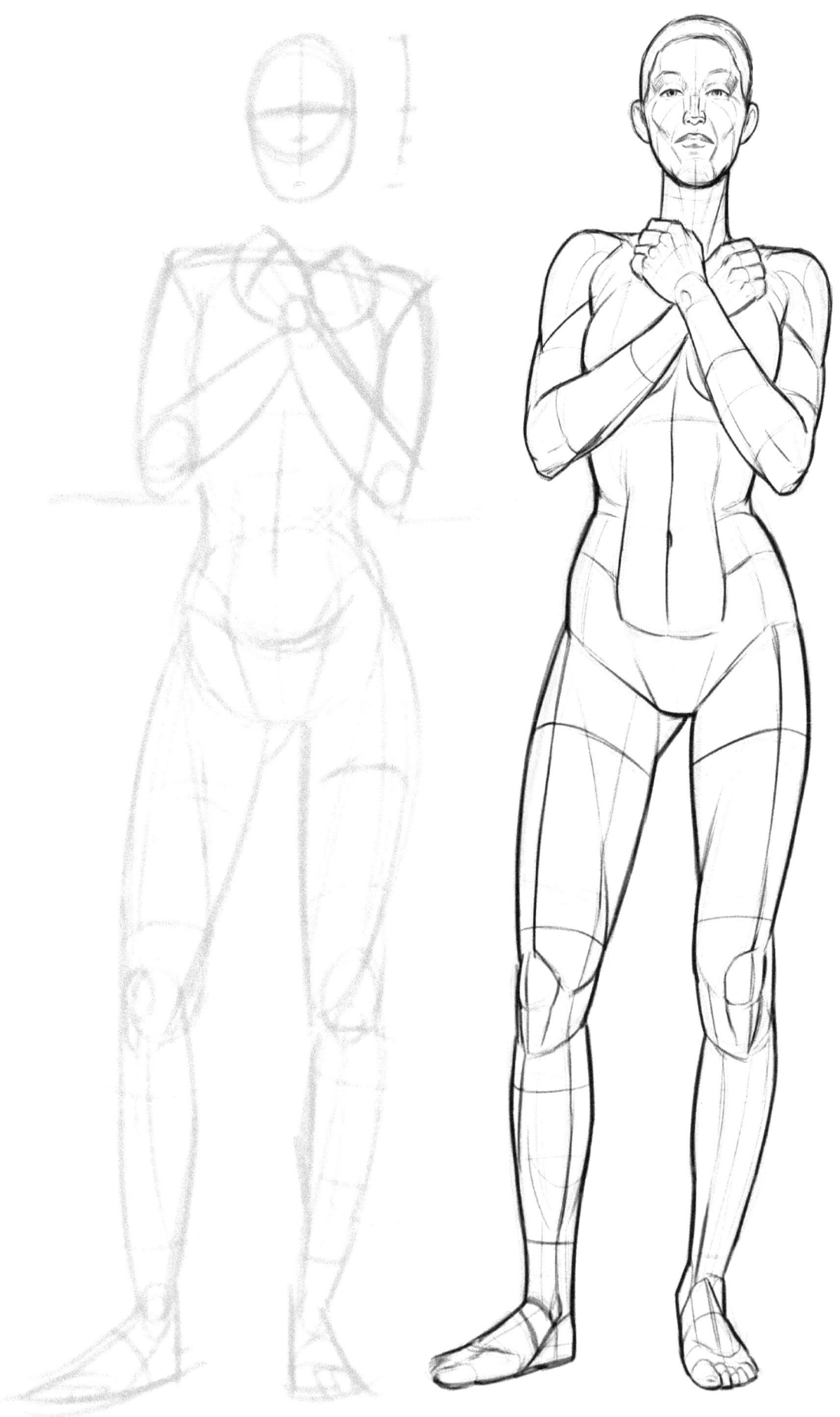

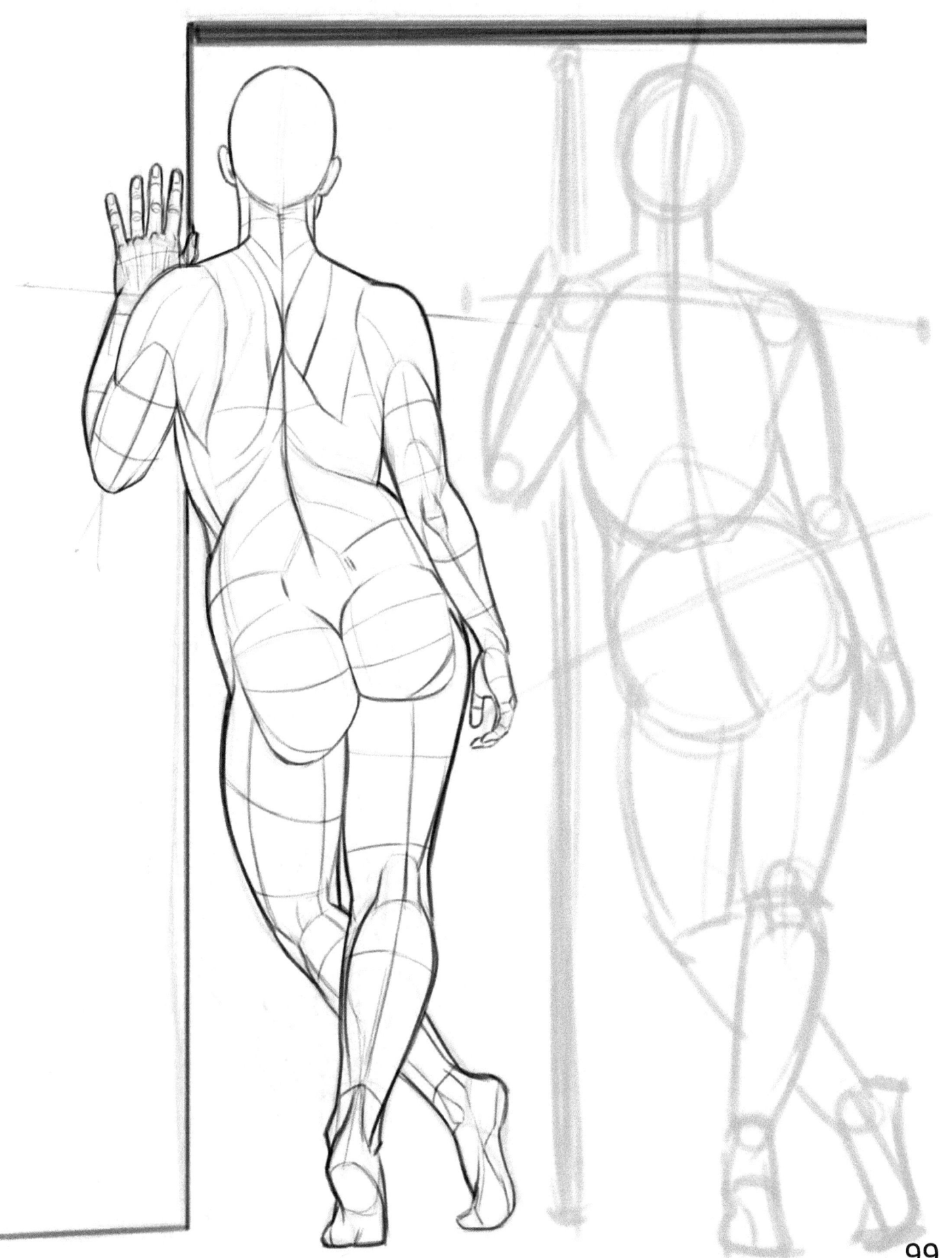

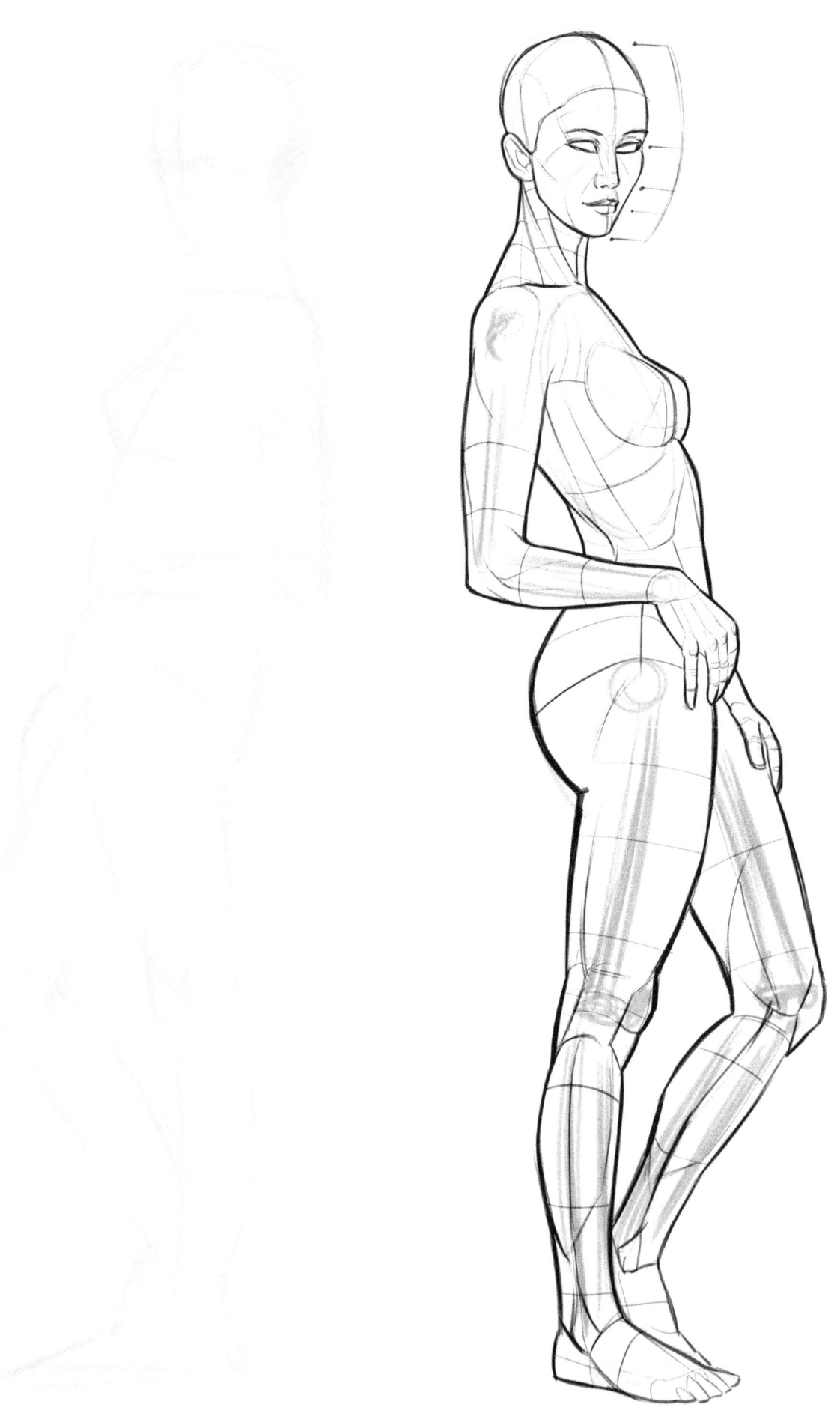

100

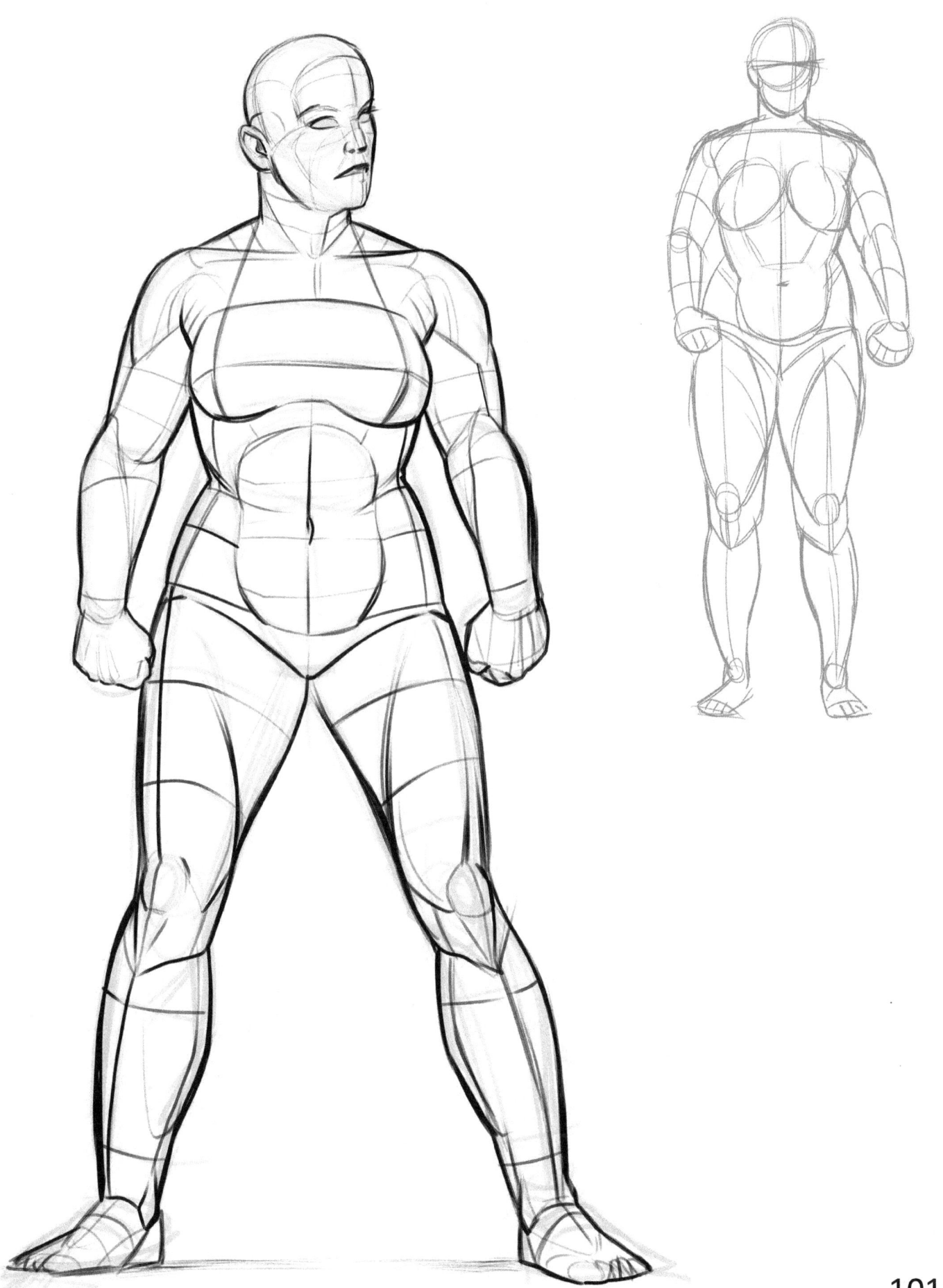

101

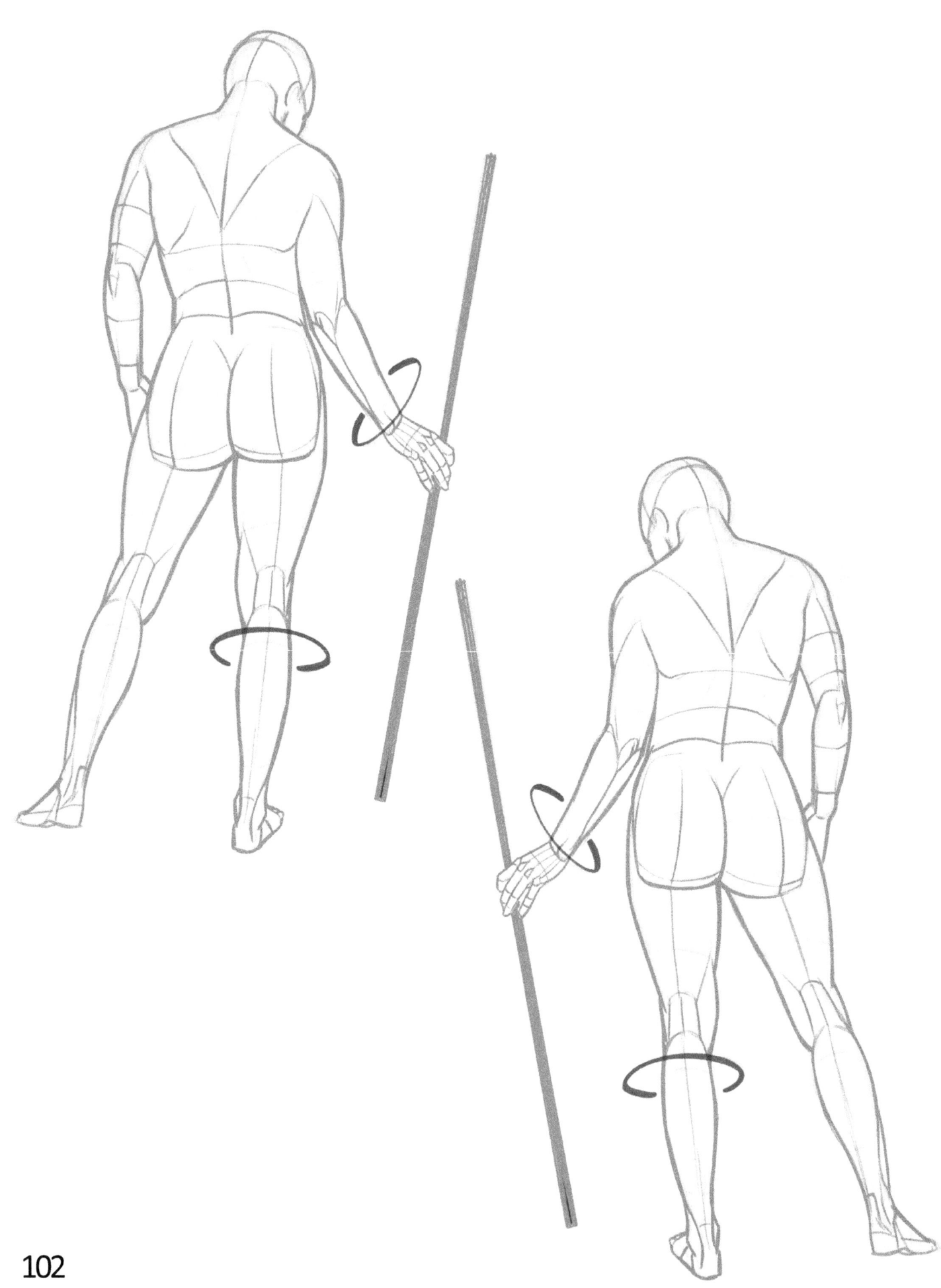

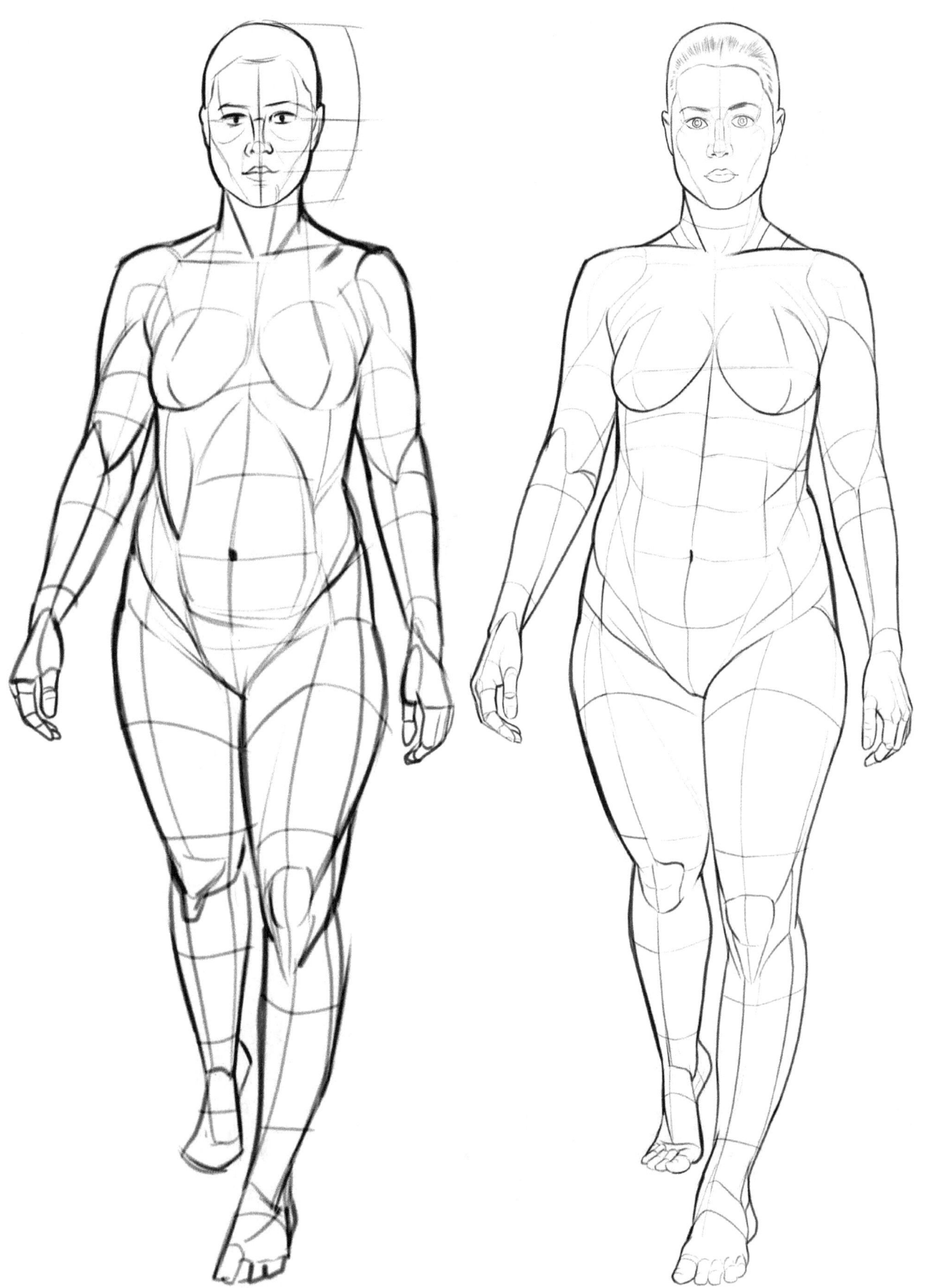

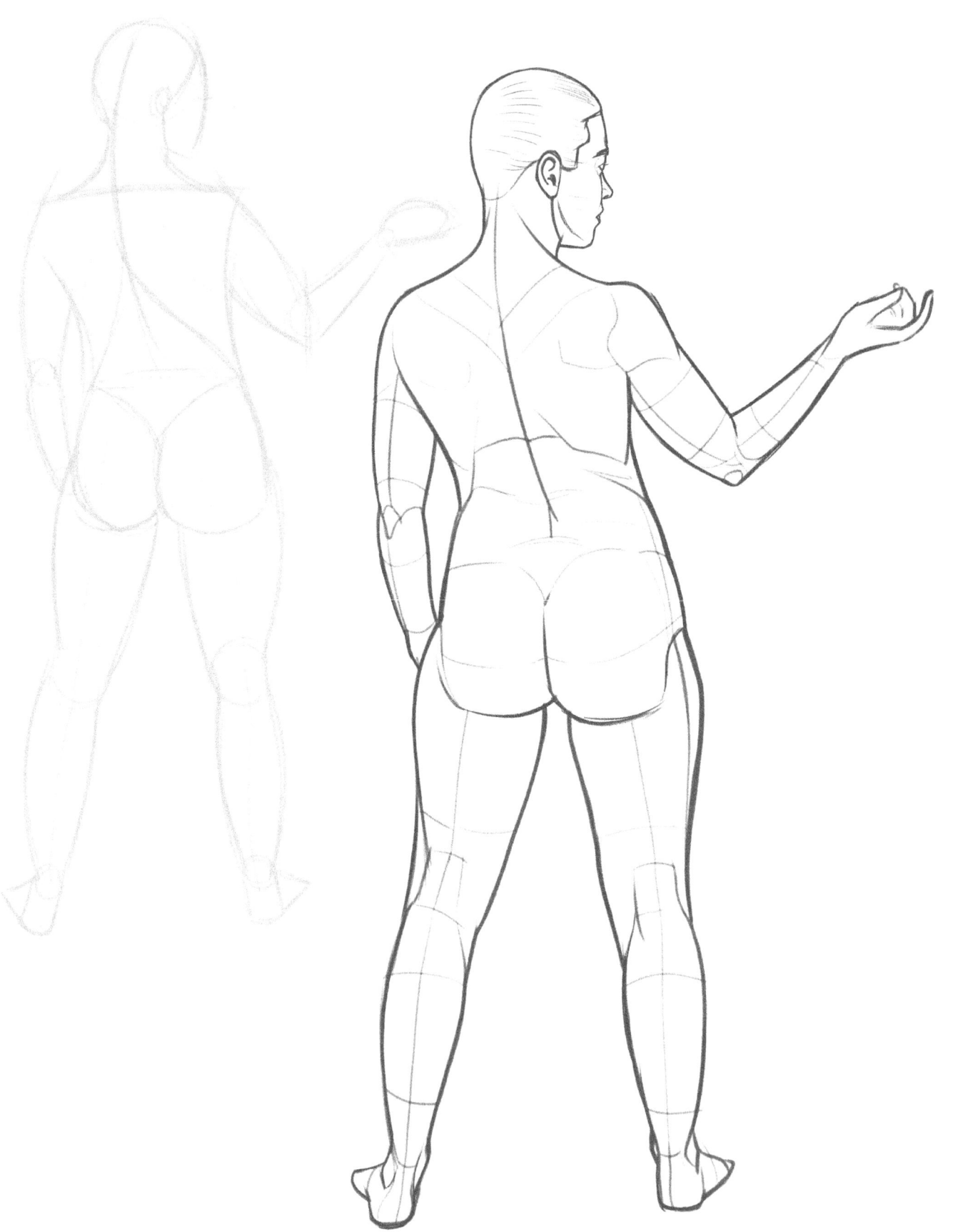

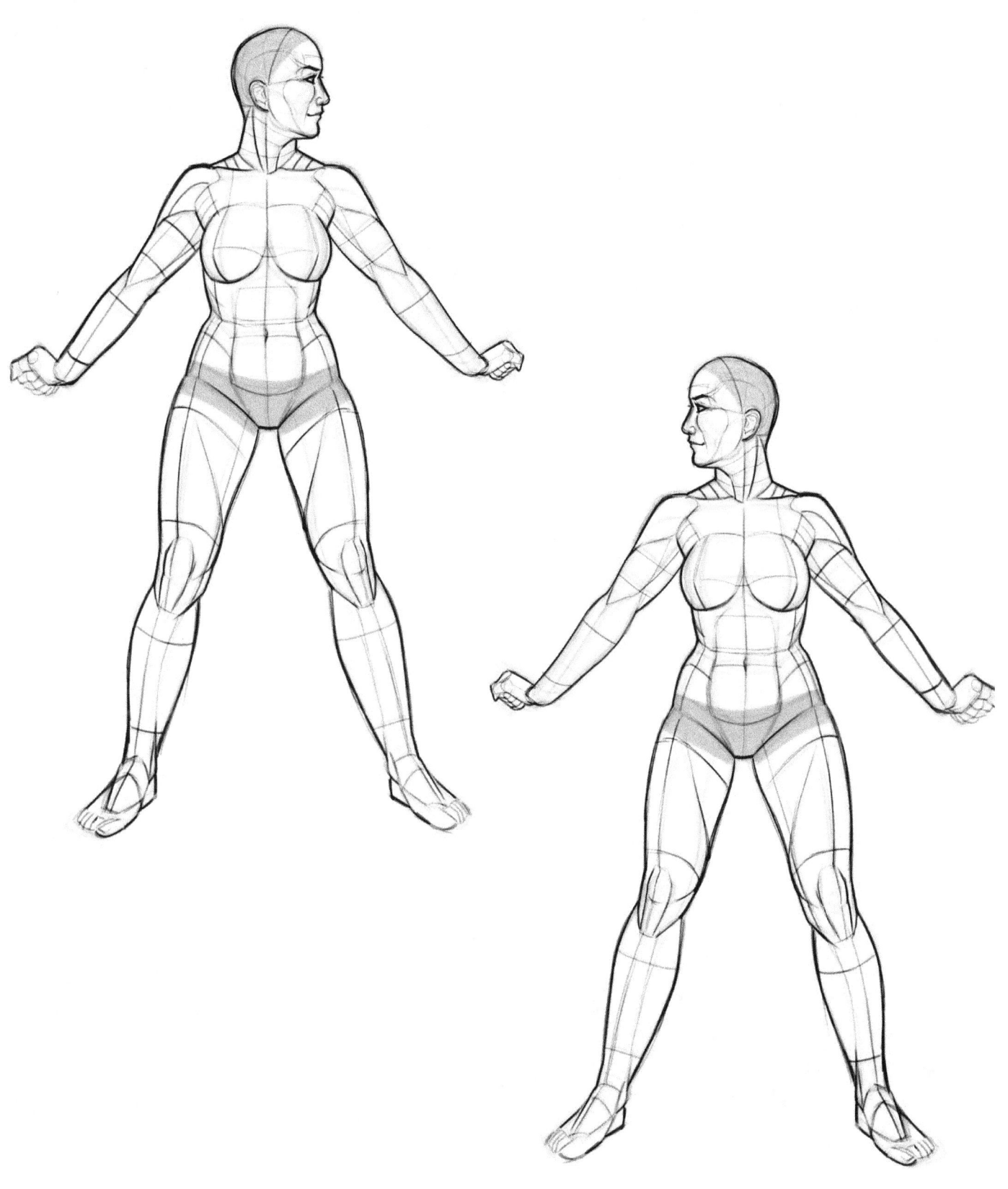

Hands

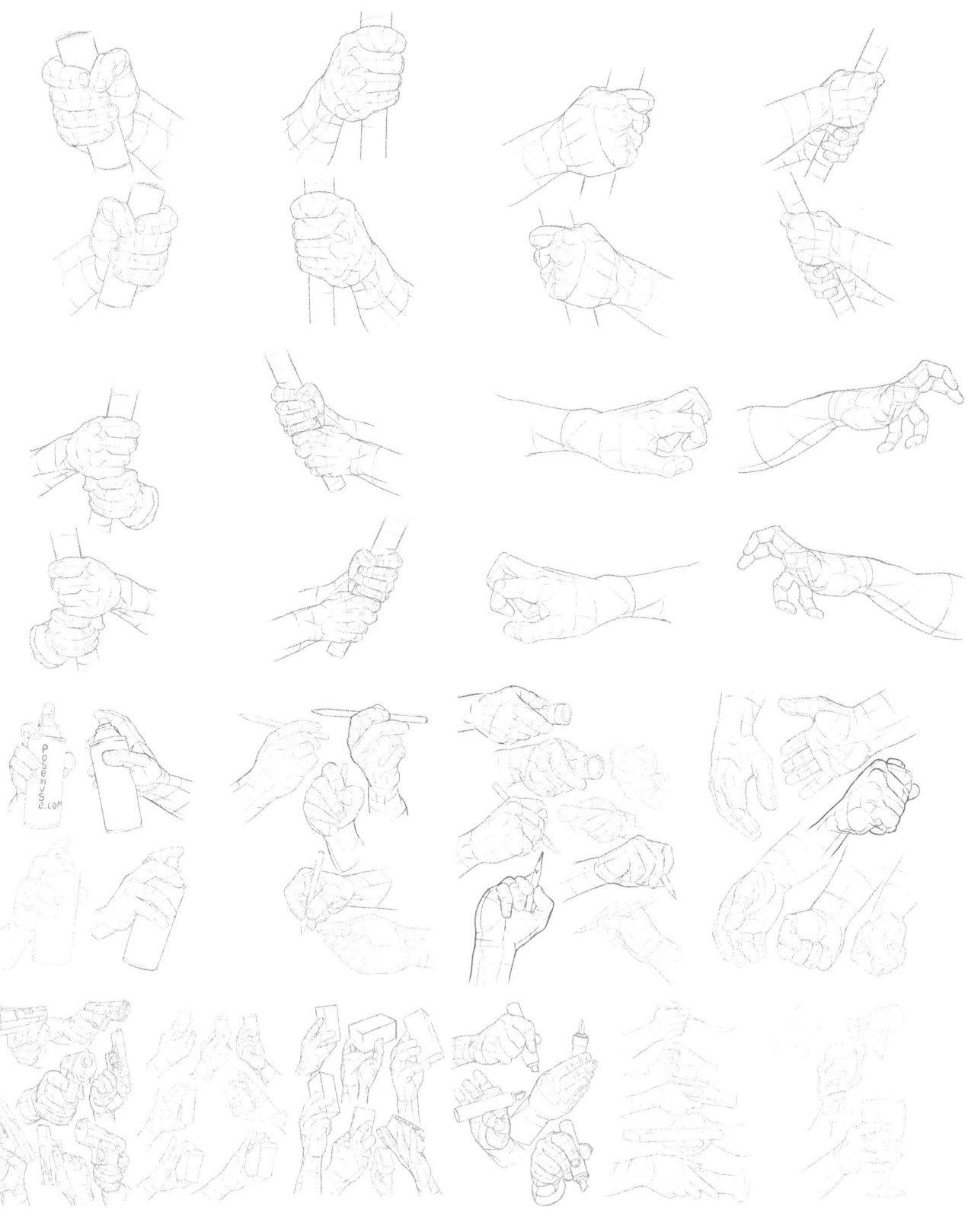

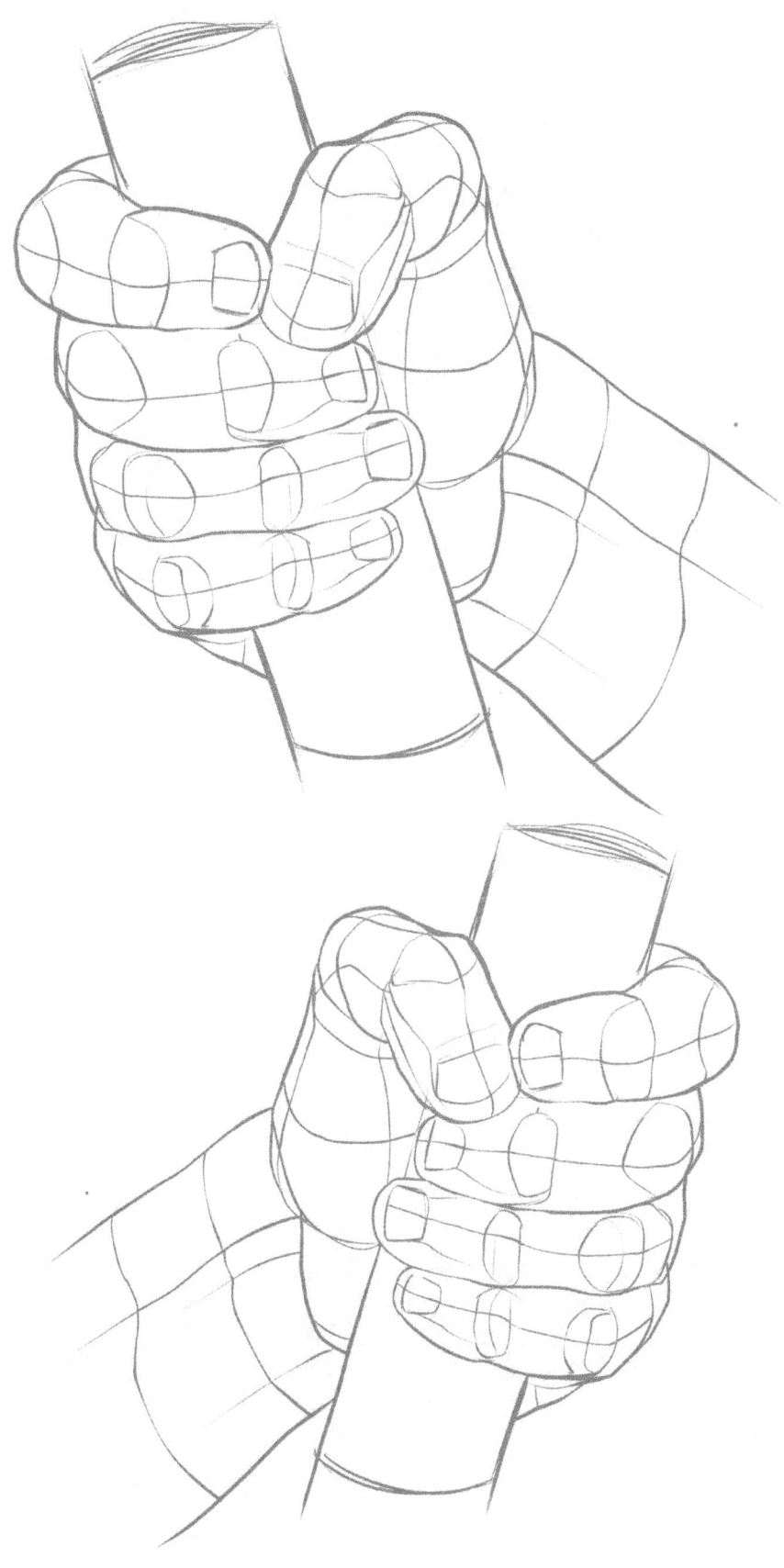

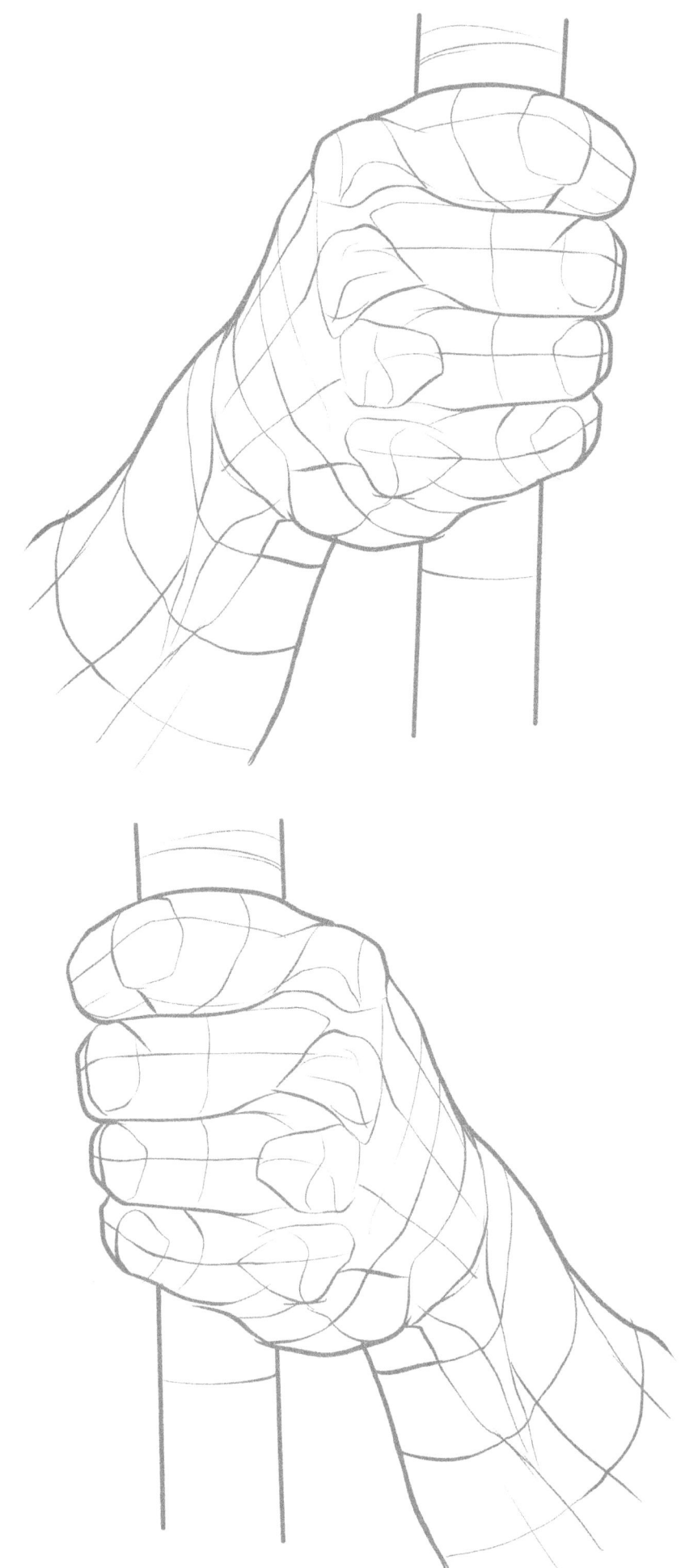

108

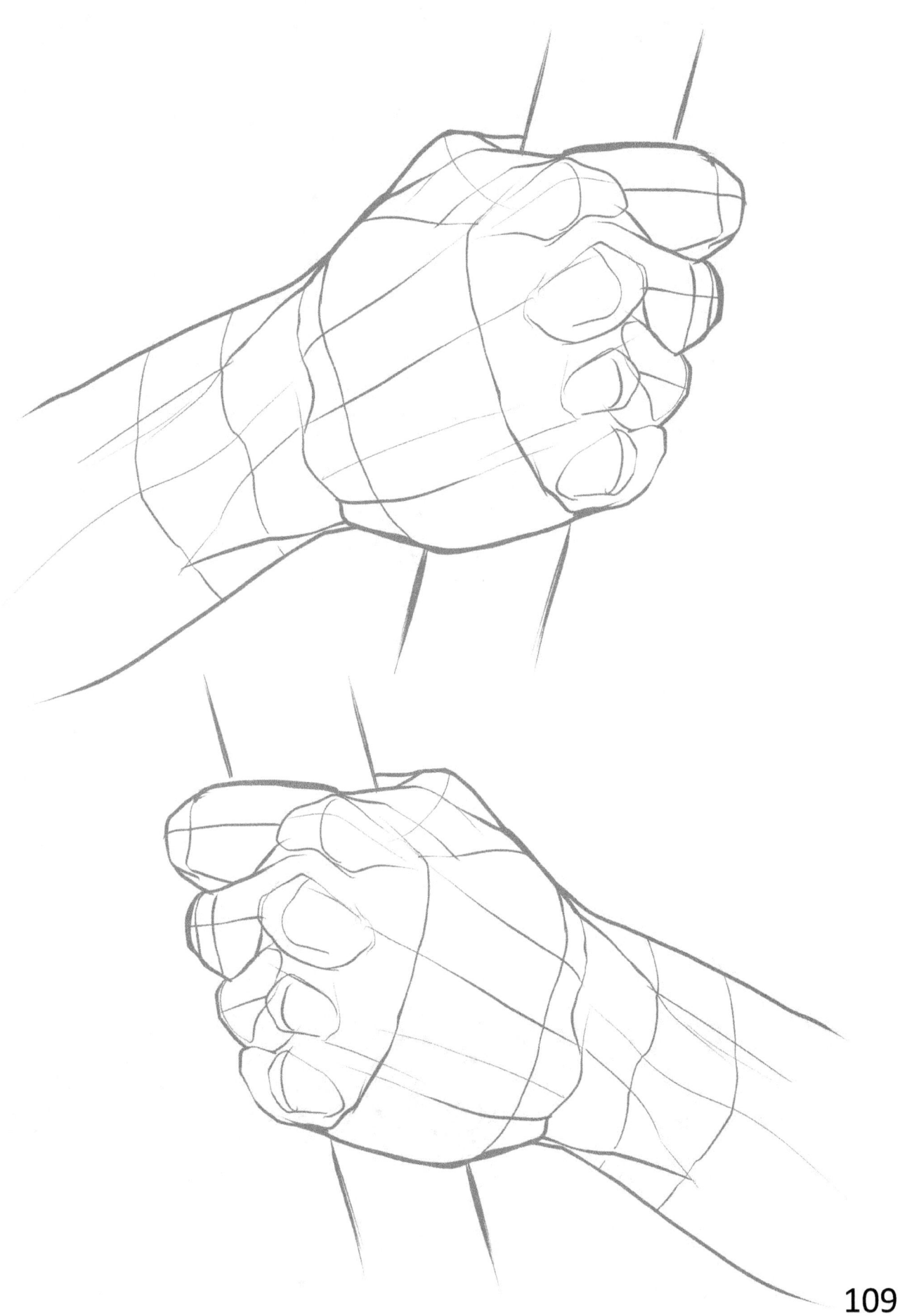

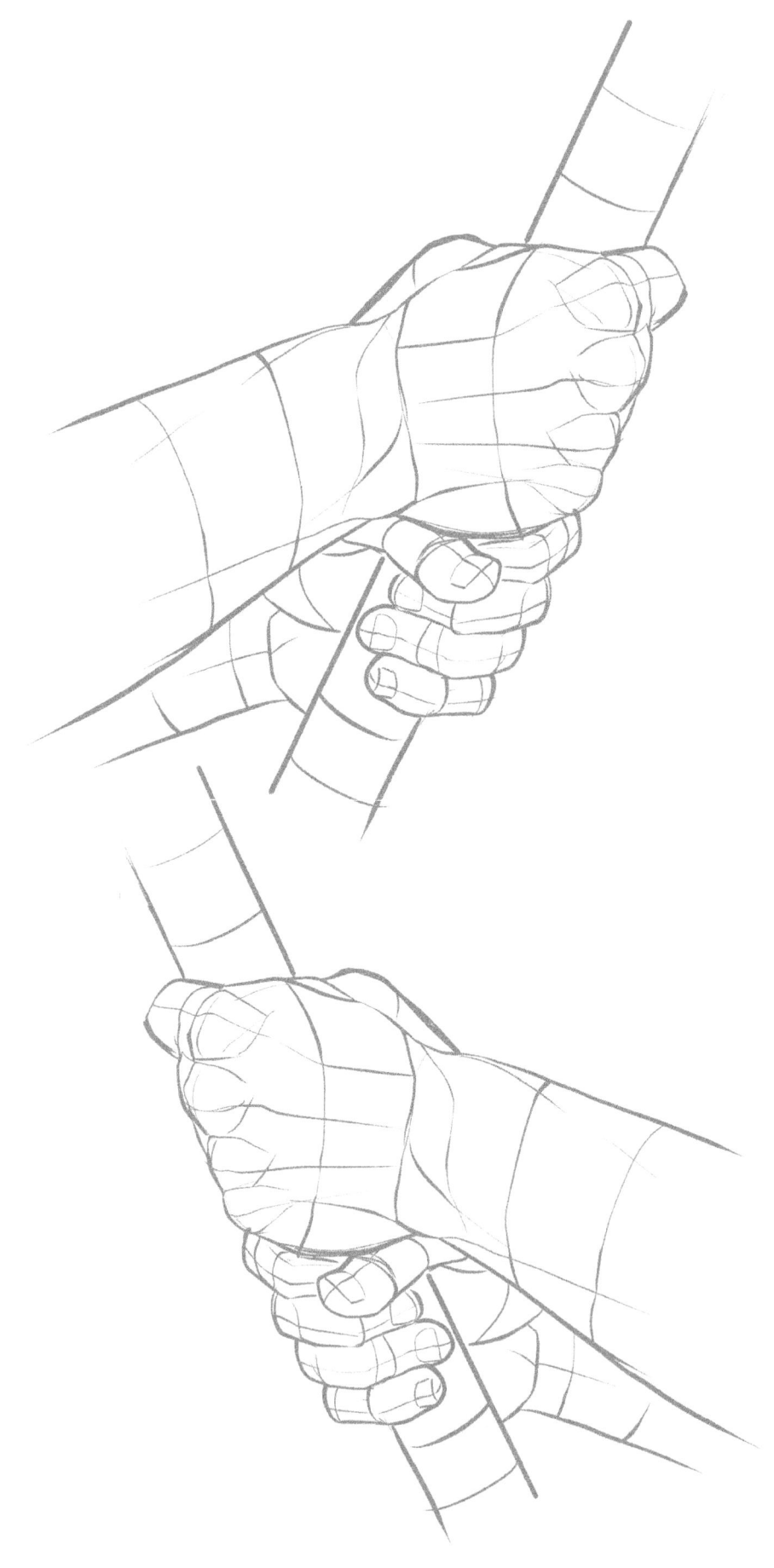

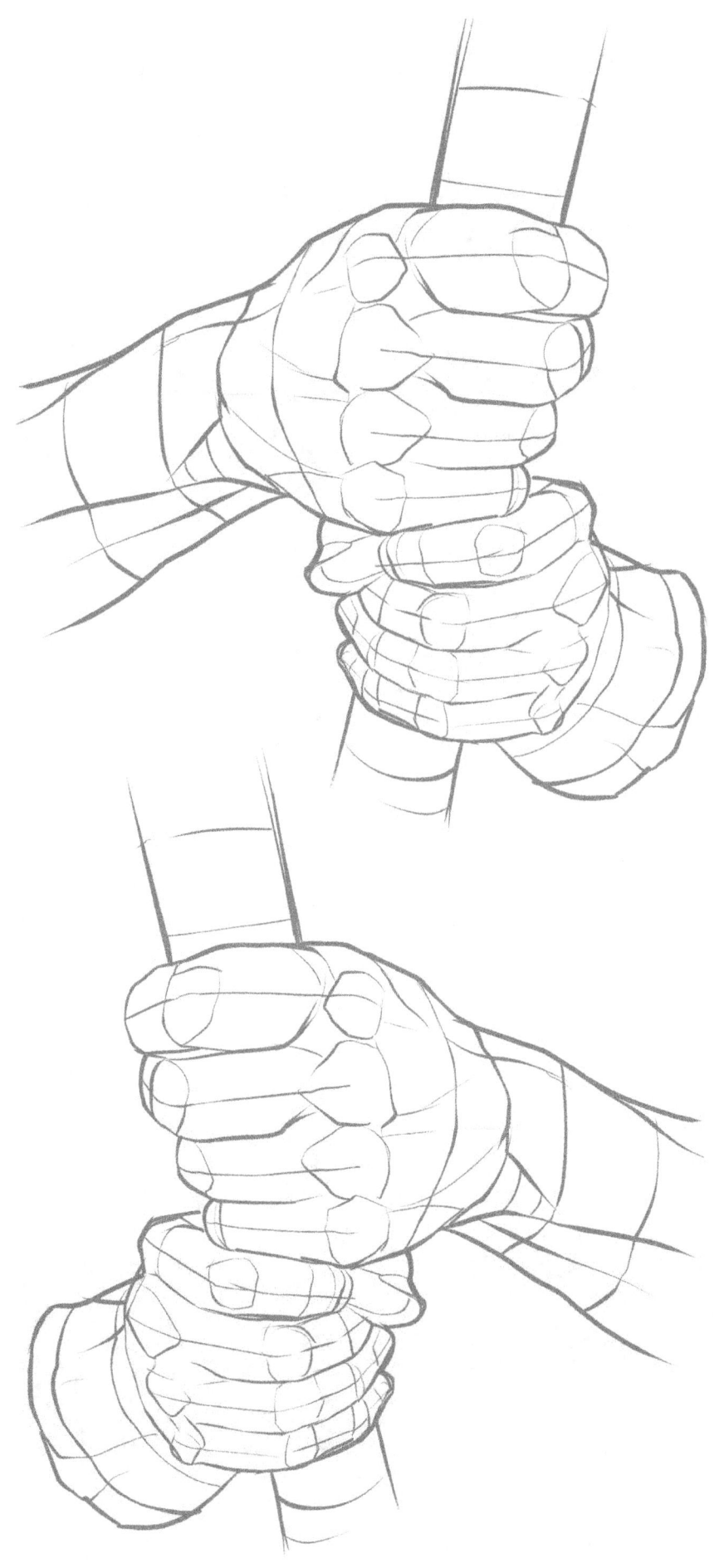

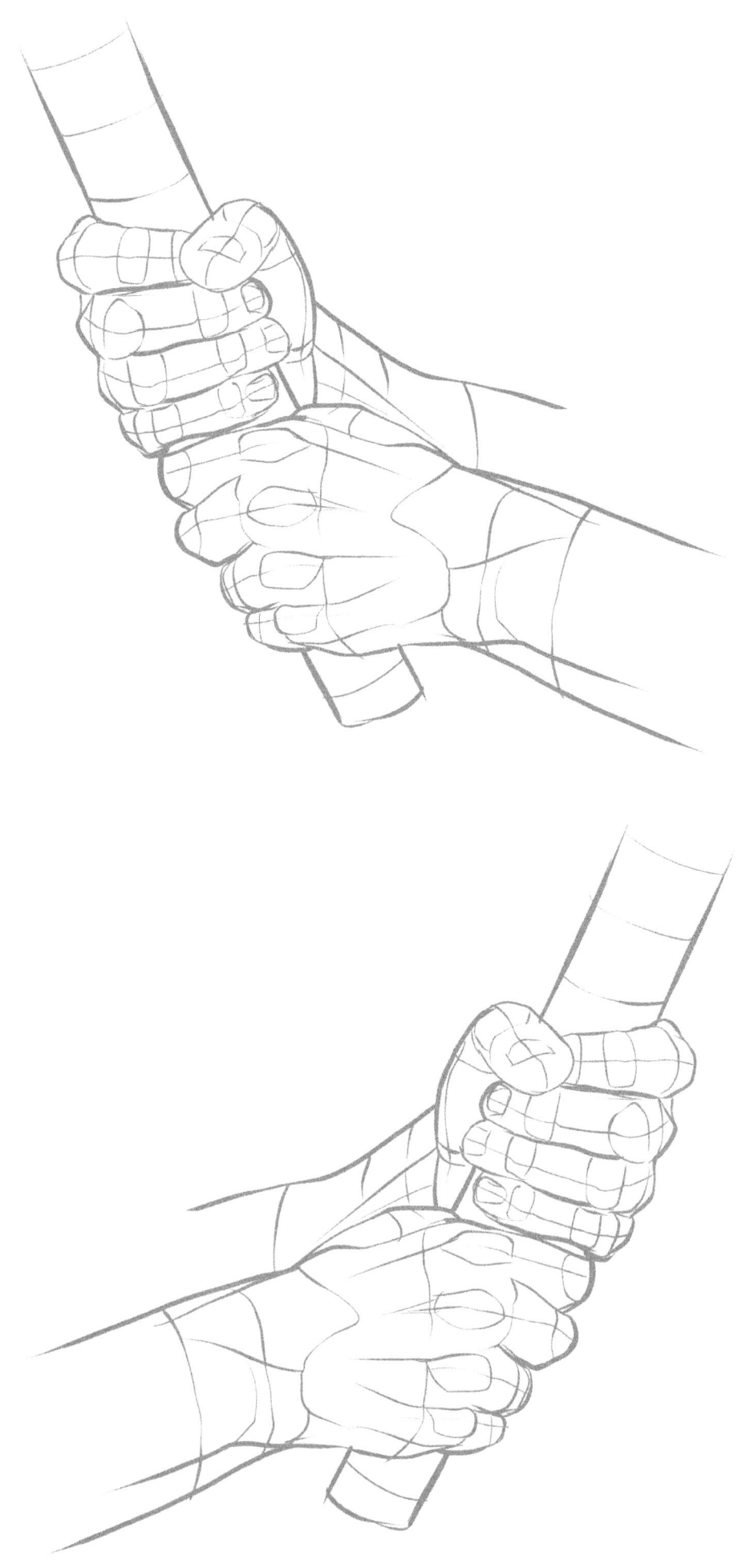

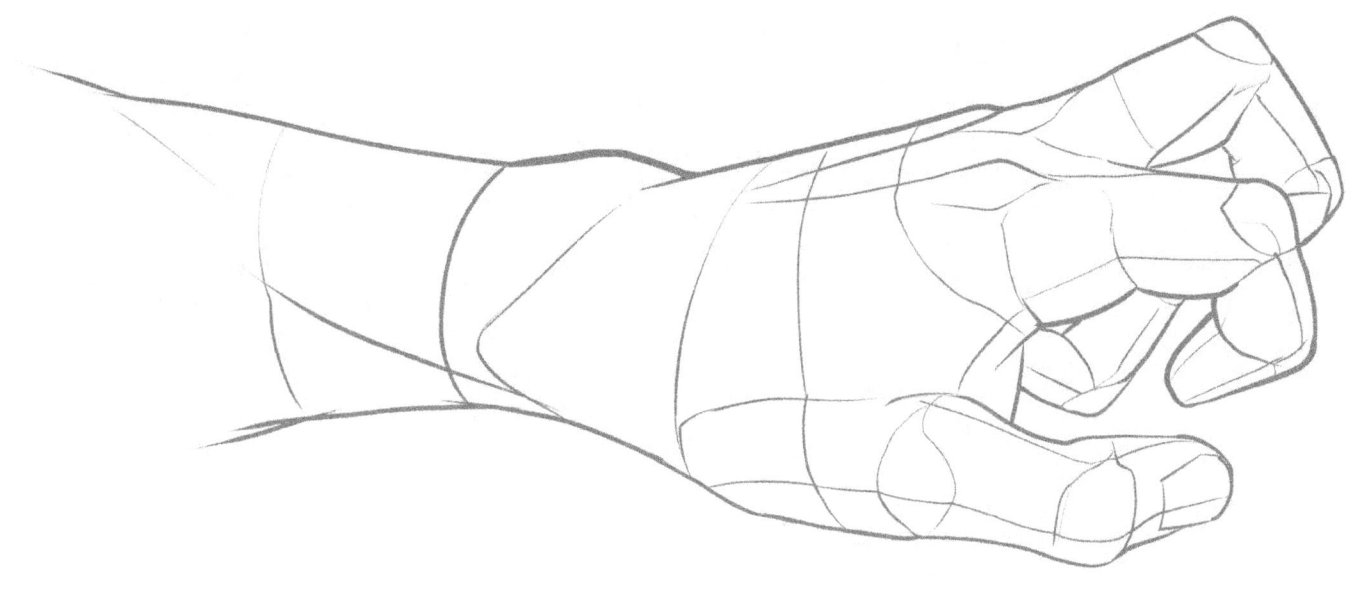

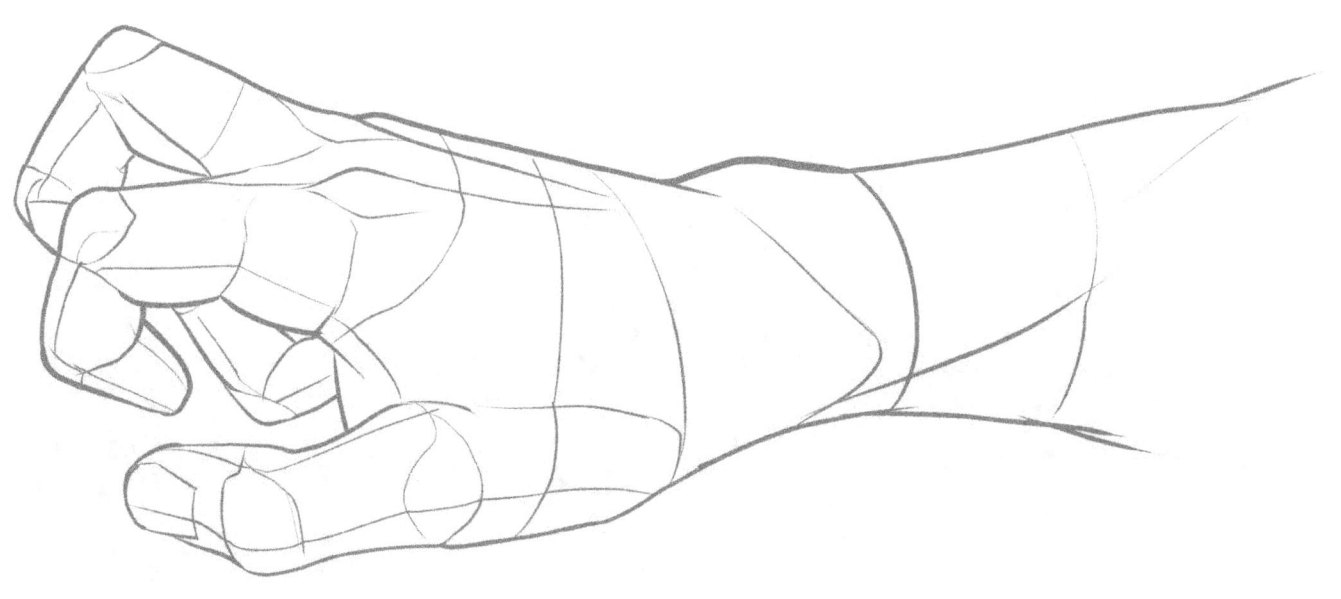

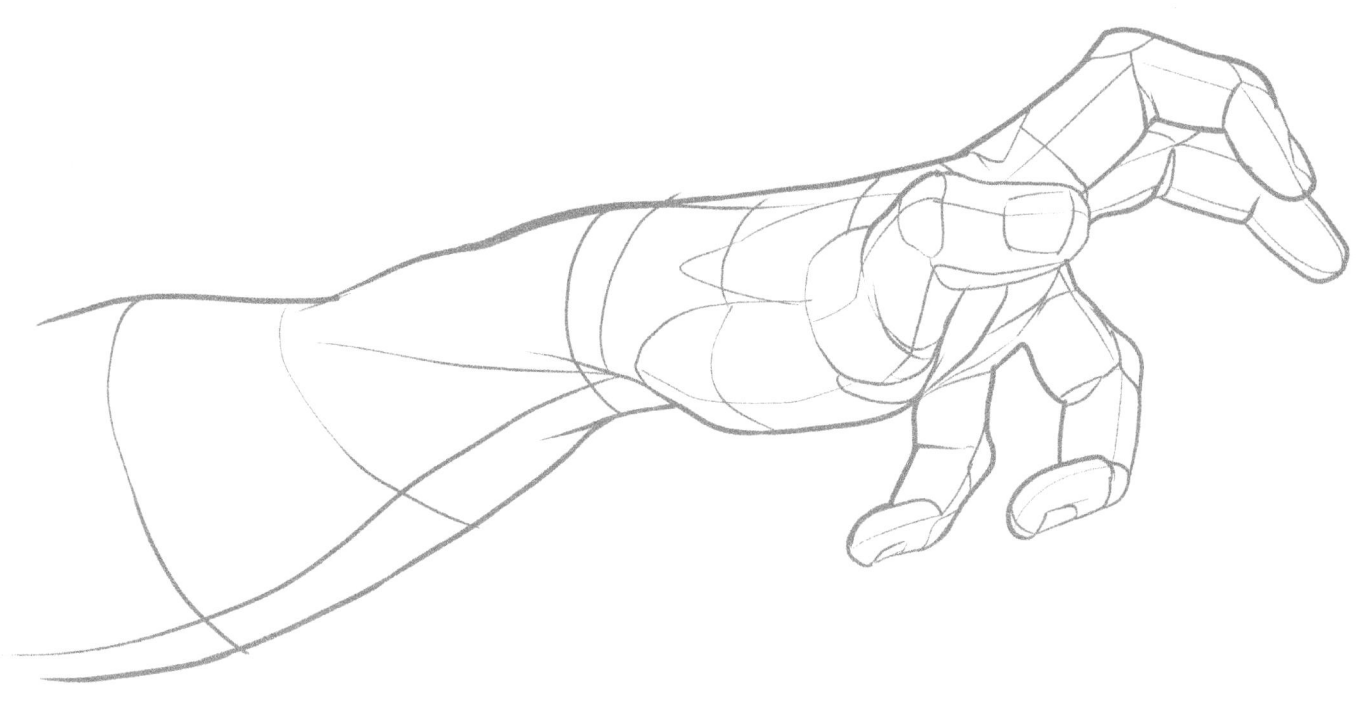

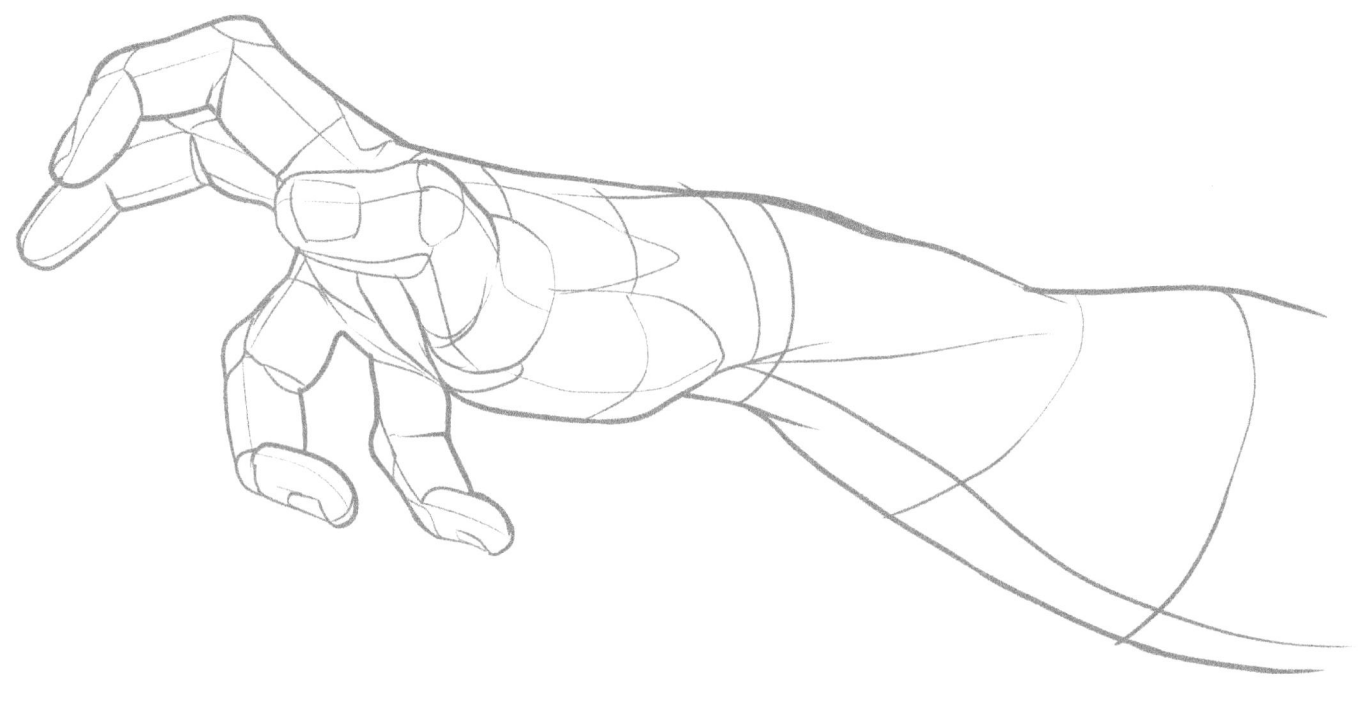

114

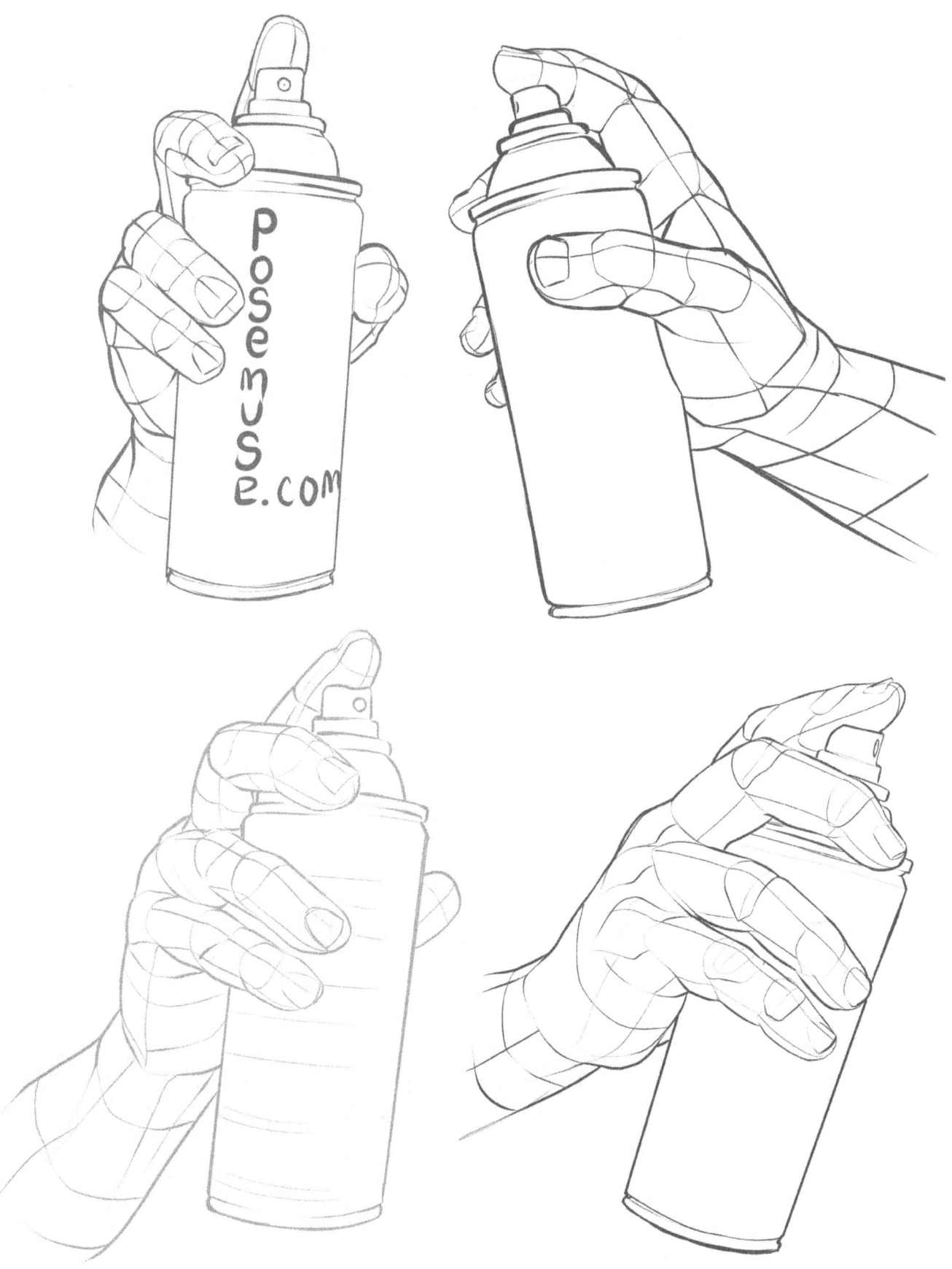

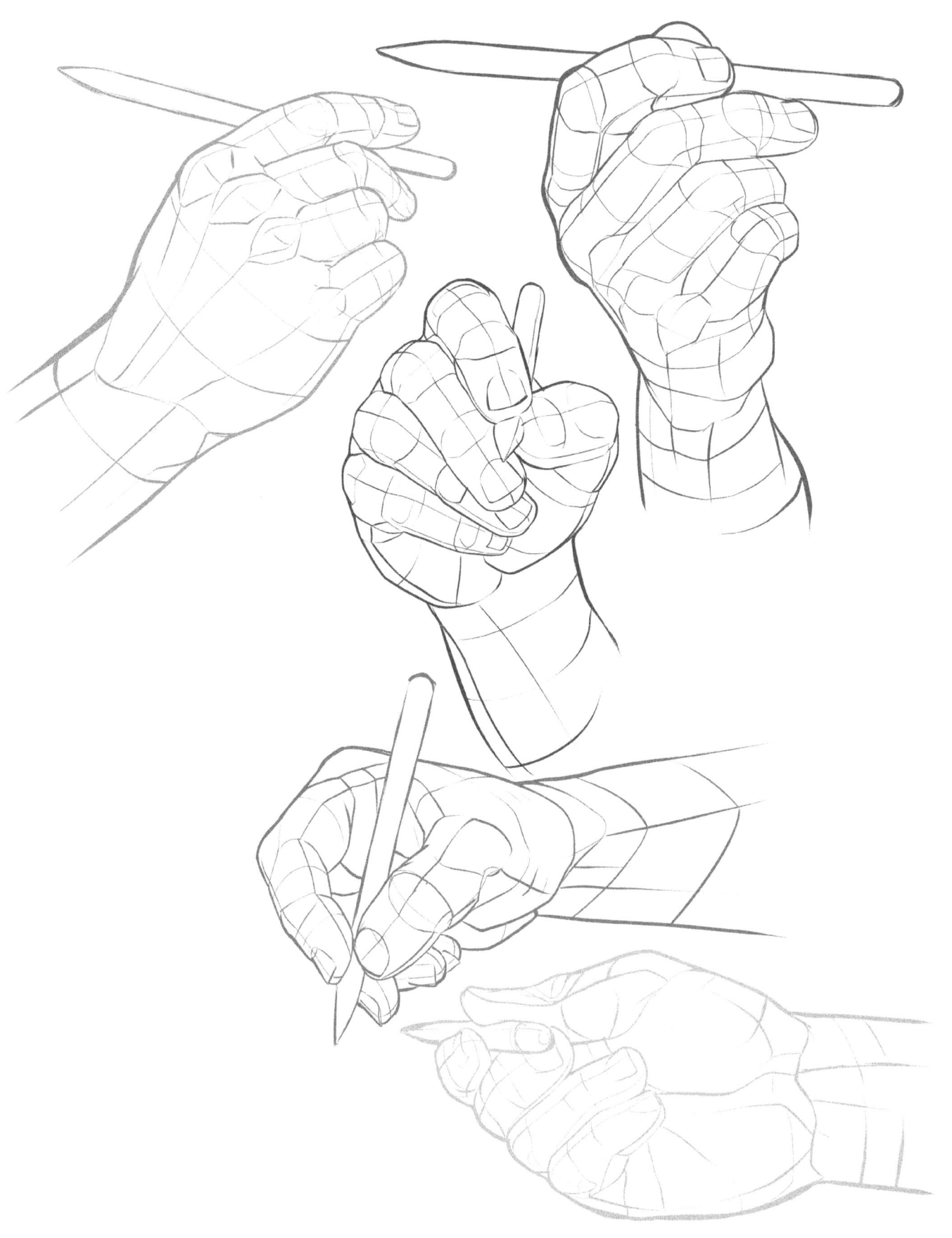

116

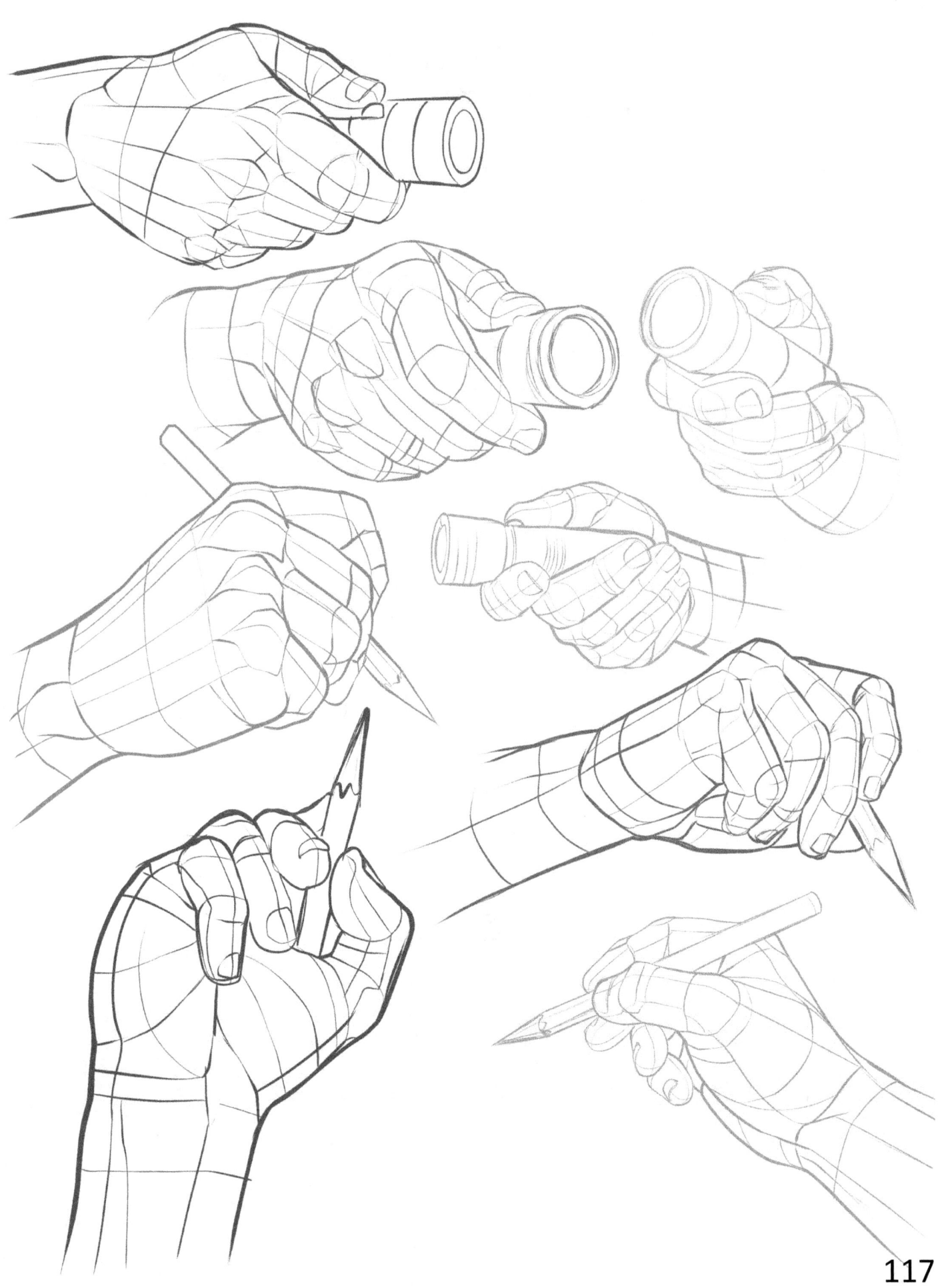

117

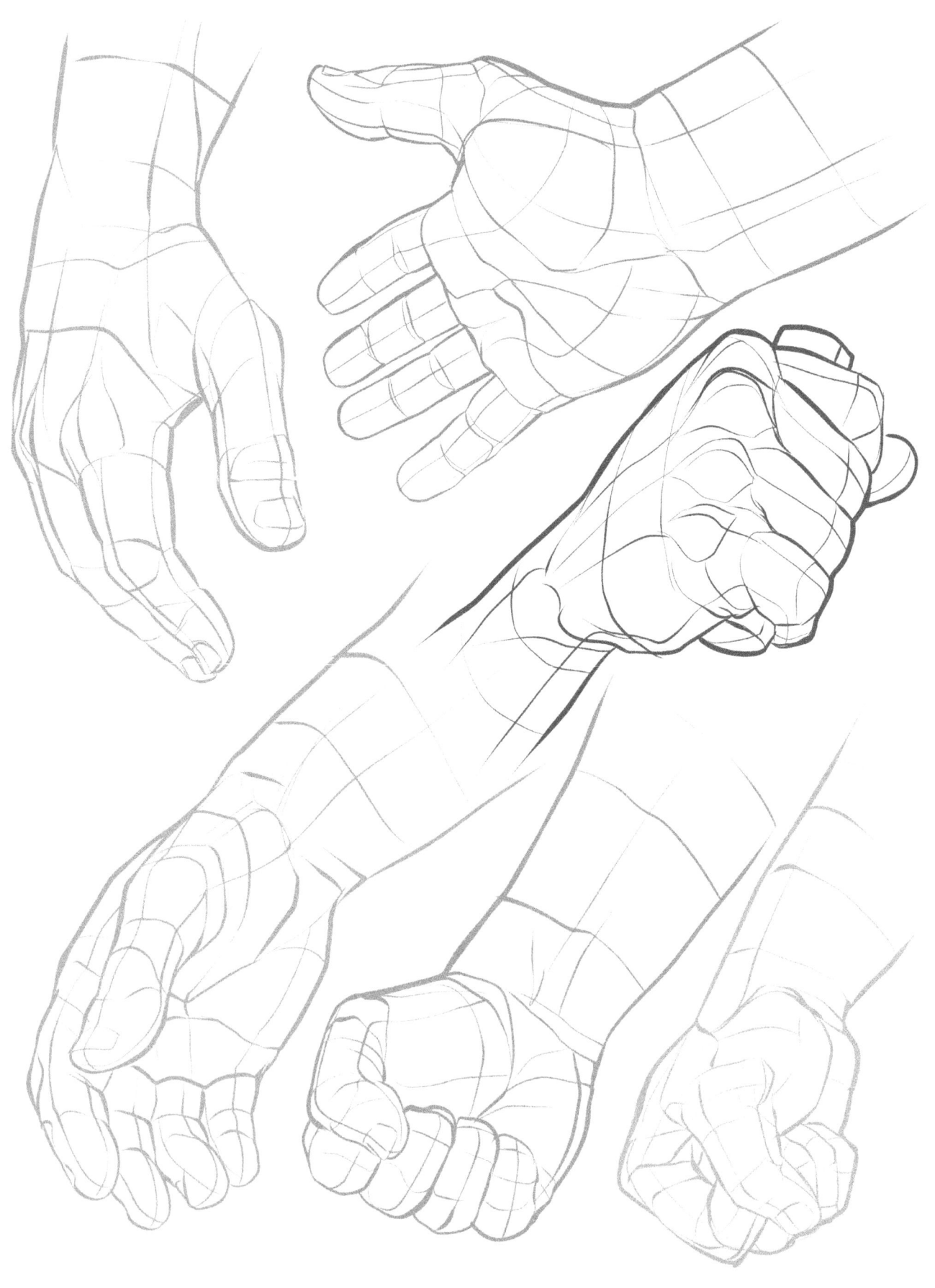

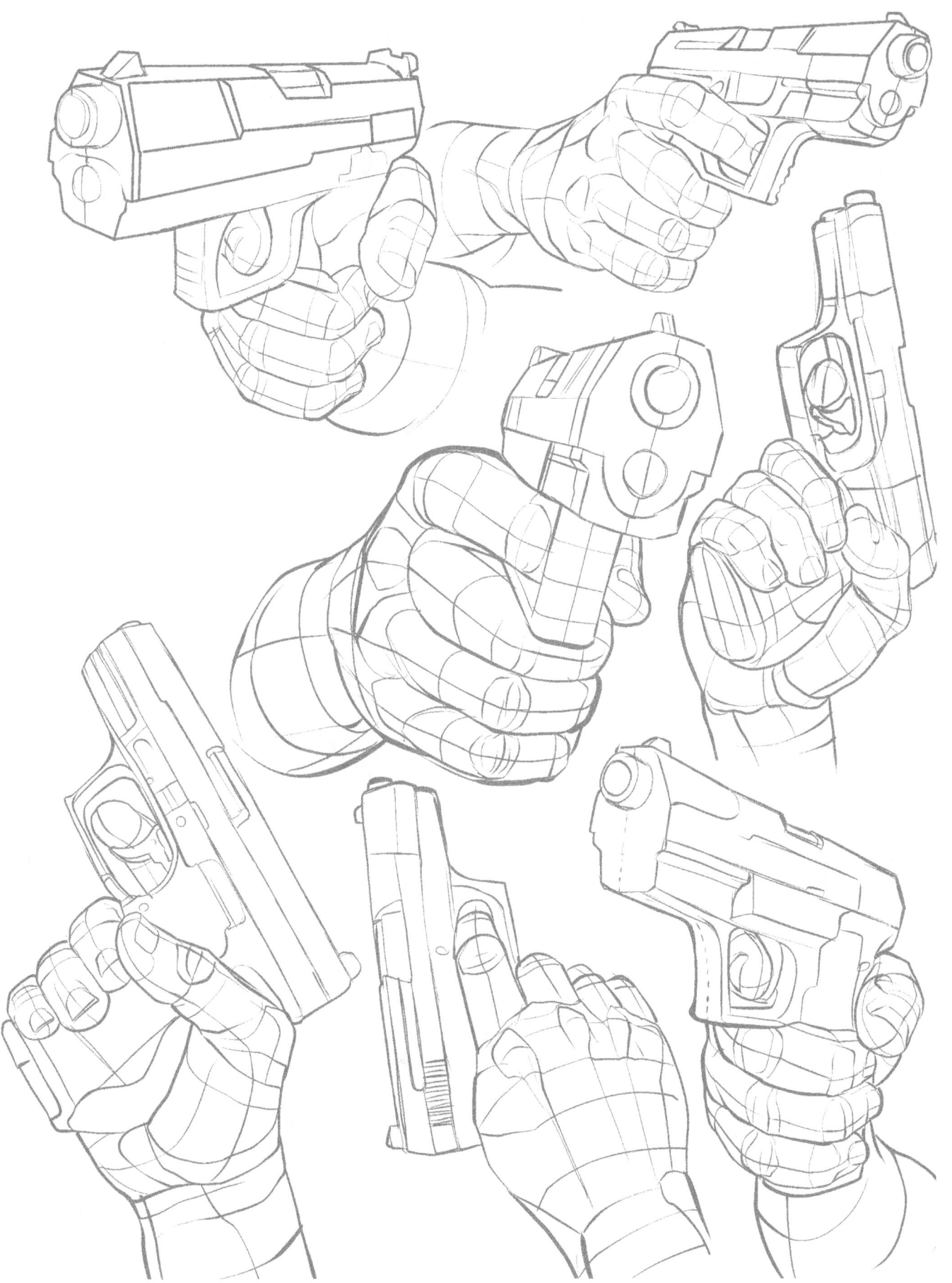

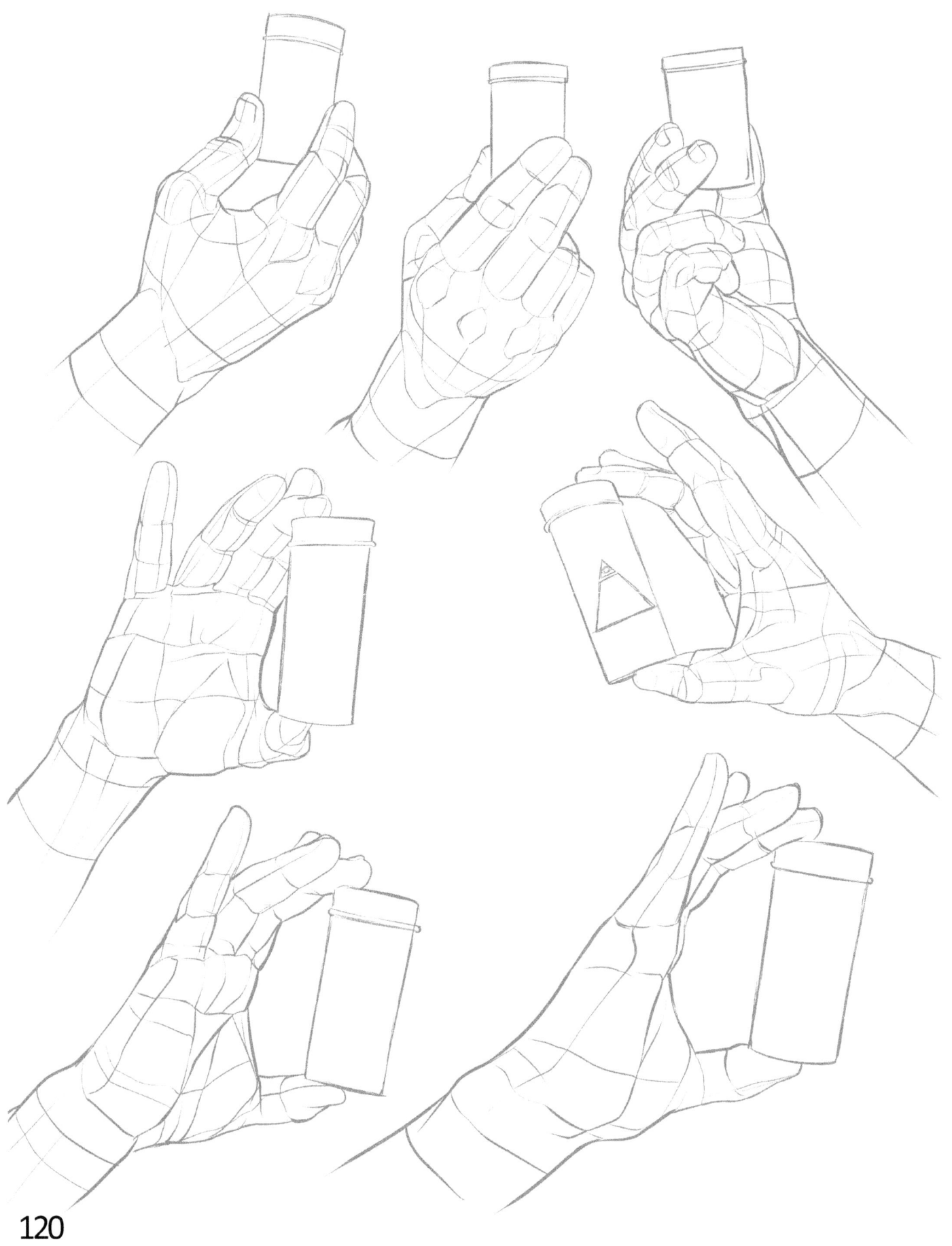

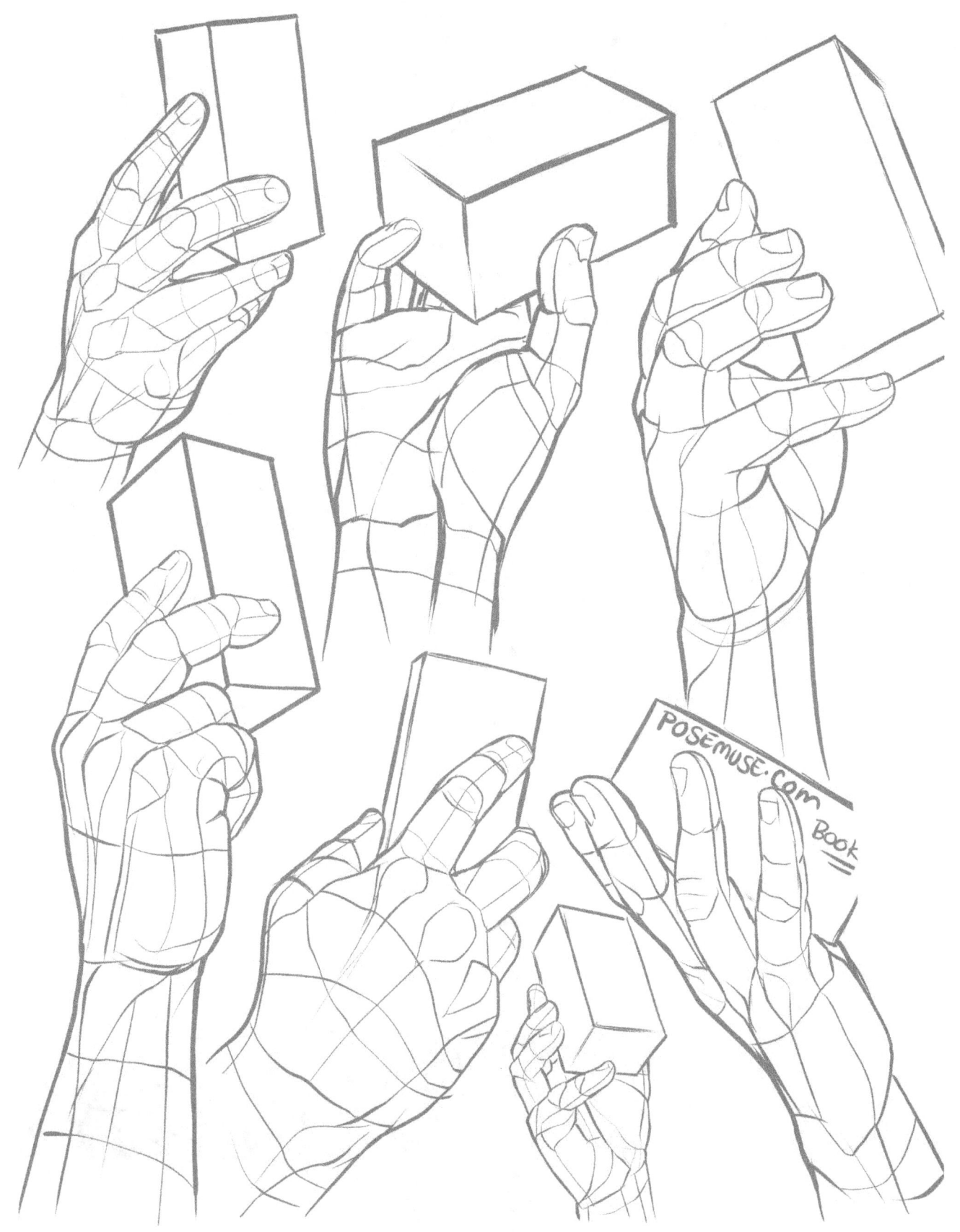

POSEMUSE.Com
Book

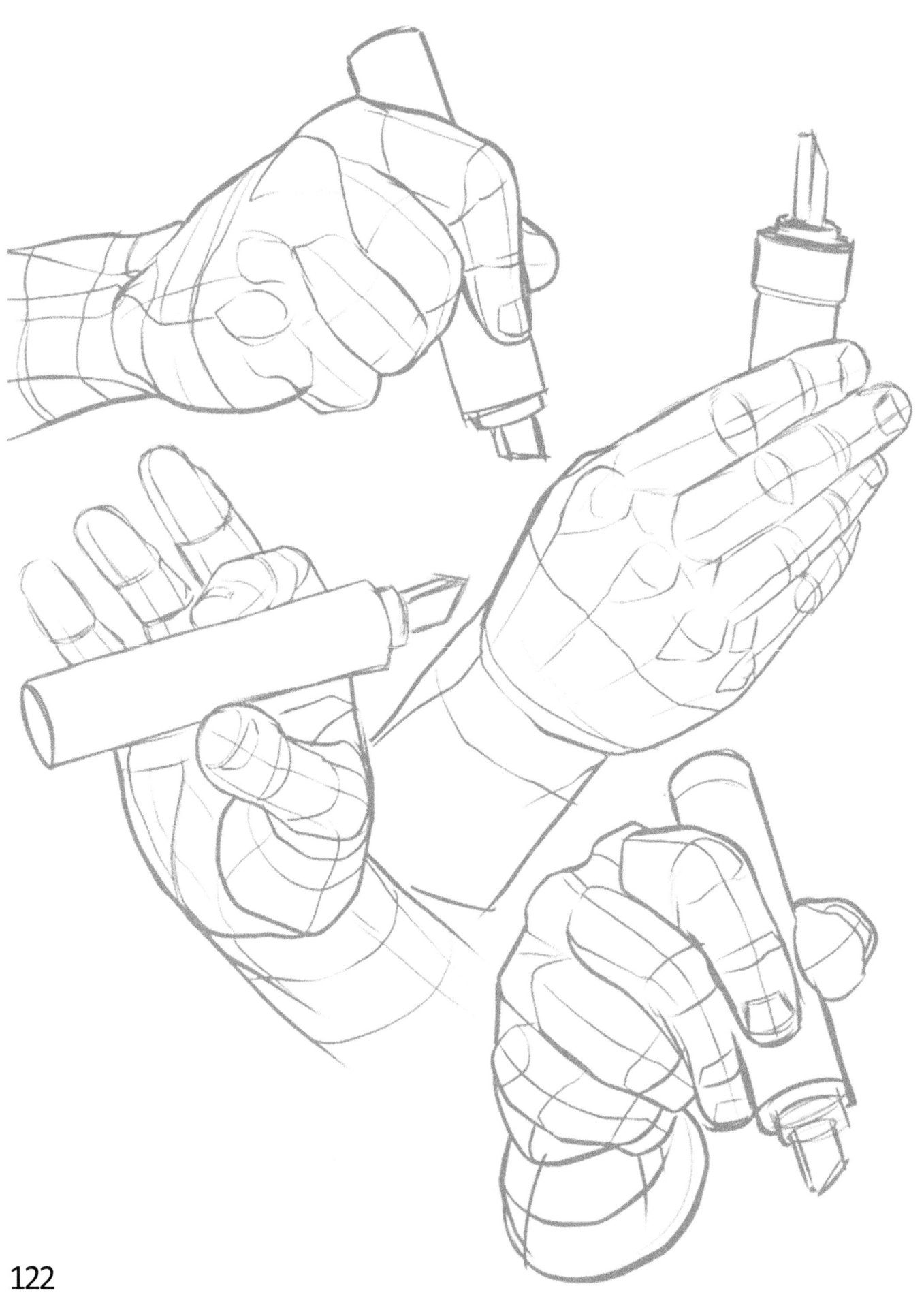

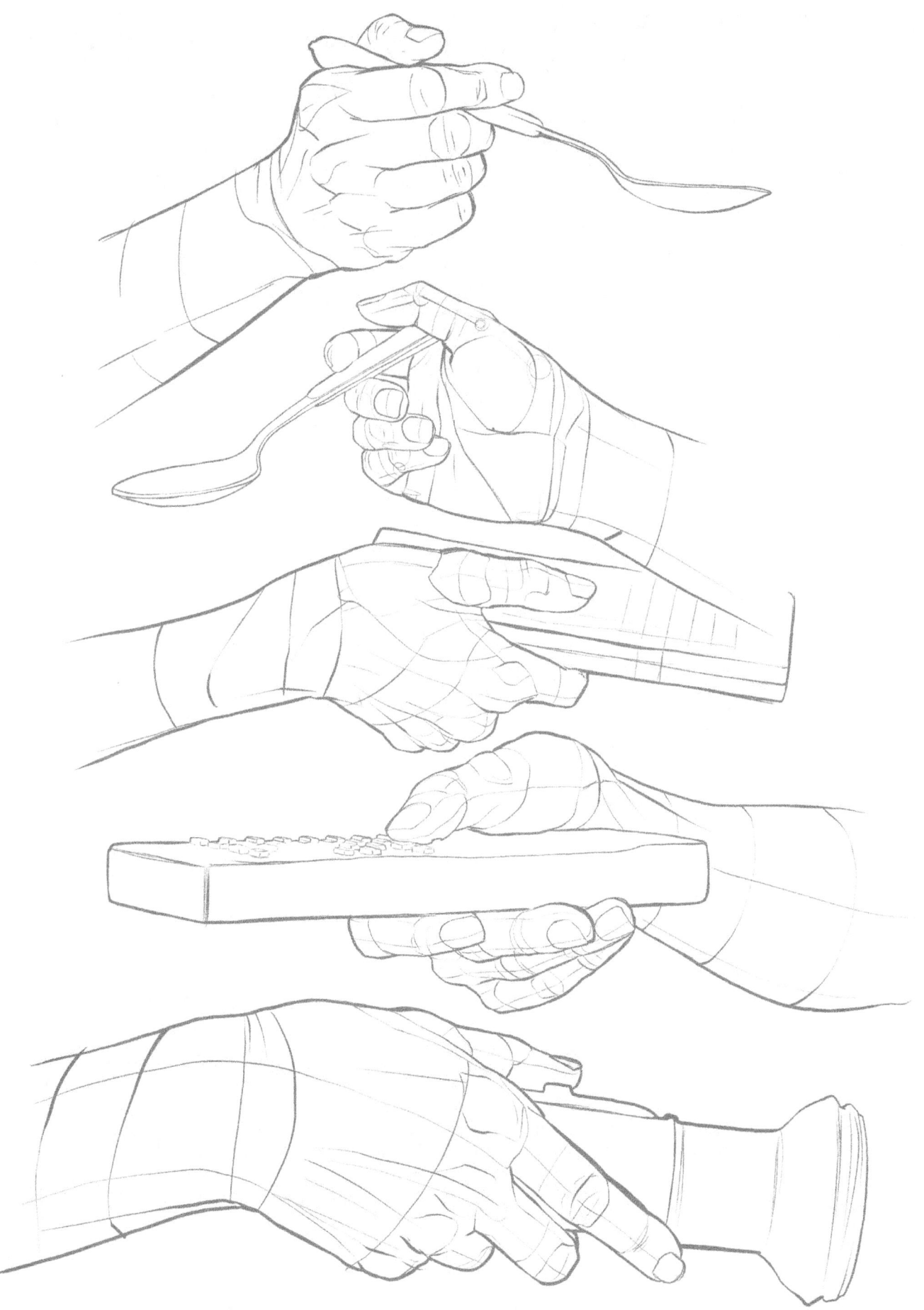

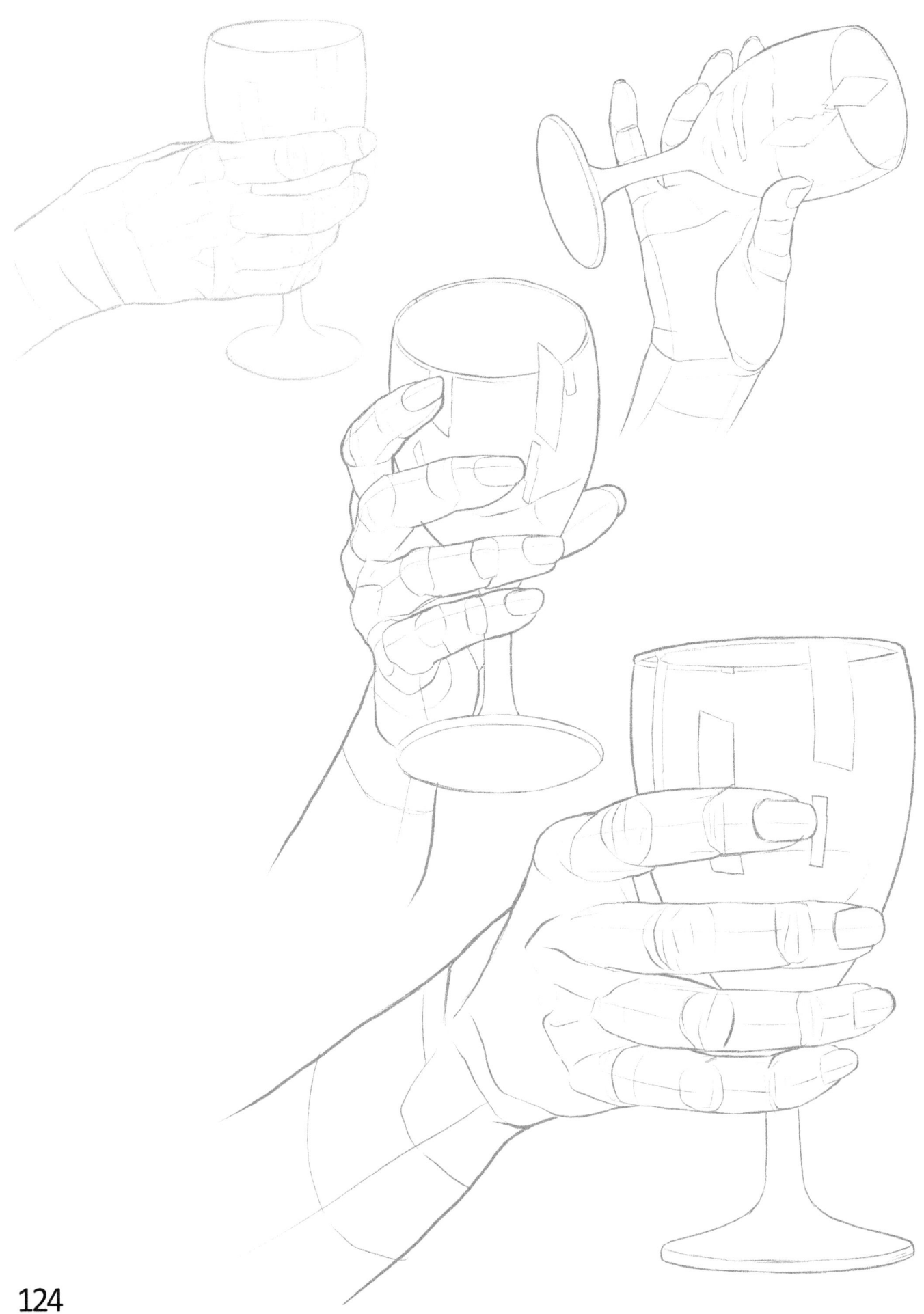

Male Poses

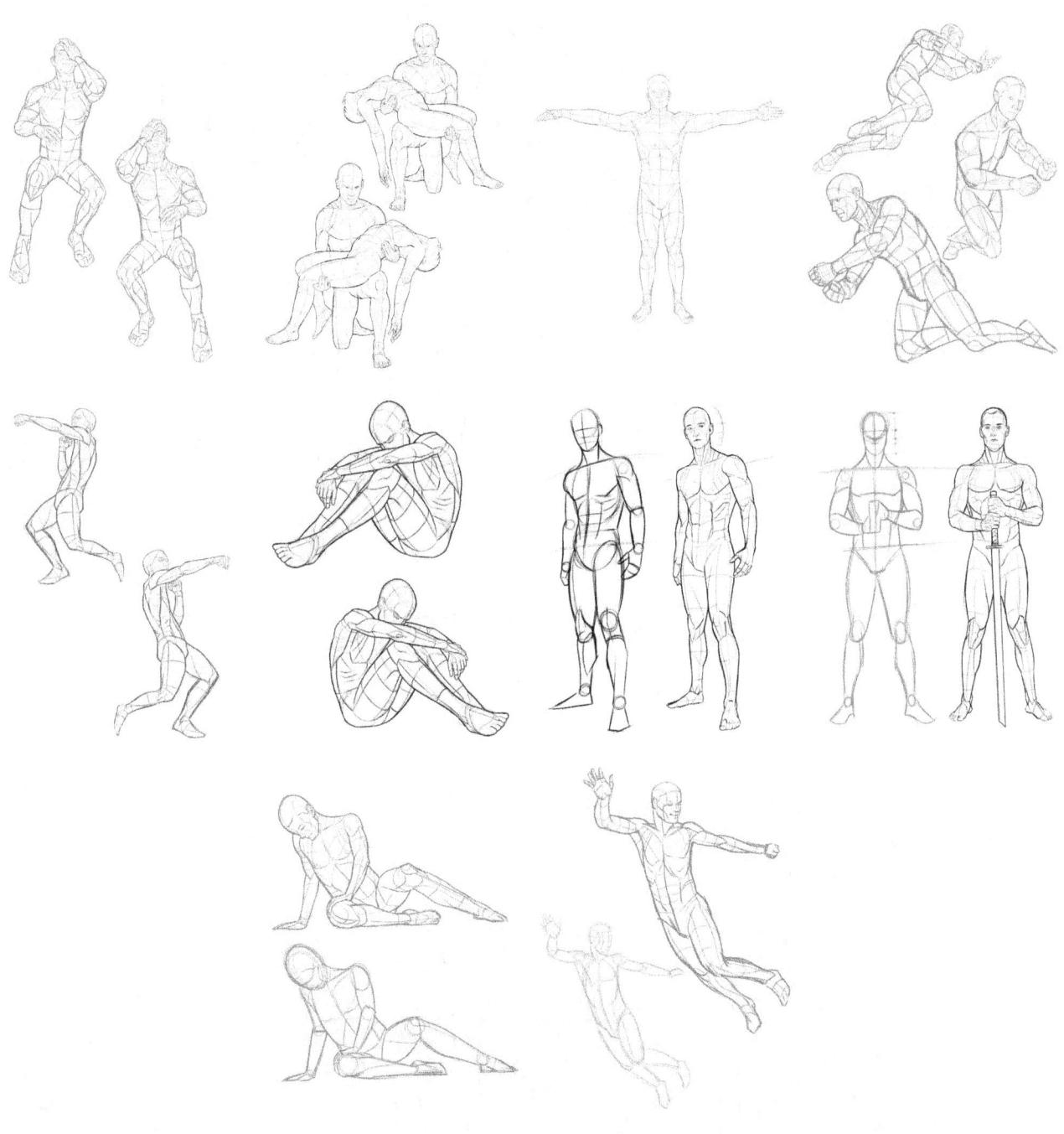

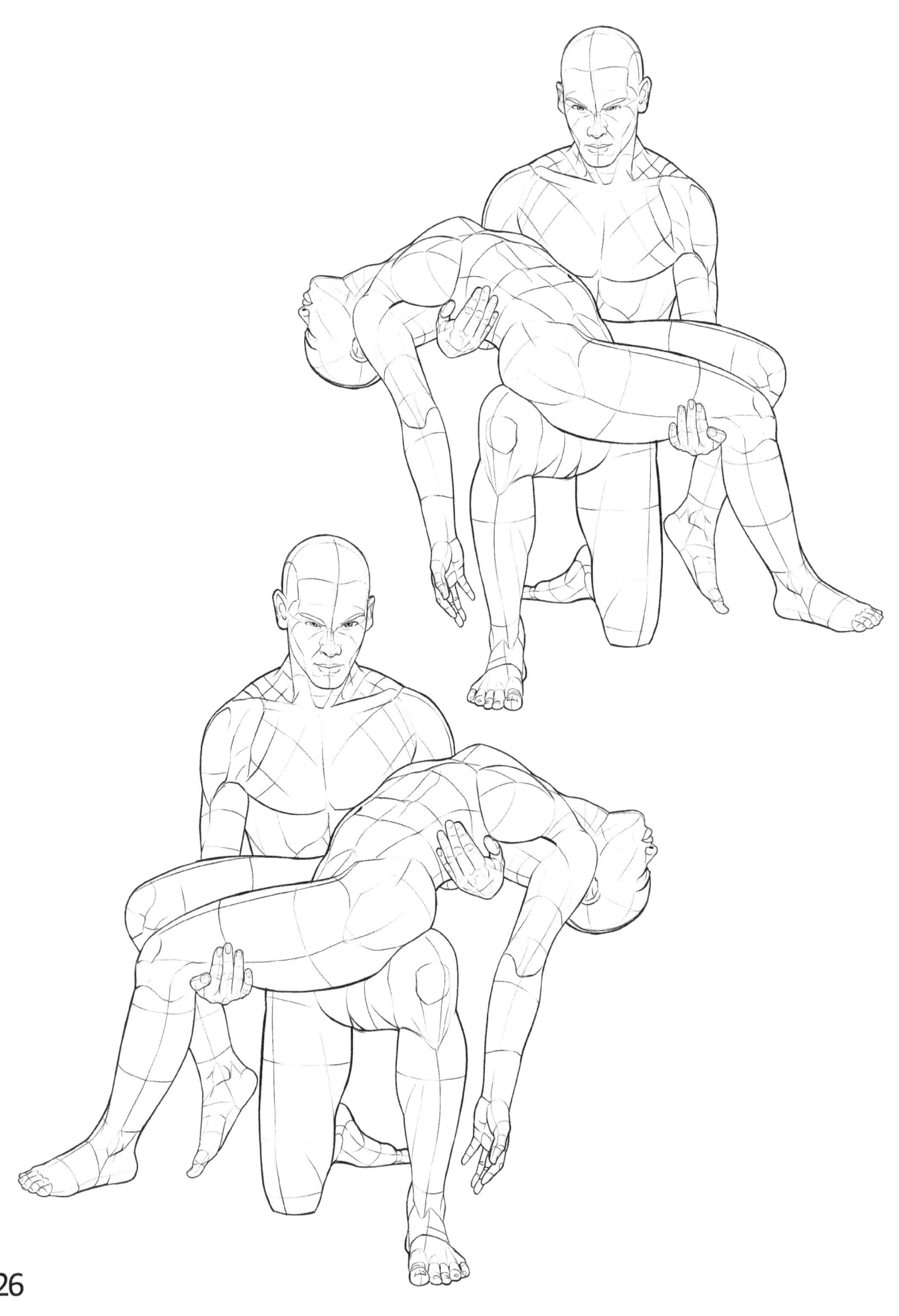

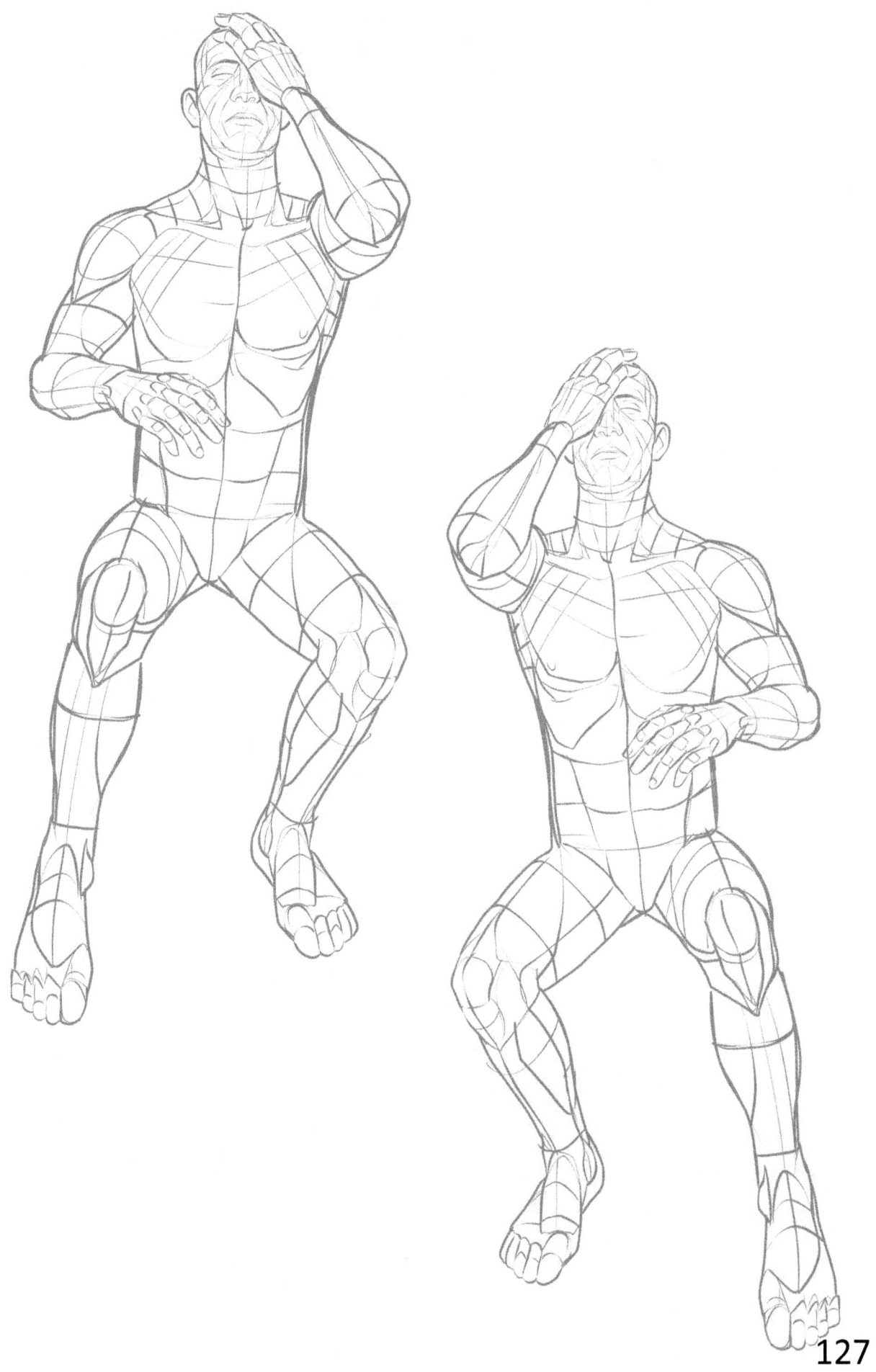

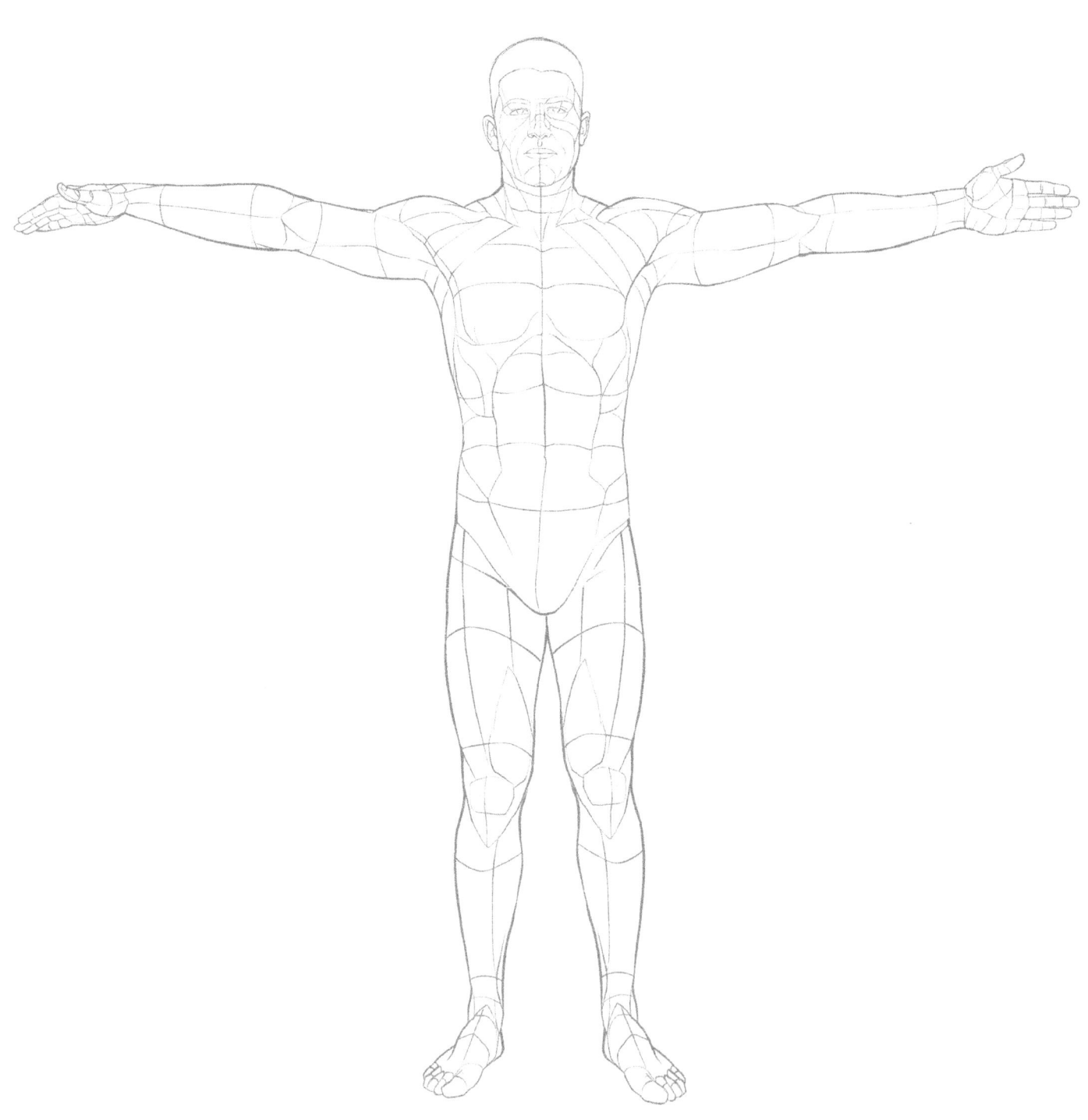

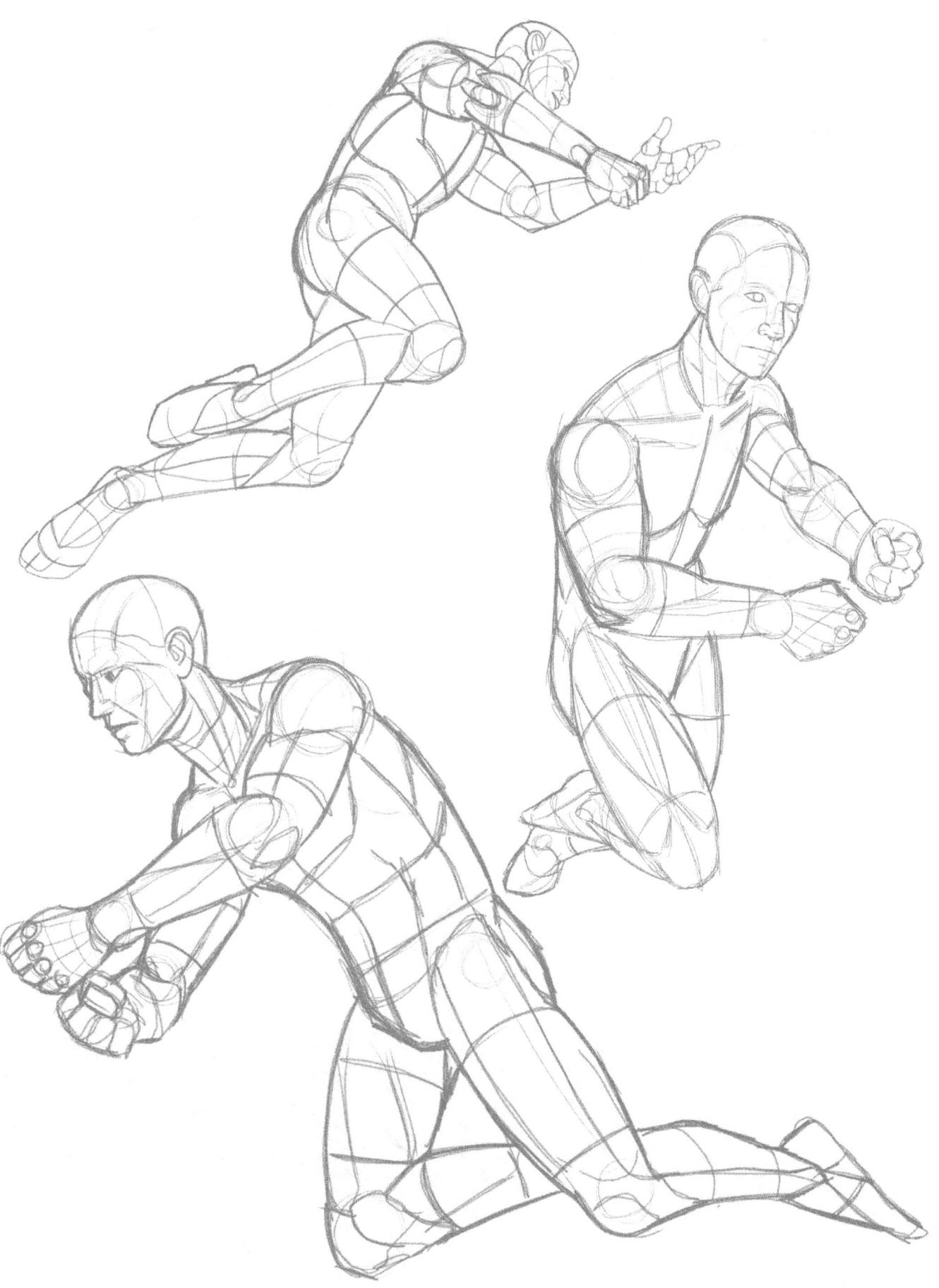

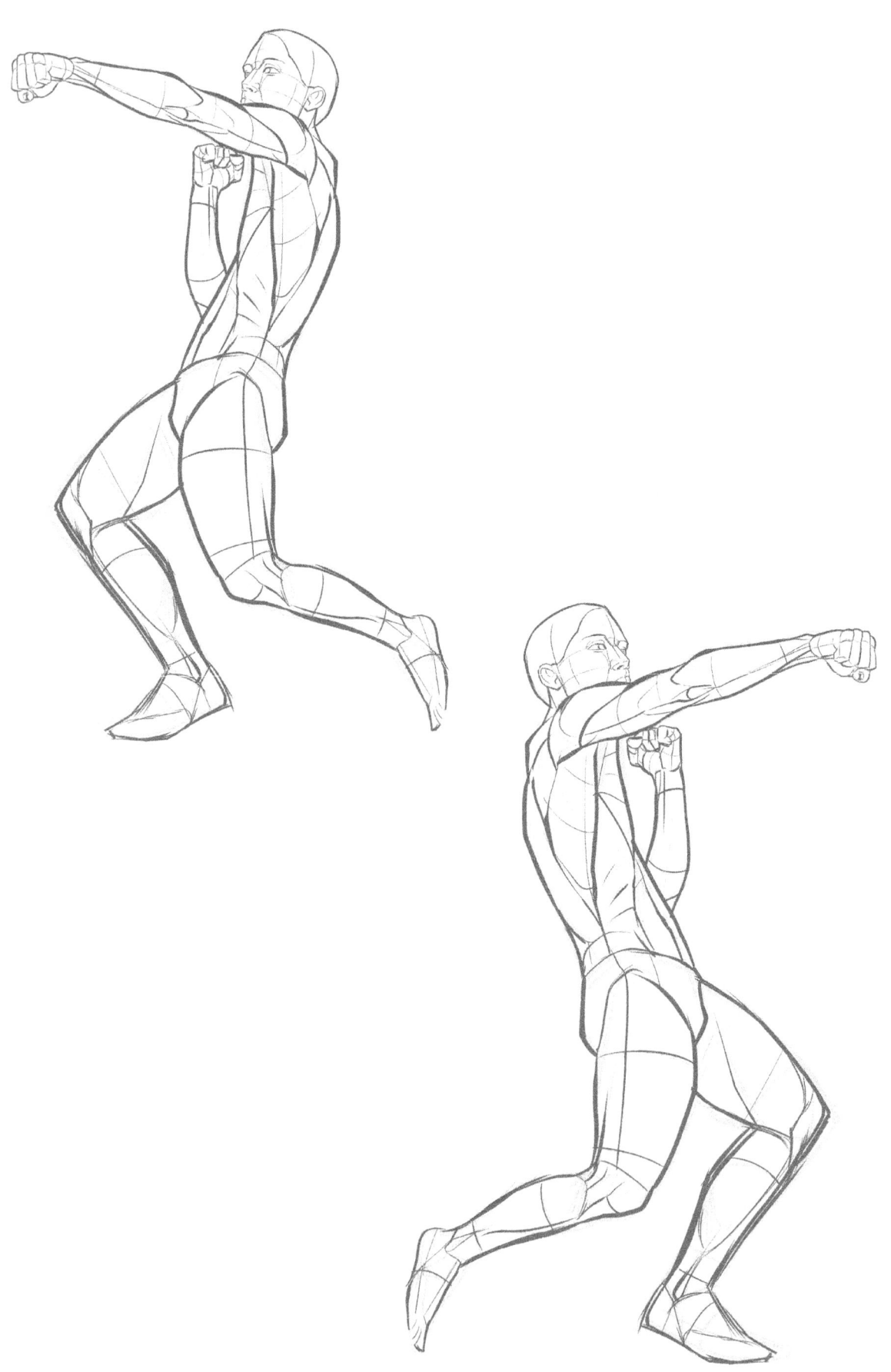

130

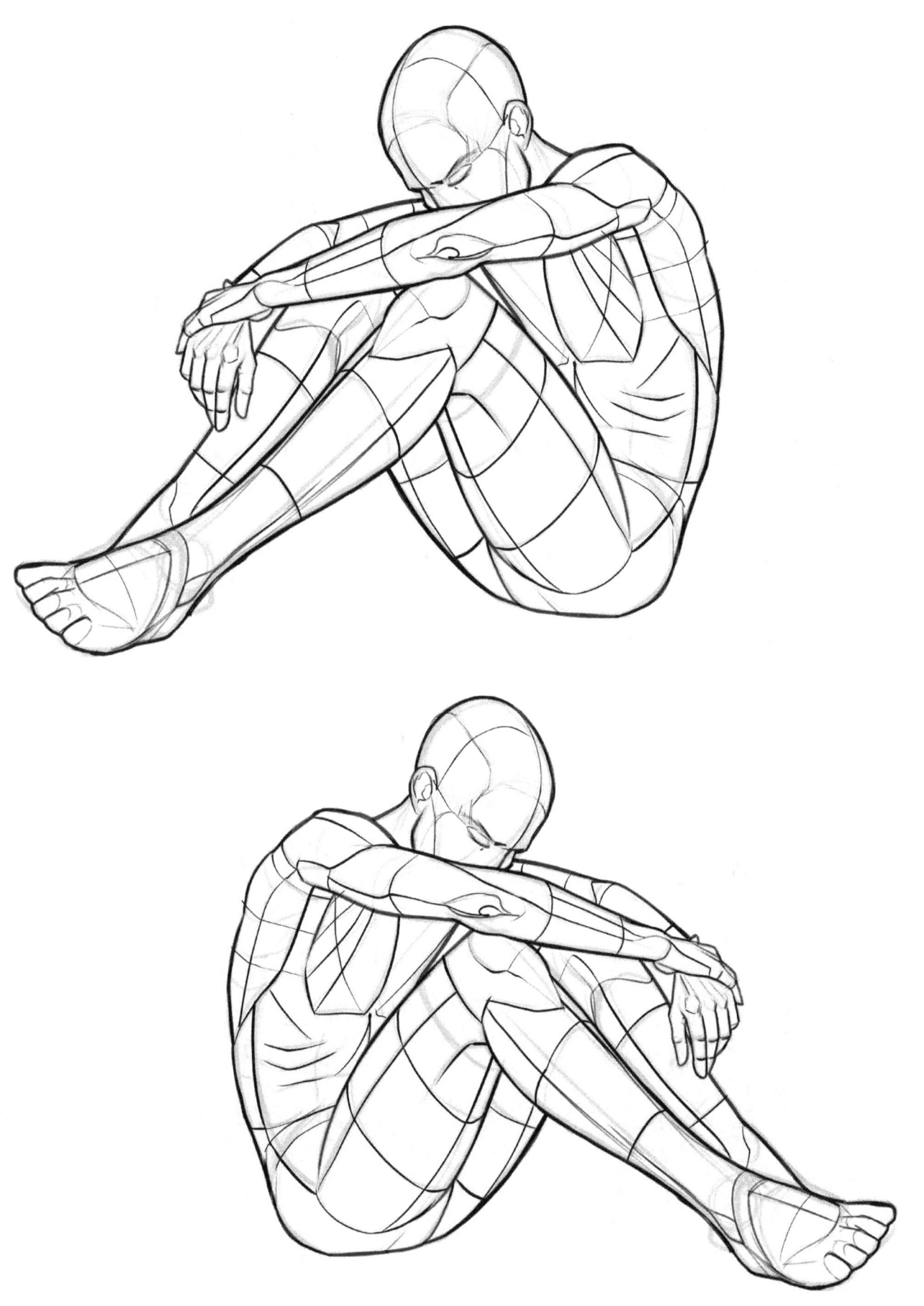

131

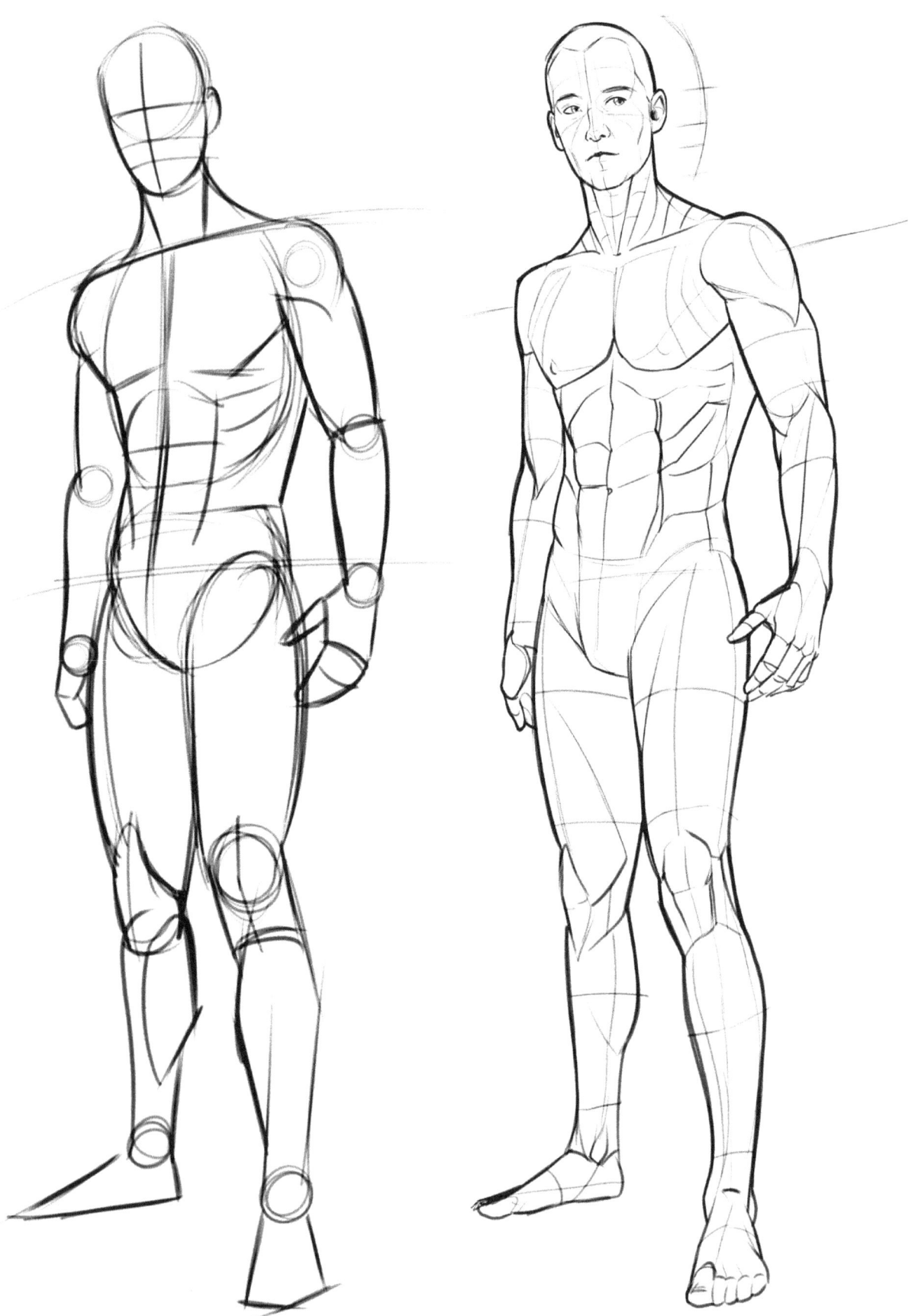

132

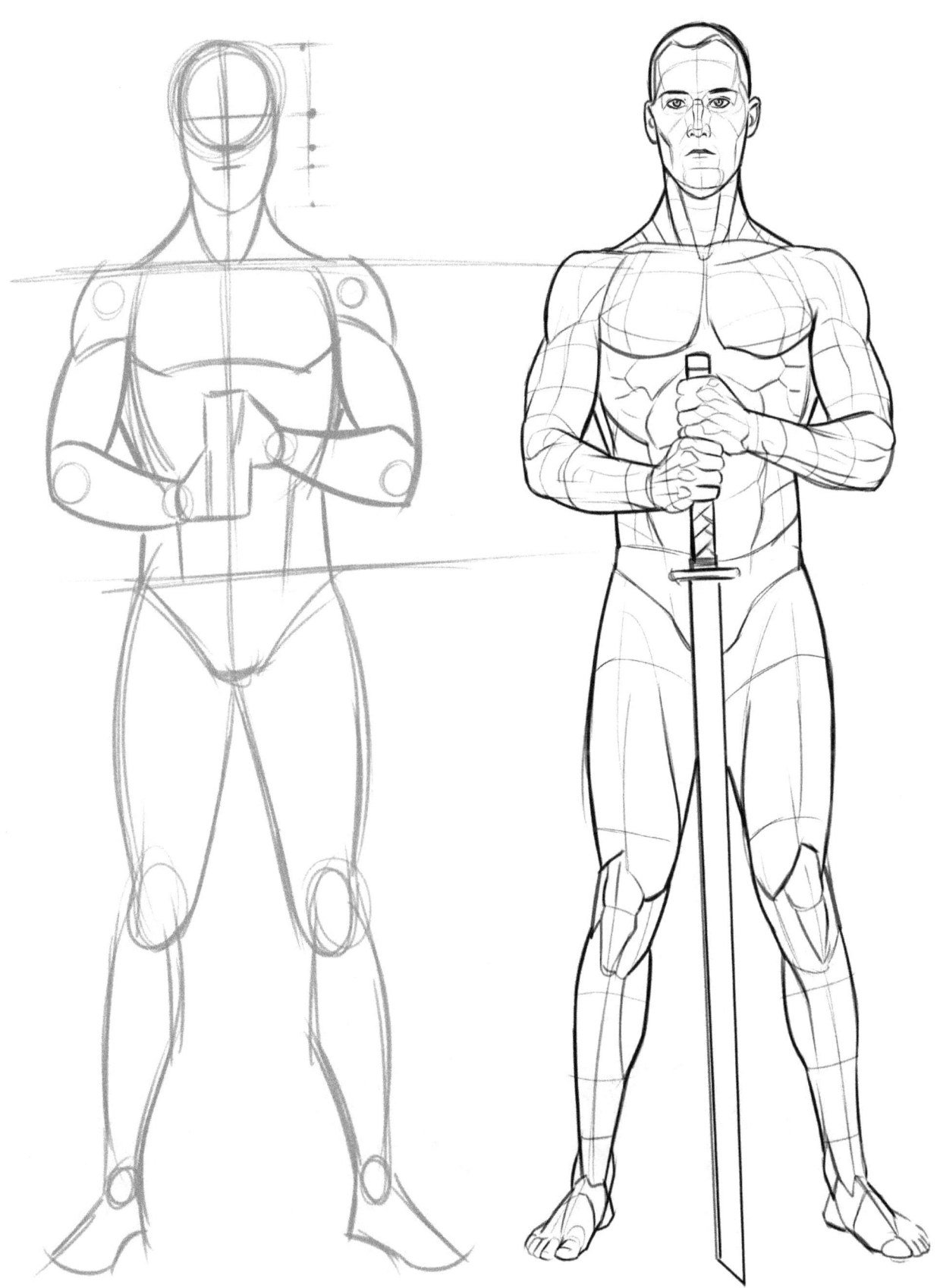

133

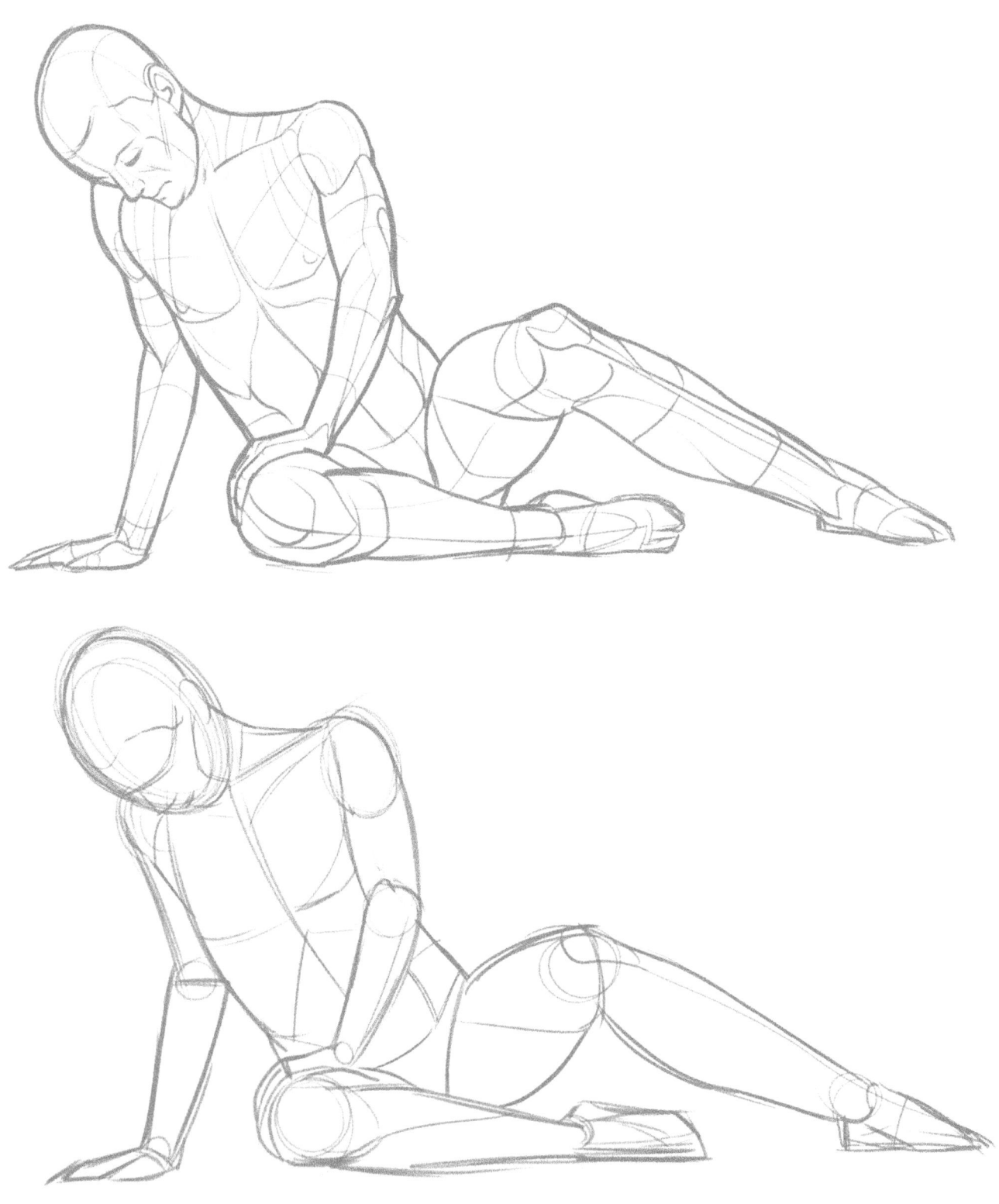

134

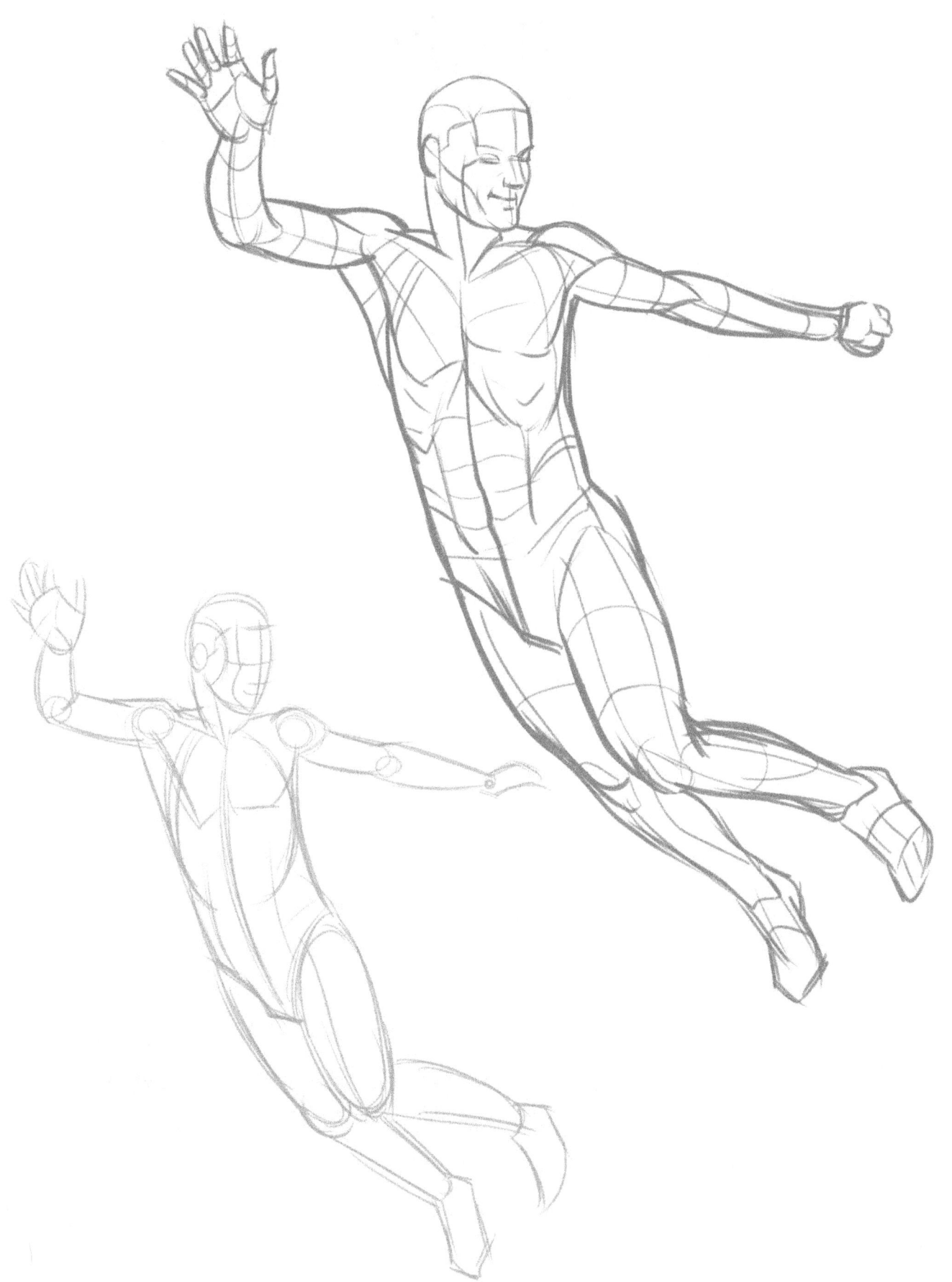

Skulls

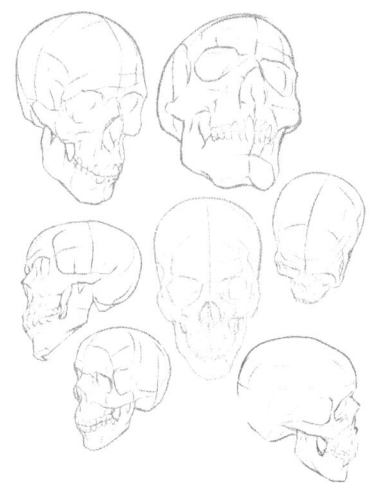 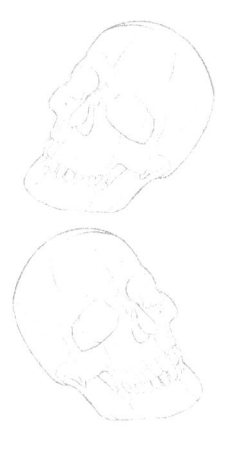 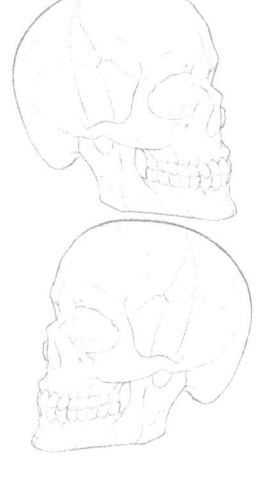

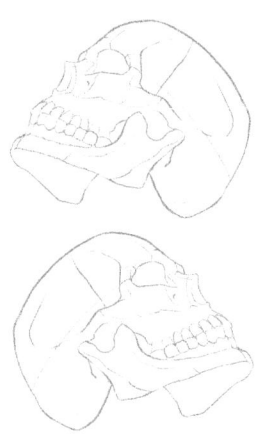

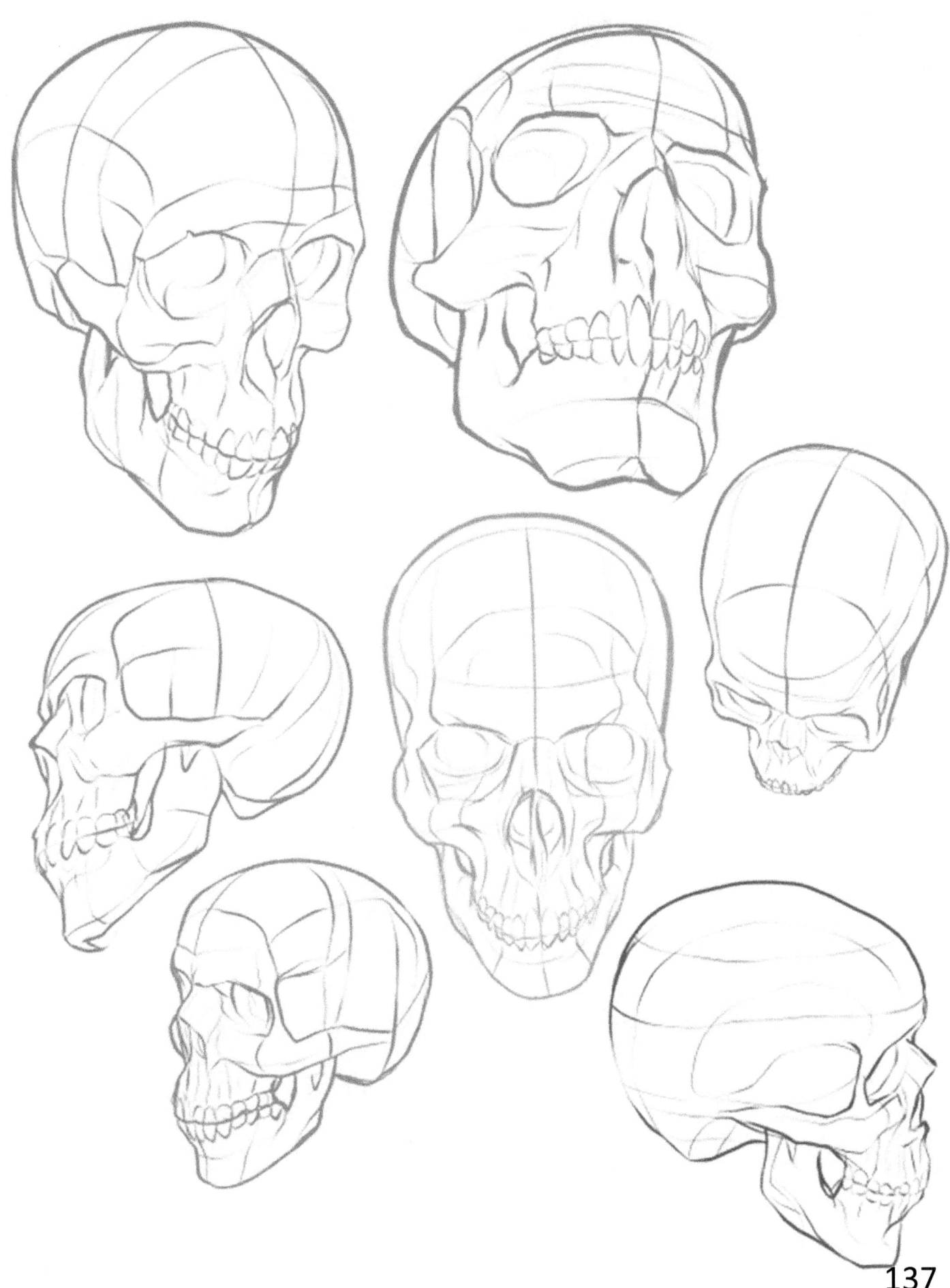

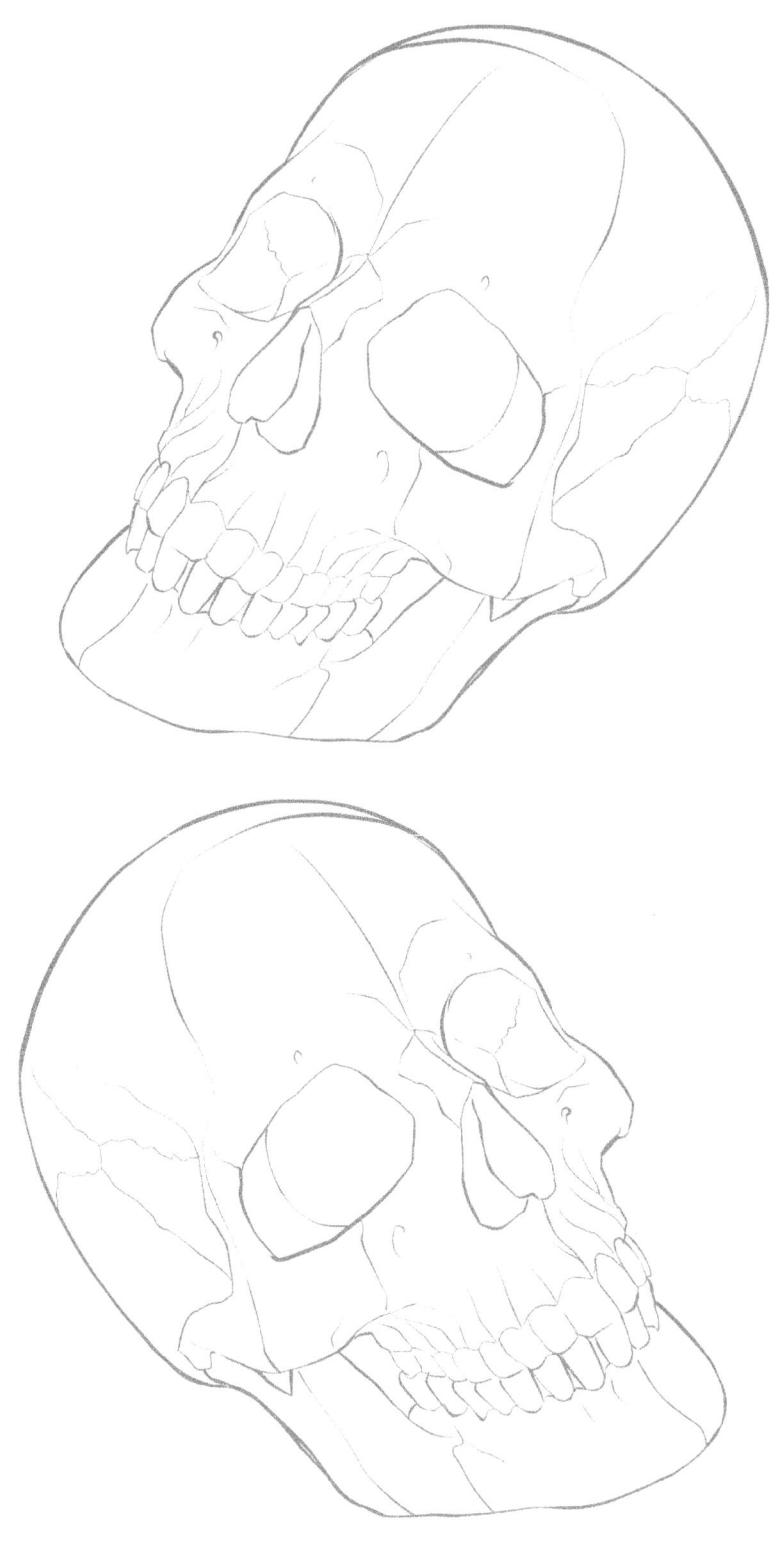

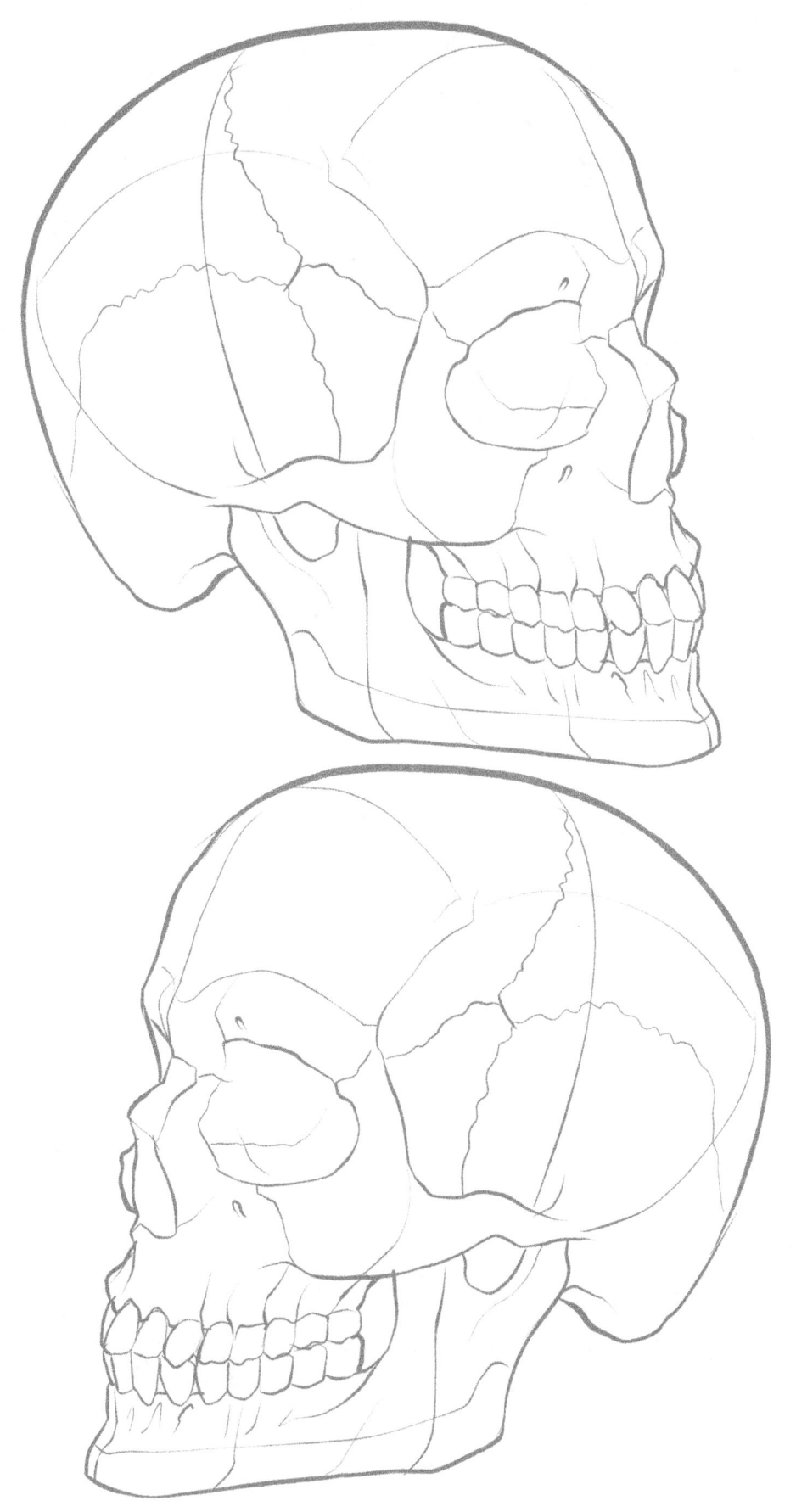

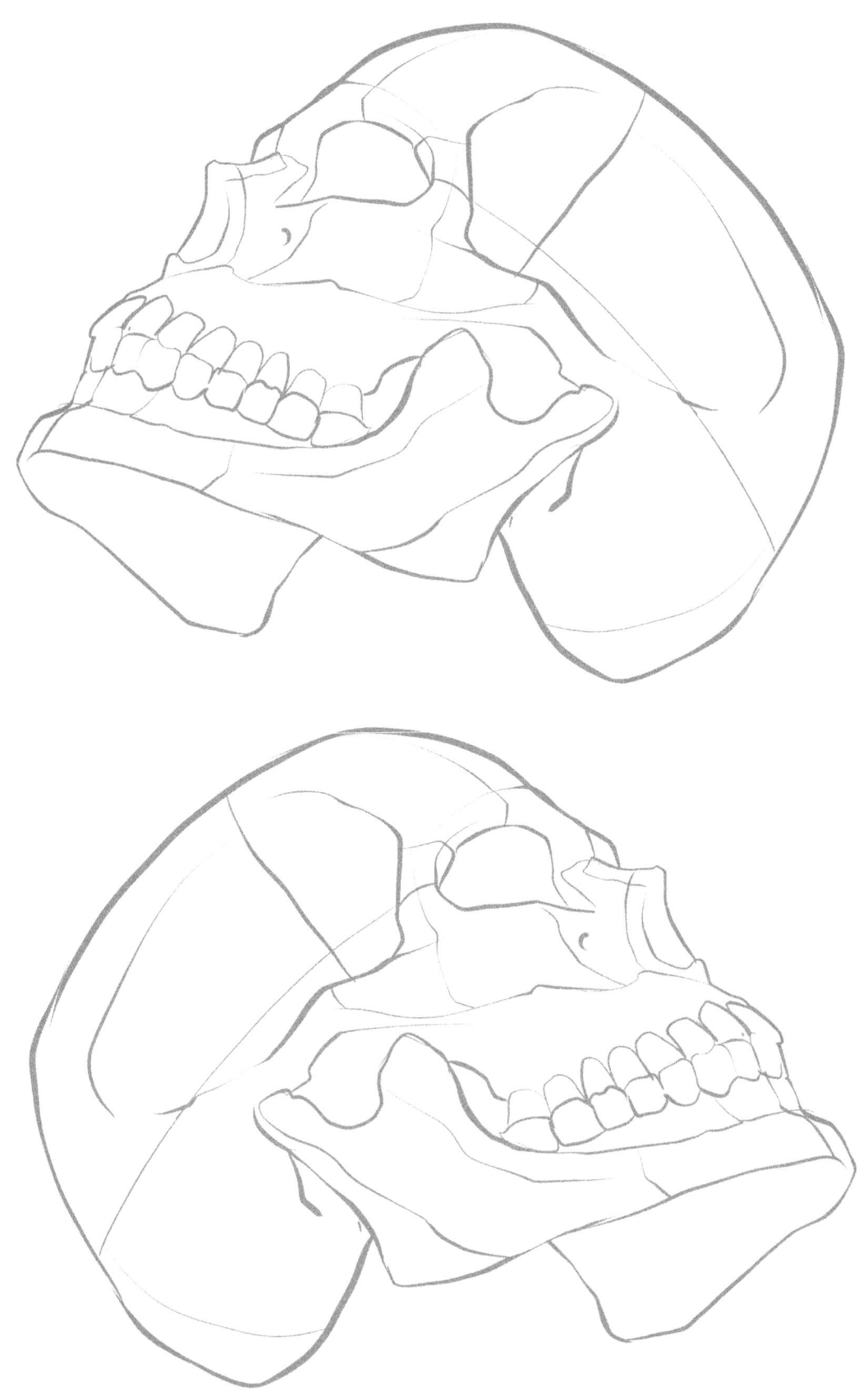

Kneeling Poses

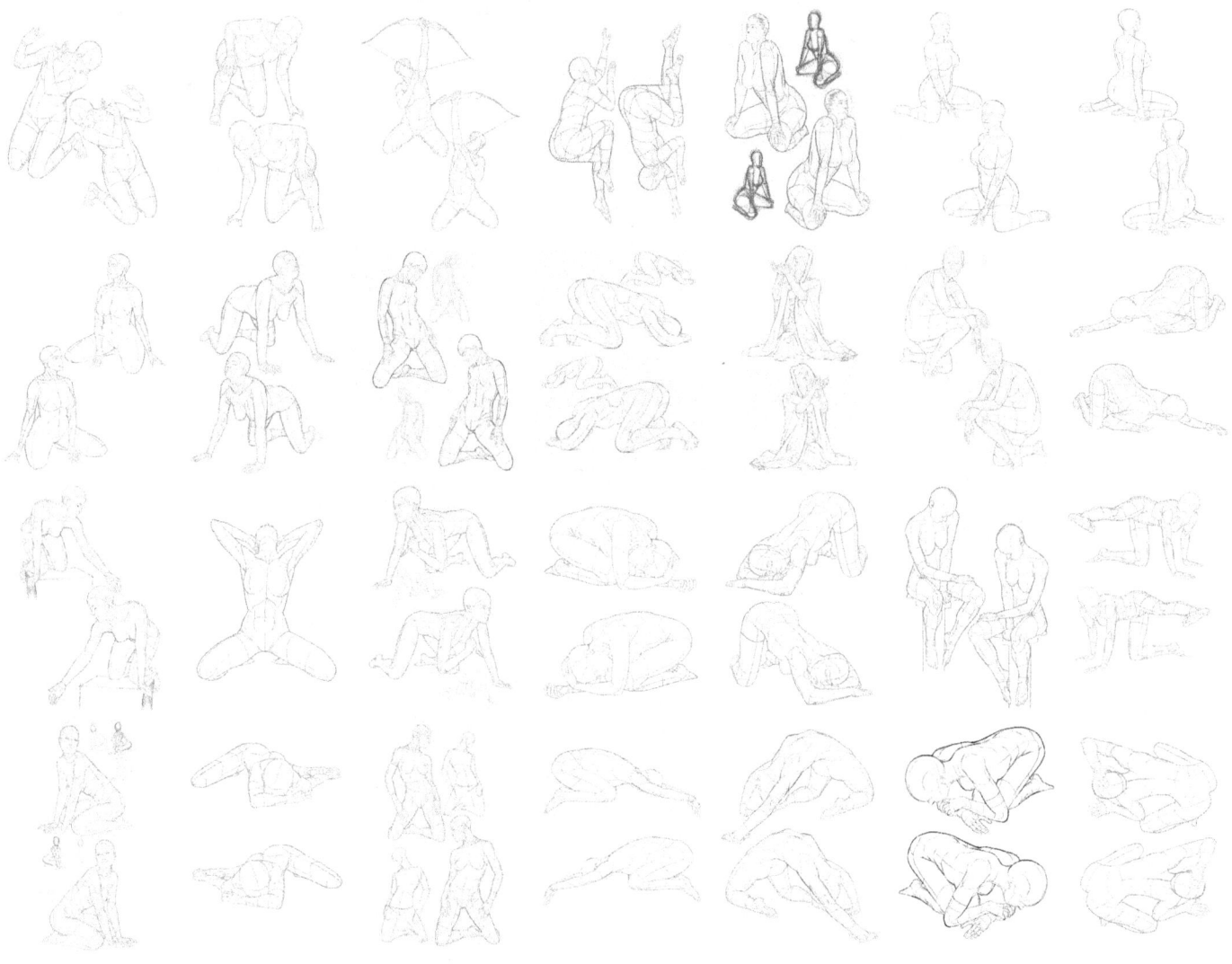

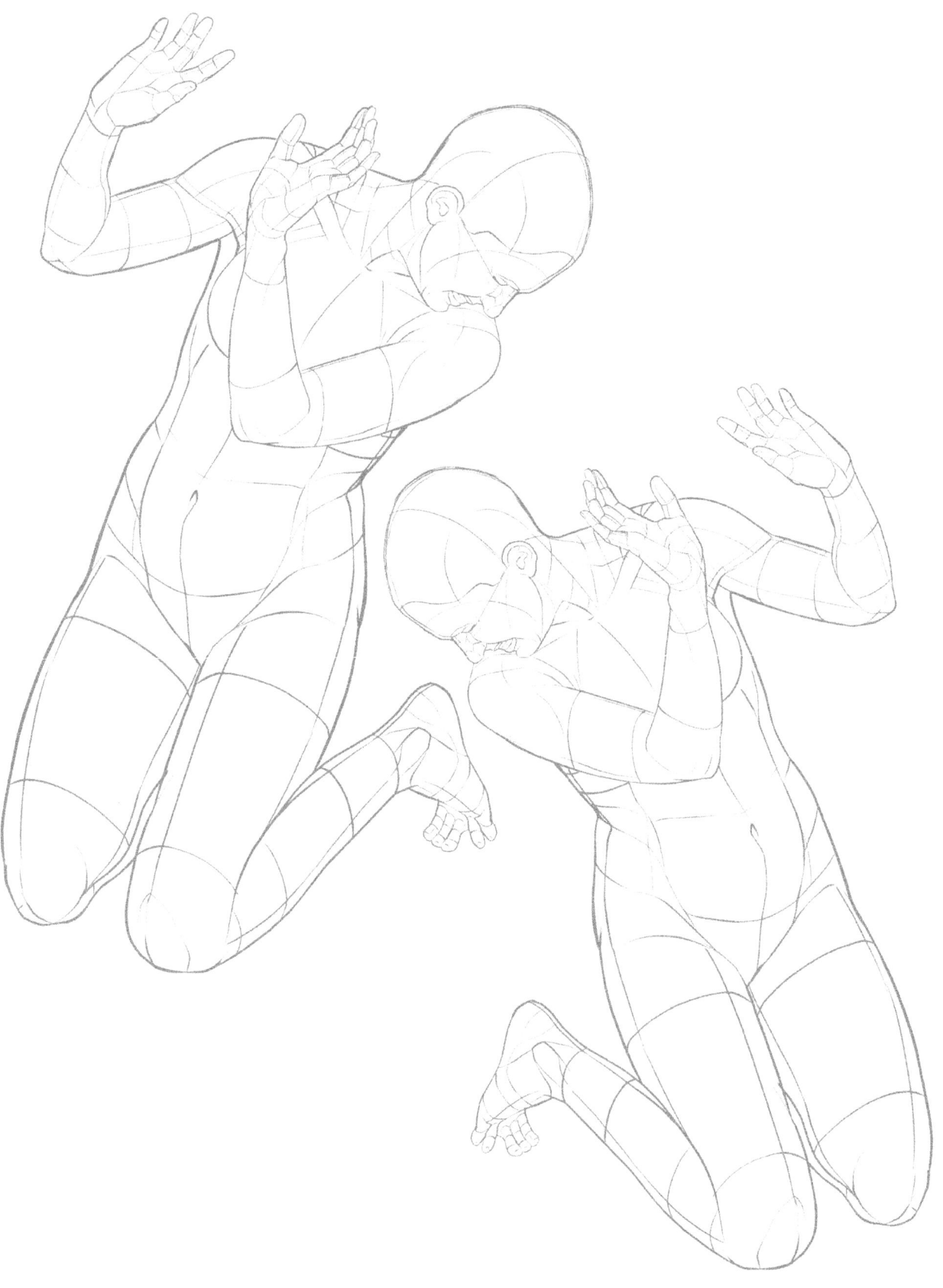

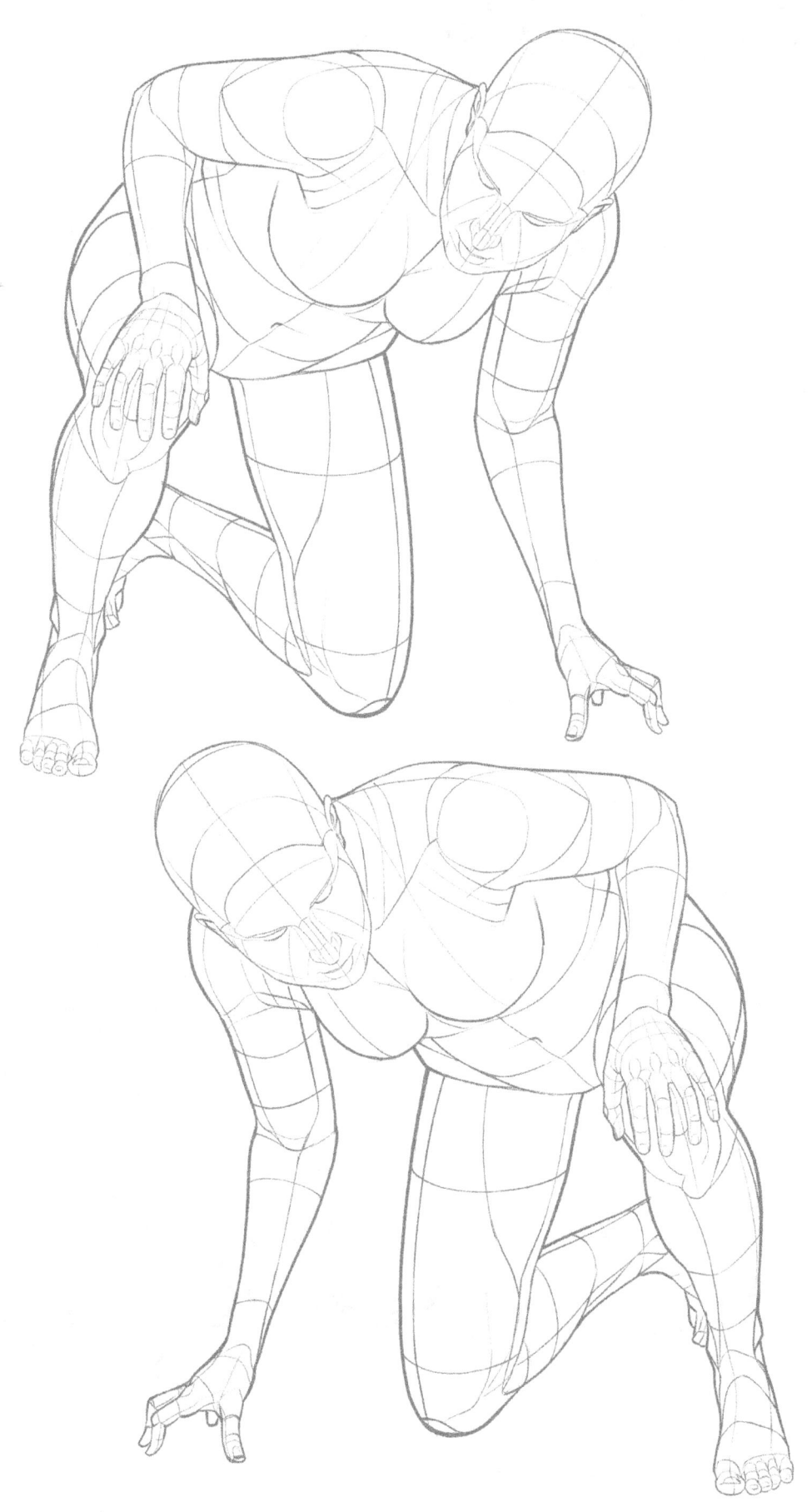

143

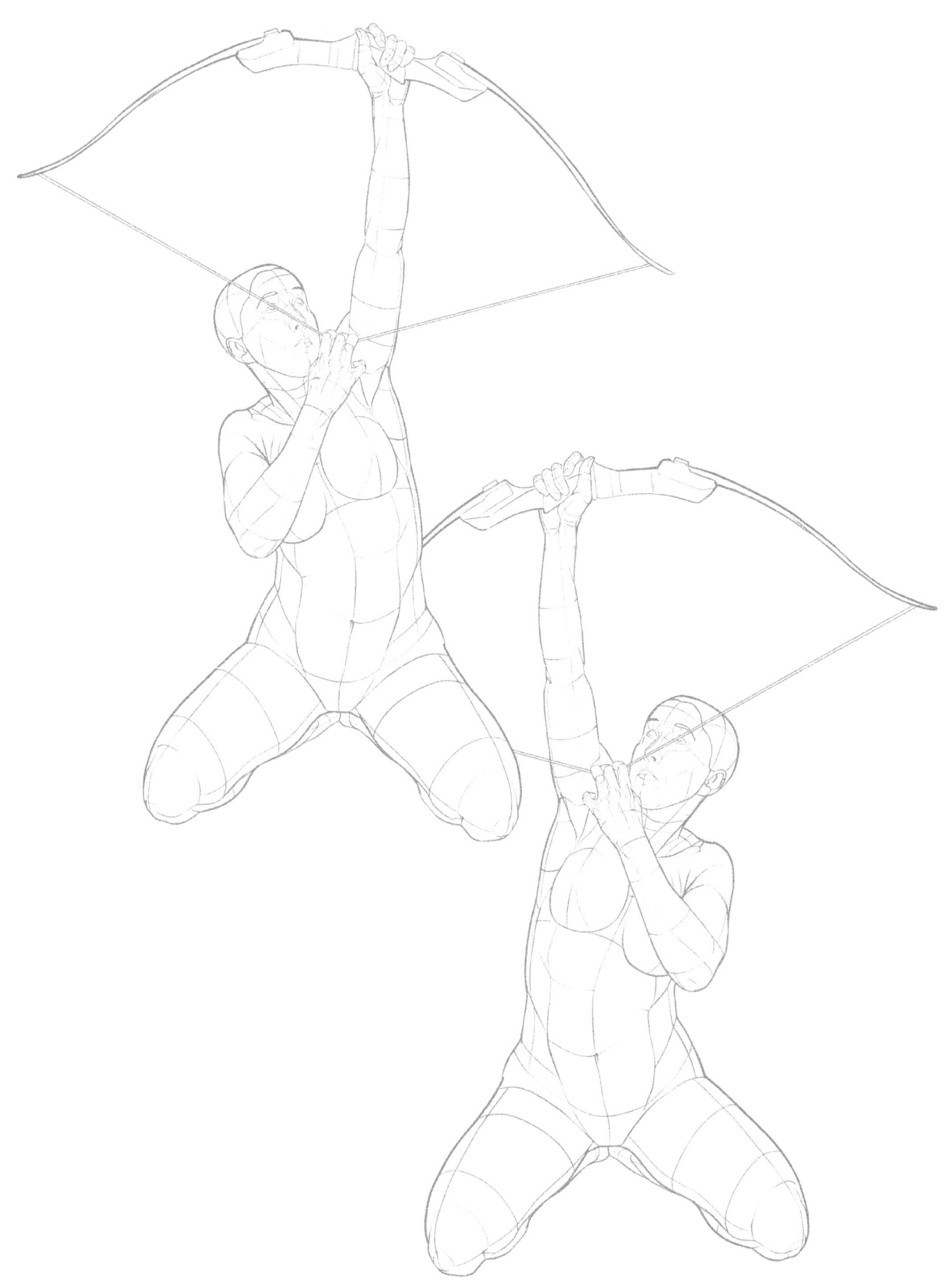

144

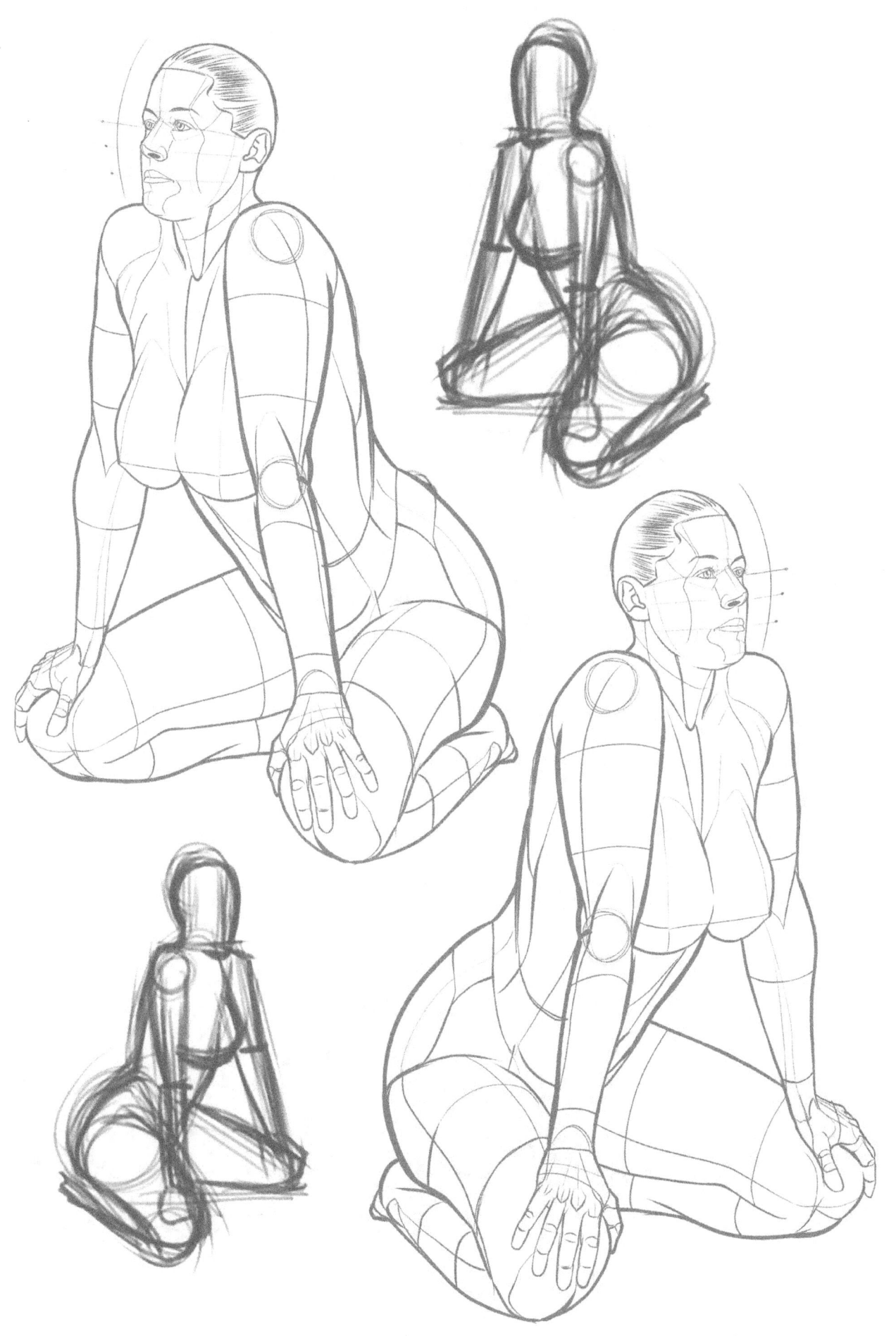

145

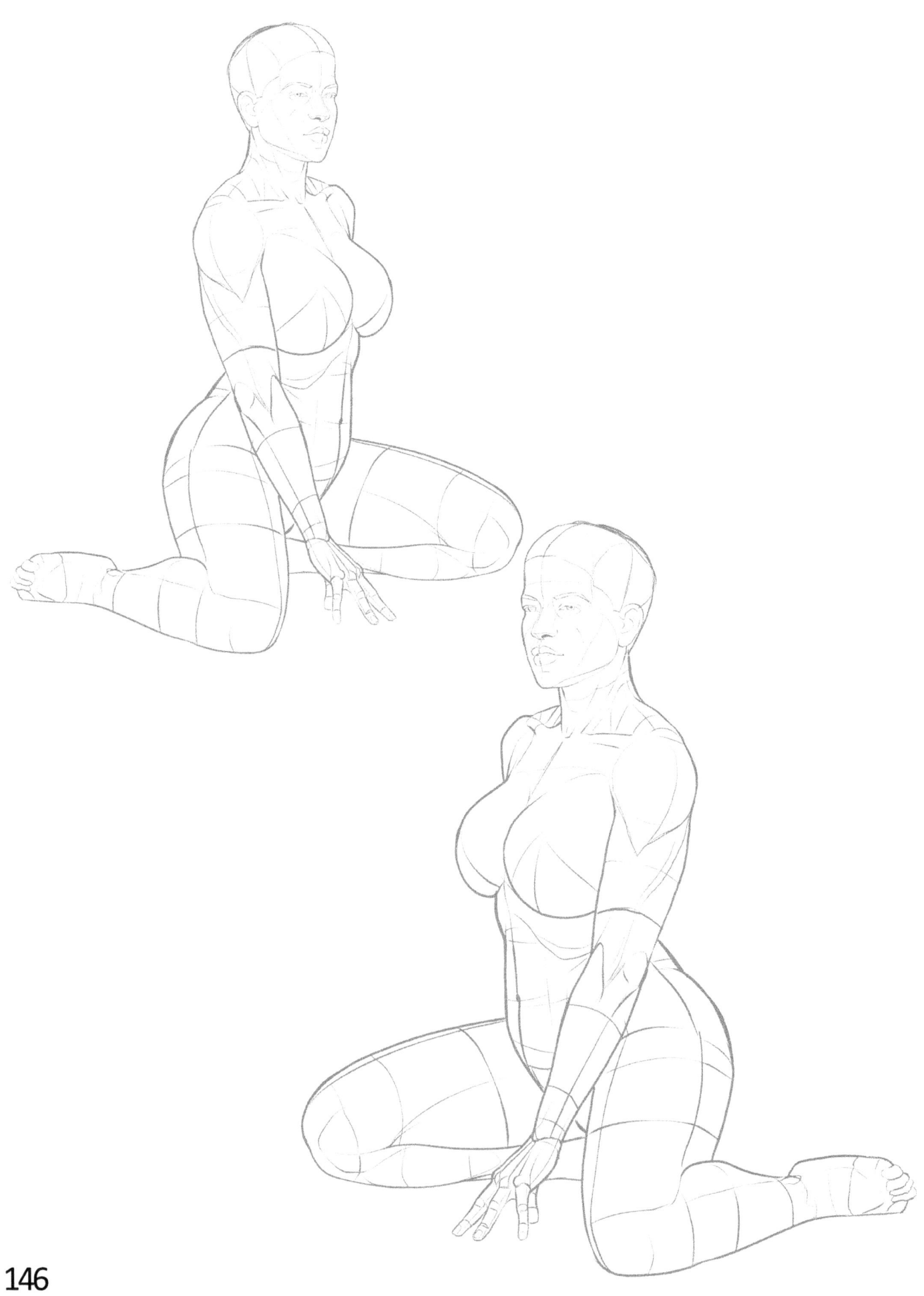

146

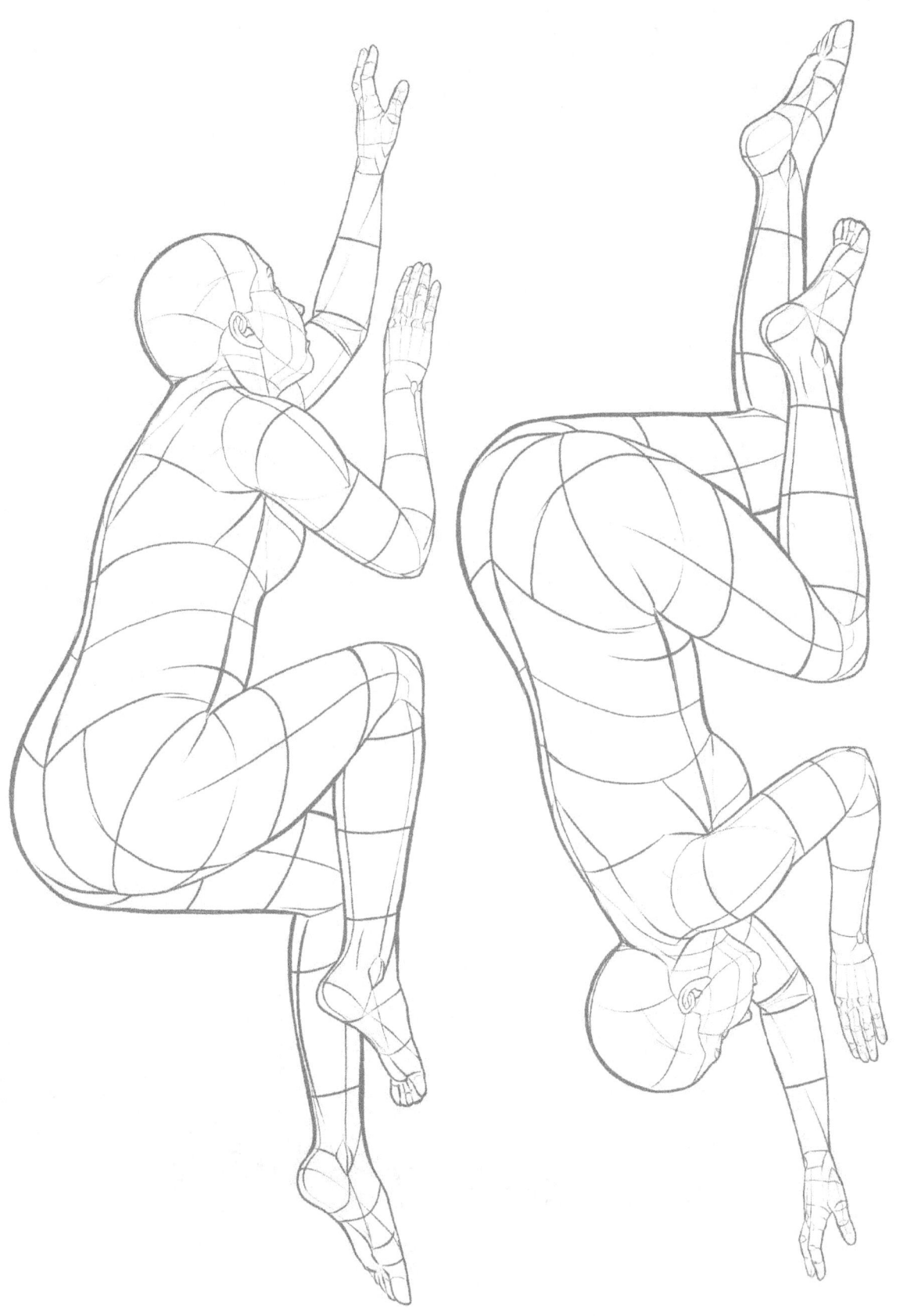

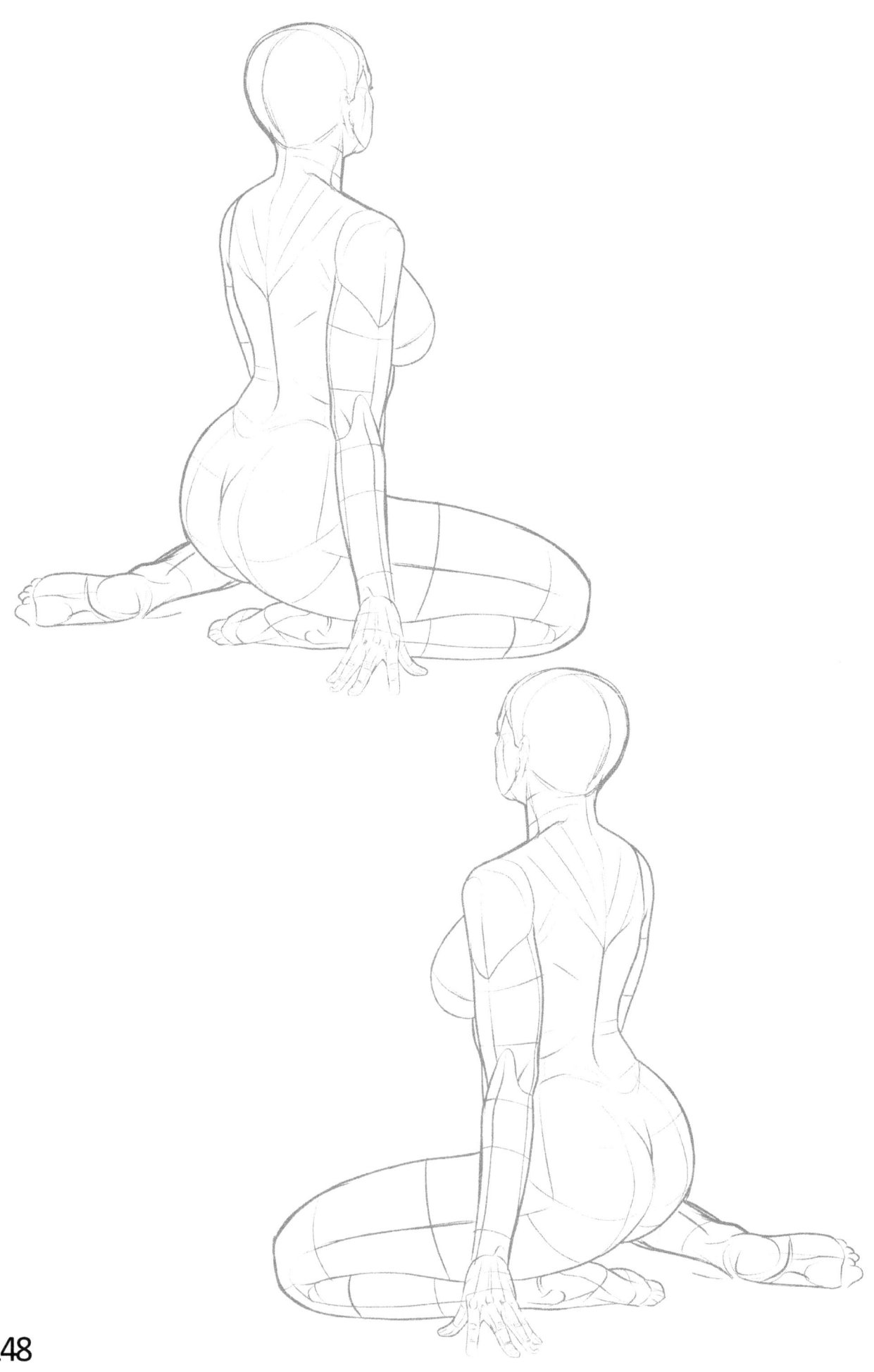

148

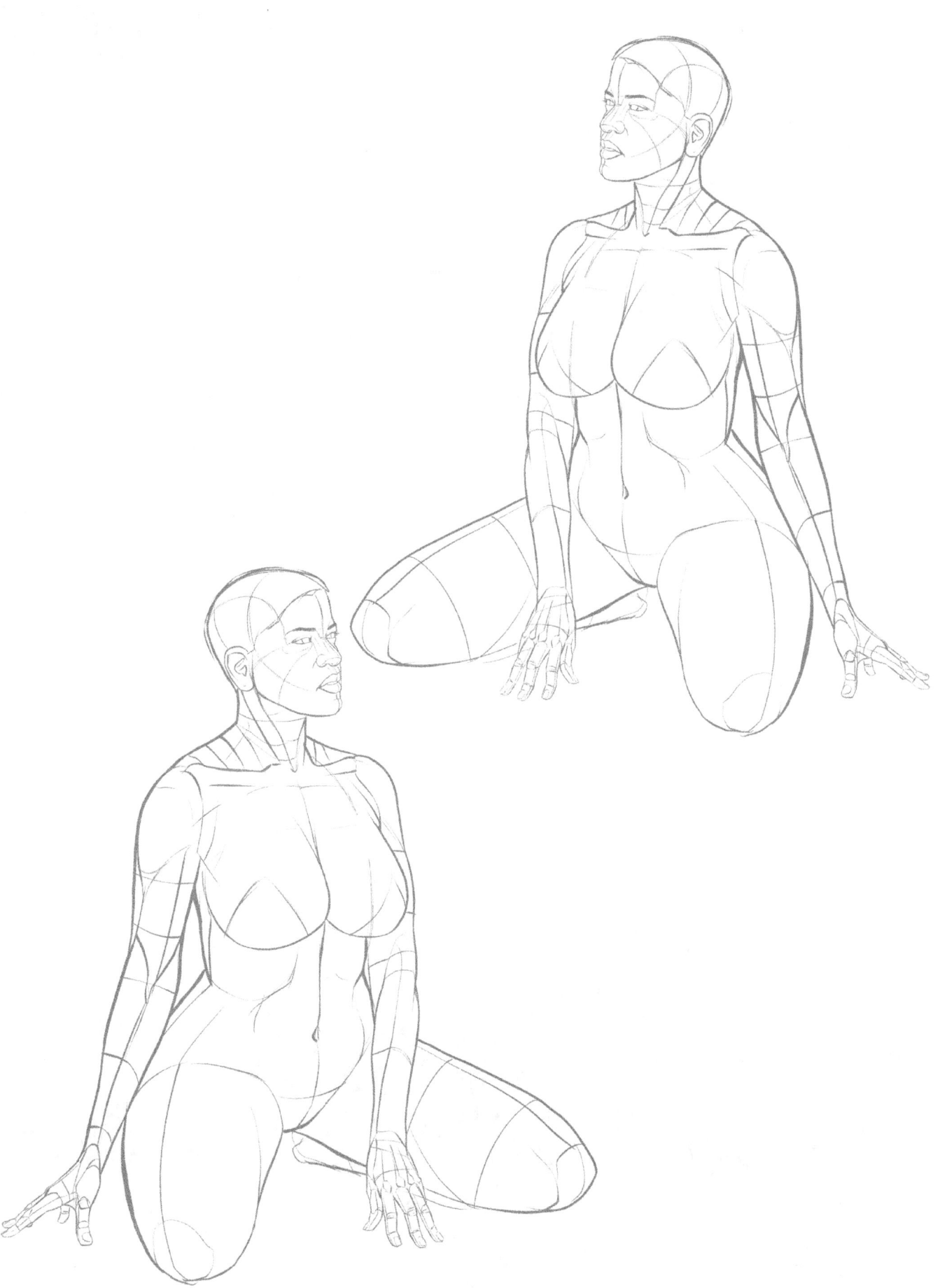

149

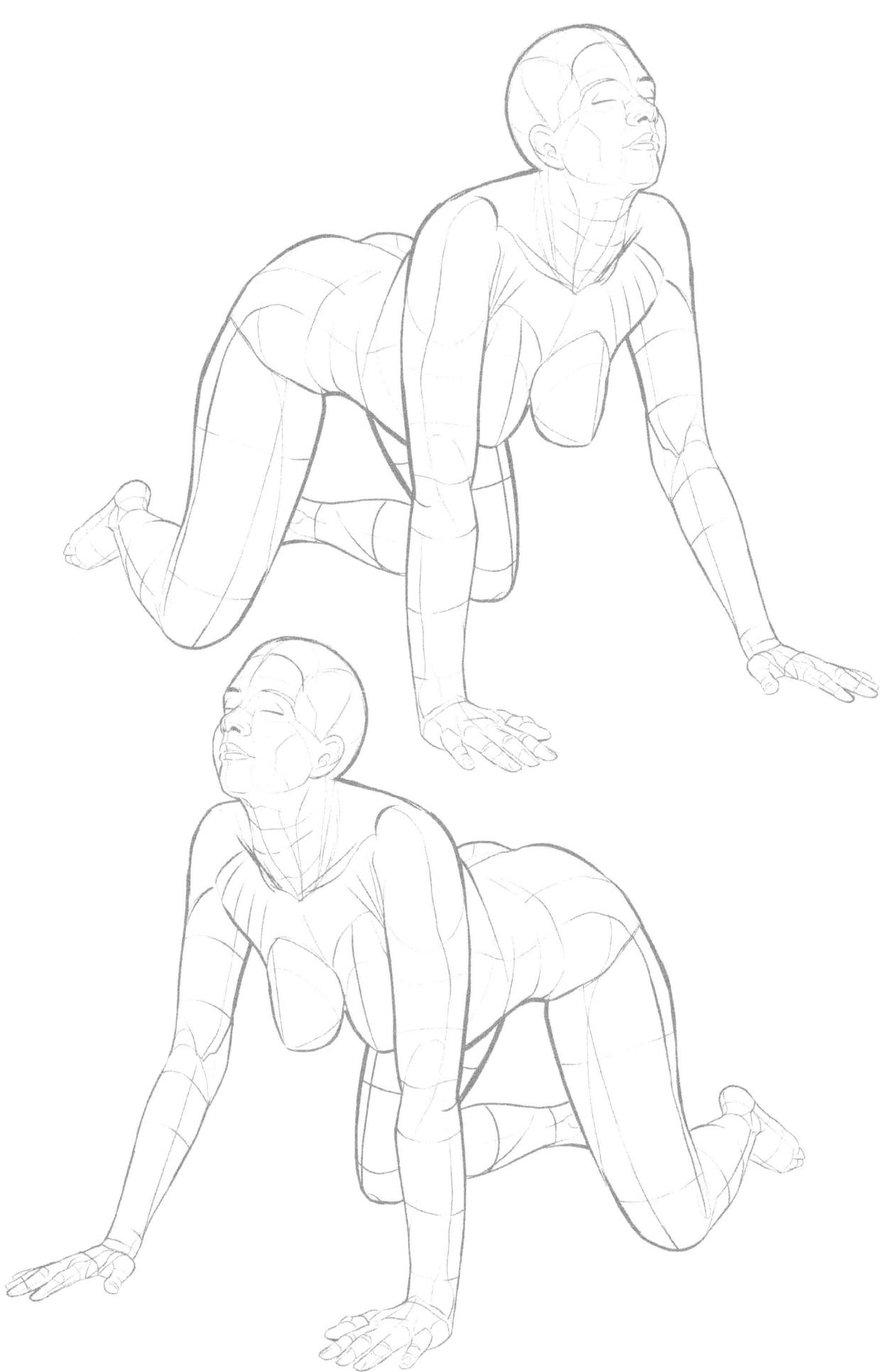

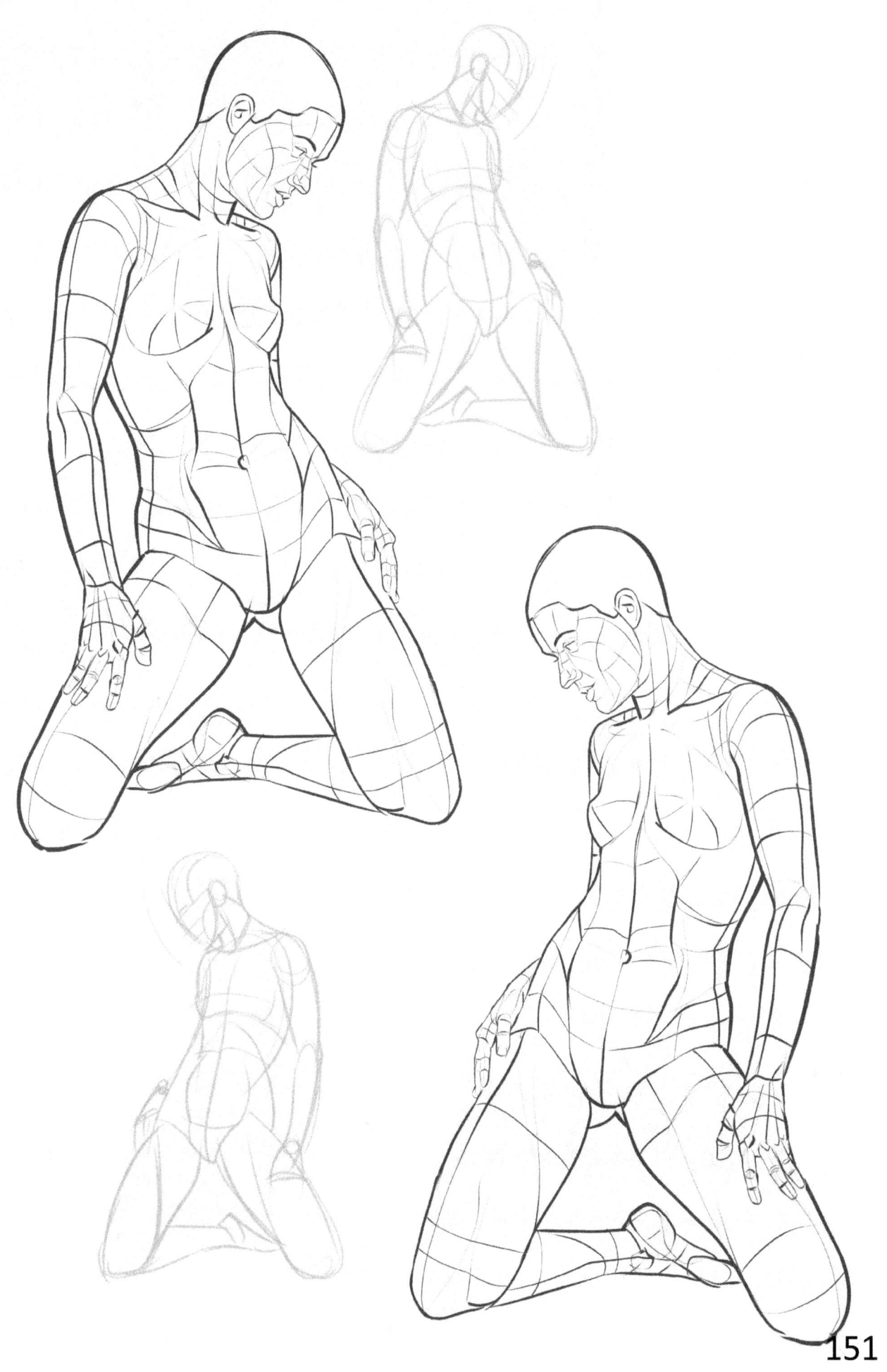

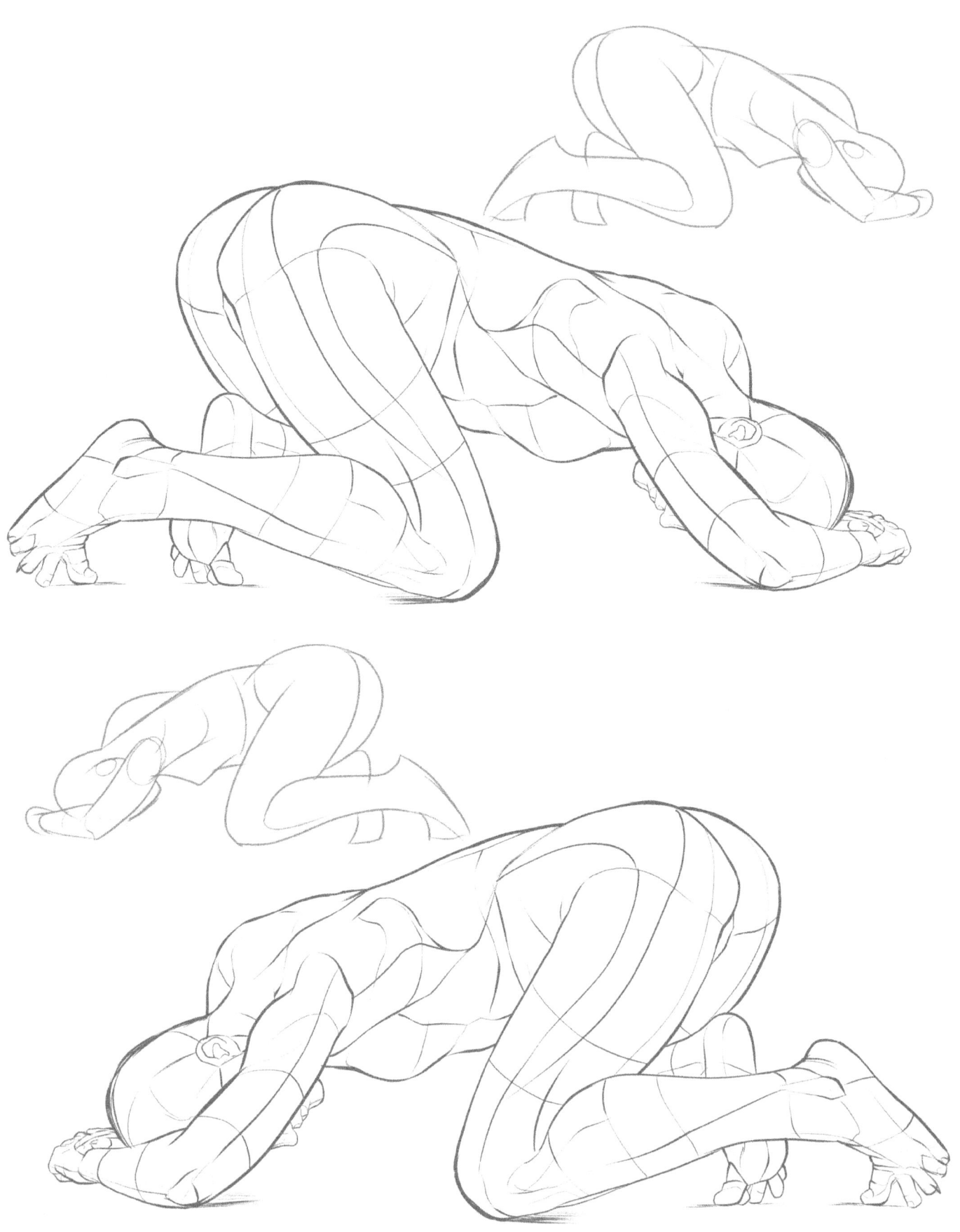

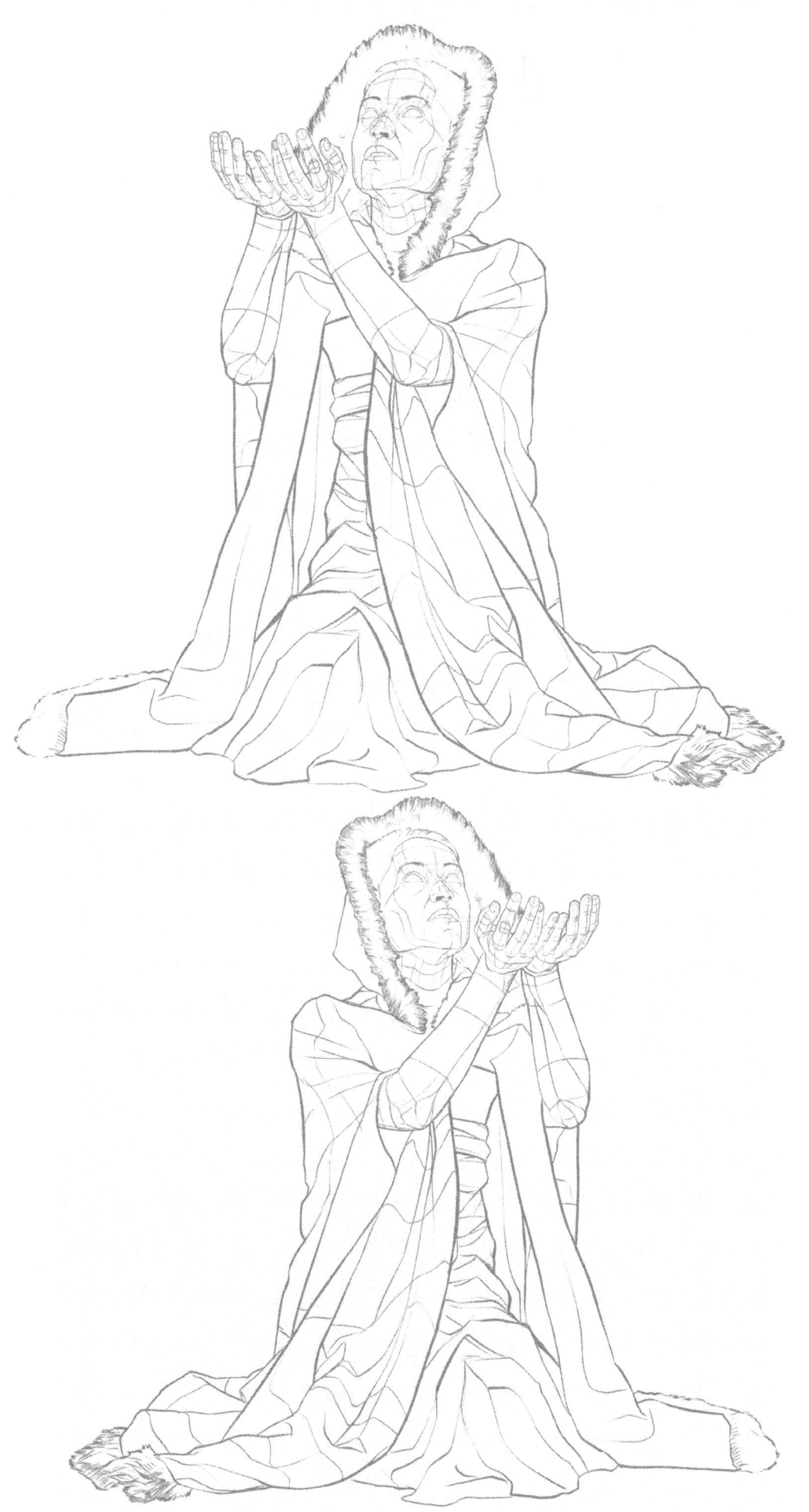

153

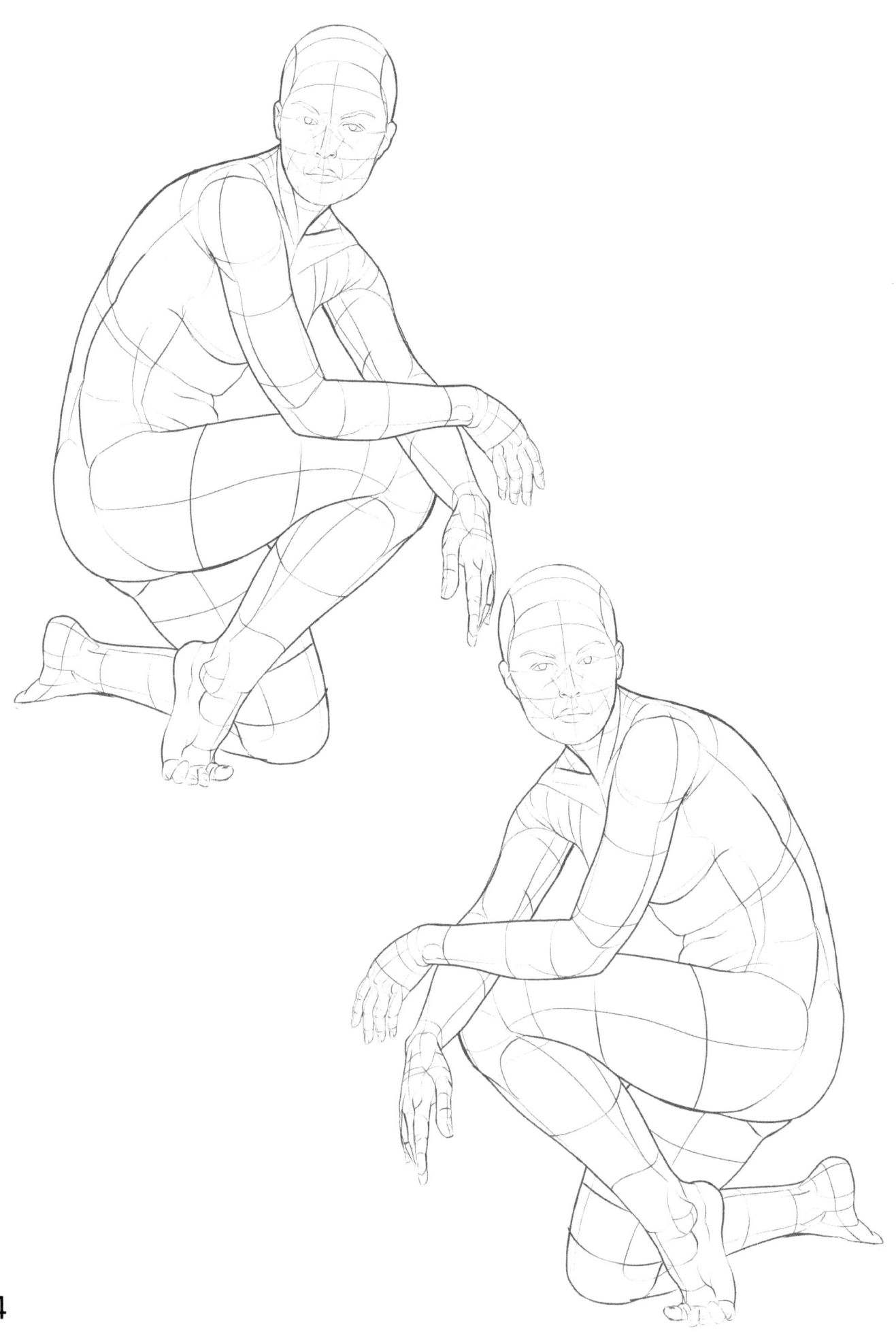

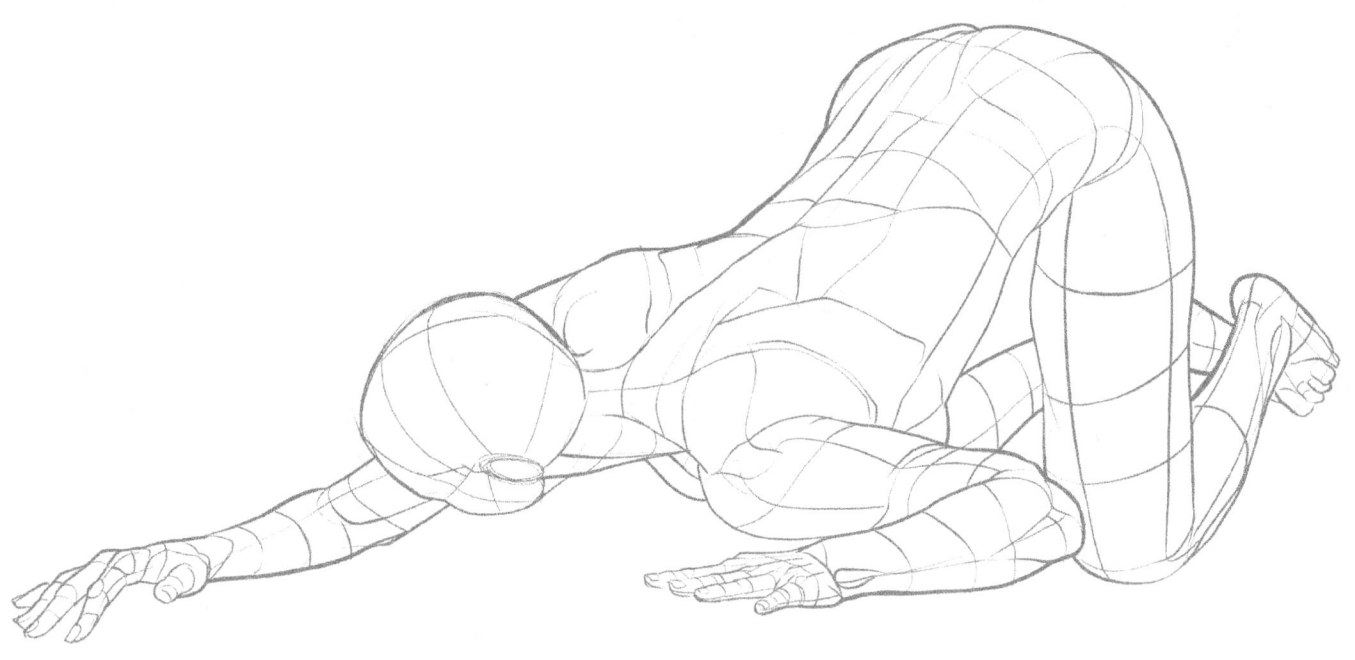

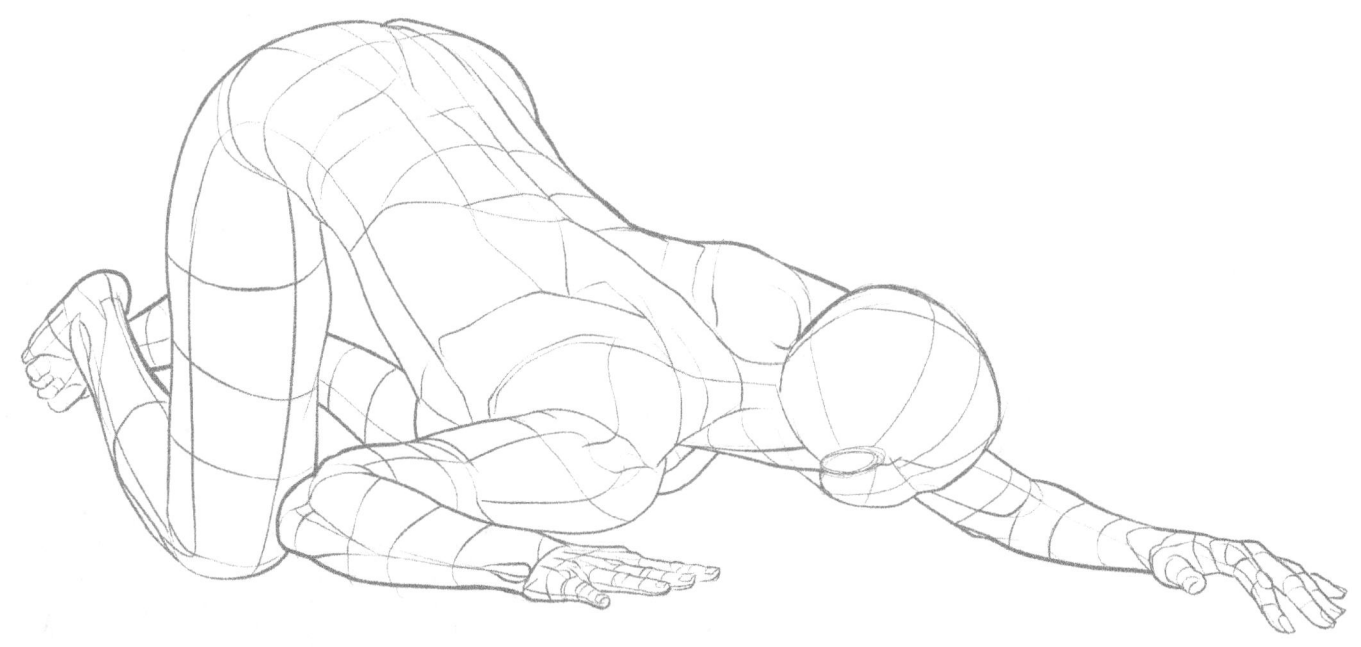

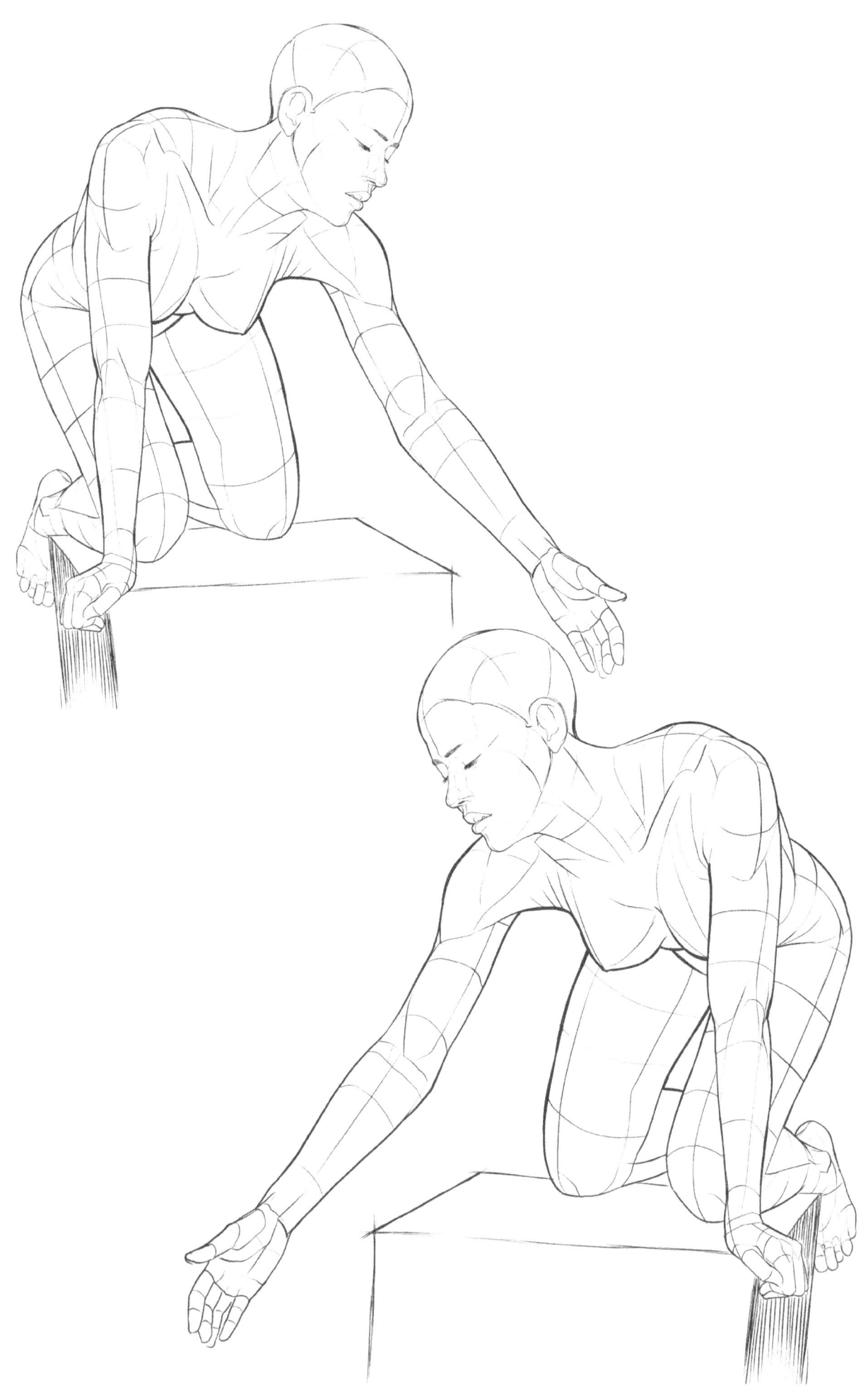

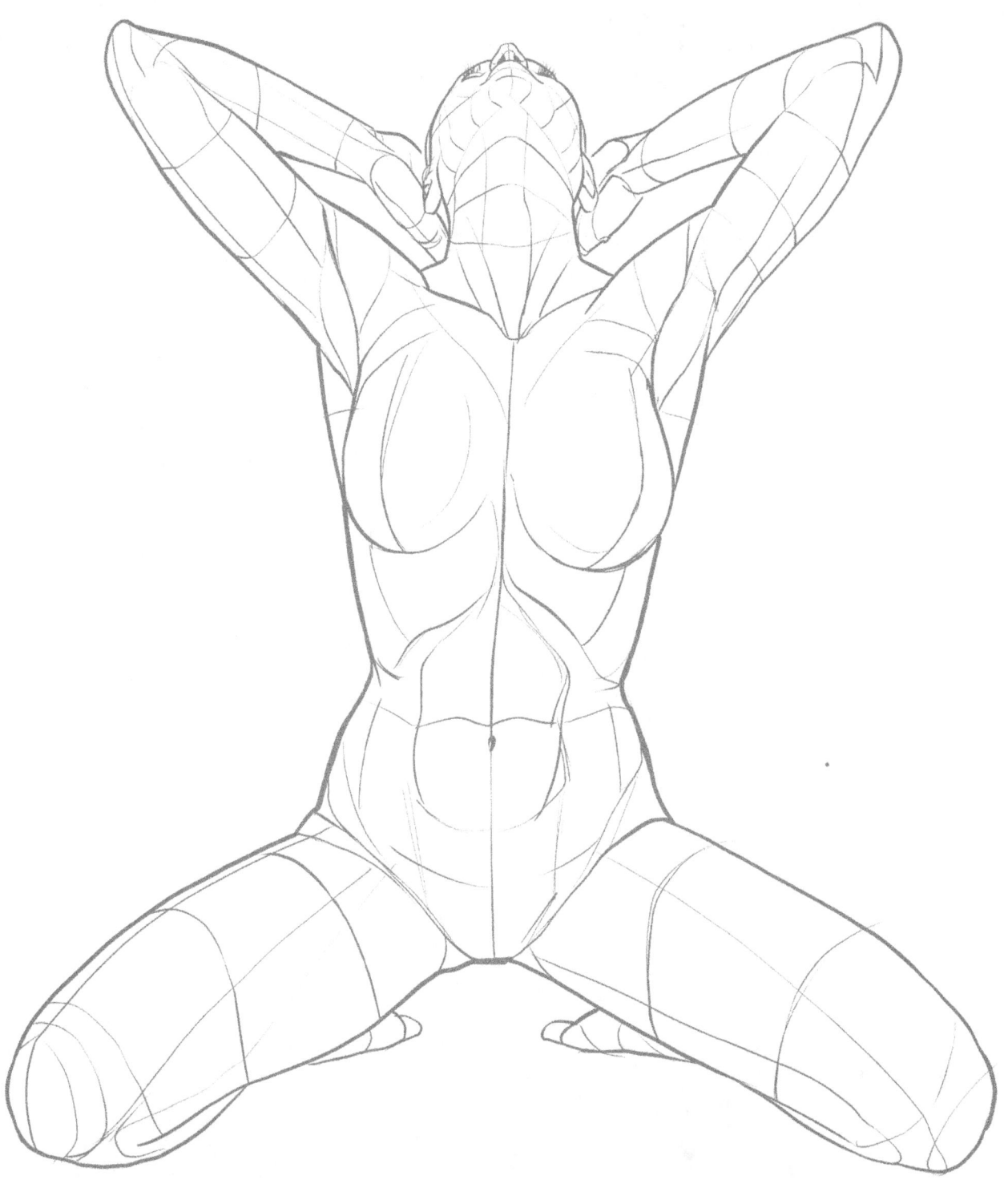

157

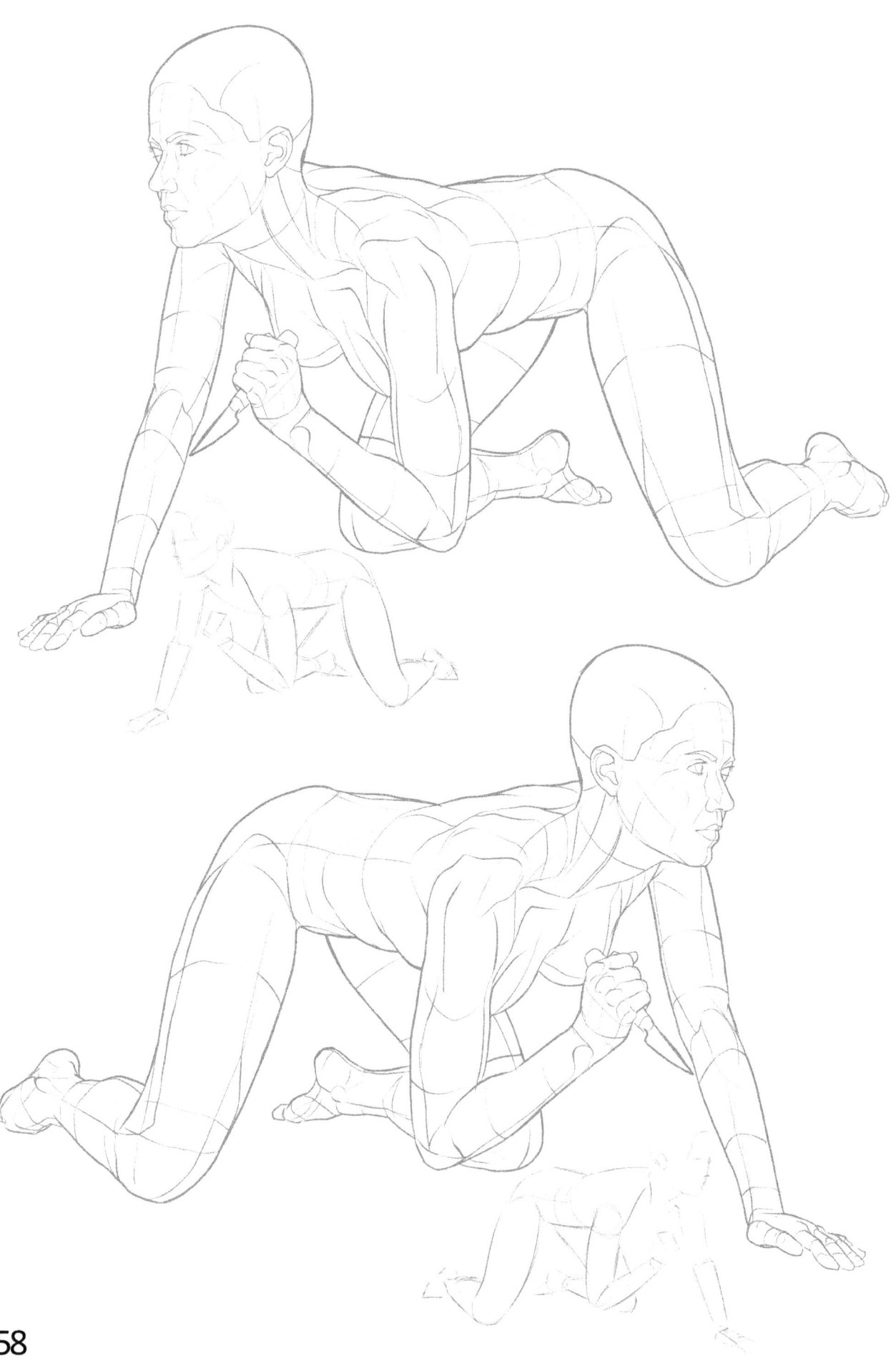

158

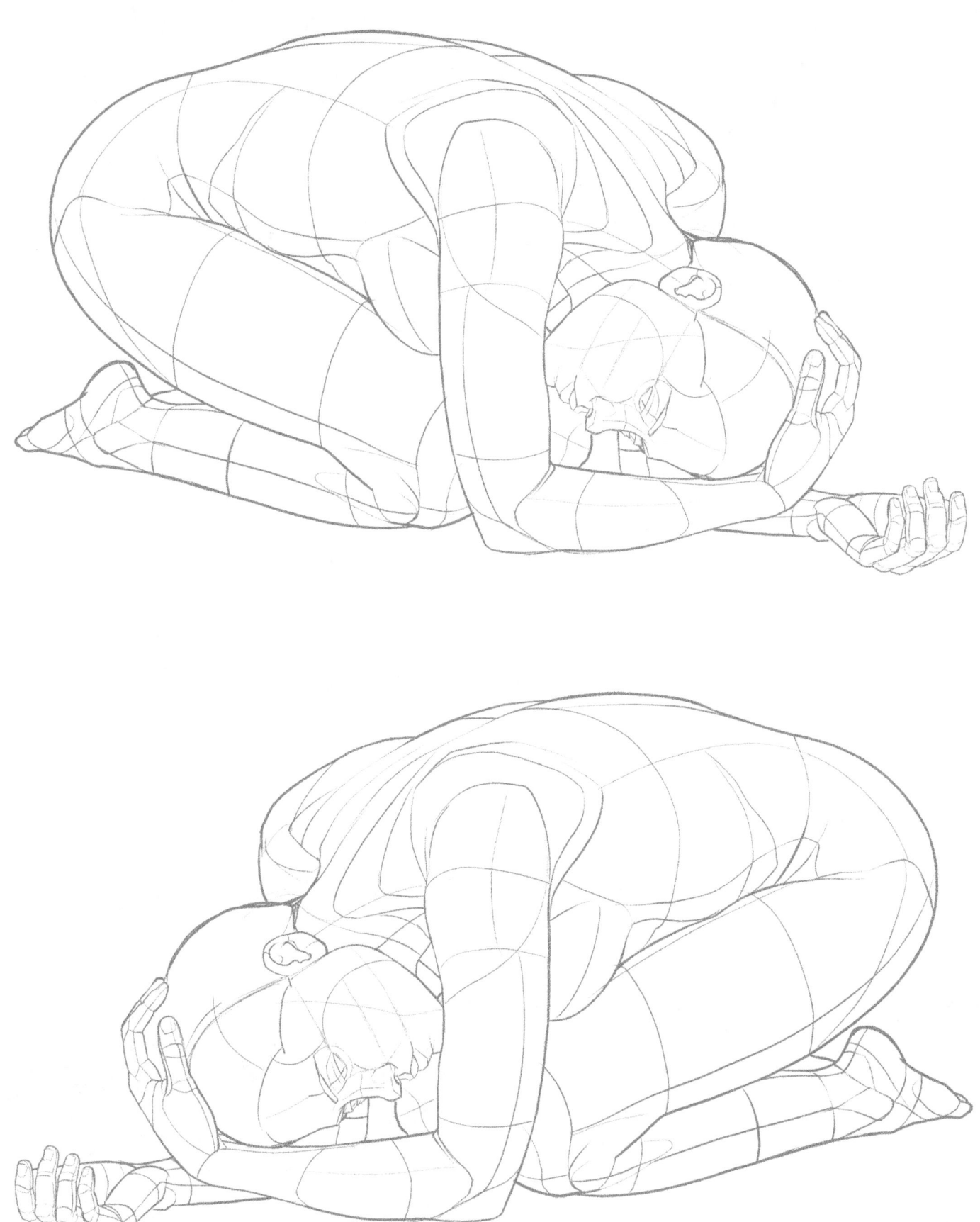

159

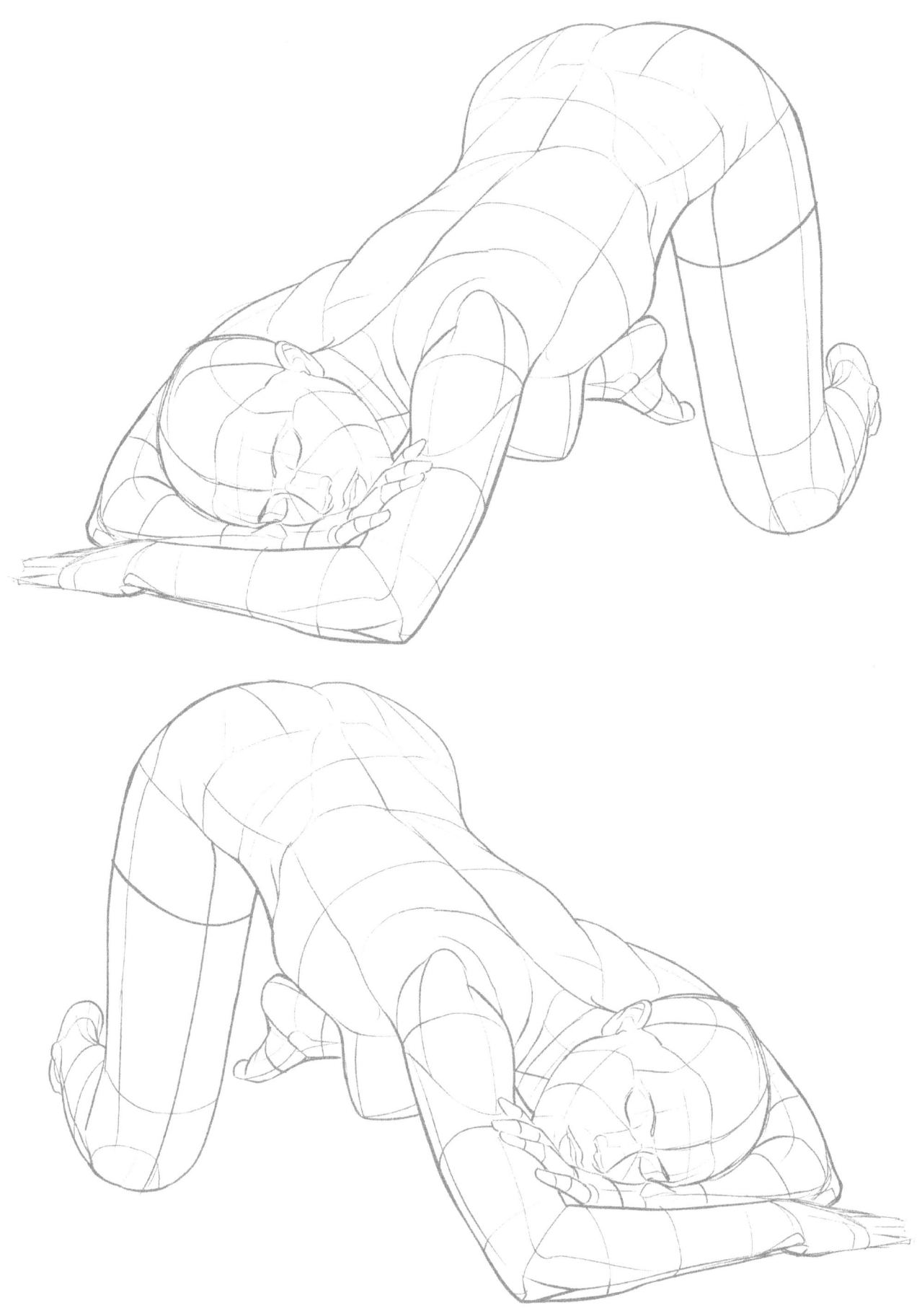

160

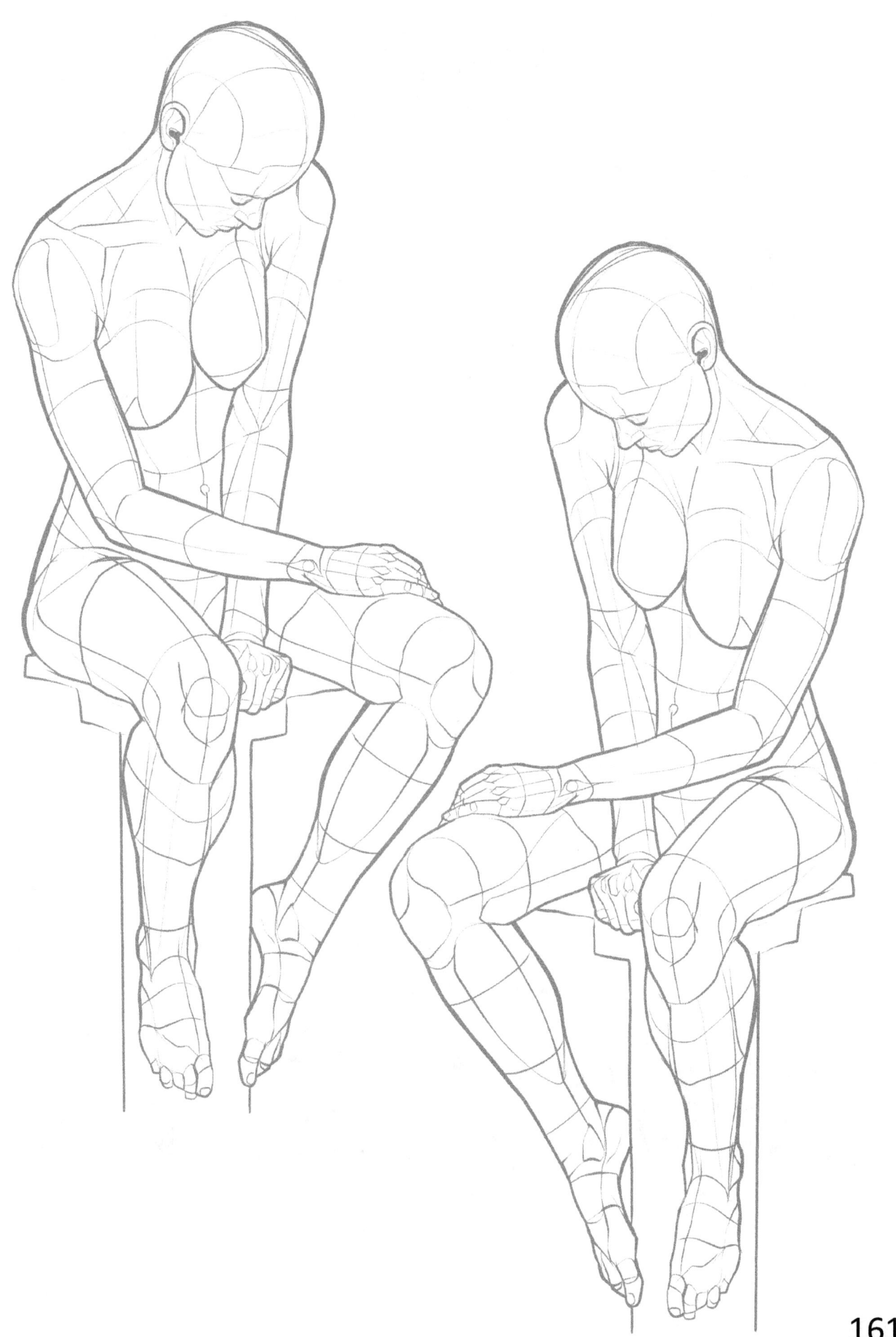

161

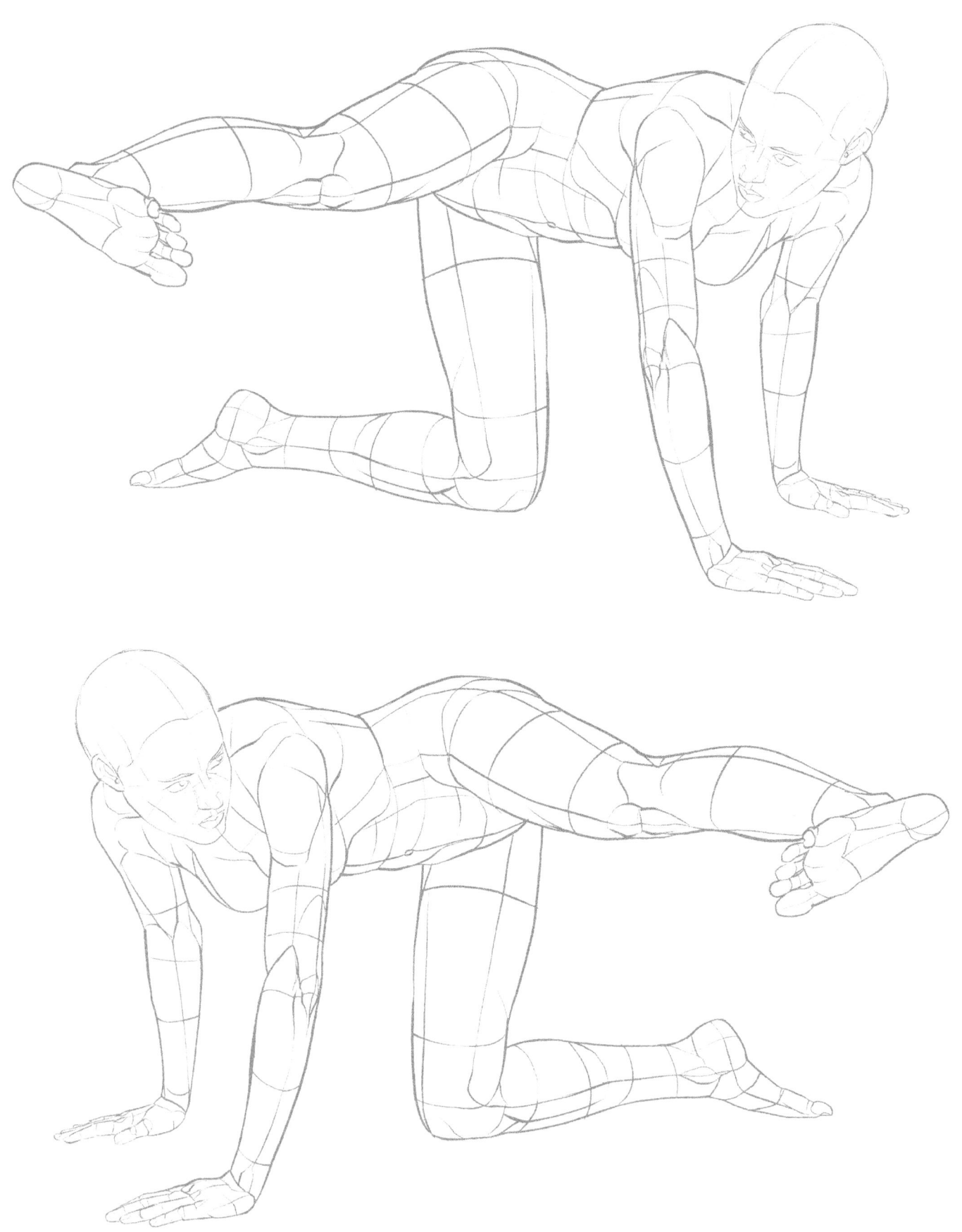

162

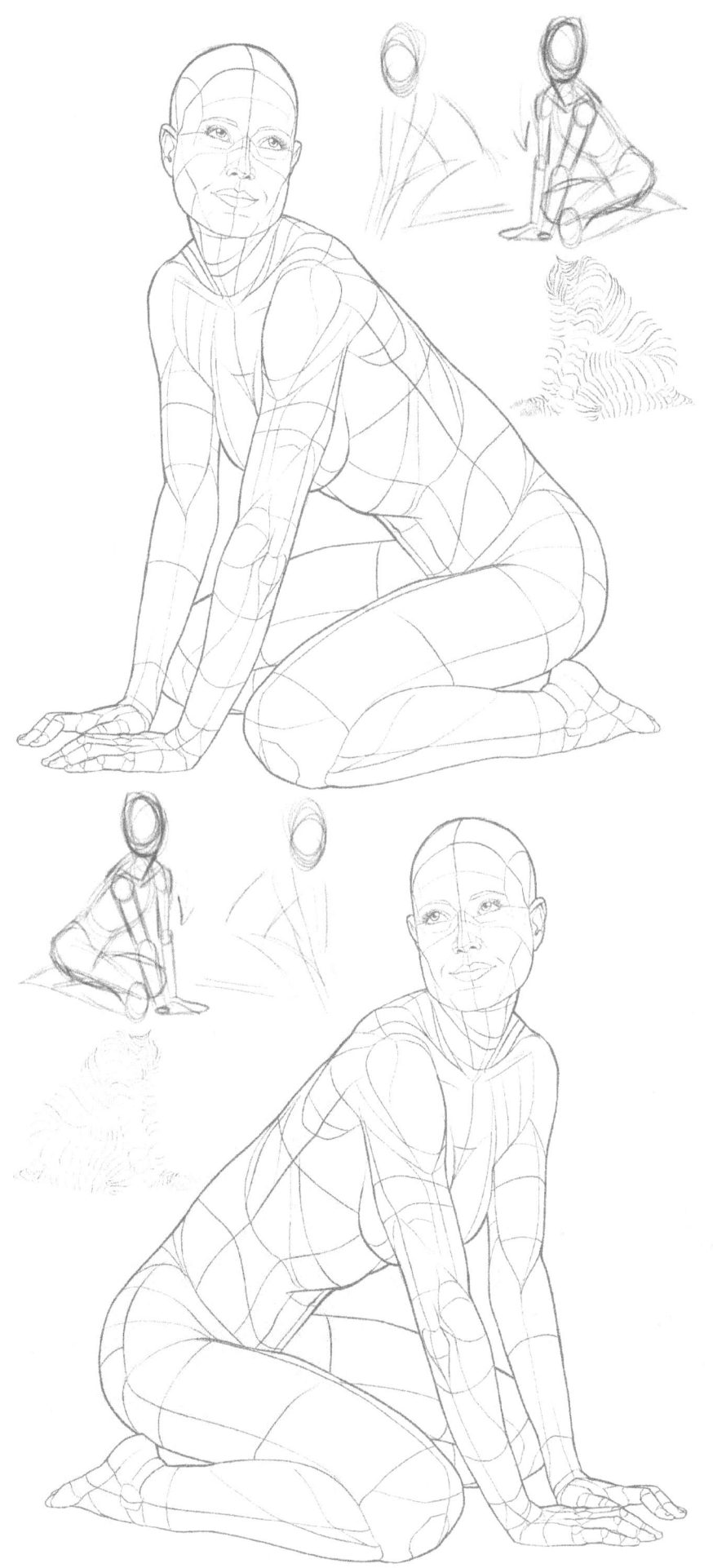

163

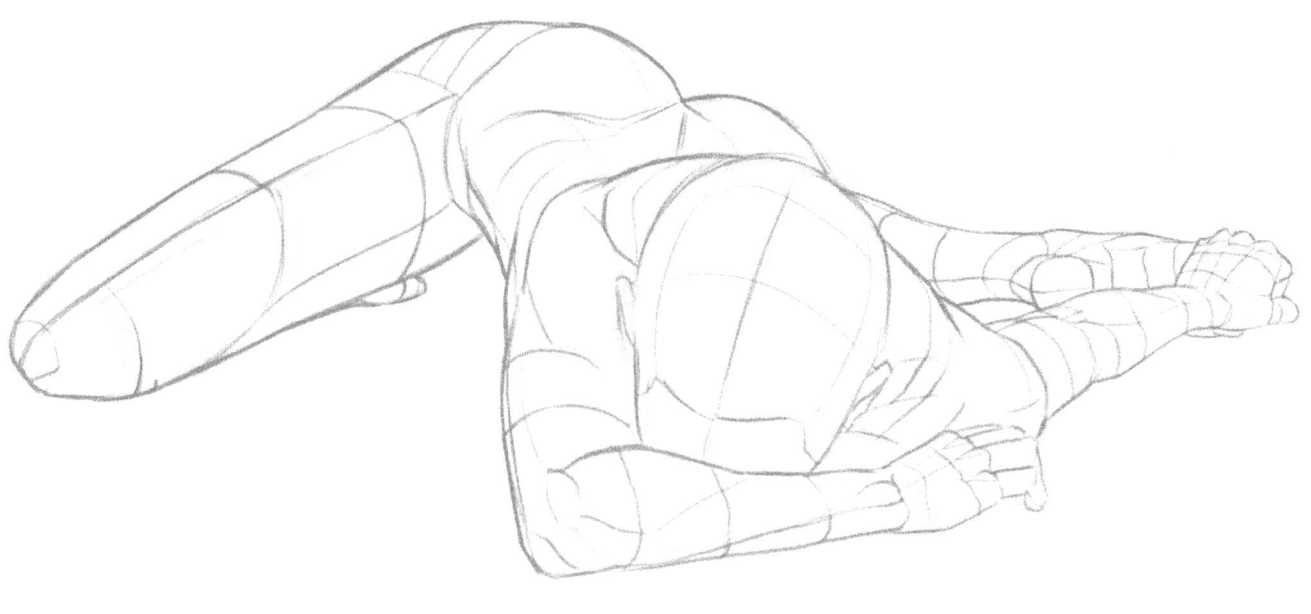

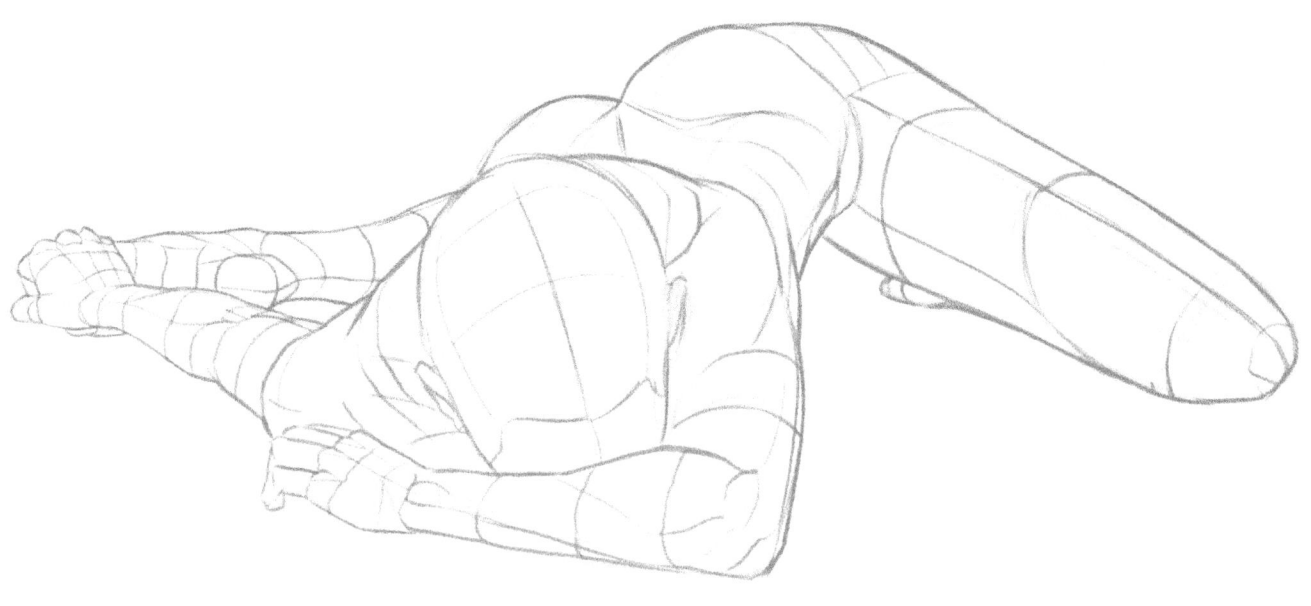

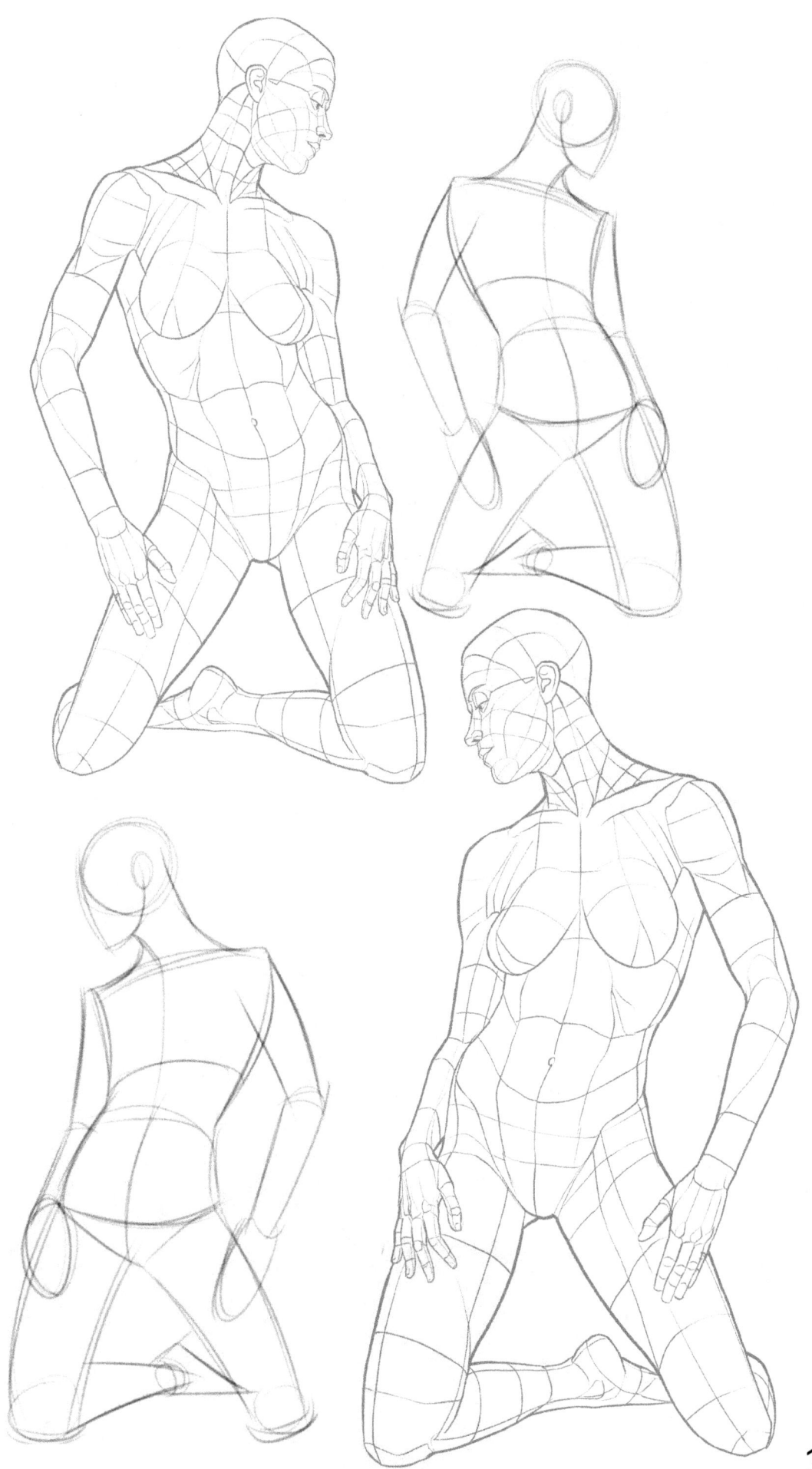

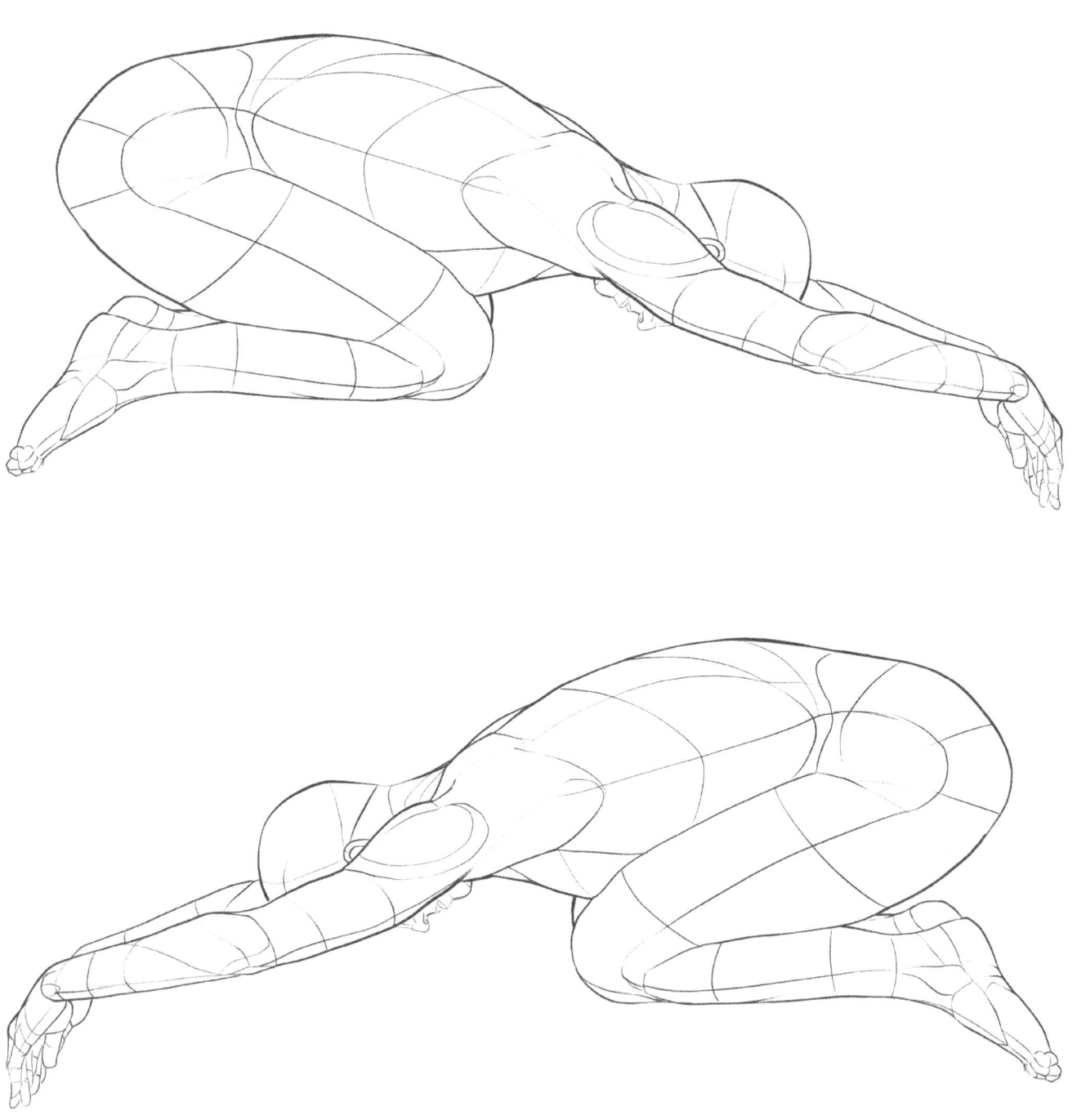

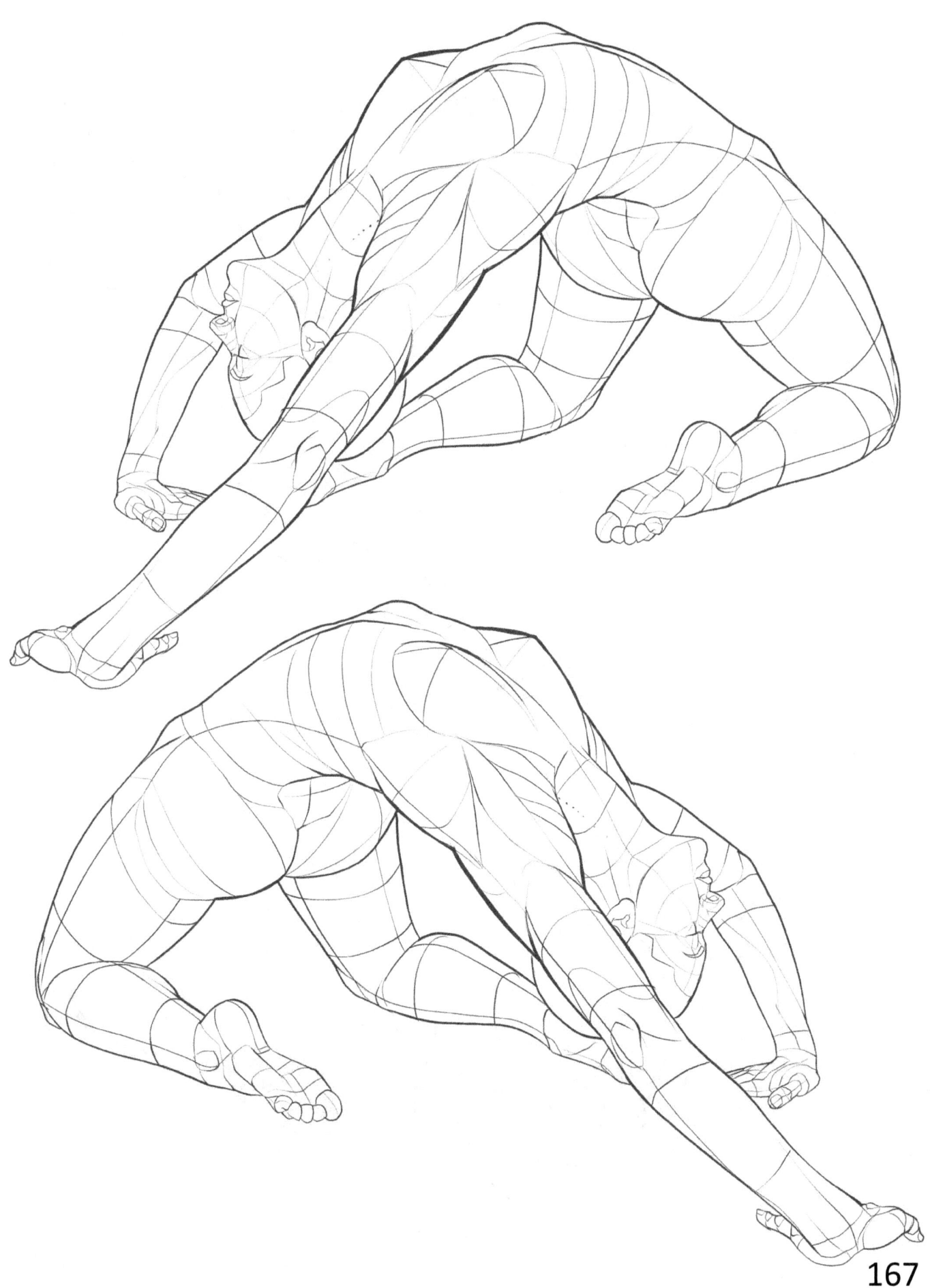

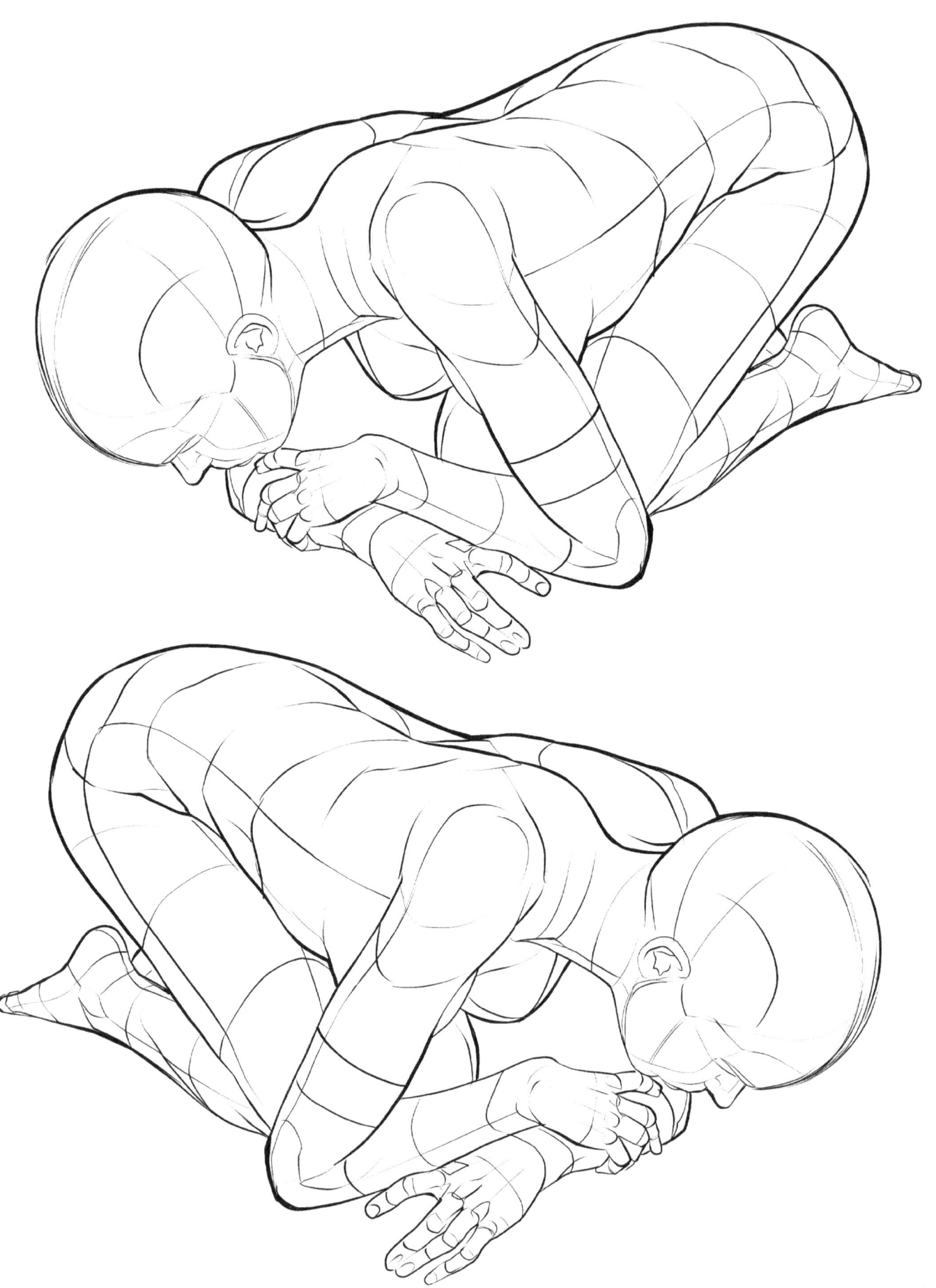

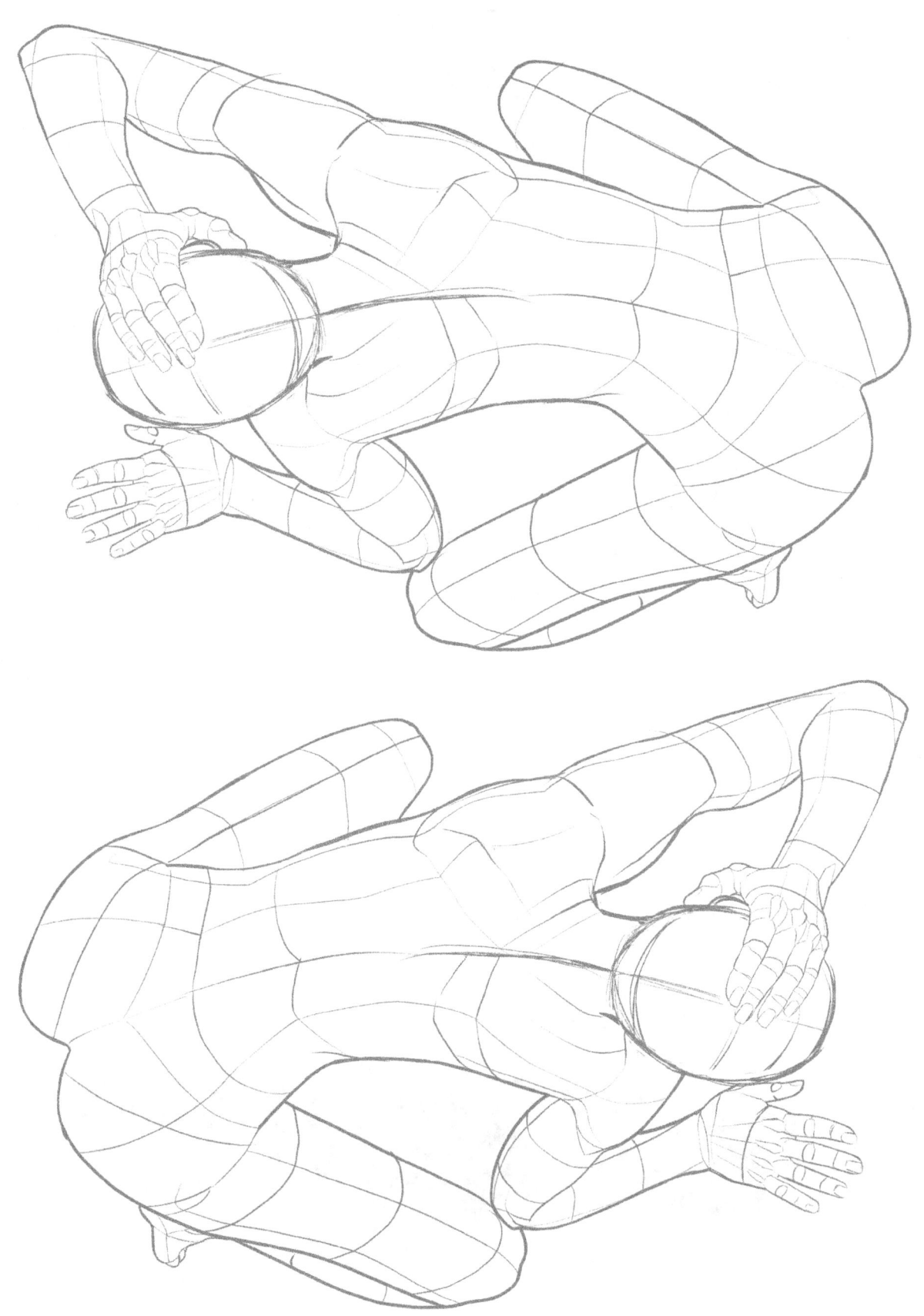

169

Flying Poses

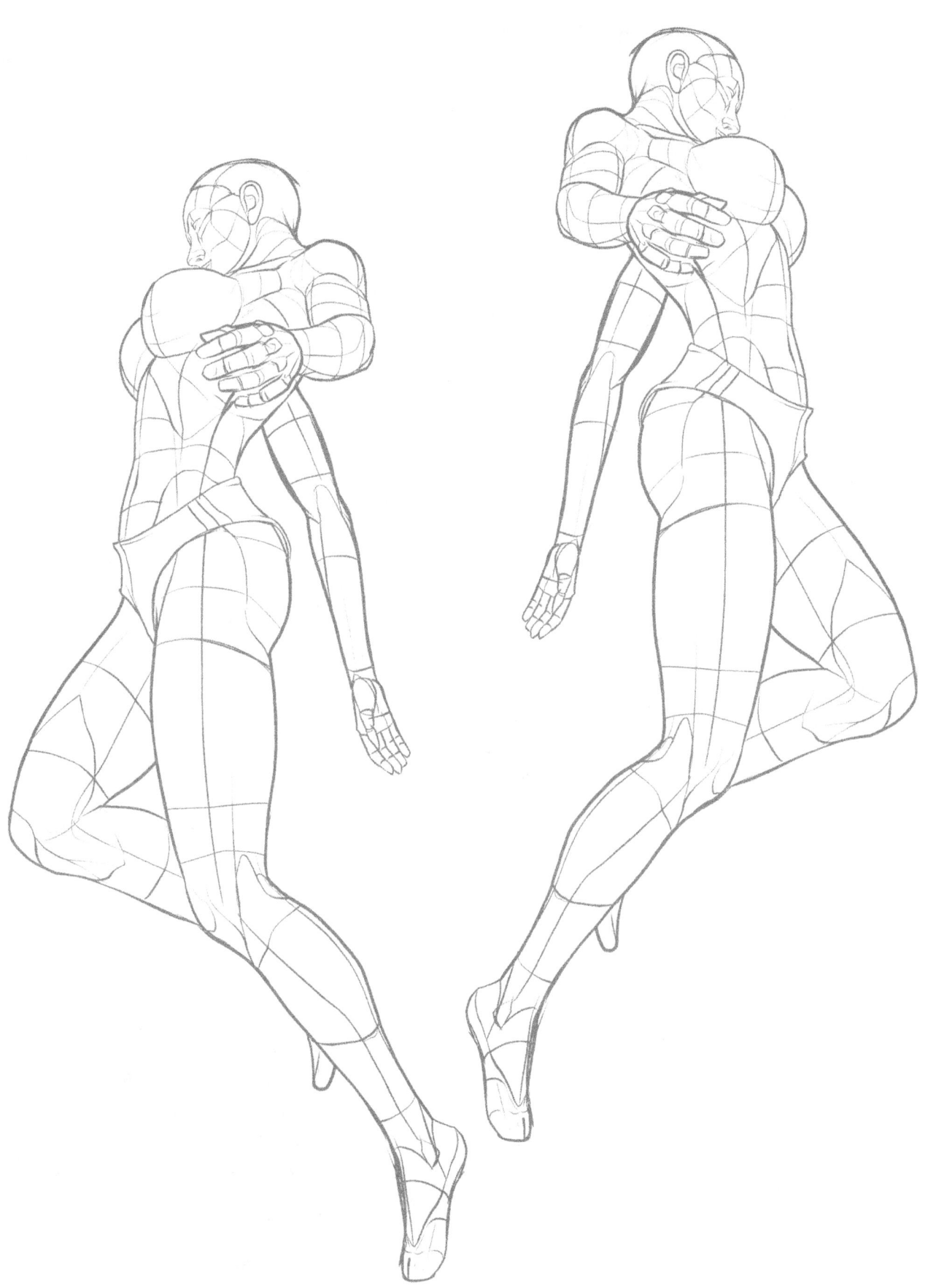

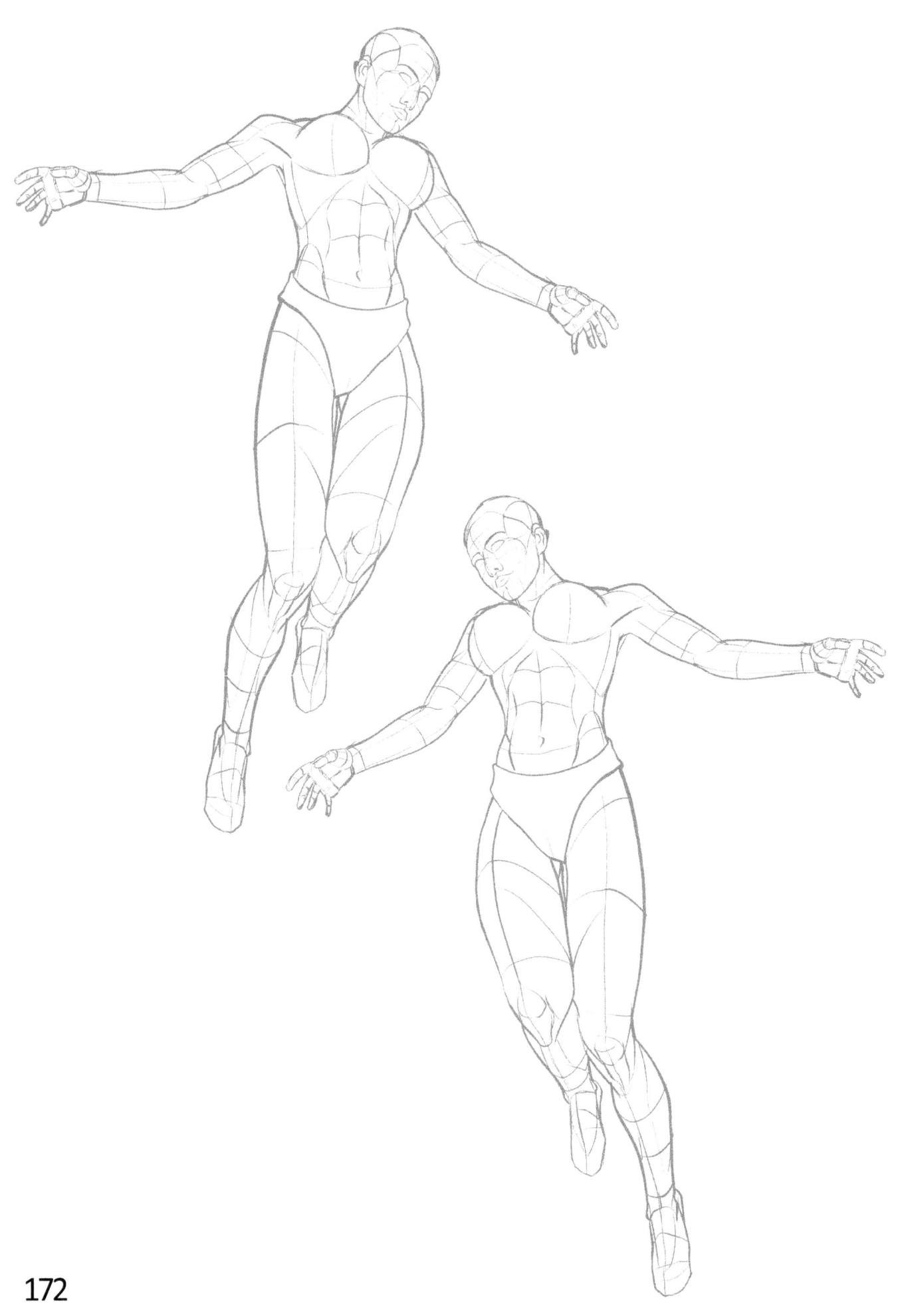

172

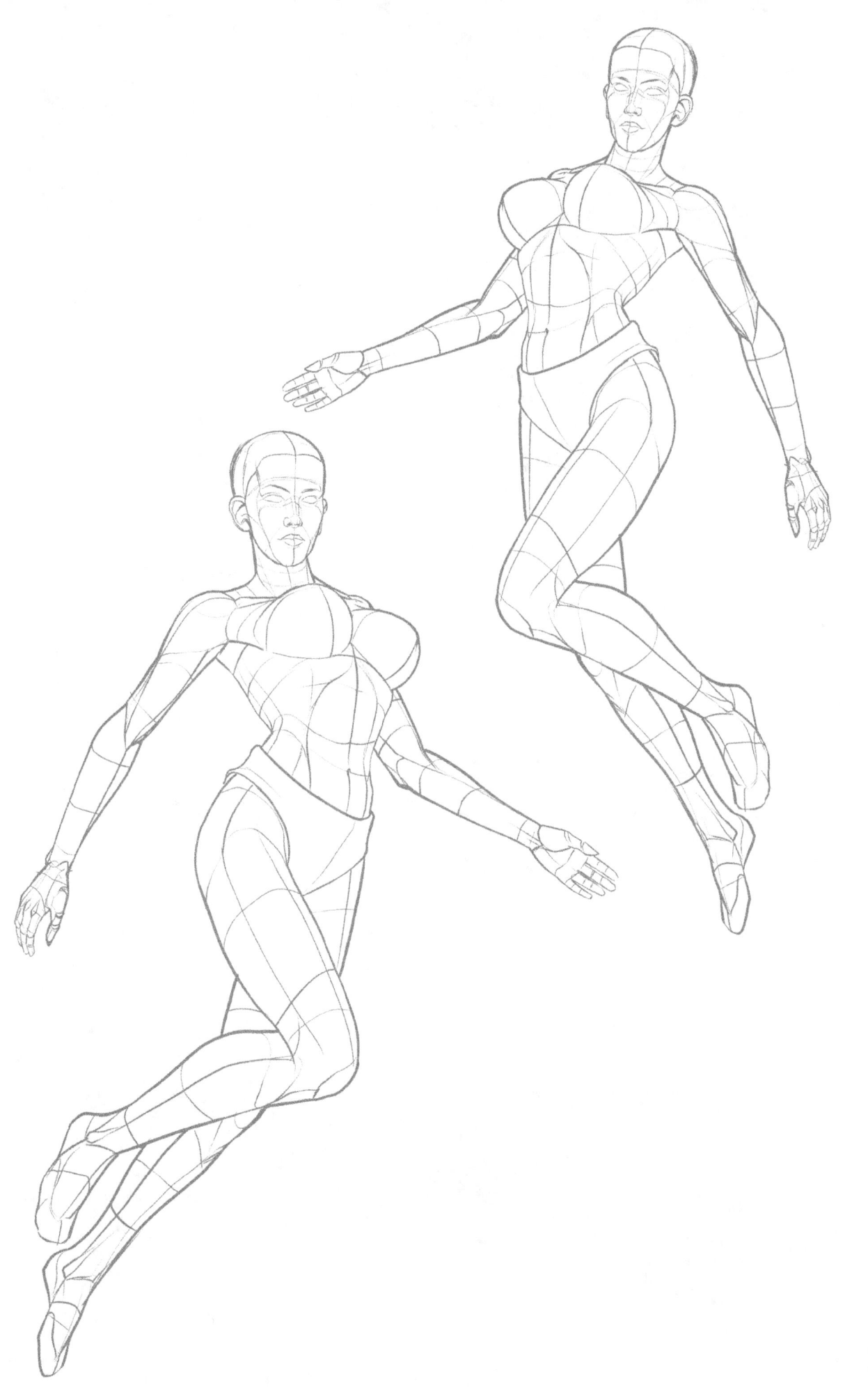

173

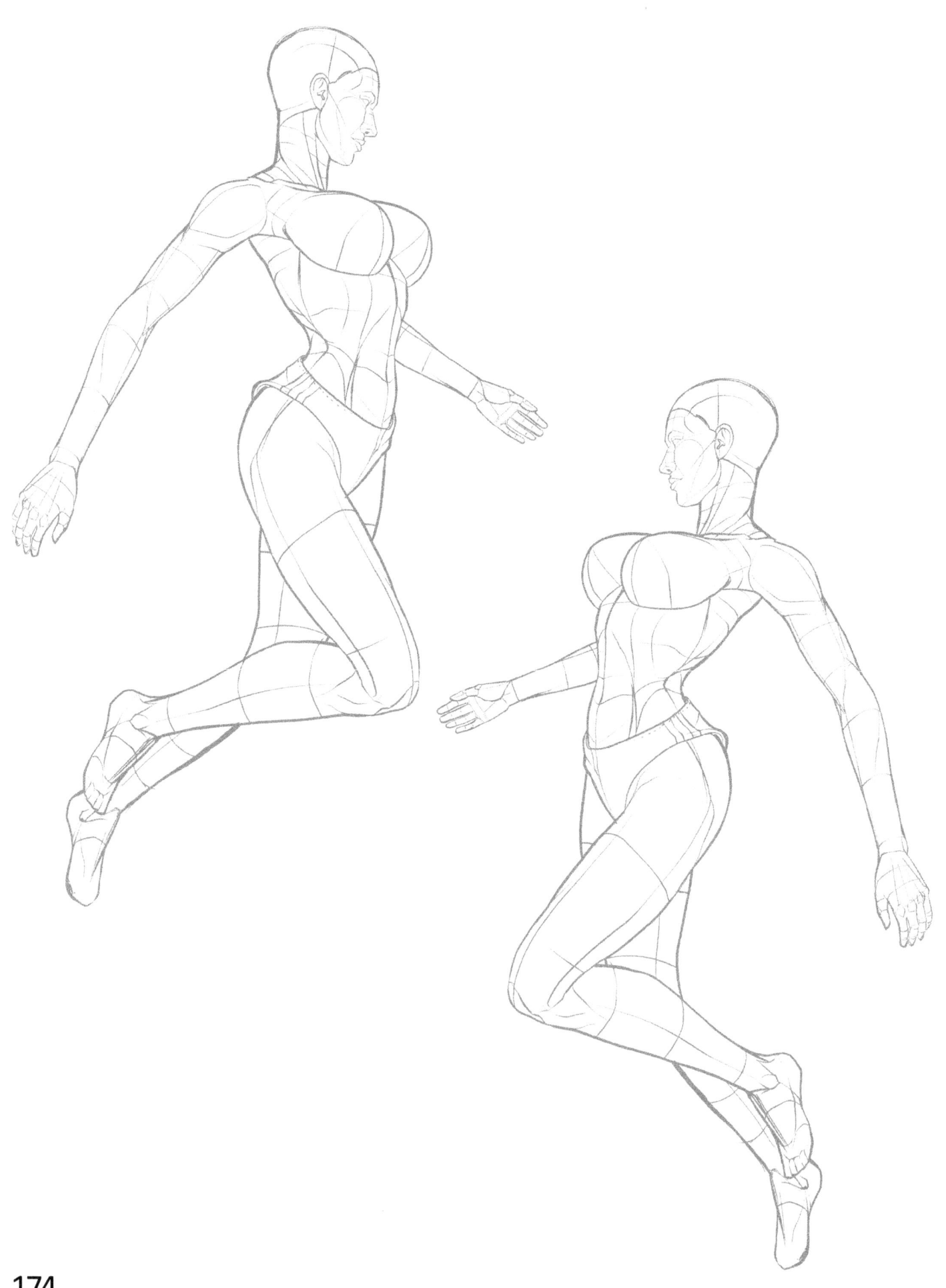

174

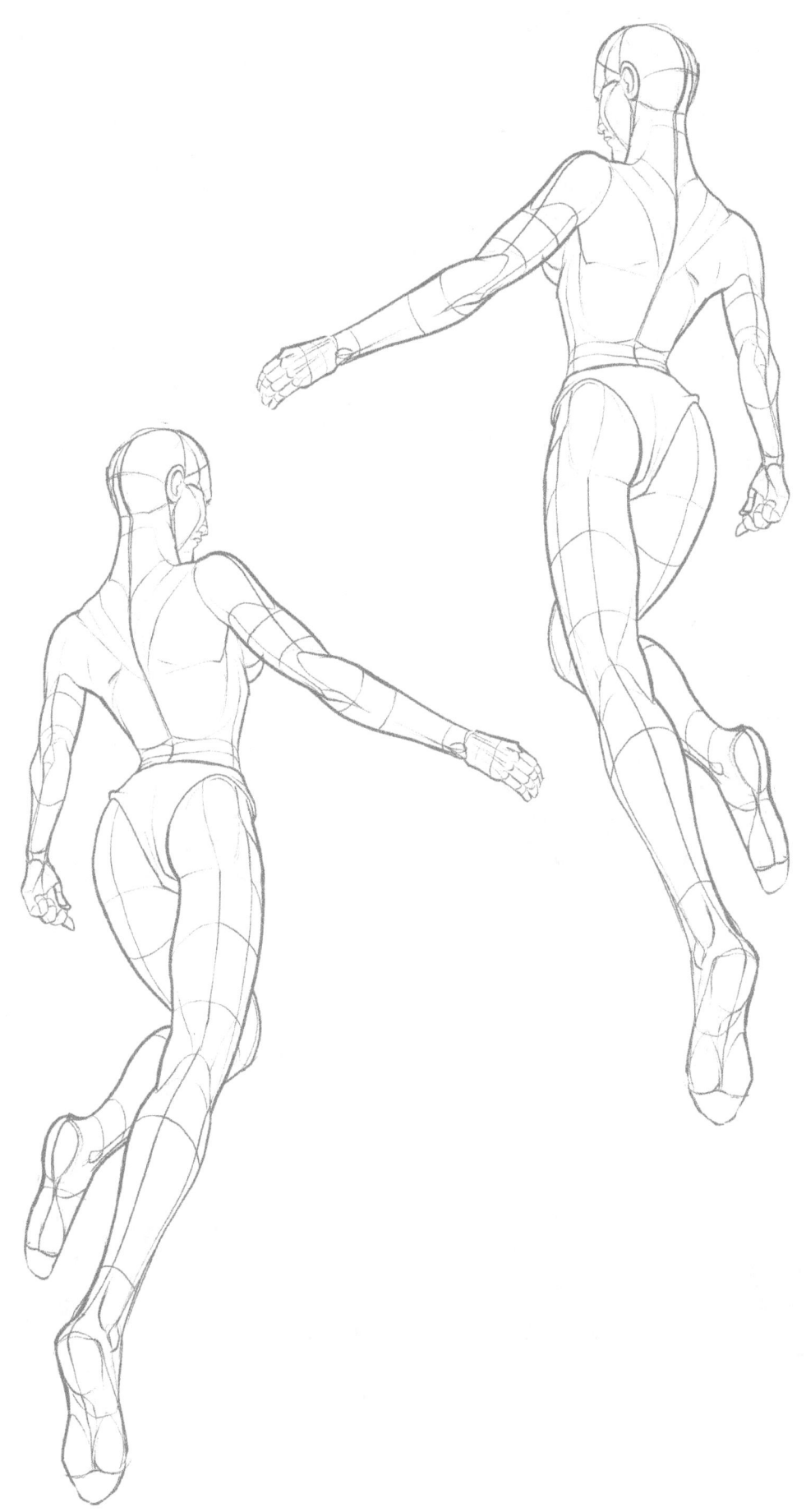

175

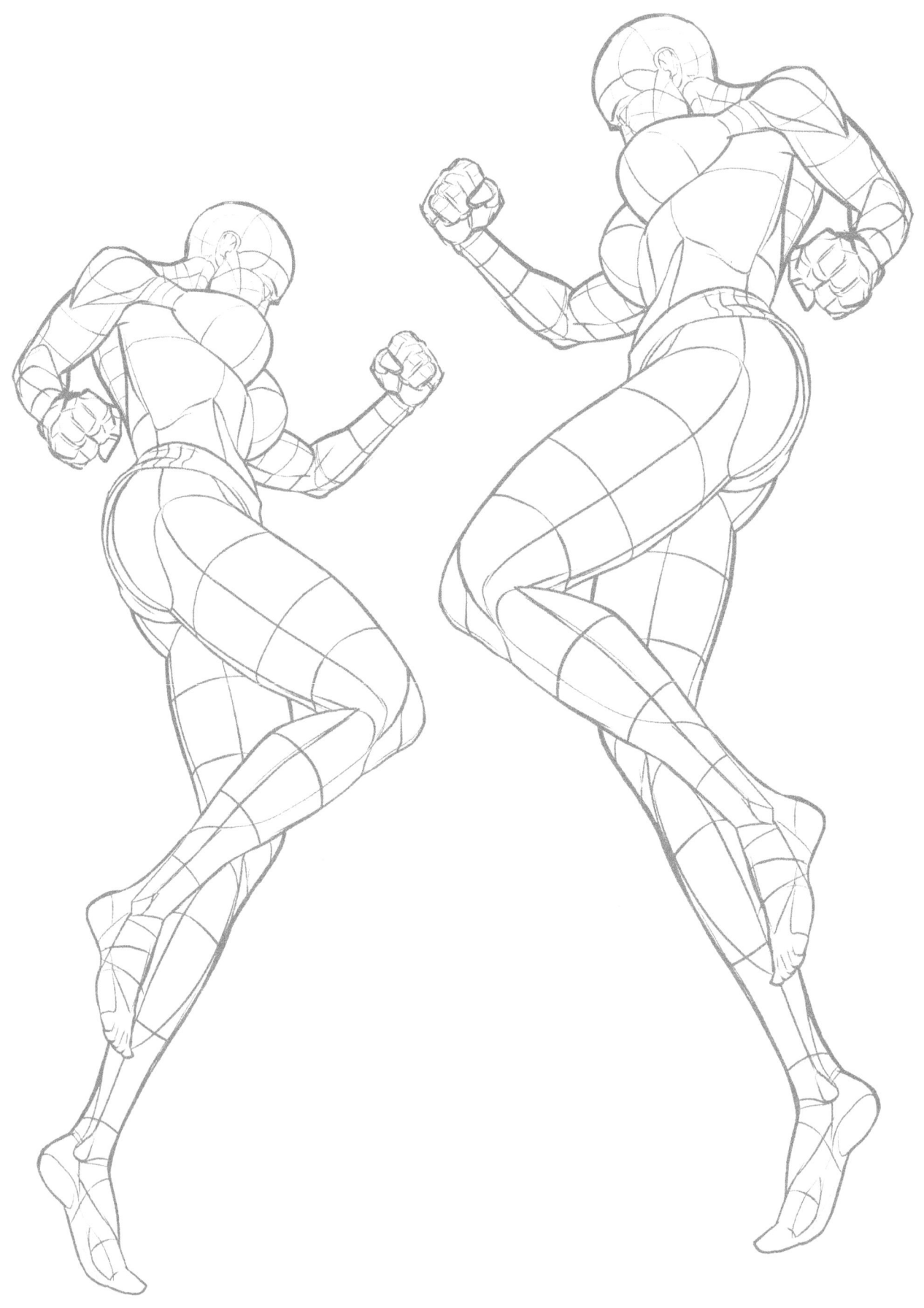

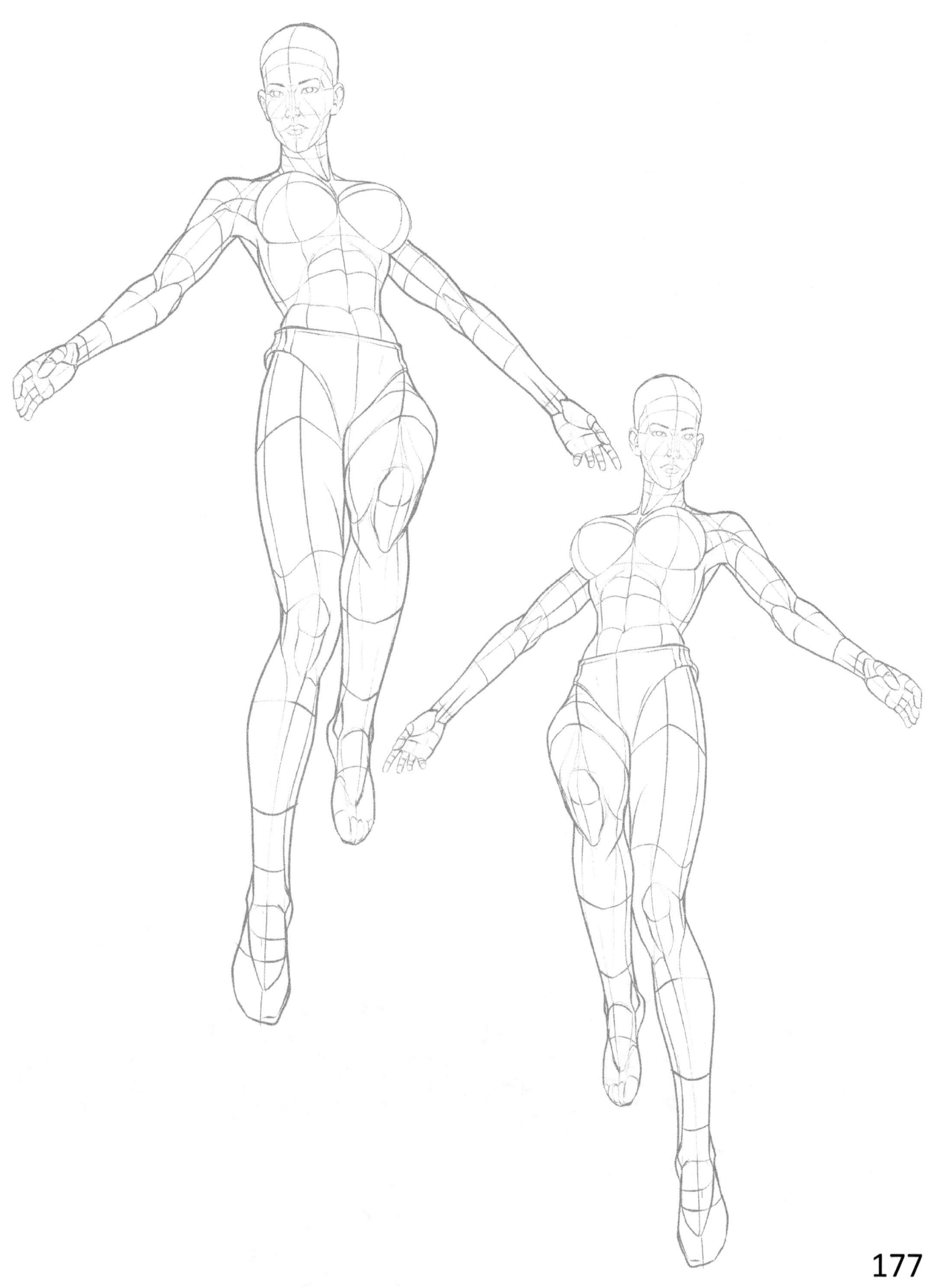

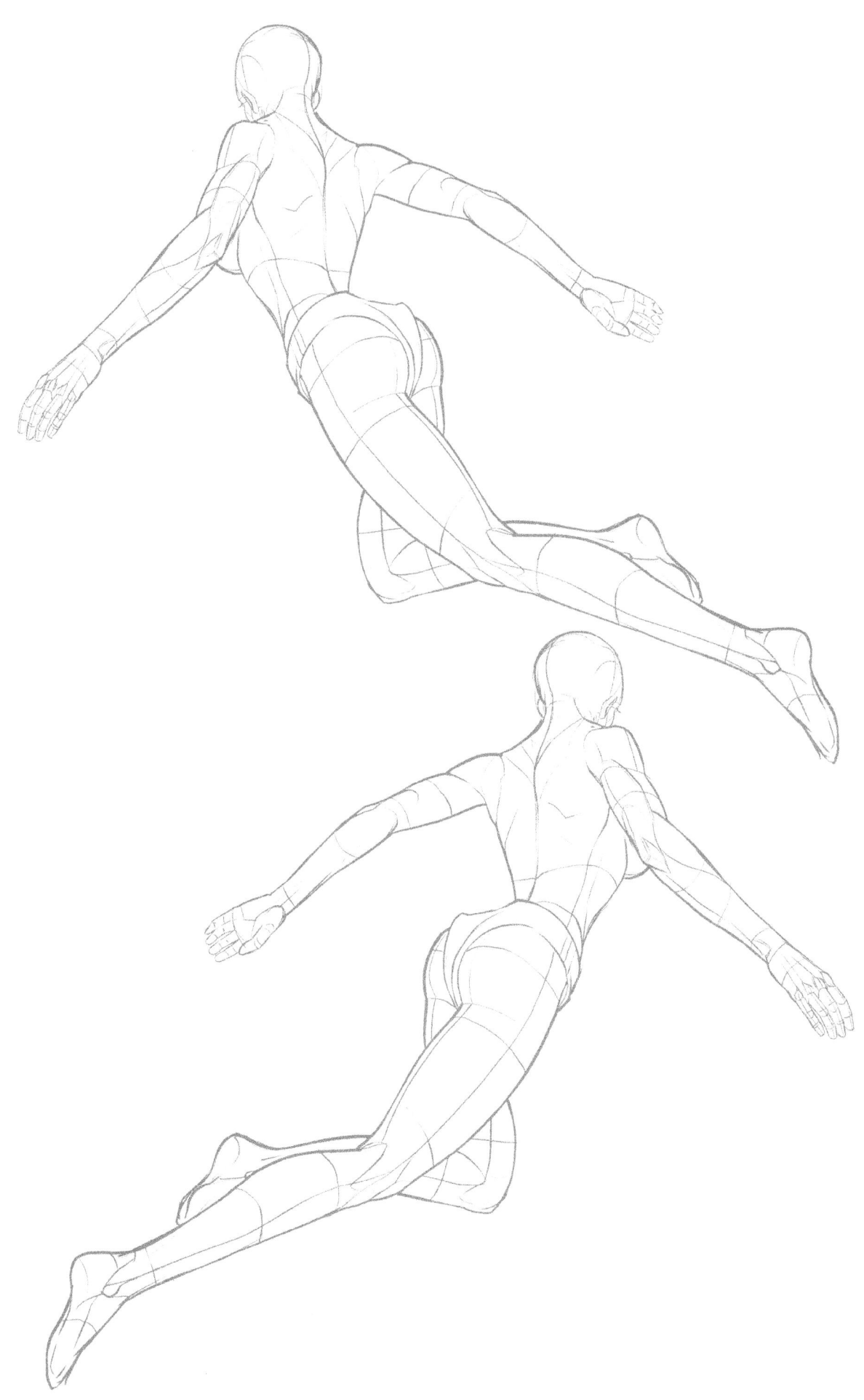

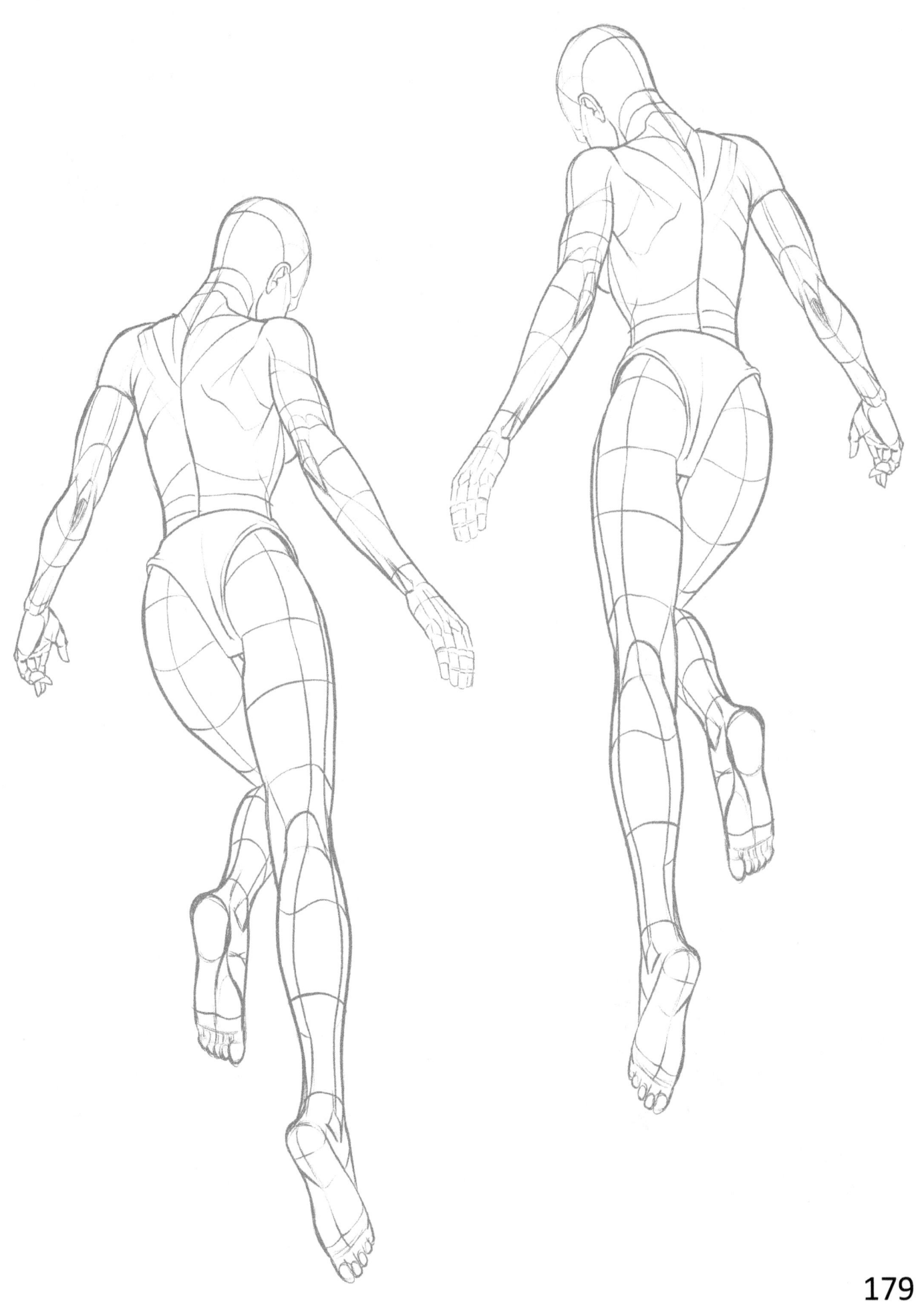

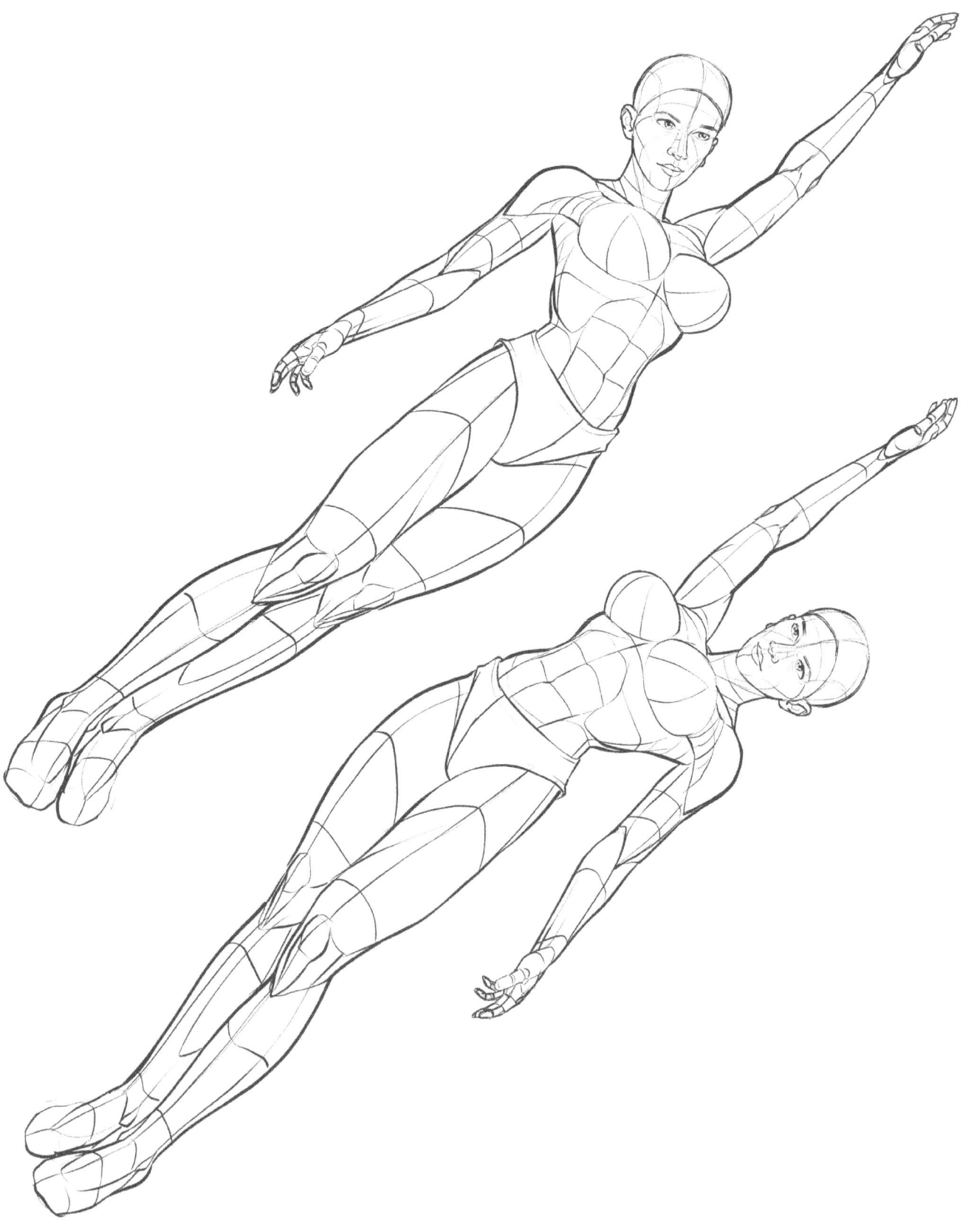

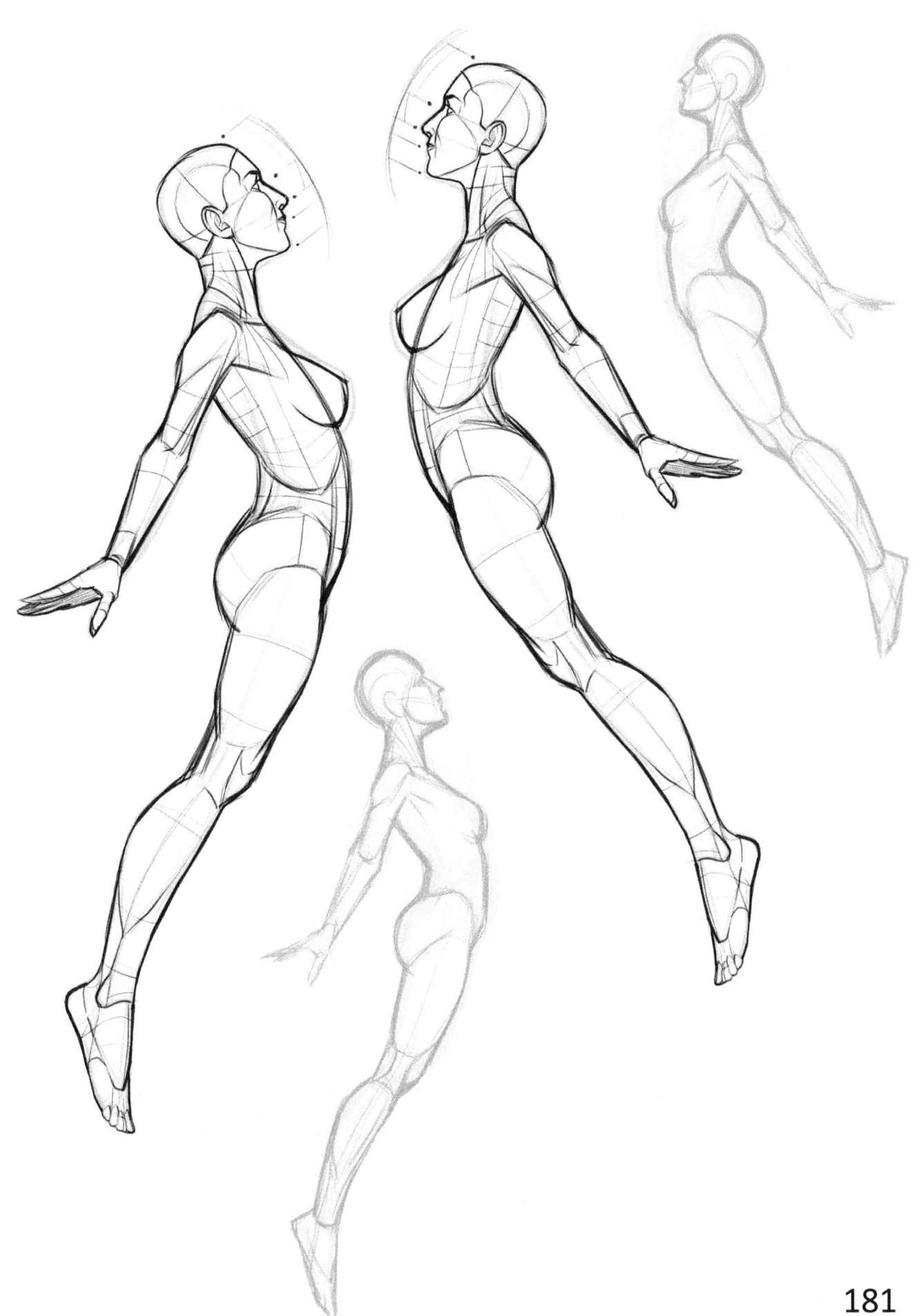

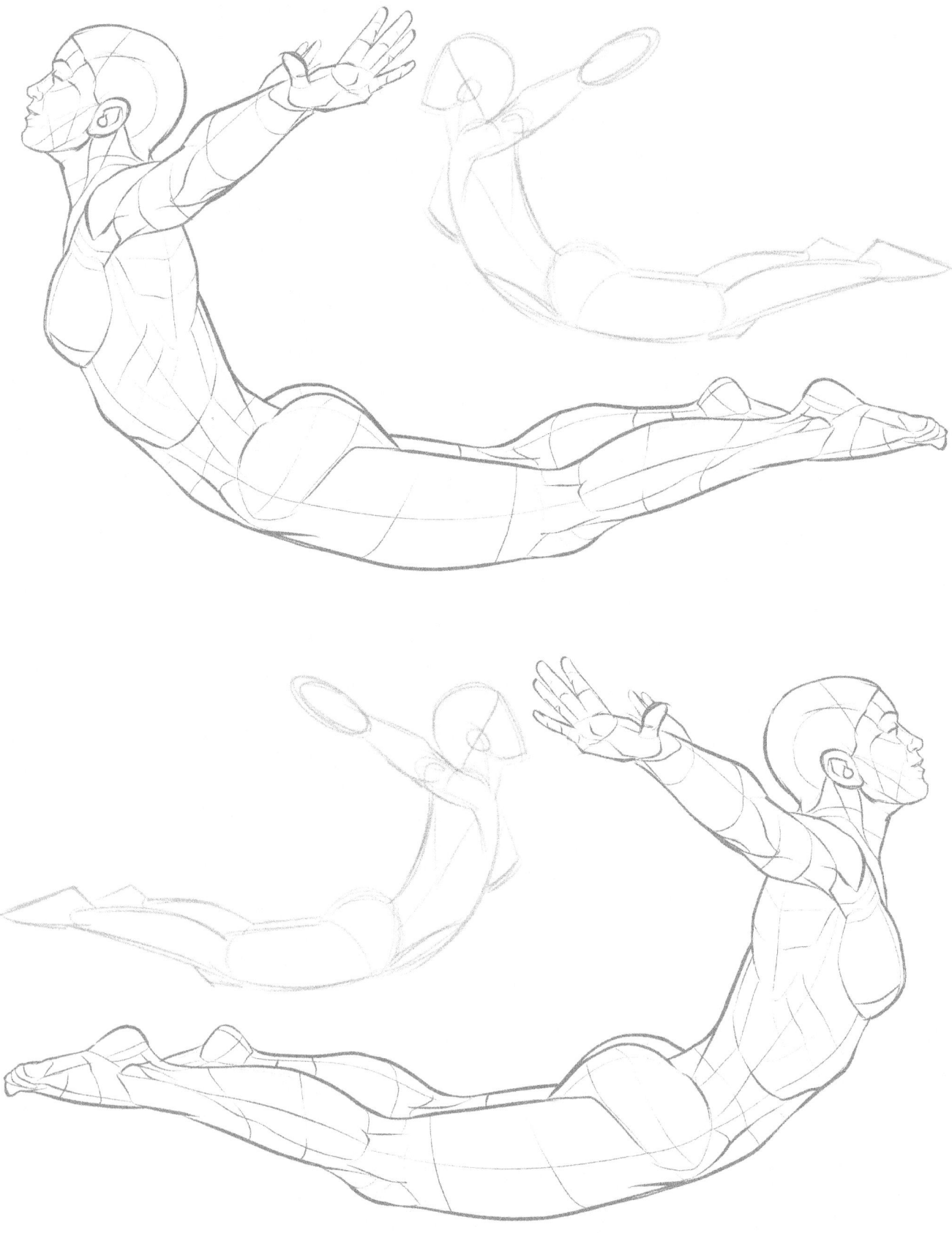

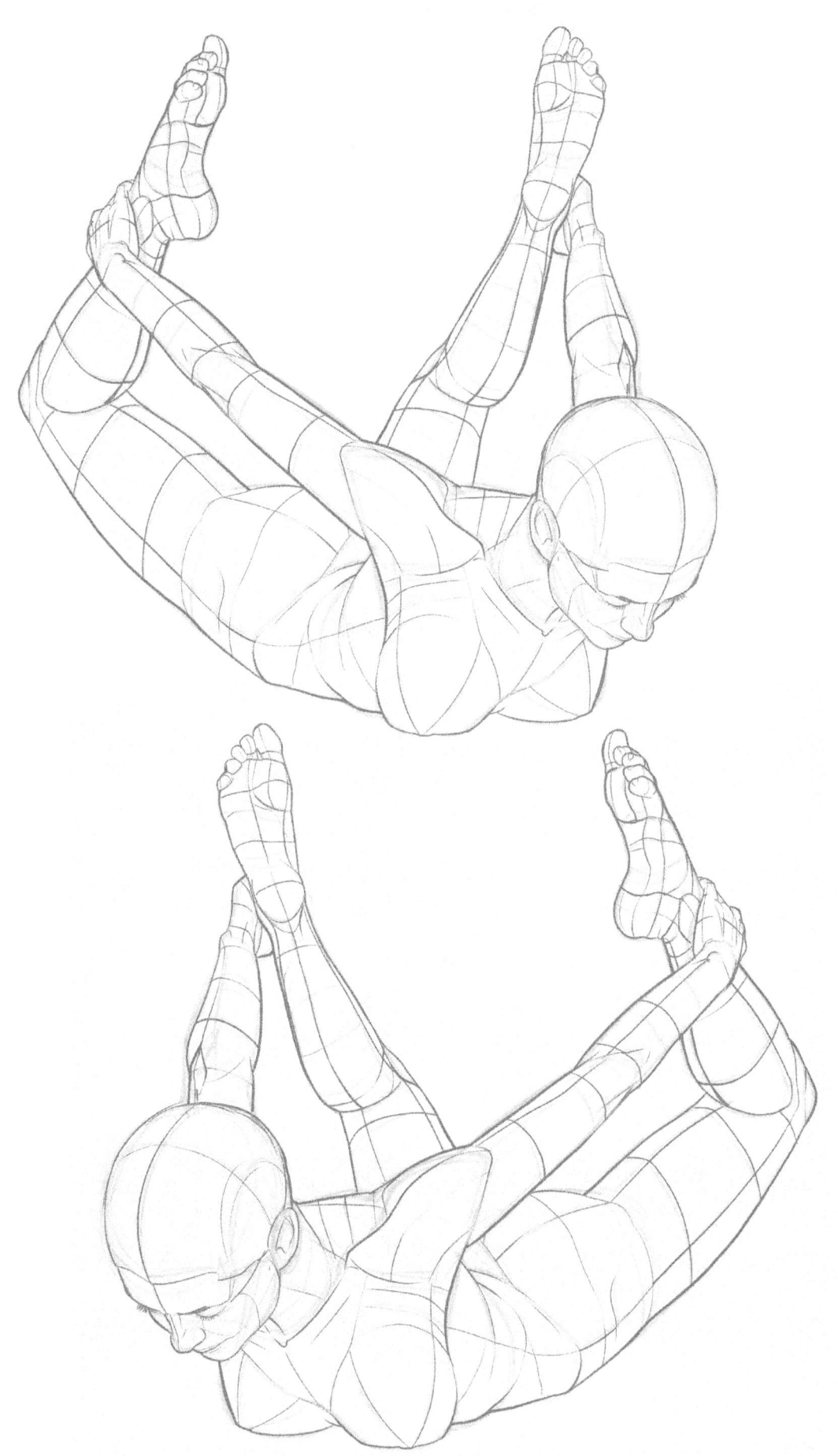

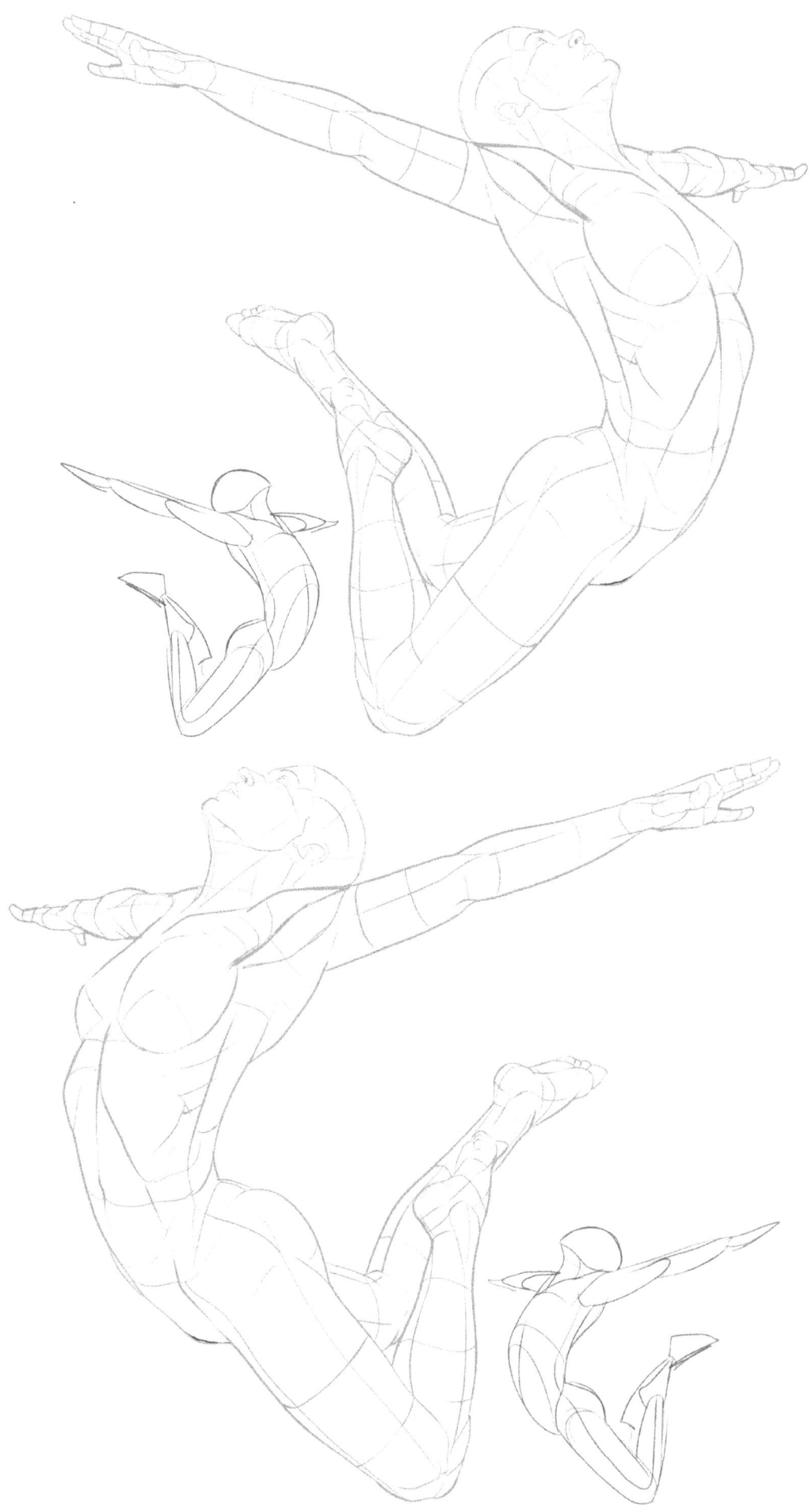

184

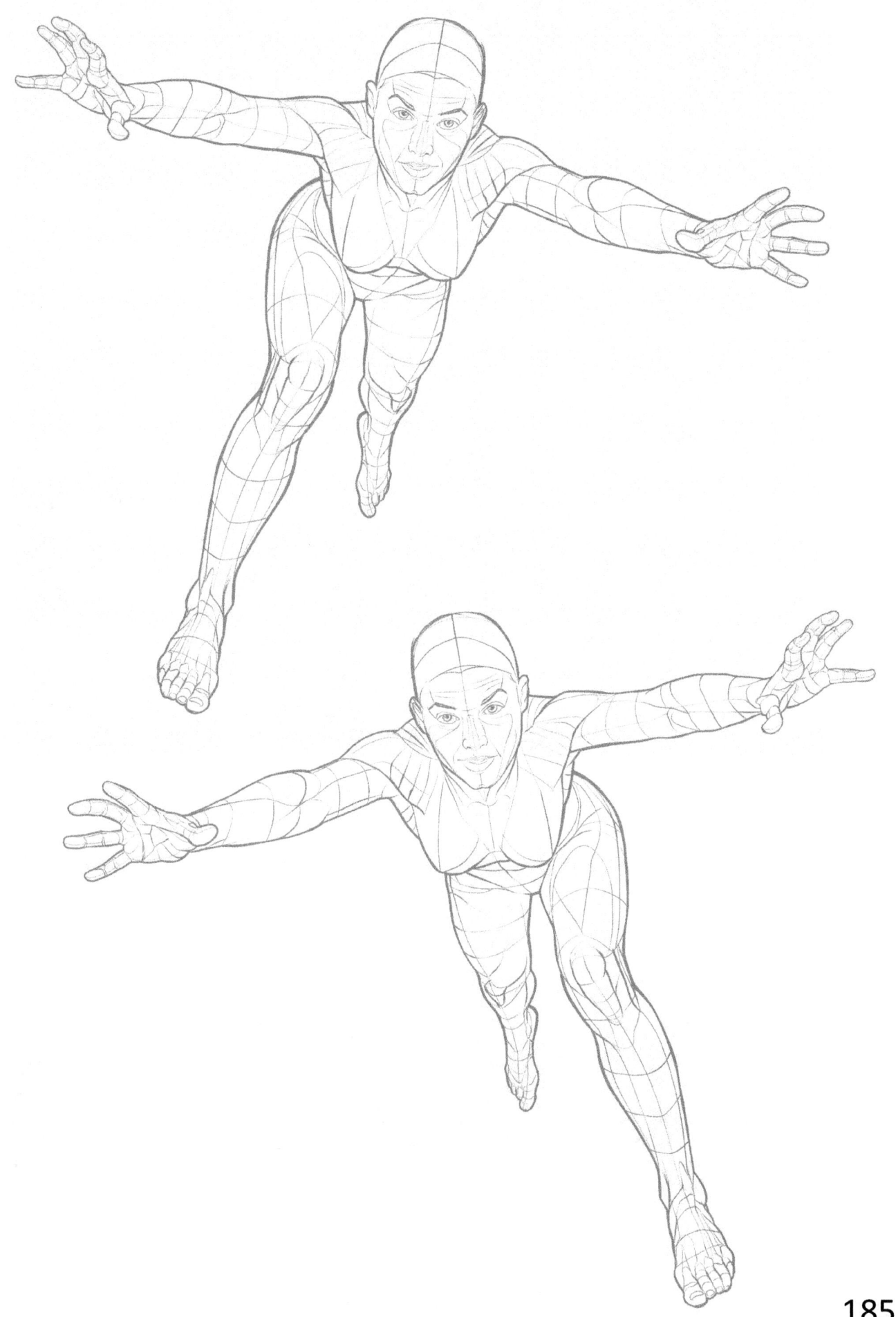

185

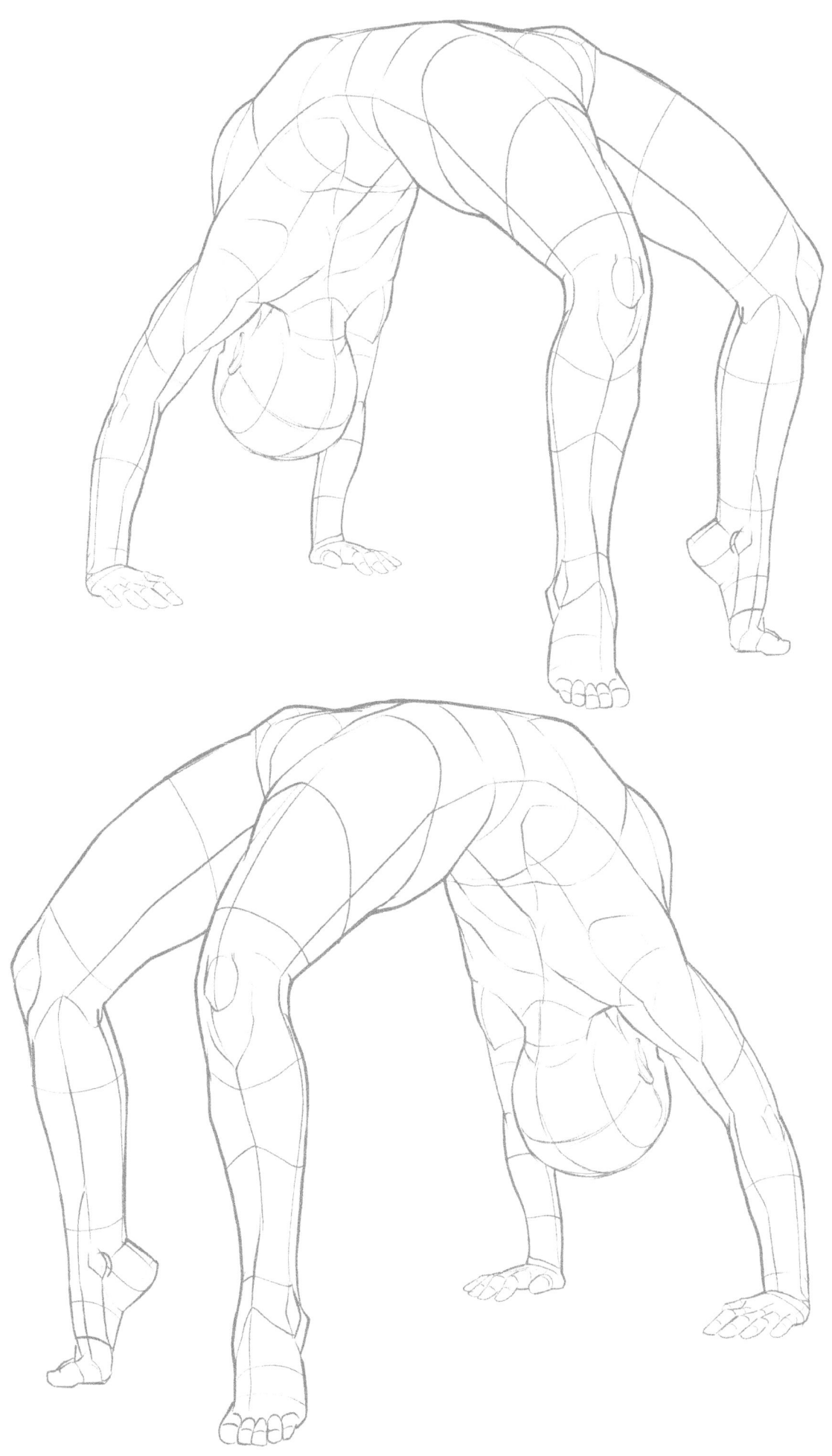

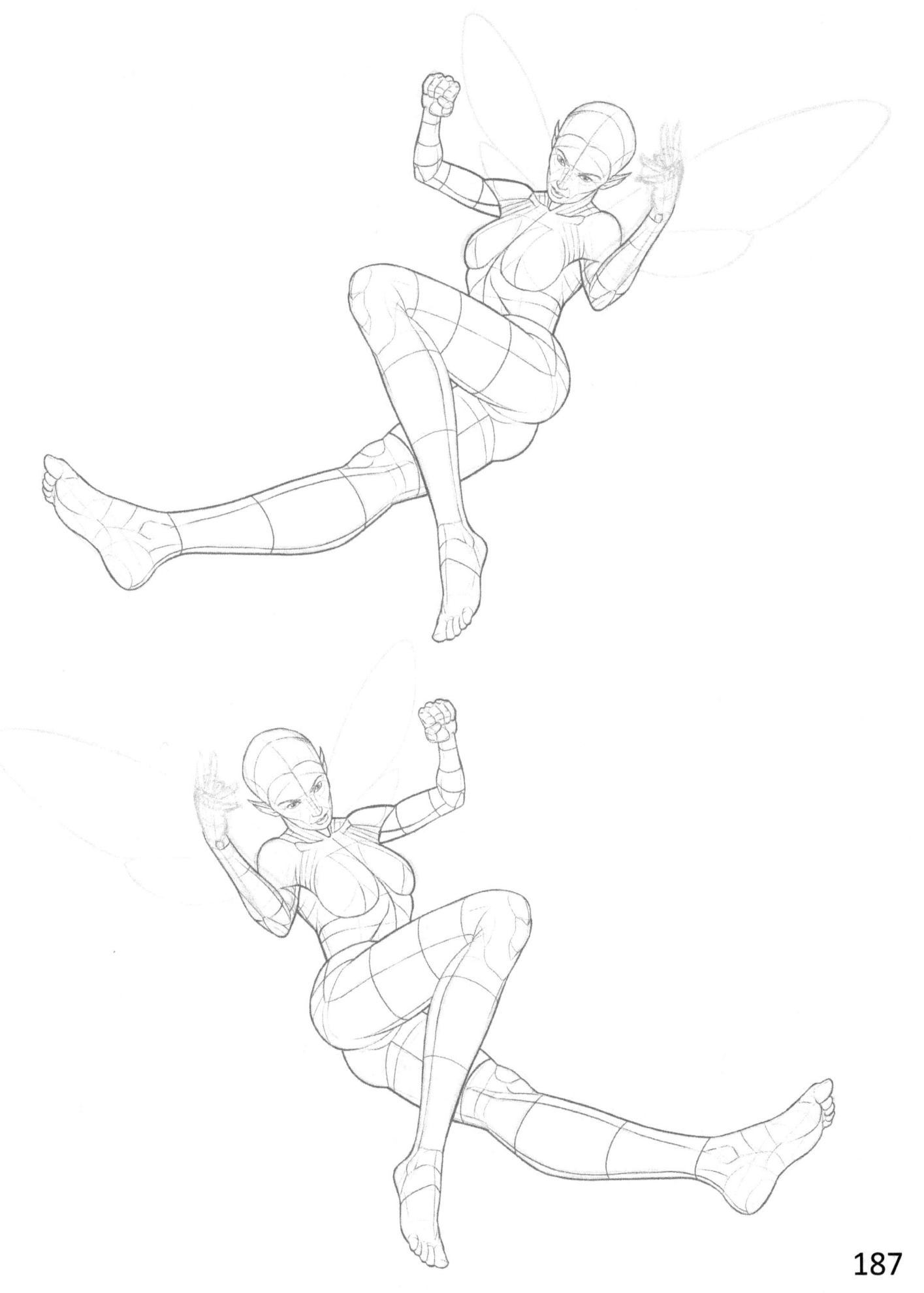

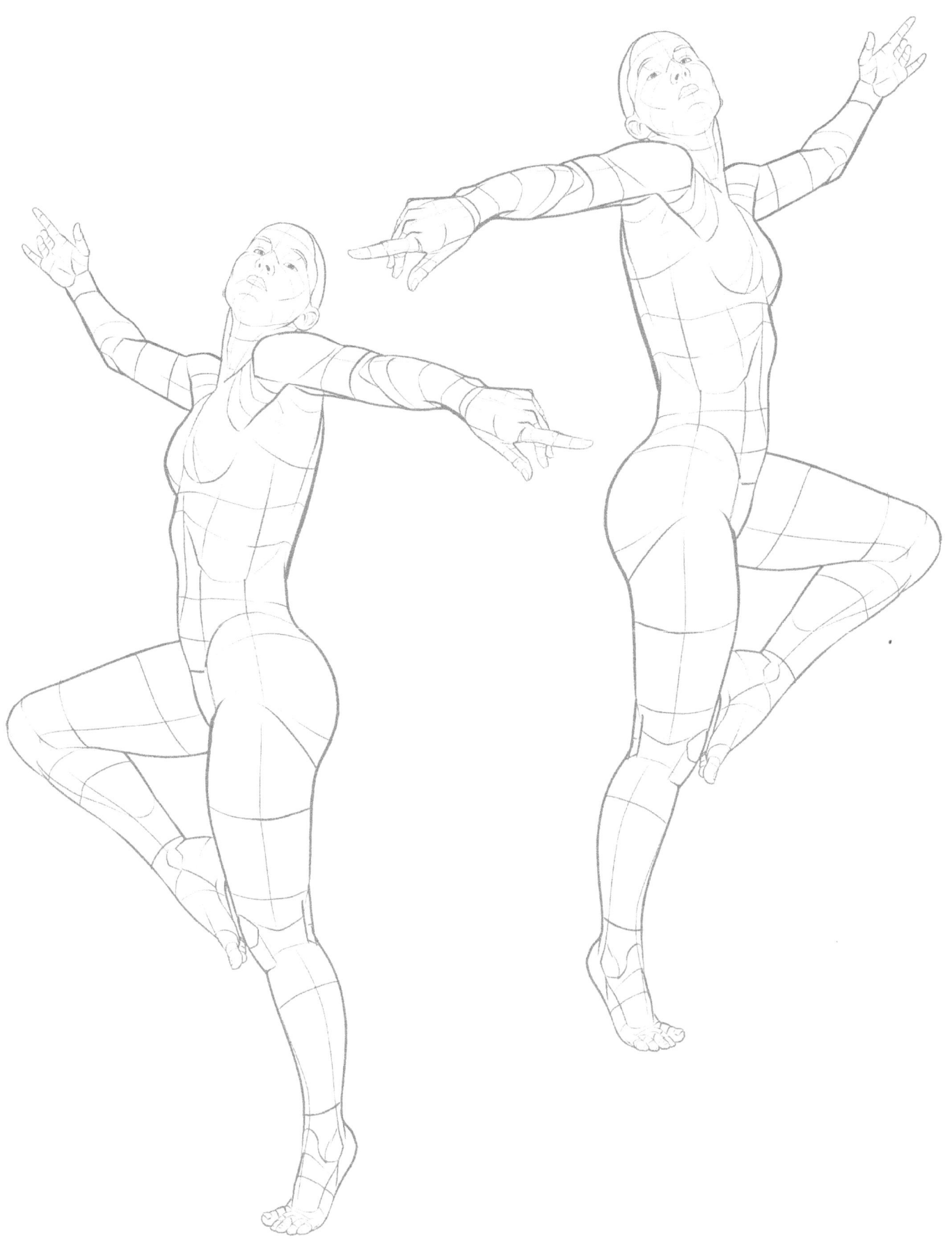

188

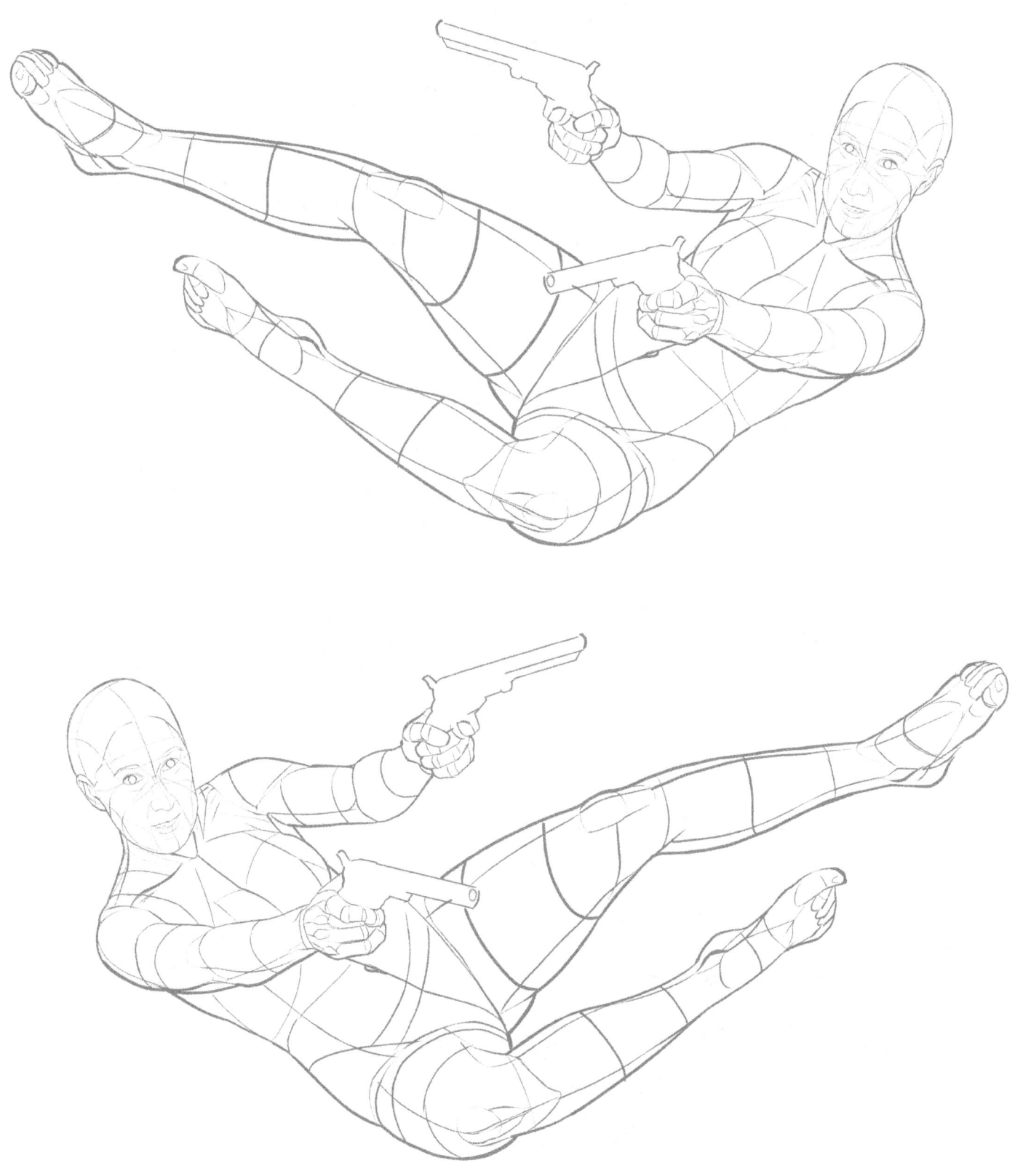

189

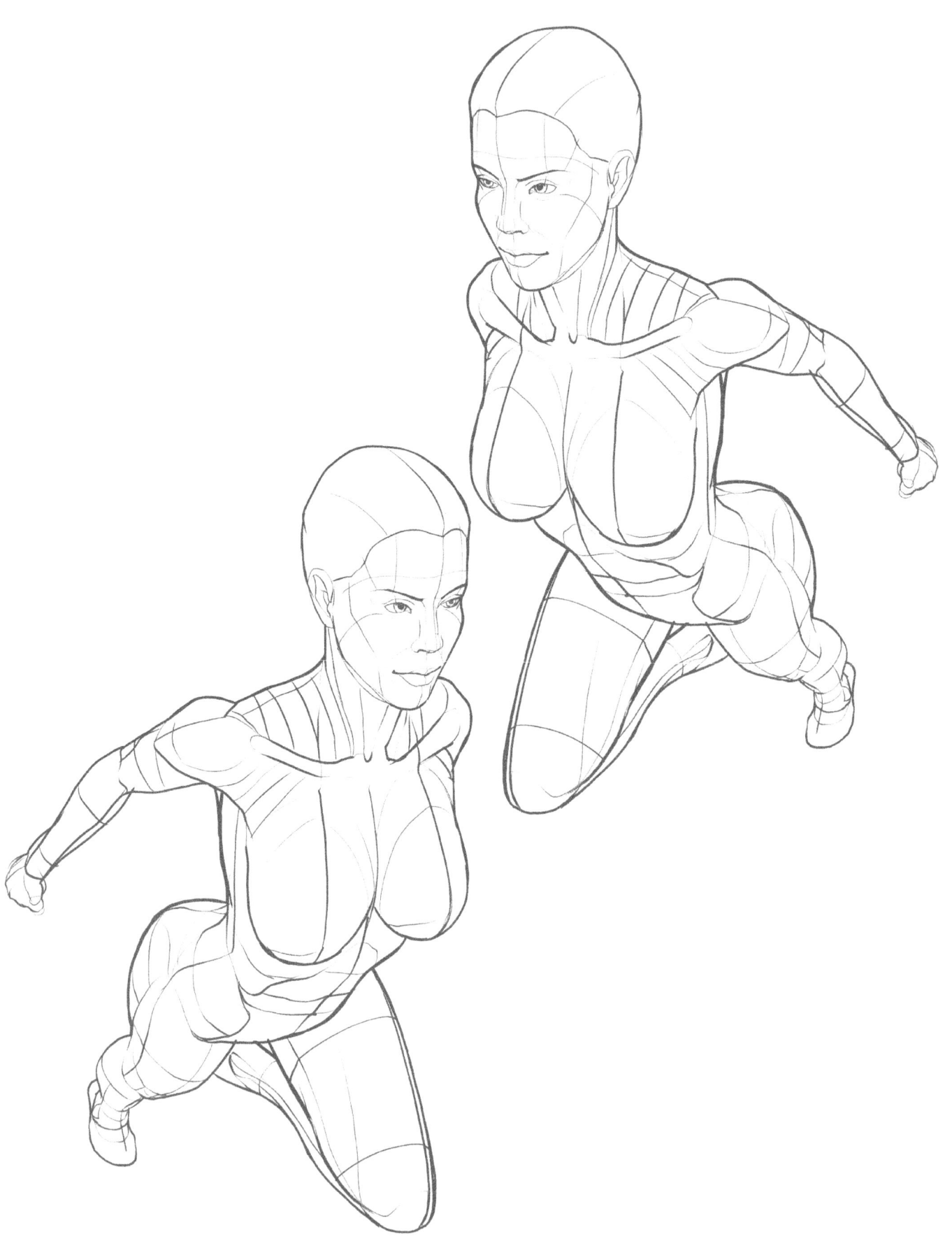

190

A special thanks to all those who helped bring this project to life below. Thank you SO much. We hope the book helps you create many, many works of art and that it continues to help for years to come.

All the artists, family and friends who have encouraged me throughout the years. Special thanks to, August, Terri, Sarah, Tavin, Paul, Sharon, Lary, Liz, Jay, Mom, Dad, the James', the Devericks', The Kinneys', Sergio, Stevie, Brandon, Berke Breathed, Adam Warren, Terry Dodson, Monte Moore and Jo Desimonne.

The business friends of PoseMuse:
UNSH/Manikin - Unsh.io/Manikin-app
SenshiStock - SenshiStock.com
Gumroad - Gumroad.com
ArmatureNIne - ArmatureNine.com
PoseSpace - PoseSpace.com

The backers who funded the 2019 Kickstarter campaign for Poses For Artists Volume 5 with their hard-earned money; A. K. Cyrway, Achim Meissner, Ajay Pollarine, Alex Wood, Alexandra Soraia Garcia, Alexis Ludeman, Amanda Mickelson, Amorita Malagon, Andrea Garcia, Anthony Jutz, Arlyn Ruzycki, Ashley Fouche, Ashley Alonso, Barry Southworth, Bethany MacKay, Betty Anne, Bob Covey, Brad Thingvold, Brittany Dupont, Brooke Robertson, Bunny Parsons, Caden Reigns, Callie J. Paar, Callista Johnson, Carson Cook, Cecelia Herff, Charlotte Curtis, Chelsey Carpenter, Chris Tan, Christian Malan, Christina Conte, Christine Crossley, Ciara Parizek, Claire Delavergne, Claire Burn, Cynthia Kytsora Waggamon, Dan Wy, Danielle Hunt, Dave Shelley, David Crocker, Didan Bay, Elizabeth Barnes, EM-J Hill, Emily Bell, Erica T Andreen, Fernando Islas, Florian Lengyel, Frank Sronce, Gloria Rodriguez, Greg Boyle, Jaclyn Stuard, James Parthun, Jassz Storms, Jateshi , Jeanette O'Brien, Johanna De Simone, John Truong, John Pankey, Joshua Mayne, Karen Lauzau, Kat Penman, Kate Flascher, Kathryn Davis, Katie Quinn Pershon, Kay Oliver, Kevin James Frear, Kevin Brown, Kimberly Kehaulani Montgomery, L. Cherin., Liselotte F Andersen, Lorraine "Kalleh" Pascucci, Lorraine Clarke, Lou Jacobs, Marcel Gohla, Margret Wood, Mark Krey, Martial M., Matt Turull, Meagan Blyth, Michael J. Simmons, Monte Michael Moore, Natalia Corby, Orrora Young, Phoenix Hailin De Mohun, Quicksilver Rain , Rachel Hahn, Raquel Coy, Richard Taylor, Riva Amyett, Sam Marzan, Samia Islam, Sand McUnicorn, Sarah Sakky' Ruth Forde, Seattle Street Art, Seb Robichaud, SER , Shawn Knapp, Shirah Pollock, Sicily Dietz, Sloan Howell, Stacy Sorey, Stefy Lopez, Steve Harrison, The Creative Fund (BackerKit), Thom Haupt, Tony Sturtevant, William Anderson, Zarae Do'Ghym

And everyone we missed not shown here!

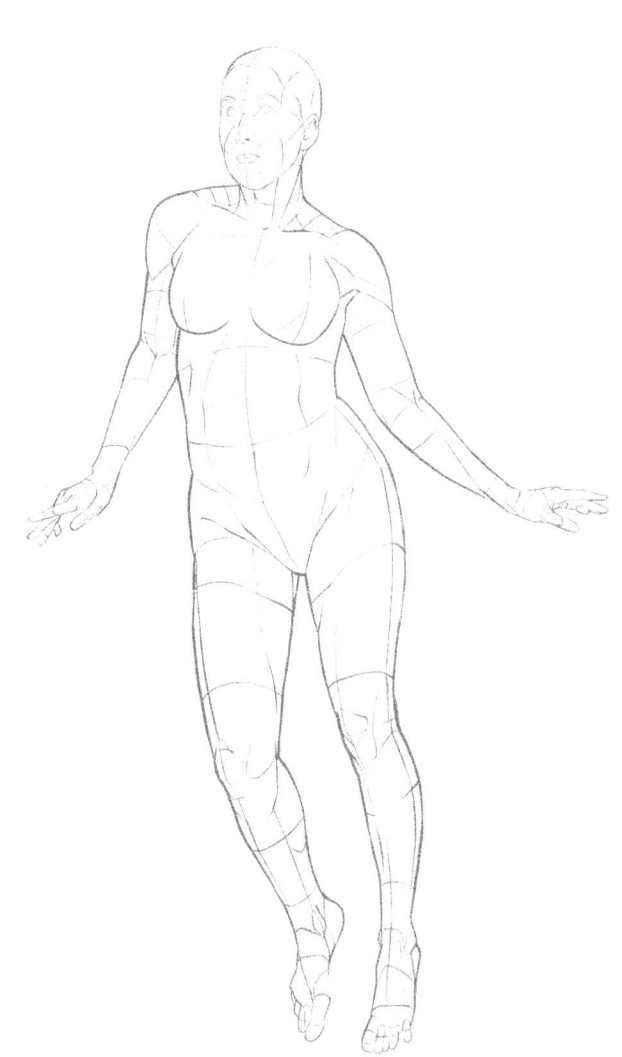